BERKSHIRE
HEROES IN WWII

WHAT READERS ARE SAYING . . .

"Another superb blend of US military history and the wellsprings of New England patriotism from a master storyteller. A must read!" — ***Admiral James Stavridis, 16th Supreme Allied Commander of NATO; author of*** **The Restless Wave: A Novel of the US Navy**

* * *

"In *Berkshire Heroes in WWII*, Pregent provides a brief history and background for twenty-eight members of the 'Greatest Generation' from a tight-knit area of Western Massachusetts. The heroes are engaged in some of the war's most historic Naval, Air, and Land battles as pilots, crew members, artillerymen, gunners, nurses, and infantrymen.

The author shares family photographs and long-preserved documents, many published for the first time, in his book. There is even an interview with a surviving veteran from the battle of Iwo Jima.

Pregent rounds out each profile with the post-war homecomings of the men and women who served so valiantly. Their stories are gripping, sad, happy, and always touching. I would highly recommend this book to anyone with a genuine interest in World War II. It keeps the legacy of the Greatest Generation alive, as it deserves to be!" — ***Thomas Luczynski, Brigadier General (Retired), Assistant Division Commander of the 38th Infantry, Commander of the 37th Armored Brigade; Served as an advisor to the Vietnamese Rangers***

* * *

"An extraordinary read! It shows you exactly what the Greatest Generation had to endure. Dennis Pregent did an amazing job in research, and it shows." — ***Wayne Soares, TV Host, Producer, Filmmaker, and Veterans Advocate***

ALSO BY DENNIS G. PREGENT

The Boys of St. Joe's '65 in the Vietnam War

Born in the Berkshires

Berkshire Patriots: Stories of Sacrifice

BERKSHIRE HEROES IN WWII

WITH COURAGE AND HONOR

Dennis G. Pregent

Berkshire Heroes in WWII

Printed in the United States of America
ISBN 978-1-956543-56-8 (softcover)

Book layout by CSinclaire Write-Design LLC
Cover by Klevur and Charlotte Sinclaire

Cover: General Eisenhower meets with Company F paratroopers, including Henry St. Pierre, on June 5, 1944, the eve of D-Day

Raleigh, North Carolina
www.writewaypublishing.com

CONTENTS

ADAMS/CHESHIRE, MASSACHUSETTS

NORTH ADAMS, MASSACHUSETTS

WILLIAMSTOWN, MASSACHUSETTS

BRANCHES OF SERVICE

AAF = Army Air Force
ANC = Army Nurse Corps
USA = US Army
USMC = US Marine Corps
USN = US Navy

ACKNOWLEDGMENTS

THANKS TO ALL WHO supported the research, writing, and publication of this book.

I am grateful to the Veterans Service agents, past and present, who serve the area's veterans. I am especially in debt to John Michael "Mike" Kennedy, Jr., a former agent who was deeply devoted to local veterans and became a good friend during the writing of this book.

Over many decades, Mike, a US Army veteran who became chief of police in Williamstown, assisted many of the heroes profiled herein, as well as veterans of later conflicts, helping them secure long-overdue pensions, medical treatment, and earned medals. And in the end, he joined the Honor Guard detail that officiated at their burials.

Mike passed away during the writing of this book. Days before leaving us, he was still sending me notes from his hospital bed. He will be greatly missed by the entire community, who recently honored Mike by renaming Williamstown's American Legion Post 152 after him.

As with my prior books, some of the most supportive sources have been Eugene Michalenko and Gene Carlson from the Adams and North Adams Historical Societies, and Mike Goodwin and Michael Nixon from the Williamstown Historical Museum. Michael Miller, a former longtime Williamstown resident, also contributed his expertise in local history.

Several local historians with a rich and abundant knowledge of the area have been significant research sources. They are Tom Boudreau from Readsboro, Vermont, John Bordeau from Adams, and Paul Marino from North Adams. Paul, an accomplished writer, has his own historical website (*www.PaulWMarino.org*).

This is my fourth book working with Jane Hobson Snyder, an accomplished editor, who has over the years helped me in so many ways from her steady, ongoing support to her great editing and technical skills—and, not the least, being available to answer my many questions. Her efforts greatly improved my manuscript by reading it carefully and rescuing readers from my mistakes.

Lee Heinrich and her wonderful team at WriteWay Publishing were a great help in managing the entire publication process. Designer Charlotte Sinclaire created the book's outstanding cover.

I am especially grateful to all the families who helped throughout the process, answering questions, responding to my numerous inquiries, and supplying original photographs and documents of their loved ones.

A special thanks to Admiral James Stavridis, 16th Supreme Allied Commander of NATO, Thomas Luczynski, Brigadier General (Ret.), and Wayne Soares, Veterans Advocate, for their kind words about this book.

And, as ever, thanks to my wife, Carol, who has lovingly endured my writing journey, offering steadfast love and support.

And a final tribute to anyone else I may have missed.

INTRODUCTION

THE WORLD'S MOST LETHAL and cataclysmic war lasted for 2,194 days, from September 1, 1939, to September 2, 1945, and saw the engagement of 70,000,000 people worldwide. Its reach seems almost too vast to fathom.

Hundreds of books have been written about World War II, trying to appreciate the bloodshed from wide-ranging perspectives. But *Berkshire Heroes in World War II: With Courage and Honor* zeroes in on how one idyllic, tight-knit county in Massachusetts, with its forested hills, stocked streams, and rich farmland, was transformed by the military service of its young people. Individual heroic stories abound, of those serving alongside family, friends, or neighbors—all from Adams, North Adams, and Williamstown. Many have gone unrecognized until now, these young men and women who served valiantly and in the spirit of their communities.

Many Berkshire towns proudly featured an Honor Roll of those currently serving in World War II. In Adams, it was a large wooden memorial on the front lawn of the town library. (Courtesy of Adams Historical Society)

Bravery, self-sacrifice, and duty were common virtues, borne out in the lives of the everyday people profiled within. While the word *hero* is in common use today, it aptly describes these twenty-eight servicemen and women, many of whom fought in the war's largest battles on land, in the air, and at sea—from the attack on Pearl Harbor, to D-Day, to the battles for Iwo Jima and Okinawa.

Here, Robert Brown of Adams poses for family, proud to be in uniform. (Courtesy of Brown family)

This book is a tribute to our former friends and neighbors, men and women, remarkable people who answered their country's call. The project takes a 1940s snapshot of the youth of the northern Berkshires who served in a noble endeavor to save the world and risked everything to defend the idea of liberty.

I, too, was born in the Berkshires, just a generation later, and though I served in Vietnam, I have always had a fascination with the stories of WWII. It began for me as a youngster eavesdropping in my grandmother's North Adams backyard during summer picnics. Her sons (my uncles) and my dad would gather around the picnic table to smoke and play cards but often ended up reminiscing about their wartime experiences. I was captivated by the exotic locales they visited and unusual situations in which they found themselves, and I never tired of hearing their stories, whether they were set in England guarding German POWs, racing across Europe liberating village after village, emancipating thousands of starving captives from concentration camps, or visiting the French can-can girls in Paris.

Most local youth like my uncles, who joined up in the early 1940s, had never been more than fifty miles from home, yet suddenly they found themselves whisked by train to camps or technical schools across the United States, some enlisting and some responding to the draft. Shortly afterwards, most would board boats, leaving the United States, their destination a mystery.

I wanted to know more about these unselfish, unsung heroes who participated in the most far-flung, destructive war in history but are now vanishing so quickly. Though seventy million men and women across the globe served in the Armed Forces during World War II, I decided to dig deeply into what I knew, drawing upon hometown contacts I've made over the decades, in order to enshrine into the historical record what happened to these twenty-eight men and women from the Adams, North Adams, and Williamstown area.

They distinguished themselves, serving in the most difficult climes, from torrid heat to 30 below zero, subject to countless diseases—and always, always with the possibility of being killed or wounded in action. Many were, in fact, wounded and decorated.

For the past year, I have spent grateful hours in conversation with veterans' agents, families, and friends, absorbing and recording stories about their loved ones. In these many months of writing and interviewing, I have hovered in a sort of timeless bubble, half in my own

The author, left, in Cheshire, Massachusetts, with World War II veteran Cheeso Massaconi, having a lively conversation about Cheeso's war years. (Courtesy of the author)

life, and half in theirs, understanding why it has been called "The Greatest Generation." Men and women unselfishly left home and family, knowingly putting themselves in harm's way to preserve the world's democracy, showing us the power of individuals coming together for a common cause.

My hope, in *Berkshire Heroes in WWII: With Courage and Honor,* is to introduce readers to the most interesting unsung heroes from all walks of Berkshire life: farm boys, teachers, machine operators, truck drivers, university students, and mill laborers among them.

From the waters of the Pacific, the shores of Normandy, or the skies of Europe, these men and women experienced different wars, whether thousands of feet in the air over the Himalayas or shivering in a wet foxhole in the Italian Alps. By taking an intimate, narrow focus on one small region, I hope the reader will better understand the realities of war and how many survived the terror and hardship by bold courage, ingenuity, or just plain luck.

I stand in awe of their extraordinary willingness and find it a privilege to be able to recount their stories. In these pages, you will meet, among others:

- **Henry St. Pierre**, the paratrooper pictured on the book's cover with General Eisenhower the night before his unit jumped into France on D-Day. Henry would be wounded, recover, fight in the Battle of the Bulge, and then become a prisoner of war.

- **Joseph Zasloff**, a wounded soldier trapped behind enemy lines, who escaped, received the Purple Heart and Bronze Star, and later became a Doctor of Political Science and a renowned expert on Indochina.

- **Roger Dennett**, an Army Air Force corporal at Pearl Harbor who returned fire with a bolt-action rifle at scores of attacking enemy Zeroes and was the first American to capture a

Japanese POW in World War II. Roger would go on to fly sixty missions over Europe.

- **Bill Linscott**, the championship skier who fought with the 10th Mountain Division and was seriously wounded in Italy, when the man next to him was killed.

- **Bernard St. John**, the Navy pilot who would sink a Japanese cruiser during one of the war's most consequential naval battles; for this, he would be awarded the Navy Cross, the nation's second-highest medal.

- **Narcheeso "Cheeso" Massaconi**, a soldier, still alive and residing in Cheshire, Massachusetts, who gives a remarkable first-hand account of fighting on Iwo Jima, one of the bloodiest battles in the Pacific.

- **Madeline Smith Beattie**, an Army nurse who withstood the still-unliberated conditions in the Philippines to treat hundreds of gravely wounded soldiers.

- **Robert Nichols**, a Navy seaman and gunner, who was present at the signing of Peace with Japan, in Tokyo Bay. He brought home a piece of a bloodied *kamikaze* windshield his crew had shot down, after half of the dead pilot landed on the deck near him.

- **Lawrence Urbano**, a Navy pilot shot down in the Philippine Sea, then rescued; his family shares his handwritten flight log, showing the exact day he shot down two Japanese planes.

- **Ferdinando Berti**, a PT boat radio operator who in a daring raid behind enemy lines manned a 40mm cannon, helping to obliterate enemy ships.

- Two farm-boy brothers, **Charlie and George Haley**: Charlie was a gunner's mate onboard ship, fighting off *kamikazes*; and George was a sergeant in the Philippines who eliminated a machine gun nest that threatened his squad of soldiers.

- **Dixon Daniels**, a Marine, whose landing on the island of Peleliu ended when a Japanese mortar hit his landing craft, enveloping it in flames.

All the participants herein are brimming with determination, unselfishness, and humility. Family recollections, oral recordings, and individual memoirs deeply enrich these narratives, attesting to the fact that young people entered the military for various reasons: yes, for the good of mankind, but also to improve their lot in life, or simply for an adventure.

Those who returned from their far-off battles did so transformed, some with lifelong physical ailments, all with a broader understanding of the world. The luckiest were strengthened and even enriched by their travails, returning to the Berkshires ready to settle down, earn a living, and reenter society.

I hope you will enjoy immersing yourself in their compelling stories as much as I enjoyed capturing them, and that *Berkshire Heroes in World War II: With Courage and Honor* will extend our memories of these honorable men and women, in perpetuity.

— DGP 4/2/24

Adams/Cheshire, Massachusetts

FERDINANDO J. BERTI
RADIOMAN
TORPEDO BOAT SQUADRON 36

After a rendezvous off the Borneo coast, eleven men on a small wooden speedboat bristling with weapons conducted a dangerous daylight raid behind enemy lines. PT Boat 528, with a continuous volley of fire, destroyed three Japanese boats, two barges, and a wooden supply ship, escaping before the enemy had time to open fire. Chief Radioman Ferdinando Berti manned the 40mm cannon, helping to obliterate the enemy ships, and he was relieved to get away just in time.

FERDINANDO JOSEPH BERTI WAS born in the small town of Cheshire, Massachusetts, on September 4, 1918, to Giuseppe (Joseph in English) and Adele (Francesconi) Berti. Giuseppe and Adele had both been born in Lucca, Italy, married there in 1913, and a month later immigrated to the United States via Ellis Island. The family quickly grew to six boys.

Giuseppe was ambitious. He found employment at the local General Electric and worked there for many years until his retirement. After settling into their new life, Giuseppe also acquired land on Furnace Hill in Cheshire, intending to start a junkyard, which Adele quickly vetoed. He then decided to become a builder, and over time, while living on Furnace Hill, he and his boys built and sold over a dozen houses. Adele supported the business and was a busy homemaker with a huge garden.

Ferdinando Joseph Berti (middle name in honor of his father) attended Cheshire Elementary School and Adams High School where he became a key member of the high school football team. He played guard on offense, nose guard on defense, and was considered an excellent punter. "Ferdie" also met a cute cheerleader, Bernadette Morris, who would years later become his wife.

Graduating in 1937, Ferdie continued playing football on tough semi-professional teams and joined Company M of the Massachusetts National Guard, playing first base for the Guard's baseball team. His unit was called into action to help the residents of Adams recover from the infamous 1938 flood, when the main business streets of Adams were inundated with four feet of water from the Hoosic River. (The devastation led to Congressional hearings that resulted in the approval of a Flood Control Project, including river dredging and flood wall construction.)

In November of 1940, Ferdie began working as a packer in the power transformer distribution center at General Electric. Not long afterward, on December 18, 1940, he enlisted in the United States Navy. Ferdie was quoted in *The Pittsfield Work News* as saying, "I thought America would get into the war, so I just got in ahead."

Ferdinando Berti as a proud young sailor. (Courtesy of Berti family)

His ninety days of boot camp training began in Newport, Rhode Island, followed by three months of radio operator instruction at Camp Noroton, Connecticut, and then ocean duty on the destroyer and minesweeper USS *Howard*, based at Norfolk Naval Base in Virginia. While on duty in the radio room, he was the first of the ship's sailors to hear about the Japanese attack on Pearl Harbor on December 7, 1941.

In the same month, he was selected to attend Patrol Torpedo Boat (PT boat) training at a small naval base on Narragansett Bay in Melville, near Portsmouth, Rhode Island. It was known as the Motor Torpedo Boat Squadron Training Center, with the impressive acronym of MTBSTC. After twelve weeks of indoctrination in PT boats, Ferdie was selected to become a radio instructor at Melville and would remain there until his deployment overseas in February 1944. He would instruct many future PT boat crews on using the boat's radio, Morse code, and semaphores (flag signaling).

In November 1942, while on a furlough home, he married Bernadette Morris, the vivacious cheerleader he had met on the Adams gridiron. After the briefest of honeymoons, she returned home to work at the Berkshire Hathaway Company in Adams.

Although assignments to PT boats were voluntary and considered glamorous, the boats and crews were considered somewhat expendable by the US Navy, which was willing to exchange one small boat and an eleven-man crew for the possibility of destroying an enemy warship with hundreds of enemy sailors.

The unarmored wooden boats with 3,000 gallons of fuel and ammunition stores were vulnerable to enemy gunfire. The crews were a hardy, independent, brave group of men who operated out of forward bases (barely developed camps with minimum support, located close to the enemy). PT patrols were typically conducted 120 to 150 nautical miles from the base and were always subject to being bombed or strafed. On high-speed patrol, the crew almost always tinkered with their weaponry or the boat's engines to ensure their highest performance.

The resilient crews embraced several mottoes. One was a derivative of words attributed to John Paul Jones (a hero of the Revolutionary War, considered the father of the American Navy): Give me a fast ship, for I intend to go in harm's way.

Many of the crews revered John D. Bulkeley, a PT boat commander known for his daring and resourceful deeds, and often repeated his simple mantra, Hit 'em hard. Bulkeley received the

Medal of Honor for his PT boat actions in the Pacific. In early 1942, in a highly publicized action, Bulkeley picked up General Douglas MacArthur along with the general's wife and staff from the Philippines. Bulkeley's boat returned them to safety on a 600-mile mission, evading countless Japanese warships.

Most PT boat crews took a pounding when riding on the waves but loved it when the boat was at full speed and would almost be lifted out of the water to plane across surfaces. Its three powerful engines allowed it to "turn on a dime." If the crew moderated the boat's speed, its fuel allowed for a range of 500 to 600 miles.

THE BOAT

IT WAS IN THE late 1930s that the Navy recognized the need for high-speed, heavily armed gunboats and, after testing, awarded a boat-building contract to three companies. The Electric Boat Company, "Elco" Naval Division, would become its major builder.

The PT fleet was established by early 1942 and, not long after, they were nicknamed "mosquito boats" as they became a nuisance to the Japanese Navy. The boats, 77 feet long and 20 feet across, were constructed of 1" x 6" boards of mahogany, spruce, or oak, fastened with brass screws. The 56-ton speedboat with a five-foot draft could reach over 40 knots and bristled with weaponry. There were four 20-foot-long torpedo tubes, two 20mm Oerlikon cannons, two twin, staggered .50-caliber machine guns, and a mortar on the transom.

PT boat crews embraced their nickname, even creating a patch featuring a fierce mosquito with boxing gloves. (Courtesy of the author)

Always looking to increase the boat's lethality, 40mm guns

replaced the 20mm cannons at one point, and most crews mounted a 37mm anti-aircraft gun on the prow (often salvaged from destroyed Bell P-39 Airacobra fighters).

A typical boat crew consisted of two officers and nine enlisted men, including a captain, an executive officer, a radioman, a radarman, three gunner's mates, one torpedo-man, three motor machinist mates, a quartermaster, a deck seaman, and (if lucky) a cook. (Usually, the cook was a "volunteered" crewmember.) All crew members were cross-trained as gunners. Ferdie, the boat radioman, manned the 20mm Oerlikon gun.

Berti, now a more seasoned sailor. (Courtesy of Berti family)

Below deck, the space was efficiently laid out. There was storage up front, a flush toilet (after flushing, the crew needed to turn off the valve or the compartment would flood), then spartan crews' quarters with four bunks and some lockers. Next came the officer's quarters with a bathroom and a galley, which included a freezer, a refrigerator, and a stove. Mid ship there were 3,000 gallons of 100-octane aviation fuel in tanks to fuel the three Packard V12 engines that powered the boat. The craft also had its own generator and batteries, carried 200 gallons of fresh water, and had many ammunition lockers.

In autumn of 1942, while at Melville, Ferdie trained Lieutenant Junior Grade John F. Kennedy, who would eventually captain PT-109, in radio communications. He found Kennedy to be a "regular Joe" and not a snobby Ivy-Leaguer as others may have portrayed him. Such in-depth training was vital: the next year, John F. Kennedy's PT boat was sunk on August 2, 1943, when attempting to ambush a Japanese task force. After days adrift and the loss of two crew members, the survivors were rescued, largely due to Kennedy's athleticism and tenacious exploration of nearby islands. Kennedy was awarded the Navy–Marine Corps medal for heroism, a notable stepping stone on his way to becoming the nation's 35th president.

Many years later, in 2002, a National Geographic Society expedition led by the famous explorer Robert Ballard located and positively identified the forward section of PT-109 in 1200 feet of water. The half-buried ship and gravesite were mapped but left undisturbed.

During Ferdie's years at Melville, he would train many other captains and crewmembers headed to the Pacific Theater of Operations. Toward the end of his tour at Melville, he was assigned to the crew of PT-528. They trained on nearby Narragansett Bay, perfecting boat tactics and firing countless tracer bullets at practice targets towed by small airplanes, always with the caveat not to hit the tow plane.

In 1944, PT-528 became part of Motor Torpedo Boat Squadron 36 (RON36), which usually had a complement of twelve PT boats subdivided into groups of three divisions. The sailors nicknamed the squadrons "RON," the last three letters of the word squadron. Shakedowns (practice runs) would continue off the coast of Florida, then near the Panama Canal, where the boats were being transported as deck cargo on large ships headed to the Pacific.

Ferdie and PT-528 were headed west: Final destination, New Guinea and the Philippines. During the trip, Ferdie and his mates underwent a longtime naval tradition commemorating the Equatorial crossing. Through a series of sometimes chastening events—eating hot sauce, shaving cream, and raw eggs; wearing clothes inside out; crawling on hands and knees across the rough deck—they were eventually "baptized by King Neptune and his court" and became official shellbacks.

The crew of the 528 resupplying at dock. (Courtesy of Berti family)

Before the Pacific arrival of PT-528 in late 1944, PT boat missions had evolved from the often dangerous and unsuccessful nighttime tactic of lying in wait in hopes of torpedoing large enemy warships to primarily barge hunting and harassing shore installations. The boats continued to conduct anti-submarine patrols, run reconnaissance missions, transport VIPS, and recover downed flyers.

At the time, trying to attack large enemy warships under darkness with the persistent problem of faulty torpedoes was particularly dangerous. The 2000-pound Mark 13 torpedoes had many problems: not launching at all, or running too deep and "porpoising," or having bad detonators, or being launched at wrong angles. While electrically fired from the cockpit, a crew member needed to be near the torpedo tube to whack it with a hammer as a backup. Many torpedoes failed for one reason or another.

The torpedoes were powered by a two-stage turbine that used alcohol as fuel. As the usefulness declined, stories abound that the government had mixed poison with alcohol to prohibit consumption by the sailors. Ferdie told the stories of innovative crews filtering the alcohol through bread, adding pineapple juice, and drinking it.

If too much of the alcohol were consumed, a released torpedo would sink to the bottom of the ocean, a natural disincentive.

In groups of two or three boats, the PTs constantly harassed Japanese operations and became known by the enemy as Devil Boats. Camouflaged, using shades of grey and green, the boats were tough to detect as they patrolled and anchored near jungle shores. While the PTs are credited with sinking several warships and a submarine, their biggest successes were against armored Japanese landing craft (Daihatsu) and interdicting their efforts to resupply isolated bases. With the addition of radar in 1943, the boats often surprised Japanese ships creeping along coastlines. Both sides with considerable firepower provided for violent to-the-death battles. The Daihatsu sometimes carried up to 100 enemy soldiers who could get into the fight with their personal weapons.

The PT boat's most lethal enemy was the Japanese floatplane, especially at night when the boat's propellers would churn up marine life and leave phosphorous wakes that acted like a searchlight pointing directly at the boat. High above and sometimes miles away, Japanese floatplanes would spot the phosphorous trails, drop a flare, and then bomb the boat.

PT-528 had barely arrived in the Pacific when its squadron was called into action to rescue President Osmeña of the Philippines. During this harrowing journey, wearing helmets and kapok life vests, they made every effort to avoid enemy warships. PT-528 crept into a harbor under darkness and rescued President Osmeña, his family, and five Philippine guerillas whom General MacArthur wanted to meet. PT-528 transported the group from Cebu to Leyte out of the reach of the Japanese, becoming part of the government in exile. President Osmeña lauded the gallant crews for their courageousness; he later sent each one a personal letter.

Ferdie continued to expertly man radio/radar and navigation equipment. The radio's 20-foot whip antenna near the cockpit allowed him a broadcasting distance of 70 miles, although its use was often kept to a minimum to avoid detection.

At one point, the crew discussed naming their boat, but quickly nixed the idea, having seen several nicknamed boats sunk and wishing to avoid bad luck. PT-528 sounded good enough.

Right after President Osmeña's rescue, RON36 and PT-528 were involved in the Battle of Leyte Gulf, the largest naval battle in World War II. In October 1944, PT-528, part of a 200,000-strong naval force, served picket duty guarding America's fleet, protecting carriers as the Japanese forces were defeated. It was at Leyte that Ferdie witnessed America's first experience with organized *kamikaze* attacks.

While protecting the warships, many miles from land, PT-528 came across a Japanese sailor (presumedly from a sunken ship) clinging to a log. Parched and black from the sun, he was left to his fate, and they continued their mission. No prisoner-of-war holding facilities were on board, and no one wanted to expose the boat to attack while rescuing an enemy combatant.

Life aboard PT boats was austere. After returning from all-night patrols, the sailors shared four hot, sweat-soaked racks (called "hot bunking"). They were constantly wet from the oppressive humidity. Bathing and laundry were done off the boat's transom. Then, from November to April, crews endured the rainy season, and also boredom, poor food, malaria, uncharted reefs, and tropical skin diseases. One in particular nicknamed "creeping crud" was the mainstay of their days.

Coffee and cigarettes were treasured items. Meals were often variations of SPAM, Vienna sausages, powdered eggs, baked beans, often eaten from a can, and Navy rations. Fresh fish was readily available via hand grenades. Treasures were real eggs, or O'Henry candy bars, often comshawed off others. When Ferdie returned home, he never ate SPAM again.

When not patrolling, the boats were supported by torpedo boat tenders. Converted, large LSTs (Landing Ship, Tanks) acted as mother ships and provided ammunition, berthing, repairs, medical treatment, laundry, and bathing. When not in action or tethered to a tender, the PT crews lived ashore, usually tented in hot, humid, rainy conditions, exposed to malaria and other jungle diseases. The crews became adept at living on very little as a group and had a reputation for scrounging or stealing from other Navy units.

In Ferdie's letters home to his sweetheart Bernadette, he would cleverly code his location by varying the middle initial of his signature, signing his letters Ferdinando B. Berti, Ferdinando O. Berti, Ferdinando R. Berti, Ferdinando N. Berti, Ferdinando E. Berti, and Ferdinando O. Berti, spelling out in this instance, Borneo.

The crew continued to update weaponry, trading 20mm for 40mm guns and adding a 37mm cannon on the front of their boat. The 37mm, made by Oldsmobile, with good magazine design, could fire ten rounds a minute.

There were now thirty-two squadrons operating in the southwest Pacific, primarily in the Solomon Islands and the Philippines. Squadrons from the south and southwest worked together.

Even with the end of war in sight, the 7th Fleet continued their attacks on Japanese shipping. In late April 1945, with P-38 Lightning airplanes providing air cover, PT-528 participated in a daring daylight raid into the Japanese-held Cowie Harbor. It was a particularly dangerous raid off Borneo's coast, striking under enemy-held heights around the harbor at noon. PT-528 and another PT boat took fire and sank a Japanese lugger and two lighters (barges). Ferdie was manning the boat's new 40mm cannon.

The crew taking a pause, with Berti on the far right. Note the stenciled images, called victory decals, indicating the number of ships sunk. (Courtesy of Berti family)

This was one of the last of Ferdie's 18 combat patrols during his twelve months in the South Pacific. An interesting postscript is that, in August of 1945, while his crew was resting at a PT boat tender, Ferdie overheard another boat sending Morse code noting that atom bombs had been dropped on Japan and that the war was over. In an eerie repetition of his experience years earlier informing his shipmates that Pearl Harbor had been bombed, he was able this time to announce the war's end.

Ferdie had been with PT-528 his entire deployment. With some reticence in leaving his crew, but anxious to be home with Bernadette, he started his return trip in October 1945. With his seabag in tow containing a Japanese flag, an officer's sword, and a helmet, Ferdie headed home by boat, landing in Boston, and was officially discharged with the rank of Chief Radioman on October 29, 1945. Taking the train home, Ferdie quickly and happily returned to civilian life, served several more years in the local National Guard, and worked briefly at Arnold Print Works and General Electric before beginning a thirty-three-year career with John Hancock Life Insurance Company.

Ferdie enjoyed visiting his life insurance clients to collect their monthly premiums. Sometimes, their payments were left in the mailbox or on the porch, but most times, the collection was in person, which gave him a chance to establish relationships; this fit well with his outgoing, gregarious nature.

Not long after returning home, his dad and brothers helped him build a house on 6 Potter Street in Adams, near St. Stanislaus Church, where the family attended services. He and Bernadette would go on to have two sons, Ronald and Richard. The Adams High footballer and his cheerleader sweetheart would be married for 56 years.

Over the years, Ferdie seldom spoke about the war, although his children remembered visits from Bob, one of his former crew members from Fall River, Massachusetts, who always brought fresh clams and talked about the war years. The kids would sneak up under the cover of darkness and avidly listen to the two old sailors recount their war stories.

Family vacations were taken in their four-door, beige Chevrolet II Nova. They visited popular regional spots such as the Catskill

Game Farm, Frontier Land, and "the North Pole," located in New York's Adirondack Mountains, a Christmas Village where Santa and his workshop could be "discovered" by children. Several of their most popular trips were to Hampton Beach in New Hampshire, where Ferdie and his brothers and their families rented cabins and enjoyed the beach, boating, some fishing, and central dining.

Ferdie seemed to know everyone. He was outgoing and always had a good word or joke for each person. His sons described him as "the life of the party." His good nature and ability to speak to a crowd often found him as a requested master of ceremonies. He is remembered for his ability to captivate an audience with Italian songs and masterful jokes. Ferdie also sang on WMNB, the local radio station, as part of the "Adams Hour" and at different local halls, usually with an accompanist.

Ferdie eventually retired from the insurance business in 1978 and Bernadette retired in 1982 from the Sprague Electric Company after her twenty-three years in their sales department, and the two of them enjoyed retirement together. Ferdie in particular loved the outdoors. He has been described as a "total outdoorsman, 12 months a year." He relished going hunting, fishing, and hiking with his family and close friends. He fished local lakes and the Deerfield River for trout. His sons remember Ferdie traveling to Nova Scotia for salmon season and bringing home a cooler full of fish. Over the years, Ferdie owned a series of Beagles that helped with his cottontail and snowshoe rabbit hunting. In pursuit of deer, he and his buddies rented a simple cabin in Vermont and aptly nicknamed it "the dark & dirty." Once, his family visited the cabin and found what has been described as a "tarpaper shack with a coal stove, bunk beds…probably only good for hunting, drinking, and poker." The family's visit required crossing a river to get to the cabin, only to find a rattlesnake occupying it. Ferdie dispatched the snake quickly, but it was the family's last visit.

Ferdie was also known locally as the "Mushroom King" because of his knowledge of mushroom species. He knew the seasons in which they could be picked safely and the best locations for finding them. Often friends and neighbors stopped by his house asking for advice on some mushrooms they had picked—most importantly, whether they were edible. He led many local forays with friends searching for mushrooms.

Ferdie remained engaged with football. He and two friends founded the Pop Warner football league in Adams, and the community recognized him for serving over thirty years as a football referee officiating at many Berkshire County games.

Ferdie also served as Chairperson for the Adams Board of Registrars for many years; was President of the Insurance Agents Union, local 58; and belonged to Trout Unlimited and the Adams Sportsman Hound and Hunt Club.

At one point, well into his 80s, he and his boys visited one of the few preserved PT boats. It was an Elco PT boat, a replica of that which Ferdie had sailed on many years ago. Postwar, the Navy had little use for the battered and worn boats, and over a hundred were beached, stripped, and burned in the Philippines. A few were sold to other countries or converted into sightseeing or fishing boats.

The boat Ferdie visited is located at the PT Boat Museum at Battleship Cove in Fall River. He nostalgically acted as the tour guide that day, remembering the countless hours spent in his radio shack, the crew's quarters, and at his gun station.

Ferdie passed away in 2005, and his funeral prompted a celebration of his life by many friends, all of whom had a Ferdie story or joke to tell. It was a life lived well.

During World War II, seventy of the five hundred PT boats in service were lost to enemy action, friendly fire, or accidents, resulting in the deaths of over three hundred sailors. Ferdie, one of the survivors, was awarded the American Campaign Medal, Asiatic–Pacific Campaign Medal with two battle stars, the Philippine Liberation Ribbon with one star, and the World War II Victory Medal for gallantry.

Robert I. Brown
Artilleryman
287th Artillery Observation Battalion

His unit landed on Okinawa in support of the 96th Army Infantry. Initially opposed by occasional artillery bursts and snipers, as the division proceeded inland, it came under bombardment from Japanese spigot mortars that launched massive 660 bombs: five-foot-tall, finned explosive rounds that left craters the size of a living room. Robert's unit needed to immediately determine their locations before the fearsome "screaming missiles" decimated the nearby front-line troops.

ROBERT IRVING BROWN MADE his unplanned entrance into the world on his mother's dining table at their Burham Street home in North Adams on February 11, 1920. On what his mother described as one of the "snowiest days of the year," a midwife successfully unwrapped the umbilical cord from around his neck. They would later attribute his bouts with bronchitis to his difficult birth.

Robert's parents were Forrest Irving Brown and Mary Agnes (Bovie), one with roots in New Hampshire and the other in Vermont, who moved to North Adams seeking work. Both found work at New England Telephone and Telegraph, and Forrest met Mary Agnes when installing equipment in the telephone office. They were married on November 17, 1914.

Forrest would work forty-three years for the phone company as an installer, and Mary Agnes would become a homemaker and manage the family's small farm and apple orchard.

The family of four lived on Burnham Street in North Adams,

purchased with the help of Forrest's elderly father, who required life tenancy for the $2,000 gift, a deal Mary Agnes later regretted. At one point, Mary Agnes was able to purchase an adjacent fourteen acres of land for $500, and the family built a barn and bought their first cow.

One of Robert's first childhood chores was milking the cow at five a.m. before school. His mother would wait for him in the doorway to come across the backyard with the fresh milk. Sometimes, he would sneak a sip of the cream that rose to the top of the pail, and his mom would correct him because she needed it to make butter and for his dad's coffee.

Robert attended Notre Dame Grammar School, and his best friends were Johnny, Olympio, and Louis. They nicknamed him "Brownie" and together fished creek bottoms for suckers. When not fishing, they threw firecrackers in the creek, waxing the wicks so they would go off. They also liked to hide behind headstones at the cemetery and watch the rituals associated with Jewish burials.

Brownie graduated in the class of 1939 from Drury High School. He had excelled in mathematics and had belonged to the French club and traffic club. He continued to help on the farm with the livestock and worked part-time at the local J.C. Penney.

Like many of his generation, he vividly remembered how he first learned of the attack on Pearl Harbor on December 7, 1941. Returning home after an argument with his girlfriend, he found his mom sitting near the radio, visibly upset. She had just heard about the Japanese attack and said the terrifying words, "We are going to war."

Less than two months later, in early February 1942, Brownie, with twenty-three other men, was part of the largest draft call of its time. The troop went to Fort Devens for official induction, followed by haircuts, inoculations, and the issuing of uniforms. Not long after, they were sent by train to Fort Bragg (now Fort Liberty), North Carolina, for additional training. Brownie remembers stopping in North Adams on the way to Bragg; it was the middle of the night, just a few minutes from home, yet he could not disembark. He described it as the loneliest night of his life.

Scoring high in math on his aptitude test at Fort Bragg, Robert was designated a Field Observation Artilleryman and sent to Fort Sill in early 1942 to learn his new job. Training ranged from eight to twelve weeks. Instructors taught him how to operate different artillery pieces; procedures for safely handling ammunition, setting charges, and lighting fuses; and, most importantly, how to calculate the distance to targets both manually and with instruments. As part of this new position, he was trained to work closely with infantry, calculating and calling in the distance to enemy artillery batteries.

Robert home on leave from Fort Bragg (now Fort Liberty), visiting his folks at 51 Burnham Street in North Adams. (Courtesy of Brown family)

Fort Sill, Oklahoma, was created shortly after the end of the Civil War. Initially established to defend settlers during the Indian Wars, its cemeteries contain tribal chiefs who were laid to rest next to 10th Cavalry "Buffalo Soldiers" and their families. The most famous residents are Geronimo, the Apache chief; a renowned Kiowa chief named Satanta (also Set'tainte, meaning *White Bear*); and a Comanche chief, Quanah Parker.

The School of Artillery at Fort Sill was established in 1911 and still operates there today on 15,000 acres, allowing open space for target practice and tactical exercises. When Robert attended the school, it had just replaced the old 75mm French-designed howitzer that had been standard in the US Army since World War I with the

105mm howitzer, which became World War II's most used artillery piece. The 105 could fire a much greater distance and was easily transportable via a 2 1/2-ton truck.

Fort Sill was also the home of World War I military combat aviation. In World War II, it championed air observation and began testing a small, two-man, unarmed airplane to help coordinate artillery fire. Known as L-4s and nicknamed "grasshoppers," they could be airborne in less than 100 feet, were painted olive drab, and equipped with radios. Each battalion had two planes. The planes would greatly aid on-the-ground observers who could only see nearby targets. So effective were the aircraft that enemy batteries would cease firing when the planes came overhead so as not to reveal their positions.

During the war, Fort Sill also served as the Army's boot camp for thousands of soldiers, an internment center for Japanese, and a stockade for German POWs.

Three artillery batteries of twelve 105mm howitzers were assigned to each Army division, and then one battery was placed with each of its three regiments. The batteries often supported each other, bringing concentrated fire upon the enemy.

Artillery would be one of the United States' significant military advantages. Germany, among other countries, still relied on horses for movement of their artillery, which significantly slowed reaction time and mobility. Horses needed rest and could only move field guns about 25 miles a day, whereas the United States could quickly transport the 105mm howitzers 150 miles by truck.

General George Patton is quoted as saying, "I do not have to tell you who won the war. You know the artillery did." Artillery would become one of WWII's deadliest weapons because of communications with observers on the ground and in light planes, allowing commanders to control multiple batteries and bring down massive firepower upon enemy positions. The Japanese and Germans were focused on building bigger guns, while United States efforts were directed at building a better system with interacting components, which worked.

In November 1942, Robert saw the Bob Hope Show at Fort Sill. He probably attended it at the now-historic Artillery Bowl, a large amphitheater-like area reserved for ceremonies and sports events. When he was watching, the temperature was 28 degrees.

During his training, Brownie became an expert at "sound ranging," a technique that began in WWI measuring the sound of live fire from enemy guns to locate them. Robert and his unit of observers would use this method very effectively in the upcoming battles of Leyte Island and Okinawa. It was particularly valuable when locating artillery pieces hidden from observation by camouflage, trees, or fog.

"Brownie" and friend training on the radio. (Courtesy of Brown family)

Brownie's unit would use microphones connected to field telephones and evaluate the sound waves from the noise of shell bursts to identify enemy positions. Each microphone received an electrical impulse that allowed observers to plot the coordinates of the origination of incoming fire. The optimal situation was to use three microphones placed in a triangular shape, hanging on a tripod slightly below the ground about 20 feet apart. A combat observation team could set up a "hasty" sound base in forty minutes to respond to urgent combat needs.

Once the enemy location could be determined, the data would be fed to US counter batteries by field telephone to its battalion fire direction center. This coordination allowed commanders to bring massive firepower from different artillery battalions onto one hostile location. Germany and Japan feared the immediate, devastating, and massive firepower unleashed by the Allies' coordinated artillery responses.

During 1943 and 1944, Robert, now adept at sound ranging, moved between Army forts, instructing other soldiers on its application. After his time at Fort Sill, he returned to Fort Bragg several times, as well as Camp Bowie in Texas, and then on to Fort Polk in Louisiana, where he trained artillery battalions. By this point, he had been promoted several times and was now a Staff Sergeant assigned to the 285th Artillery Observation Battalion.

At one point, just before embarking overseas with the 285th, Robert and several MPs were sent on a trip to retrieve a soldier who had been AWOL (Absent without Leave). Upon Robert's return, his unit had already left for Europe, and Robert was reassigned to the 287th Artillery Observation Battalion.

Robert first left the United States from Seattle, Washington, on D-Day (June 6, 1944), headed for the Pacific Theater. He traveled on a Liberty ship that stopped in the Marshall and Admiralty islands; unknown to him at the time, he was headed for the Philippine island of Leyte and his first major battle.

On October 20, 1944, Operation King II began with the invasion of Leyte Island. Leyte is 115 miles long and at various points measures between 15 to 40 miles wide, and it was occupied by an estimated 20,000 Japanese soldiers. The 7th and 96th Infantry Divisions landed on the southern half of the island, near a town named Dulag, establishing a beachhead. Once the beaches were secure, the divisions moved westward to seize the Dulag airfield and then continued on to capture the island's three other fields.

Brownie's group began working closely with the Army's 96th Infantry as they slugged it out with the Japanese 9th Infantry Division.

Held on ships until the beachhead was secure, Brownie's 287th Observation Battalion and two artillery battalions landed on the swampy and muddy Blue Beach on October 22. By nighttime, they were on the outskirts of Dulag. The 287th Observation Battalion established a position north of Dulag, and by October 24, all were in place to fire in support.

The conditions on the marshy ground made movement miserable, if not impossible. Heavy rains immobilized artillery pieces, and the units came under aerial attack at different times. The 287th was very close to the front lines and subject to *banzai* attacks by Japanese forces. Snipers were a real nuisance, cleverly shooting right when the artillery pieces fired in order to disguise their locations.

Simultaneously with the battle on land, the Japanese determined to keep the island and engaged US Naval forces in the Leyte Gulf. Over three days (October 23 to 26), their fleet would be decimated with the loss of four carriers, three battleships, six heavy and four light cruisers, and nine destroyers. At the beginning of Leyte Gulf, few knew there were doubts about its outcome, and the general in charge of artillery on the island had two 155mm howitzer battalions train their guns on the ocean.

At Dulag, Robert set up his observation team under mortar and artillery bombardment. Using range sounding, the team dug three holes, set up tripods over each, and, with microphones, began using percussion information from the three points to calculate the distance/location of Japanese guns. Then they called in artillery to destroy them.

With visibility poor and the Japanese initially holding the high ground, the 287th also had observers on L-4 artillery spotter planes. One pilot got lost in a rainstorm, landed in Japanese territory, and had the presence of mind to bury operational plans, hide his aircraft, and make it back to friendly territory. Days later, once the area was in friendly hands, he returned, dug up the plans, fixed the plane, and returned to Dalag airfield.

The Japanese continued to send thousands of reinforcements

to the island from October to December, and the 96th Infantry was in the center of these battles, always supported by Robert's 287th Observation Battalion.

Most of the island was secured by the end of November. Still, in one last effort the early morning of December 6, the Japanese infiltrated an area adjacent to the 287th in an attempt to retake an airfield, and 150 Japanese paratroopers landed nearby. It took two days of fierce hand-to-hand combat to eliminate them.

Pockets of resistance continued to exist, and in late December, Robert and his team were on a nighttime Christmas Eve mission to replace wire for microphones that the Japanese had severed. The trailer holding the large roll of wire slid off the muddy road into a mud hole. They were able to winch the trailer out and resume the mission, although the cable had been nicked, and as it unspooled too rapidly through the hands of a soldier, it pierced both of his hands. Robert would later tell his son in graphic detail, "It tore up his hands like hamburger!"

The man's screaming quickly brought heavy enemy fire from a Japanese patrol. The group ran for cover and Robert began trying to recite the *Hail Mary*, a prayer his mother had taught him, but, in the pandemonium, he could only remember "Hail Mary, full of grace," so he kept repeating those words.

In his scramble to escape enemy fire, he fell into a rice paddy and swallowed a mouthful of mud and buffalo dung. He got to his feet and continued running but began to feel sick and was about ready to accept his fate when some kid in his outfit grabbed him and said, "C'mon, Sarge, not tonight, not tonight!"

He recalled, "I guess the blessed mother heard me that Christmas Eve, even though I couldn't remember her prayer. I was so scared that night, I couldn't stop crying!"

On another occasion, Brownie was talking with a local man who had captured a Japanese soldier. In the middle of their conversation, with the hand-tied soldier nearby, the local native (whom the Japanese had tormented) turned around and cut off the prisoner's ear.

Robert was shocked by the rapid action, and the mutilated, screaming prisoner was taken away by the Leyte man, his fate relatively sealed. Later, the same native returned and gave Robert the knife with sergeant stripes carved in the wooden sheath. By December 1944, securing the island was in its final phase, although some Japanese holdouts would fight on for five more months. Back in Europe, friends of Robert were losing their lives. His close childhood friend Johnny was killed while crossing the Rhine River with the US Army. Then, on December 17, 1944, near the city of Malmedy, Belgium, thirty vehicles from the 285th, Robert's former battalion, were taken under fire by German SS tanks during the Battle of the Bulge. With no choice, the troops surrendered. Shortly afterward, the SS troops lined up the American POWs in a farmer's field, machine-gunned 84 soldiers, and executed any wounded with a shot to the head. Almost all of the slain were from Battery B of the 285th, the same men Robert had served with at Fort Sill. He would never forget the faces of those he had lived alongside for months. The war crime became known as the Malmedy Massacre.

It was later discovered that SS troops had murdered 500 to 700 POWs during the month-long Battle of the Bulge. At war's end, trials were held at the Dachau concentration camp, and the war criminals were sentenced to death or imprisonment. Not one of the death sentences was carried out, ultimately.

For Robert and his unit, there would be several months of rest, refitting, and training of replacements before the 287th would again be engaged in one of the defining battles of World War II: the invasion of Okinawa, known as "Operation Iceberg." The 287th would be a valuable part of World War II's Pacific strategy, simply Army and Marines island-hopping en route to Japan. The capture of Okinawa would bring Japan well within range of heavy bombers.

The USS *Audrain* brought the 287th to Okinawa. They paused offshore for seven days after the infantry landed on April 1, 1945 (Easter Sunday). While waiting for the beachhead to be secured, they were subject to Japan's newly introduced weapon—the deadly *kamikaze*, a bomb-laden plane suicidally flown into a target. During the battle of Leyte Gulf, over 400 US ships were sunk or damaged, and thousands of sailors were killed.

Once able to disembark, they met very little resistance, but within a few days, all hell broke loose as his unit followed the 96th Army Infantry Division across the island and southward into the island's most heavily defended areas.

Initially, the artillery batteries were located near the hospital tents on the beach while the observers ranged forward behind the advancing infantry. Robert and his team were often with the infantry units, who greatly appreciated the firepower they could provide to suppress the enemy quickly.

The battles were vicious, with no quarter given as they captured Cactus and Kakazu Ridge, fought along the Shuri line, and numerous other unnamed knolls where thousands died. Robert's unit quickly identified enemy emplacements and artillery locations to be extinguished by 105mm howitzers. Concrete burial tombs cut into hillsides often harbored enemy guns and were destroyed as units pushed on.

Surrendering was not an option for many Japanese, who often dispatched themselves with a grenade or shot to the head. When the Japanese 24th Division headquarters was located in a cave with over 200 Japanese in it, the Americans broadcasted a surrender request, but to no avail. Over 1,500 gallons of gasoline and 300 pounds of dynamite were used to seal the mountain redoubt.

As they proceeded southward, his unit passed by stripped-down Japanese prisoners wearing loincloths, or naked, being thrown into trucks to be taken to an internment center. Too often, the trucks would be back sooner than expected. Robert later told his son that he presumed they'd all been shot.

During the battle, Robert came across a dead Japanese soldier who had bled from his ears and apparently died from an artillery concussion. Noticing his helmet nearby and checking it for booby traps, he found a flag in its lining and retrieved it as a war souvenir, which he later brought back to the States.

Robert takes a break on his unit's Jeep, with a souvenir from the recent battle. (Courtesy of Brown family)

The fighting continued, increasing in intensity. At one point, under an extended period of shelling, Robert was sharing a foxhole with one of his young soldiers, who was crying. He encouraged the soldier that they would get through it. After a moment, the man told him, "Sarge, I'm crying because I shit in my pants."

Fighting on the island concluded in June 1945, and the 287th became part of the occupying force, processing prisoners, collecting weapons, and preparing for their next battle, which was to be the assault on Japan. Over 12,000 Americans were killed and another 36,000 wounded in the fight for Okinawa, the bloodiest Pacific battle. Also dead were 110,000 Japanese military and 100,000 civilians.

Many military and diplomacy experts have concluded that the high human cost of capturing Okinawa and the anticipated difficulty that would be experienced in invading Japan led to the use of atomic bombs on Hiroshima and Nagasaki in early August 1945. It can't be known whether traditional warfare would have been preferable to the horrors of atomic warfare, but Japan's unconditional surrender took place in September 1945.

By now, Robert had accumulated enough points to be released from duty. He headed home in December 1945 with the rank of 1st Sergeant, and he was discharged at Fort Devens in January 1946. In March, at his sister's wedding, he met a young woman by the name of Margaret Mary St. John, who worked for the telephone company. She would become the future Mrs. Robert Brown.

The couple were married on April 12, 1947, at St. Thomas Church in Adams, Massachusetts, and would have nine children over the next twenty-plus years. After his return home, Robert was hired by the New England Telephone Company and, for many years, worked as a lineman and then an equipment installer. He found the electronics and wiring similar to his artillery work. The telephone company was a bit of a Cupid's bow: Robert and Margaret, as well as his parents, all worked and met there.

To provide for nine children, Robert had a second job creating and painting signs for local businesses. On the weekend, Greylock Ice & Fuel Trucks would pull into his driveway, and he would design and letter them. He also made signs for local supermarkets and ice cream parlors. When money was scarce at Christmas, he would make toys in his workshop. His son also remembers Dad handcrafting 2' x 3' garages, toy cribs, and many painted rocking horses for his brothers and sisters.

Robert's second job also fed into his love of painting. His medium was oil and acrylics, and he loved doing caricatures, painting scenes of everyday life, and crafting beautiful portraits of well-known figures such as Pope Pius X and George Washington. His artistry and sense of humor carried over to work at the telephone company. If he had a bad day at work, he would come home and render a comedic sketch, not necessarily flattering of the person who upset him. This usually made him feel better.

Robert, a self-taught violinist, appreciated all types of music, from Arthur Fielder's Boston Pops Orchestra to "The Lawrence Welk Show" and "Sing Along with Mitch" on television. He also enjoyed musicals, opera, and ballet. He was an enthusiastic sound man for his son and daughter as they played at weddings and Masses for local churches.

At his two-story home on Randall Street, Robert had a den upstairs in the back of the house with a sign on the door that read *War Room*. In his retreat, he painted and displayed some of his creations. Central on the back wall was the Japanese flag from Okinawa. In addition to his desk and VCR, there was also a Japanese rifle, a disarmed grenade, and a timer from a Japanese bomb.

Family vacations were taken in a packed, four-door green 1962 Chevrolet Bel Air station wagon. If headed to Lake Sebago in Maine, the family would haul an Apache trailer. When the children were young, weekends often included trips to the Catskill Game Farm, Gaslight Village, Storytown, nearby picnic grounds, or Anthony's Pond in Adams.

His children describe Robert as always loving a good joke, a devoted family man who garnered their respect. They joke about Dad the Army man, always inspecting their cub or boy scout uniforms before they left for a meeting.

The horrors of war were never too far away. When Robert bought his first computer and researched the Malmedy Massacre, he had tears as he read the names of close friends he soldiered with for many months. Margaret, his wife, often said, "It was the hand of God that interceded for him."

A few copies of Robert's letters from the Pacific remain. Below are some abridged notes from them:

November 10, 1945, in the rear echelon: *Platoon has a cute puppy. He loves beer but gets very unsteady from it…also eats apples and oranges. We do want to move back to the beach. We'll have Quonset huts to live in instead of tents….*

November 13, 1945, processing to go home: *After you receive this letter, you can stop writing me…. I must have 69 points. It will be a great day for me when I see the good old U.S.A.*

November 14, 1945, written from the 25th Replacement

Center: *Waiting until I'm called to get on a ship to go home…slim chance of being home with you for Christmas…. If you can buy any undershirts and broadcloth shirts, will you get them for me, please? I've heard they are very scarce.*

One of Robert's sons described his dad in glowing terms: "My dad is the greatest man I ever knew…. [I] compared all others to him. He was honest, decent, kind, gentle, and he was a warrior." This family man and warrior passed away in his recliner in the year 2000, listening to his favorite Irish melodies.

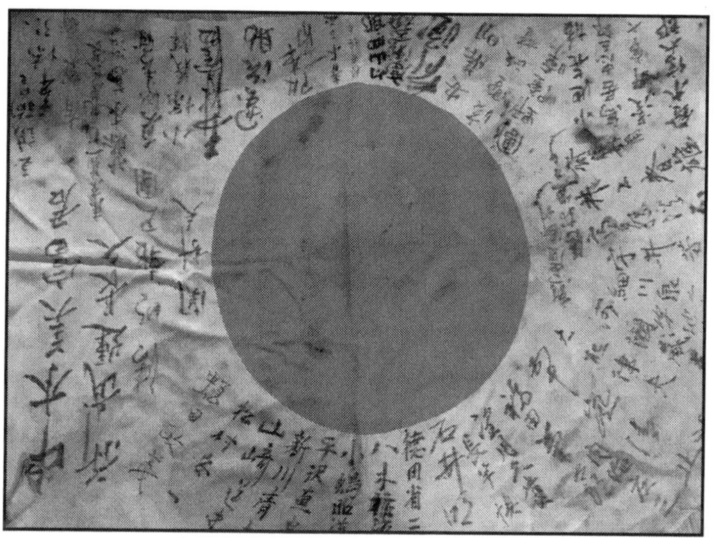

The flag from a Japanese soldier's helmet: captured in war, returned in peace. (Courtesy of Brown family)

POSTSCRIPT

AFTER ROBERT'S DEATH, HIS son contacted the OBON Society to locate the deceased Japanese soldier's family. The OBON society's mission is to return "good luck flags" to their families in Japan. He described, based on his father's memory, where and how it was obtained and sent a picture to them.

The good luck flags (Yoshiaki Hinomaru) were smaller replicas of the Japanese national flag. They were signed by family and friends, often with a short message for the deploying soldier wishing him good luck and victory. The text, written with a calligraphy brush and ink, radiated from the flag's central red circle to resemble the sun's rays. It was something of a work of art, and quite personal. Whenever the deployed soldier unfolded it, it reminded him of his community and the prayers being offered for him.

Remarkably the flag was identified as having belonged to Mitomi Nakamoto, a soldier killed in action. His brother Tomiyasu Nakamoto, living in the Kyoto prefecture, recognized many of the signatures and wished to have the flag returned. The Brown family mailed it to OBON, who repatriated the flag with its family.

Dixon H. Daniels
Communications Officer
1st Marine Division

From a mile's distance, the black mortar puffs in the sky did not seem that threatening as his amphibious vehicle approached Peleliu's beach. As he and his fellow Marines closed in on a reef 700 yards from shore, the explosions became deafening, and massive blasts of water started to appear on all sides of their boat. The Japanese had accurately pre-registered their mortars, and suddenly, his boat was enveloped in flames.

DIXON "DIXIE" HALL DANIELS was born in Adams, Massachusetts, on September 30, 1921. His parents, Rupert and Marjorie (Wellington) Daniels, would have one daughter and four sons, most of whom went on to serve in World War II.

Rupert was an executive with the L.L. Brown Paper Co., which his family had managed for decades. The company had been founded in 1849; before Rupert, his father led the company for more than half a century. Family history recounts that the eldest Daniels started as a sweeper, borrowed money, and eventually bought the business. Rupert, who had been a three-star high school athlete, became a community leader and sang every Sunday in the First Congregational Choir. Marjorie, well known for her gracious hospitality, was an active community volunteer and homemaker.

Dixon attended a local grammar school and, like many of his friends, spent most of his time outdoors. When he wasn't fishing, he was likely to be off on an adventure with his BB gun. Even today, Dixon's son remembers Dixon describing how he would "buy a scoop of BBs at the local hardware store and fill both his pockets for 3 cents and be able to shoot all weekend."

Early on, Rupert introduced Dixon to what would later become his passion in life: golf. As an adolescent, he played many rounds at the Forest Park Country Club and just missed winning the junior member club championship in 1938, losing to his brother.

On Sundays, Dixon would scrub for church and sing every week in the First Congregational Church on Park Street, right across from the Adams Diner. As he grew older, his dad often found him part-time janitorial work at L.L. Brown, which competed for his time on Sundays.

Dixon graduated from Adams High School in 1939. "At high school he was a member of the Pro Merito society, an outstanding athlete and three-letter man and a member of the debating team, the Hi-Tension staff and the executive committee of the class," wrote the local paper of record, *The Transcript* of North Adams, in December 1942. At graduation, the Alumni Association awarded him a scholarship of $50 for being a student "who [in] the belief of the teachers will reflect the greatest credit on Adams High School by their future accomplishments…." (*Transcript,* 6-24-39).

His oratorical skills were also well displayed when he was selected to recite the Gettysburg Address during the town's well-attended 1939 Memorial Day celebration.

Dixon was accepted to Dartmouth College in Hanover, New Hampshire, and quickly settled in as a bright student, athlete, and member of the DKE fraternity. He played varsity football, basketball, and baseball. His 1940 freshman basketball squad was recognized for having a perfect season. One of his fondest memories was as a junior playing and beating Williams College baseball team 10 - 8. He played right field and had two of Dartmouth's seven hits.

With the crescendo of World War II increasing, Dixon remained at Dartmouth for summer studies "so that his graduation may be advanced to December instead of taking place next June, as he is anxious to enter the armed forces of the country as soon as his college career can be completed" (*Transcript,* 7-17-42). In December 1942, Dixon received his A.B. Degree in History.

Dixon as a newly minted Marine Corps Lieutenant. (Courtesy of Daniels family)

After graduation, he was temporarily employed at L.L. Brown Paper Company, passed his military physical in July, and entered the United States Marine Corps in January 1943.

He began, as many Marines do, in recruit training at Parris Island, South Carolina. After six weeks of intense indoctrination, he was transferred to an Officer Candidate Class at Quantico, Virginia, for the eight-week course on leadership, tactics, and weapons. Dixon "graduate[d] and [was] commissioned a Second Lieutenant in April 1943" (*Transcript,* 4-24-43).

He was selected to be a Communications Line Officer and, after considerable training, assigned to the newly formed Joint Assault Signal Company (JASCO). JASCO units are attached to Infantry divisions and are responsible for coordinating all land and naval gunfire and close air support for infantry troops. Communication Officers with these newly formed Assault Signal Companies will be critical in the Marines' upcoming beach landings.

It is notable that JASCOs were formed after the Marines' battle at Tarawa, where lapses of supporting arms before the Marines landed caused them to fight under horrific conditions and intense Japanese fire. In addition, after landing, they suffered from a lack of communication between pilots and ground troops. JASCO was meant to be a solution and preventative measure. During the last year of the war, JASCOs were lauded as being very responsive to ground troops' needs, lifting supporting fires as the unit progressed, not at a predetermined time, and developing creeping barrages that kept several hundred yards ahead of troops, clearing the way for them. Both actions were highly successful and significantly reduced casualties.

Dixon's next months were consumed with communications training. He attended Harvard University's Pre-Radar Program for 13 weeks, then moved to Fort Monmouth, New Jersey, and on to Naval Armory, Los Angeles, California, for 22 weeks in additional communications training.

As soon as his training was completed, Dixon quickly shipped out in early 1944, and his 4th JASCO unit was assigned to the Marine 1st Division, where he was subsequently transferred to the 2nd Battalion of the 5th Marine Regiment, boasting 1,000 Marines and sailors. (The 2nd Battalion-5th Marine Regiment was formed in 1914 and fought in the storied World War I battles of Belleau Wood and the Meuse-Argonne Offensive. Its motto, "Retreat, Hell!," originated at Belleau Wood when fleeing French soldiers being overwhelmed by German troops told the newly arrived Marines to retreat. The battalion responded, "Retreat, Hell! We just got here!")

1st Marine Division Patch. (Courtesy of the author)

With the 1st Division, Dixon participated in the capturing of several small islands and was involved in the tail end of the Battle of Cape Gloucester. In later years, he recounted to his son how, on one beach landing, a lone Japanese officer came running toward his large group of Marines, firing his pistol. Quickly, he was dispatched. During another skirmish, the Marine next to him was shot through the neck and continued to fight, much to the surprise of his comrades.

After Cape Gloucester was secured in April 1944, the 1st Division was diverted to recover, replenish its supplies, and replace its casualties on the island of Pavuvu, sixty miles west of Guadalcanal. The Division had over 1,000 casualties in the Battle for Cape Gloucester, and many of its Marines were trying to recover from malaria, dysentery, and jungle rot.

The island, picked as a recovery site from the air by the Division's commanding general for its idyllic, beach-like appearance, was misleading. Home to an abandoned coconut plantation, Pavuvu was described by the men as a desolate chunk of mud and coral. There were no roads, electricity, or water, so the recovering Marines spent days chipping and crushing coral to make marginal roads and living areas. Showers consisted of the occasional rainstorm, and giant rats and crabs became their latest enemy.

Dixie was snake-bitten on Pavuvu but was quickly treated and recovered after several days in a tent hospital.

While the work details tried to make the island livable, thousands of replacements were brought in and spent many training hours assaulting life-like Japanese bunkers with grenades, flamethrowers, bazookas, and demolitions, preparing for their next battle.

The Division's only relief that summer was a surprise visit by Bob Hope and his accompanying USO Troupe. The open-air show was seen by most of the Division and was a great morale lifter. Always the jester, Hope noted that the giant land crabs, if saddled, might be racehorses.

About the same time, Dixon's hometown newspaper relayed some good news: "Brothers Meet in the South Pacific—Lieut. Dixon Daniels…had the pleasure of meeting his brother…Donald Daniels, when he recently arrived at a South Pacific Island" (*Transcript,* 8-10-44). The reunion was short-lived. Just days after seeing his brother, Dixon and the 1st Division secretly departed Pavuvu for its next battle: the invasion of Peleliu Island. Once the thousands of Marines were loaded aboard thirty large Landing Ship Tanks (LSTs, troop carriers), the convoy departed on September 4, 1944, for an eleven-day 2100-mile trip and were now part of Operation Stalemate.

The LSTs, also known to the Marines as Large Slow Targets because of their sluggish pace of between seven and nine knots per hour, were designed with huge clam-shell doors that allowed the launching of amphibious vehicles. The Marines packed on the LSTs tried to stay on deck as much as possible and avoid the dank, humid conditions below. Dixon, like others, read books, played cards, drank black coffee, and cleaned his M1 carbine to pass the time. Dixie, an expert marksman, enjoyed carrying the carbine. It weighed four pounds less than the traditional M1 Garand rifle, and the communications team, already burdened with radios and other equipment, welcomed its lighter weight and shorter design.

At Peleliu, the 9,000 infantry Marines from the 1st Division's three regiments would face an entrenched enemy of well over 10,000 combatants. Most tacticians at the time recommended assaulting forces outnumber their opponents three to one. It was not to be for this operation. Waiting for them were Japan's best troops from the Japanese 4th Infantry Division and 2nd Infantry Regiment, supported by 3,000 forced laborers.

During this pre-invasion period, Dixon, as the team's leader, met with ship and aviation members to ensure he understood the ground forces' objectives and established common radio frequencies. Operation Stalemate and the hoped-for capture of Peleliu had been designed to protect General MacArthur's right flank as he got ready to invade the Philippines. Peleliu lies 500 miles from the Philippines, providing a harbor and excellent airfield for the Japanese. The primary goal of the invasion force was to capture the island's airfield and destroy the Japanese air force. No one realized at the time that most of Japan's Pacific air fleet had already been destroyed in earlier battles; in retrospect the costly invasion was unnecessary. The previous March, Peleliu had been pummeled by Hellcat fighters and dauntless dive-bombers cratering the runway and destroying scores of Japanese Zeroes, permanently blunting any threat to MacArthur's impending invasion of the Philippines.

While Dixon was on the way to Peleliu, airstrikes were launched on the island, followed by a naval bombardment by five battleships, eight heavy and light cruisers, and fifteen destroyers. Running parallel about three miles offshore, the 16- and 14-inch guns pummeled every target they could see.

After days of bombing, both naval and from the air, there were few surface targets left. General Rupertus, the 1st Division's Commanding General, believed at this point it would only take three or four days to secure the island. What he didn't realize was that the defenders were hidden below ground in over 600 caves, tunnels, and bunkers, and that Japanese strategy had changed from wasteful *banzai* attacks to delayed responses, purposefully hanging back to wear out and bleed the attackers, causing the maximum number of casualties.

On the morning of the invasion, September 15, 1944, Dixon woke to the sound of reveille at 3:00 a.m. and was offered the traditional before-battle breakfast of steak, eggs, and coffee. Many men declined to eat, anxious about what's ahead of them. Dixie remembered his commanding officer telling him the landing would be "a tough one." At 5:30 a.m., he went below deck and climbed into his amtrac (amphibious tracked vehicle) for a slow trip to shore.

Hundreds of amtracs (also known as LVTs—Landing Vehicle Tracked) splashed out of the LST and assembled several miles from shore. They were led by heavily armored LVTs with 75mm cannons and .50-caliber machine guns designed to forge the way and suppress enemy beach fire. Dixon's group followed the waves of infantrymen.

The 36,000-pound amtracs, armed with two .30-caliber machine guns, were intended to provide protection and transportation of 24 fully equipped Marines or equipment as they traveled to shore. Once the troops disembarked, the amtracs loaded the wounded and returned to hospital ships.

Dixon's amtrac carried members of his platoon and a communications Jeep with some 55-gallon barrels of fuel. Once on shore, he planned to use the MZ radio Jeep as a relay station to communicate between his men on land, the ships, and nearby aircraft. In one of the succeeding waves were dozens of Native Americans from the Navajo tribe, "code talkers" who would radio messages in their language as it was incomprehensible to the Japanese. They could send unbreakable messages to fire support on ships and command posts on the island.

Five battalions from 1st, 5th, and 7th Regiments were to head for designated landing areas. Battalions from the 1st Regiment would land to the left on White beaches 1 and 2. Dixon, with the 5th, would land in the middle on Orange beaches 1 and 2; the 7th would land on Orange beach 3. The plan was to land abreast across an area of 2,500 yards.

Everyone knew their vehicles would pause at a reef 700 yards from shore as the amtracs ambled over the coral buffer. Few realized from that point onward the entire area had been pre-registered by Japanese artillery and mortars, and mines were strewn throughout their path.

As the waves of amtracs began their approach, black puffs in the sky appeared, and Dixon, from his vantage point, began to see huge bursts of water far ahead, all from enemy artillery. In a way, he was lucky that his battalion was in the middle of the landing forces, so enfilading fire from the flanks would be less dangerous to his group, but he was exposed to indirect mortar fire.

As Dixon's amtrac slowly approached the reef, shells began bursting nearby, sea water splashed over the side of his boat, and he heard machine gun bullets dinging its hull. Once the reef was barely navigated, he peeked over the side to see dozens of burned and blackened amtracs ablaze and corpses floating in the water. The boat's slow pace made it a tempting target for the Japanese artillerymen.

Even with Hellcat fighters flying overhead, spraying the beach with .50-caliber fire, blue and white Japanese machine gun tracers reached out from the beach from every direction, creating a withering hailstorm to run through.

The six-mile island was festooned with artillery. There were dozens of 75mm artillery pieces, heavy mortars, dual-purpose antiaircraft guns, and rocket launchers, all quickly directed at the amphibious boats. The Japanese had presumed, and they were right, that the Marines' primary objective would be its first-class airfield located just 300 yards inland from the beach.

As the amtracs continued to navigate the reef, artillery and mortar fire began coming in from the 300-foot mountain in the distance, called Umurbrogol by the Americans. Caves, with rails and armor-plated doors, had protected these fortifications, and now they unleashed fire on the approaching beaches.

It is believed fire from one of these mortars hit the battalion amtrac carrying its communications equipment—Dixon's amtrac.

Dixon remembers a deafening explosion on the left side of his amtrac as his landing craft approached the beach. The hit threw the communications Jeep up against him and many others, trapping them against the wall while at the same time igniting the boat's gasoline drums. Later in life, he told his son, "I said to myself, this is it; I'm going to burn to death before ever firing a shot!"

Dixon thinks the landing craft rolled over, which freed him, but he doesn't remember hitting the water, and he woke up in a field hospital many days later with most of the front of his body burned and suffering many cuts from the coral. He believed that no one else survived.

It appeared that he was rescued by several Marines who dragged him ashore to the battalion aid station, where he was likely given a shot of morphine by a corpsman, put on an IV to prevent shock, and then loaded unconscious onto an amtrac that carried him to the USS *Bountiful*, a naval hospital ship.

The 1st Marine Division would suffer over 1,000 casualties on the first day, and Dixon was among them. The anticipated three-day battle would not conclude for over two months, resulting in 10,000 Marine and Army casualties. Fewer than 100 Japanese survived.

Dixon was awarded the Purple Heart and his unit, the 4th JASCO, for its heroics would receive the Presidential Unit Citation and go on to receive a second award for its actions at the Battle of Okinawa.

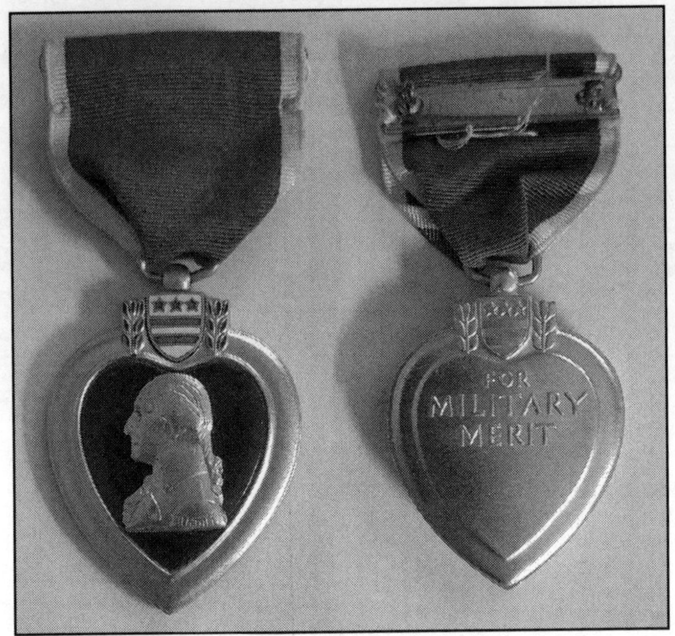

Dixon's original Purple Heart medal. (Courtesy of Daniels family)

In the meantime, Dixon was evacuated by ship to the Naval Hospital in San Diego, California. He eventually awoke to find his eyes bandaged and could tell that most of his burns were on the front of his body. His face, forearms, hands, chest, neck, and legs were covered with dressings and were horribly painful. He also suffered from lacerating coral cuts. Although unable to see, he recognized the voice of another wounded JASCO Marine in the bed beside him.

Dixon would be in San Diego for months as doctors repeatedly grafted thin slices of skin from his back, buttocks, and legs to his burned areas. Although burn victims represented only 1.5% of World War II's casualties, they required a tremendous amount of hospital care. While rudimentary forms of skin grafting had been going on for hundreds of years, the 1940s saw considerable advancement in understanding skin grafting. Removing damaged skin, followed by grafting a thin layer of skin taken from another part of the body went a long way in hastening healing.

Fortunately, Dixon was the beneficiary of recent work done

by a New Zealander named Archibald McIndoe, a doctor with the Royal Air Force renowned for his work in developing new grafting techniques during World War II. Aware that burn victims had suffered high mortality rates during the first World War, McIndoe instituted saline-bath immersions, advocated keeping wounds open for healing, and regularly changed loose, moist dressings with soothing jelly. McIndoe was also the first physician to understand the need to rehabilitate sometimes horribly disfigured men into society.

Following his release from San Diego Hospital after months of painful grafts, *The Transcript* reported: "Wounded Marine at Adams Home....at the conclusion of his leave...will report to the Chelsea Naval Hospital...for further hospitalization..." (1-4-45).

Dixon was subsequently released from Chelsea and ordered back to San Diego for more skin grafts for the following year. He underwent numerous operations before being honorably discharged in June 1946 in San Diego, California.

While Dixie was at the hospital, his dad wired him some money, so before returning directly home, he decided to purchase a car and outfitted himself with a fly rod, creel, and other equipment and even took some time to tie some flies before setting out on an odyssey that loomed large in his memory for the rest of his life: Dixie decided to "fish" his way back home, traveling from Oregon through Idaho into Montana, almost to the Canadian border, experiencing the best trout fishing of his life. He would fish for a day, stay at a nearby motel, and travel the following morning to another river. The details of the trip and the size of the trout were lasting memories for him.

Once home, he resumed working at L.L. Brown, moving between many different departments, learning the business in preparation to help manage the company in the future. Always energetic, once his wounds healed, he started playing adult softball for Chick's Café in Adams, manning the left-field position.

Never far from a golf club, Dixie met his future wife, avid golfer Margarett "Peggy" Head, at the Pittsfield Country Club while he was golfing with his brother Rupert and she with her father. A strong connection was made, and the couple became engaged, then married in June 1949.

Dixie and Peggy initially lived in a row house; after his father gave them some land, they built a cedar-shake ranch home with a beautiful view of Mount Greylock. In tribute to their love of golf, they jokingly named their home site "Niblick Nob," referring to golf slang for a golfer who tops the ball and makes an errant shot. Over the years, the couple adopted three children, a boy and two girls, and Peggy became a regular volunteer at the local hospital as well as a Cub Scout den mother.

The young couple expanded their love of golfing together and played in courses all over the East Coast, at Pebble Beach in California, and St. Andrews in Scotland. One time, they played in the National Pro-Am tournament. Dixie would go on to be the club champion at Taconic Golf Club for four consecutive years and a medalist in the state golf championship. He and Peggy would also win four state husband/wife championships.

When not golfing, Dixie continued to fly-fish all over Western Massachusetts and Vermont pursuing brown trout, his favorite fish. He also enjoyed upland bird hunting and hunted pheasants, grouse, woodcock, and ducks with his Browning 12-gauge shotgun. He often said that "you didn't want to shoot at the pheasant head-on and put too many pellets in its breast; fire at them going away," and then lamented that he often missed those shots.

As a family, they would pack their Country Squire Ford station wagon and vacation for weeks at lakes in Vermont, New Hampshire, or Maine, specially chosen places where the fishing was excellent. Brown trout for breakfast was Dixie's favorite meal.

The family also had a large vegetable garden and spent much time canning their vegetables, always sharing their renowned bread-and-butter pickles and homemade sauerkraut with friends and neighbors. One of their son's favorite memories was going with his dad to Dry Brook, a stream near the high school, and watching him knock butternuts out of trees so he could wade into the water and collect them for Mom. After the nuts were dried out and crushed, Peggy would use them to make candy and cookies and to put on ice cream. Sometimes, she would cook them in foil with olive oil and soy sauce for the family to enjoy.

Dixie, with his easygoing nature, became known as a sound businessman and civic leader and, in time, assumed the role of Vice President and Treasurer of L.L. Brown Paper Co. Mill, until it closed in 1973. After the closure, Dixie sold air filters to businesses across the state, always traveling with his fishing pole nearby. His son believes Dixie knew all the best fishing streams, lakes, and ponds from Adams to Boston.

Locally, Dixie was on the Adams Personnel Board and served as a Town Meeting Member, was President of the Lions Club, an active Boy Scout leader, and continued throughout his life to sing in the First Congregational Church choir.

Dixie never talked much about his war injuries or disfigurements. He could never grow a beard because of his burns, and even thirty years after the war, he continued having hospital procedures to remove nagging pieces of shrapnel from his arms, hands, as well as his face. At one point, much later in his life, in his seventies, his lawyer suggested Dixie apply for a long-overdue veteran's disability pension. Initially, and surprisingly, he was denied the benefit, but an appeal to the Veterans Administration corrected the mistake and awarded him a pension for his severe war wounds.

This courageous and grievously wounded veteran was described by one of his friends as "one of the most unforgettable people I have ever met.... He could tell a story like no one else." Often described as a gentle giant with broad shoulders who stood over six feet tall, Dixie was known to help anyone in need and didn't let his war wounds hold him back. In the end, he lived a full life and was married fifty-two years to Peggy, his companion in life and in golf. They rest together in Bellevue Cemetery in Adams.

Ernest A. Jaworski
Artillery Officer
451st Antiaircraft Battalion

He led his men through two viciously contested amphibious landings in Italy at Salerno and Anzio under heavy Italian and German artillery barrages and bombings. His automatic weapons platoon set up their 40mm antiaircraft guns and, despite losses, helped secure both beachheads and neighboring seaports.

They closely followed the infantry as it proceeded inland, protecting them from enemy aircraft and lowering their guns in direct fire against enemy counterattacking Panzer divisions. With toeholds created and Italy's surrender, so would begin a month-long slog that would lead to the destruction of the Nazi regime.

ERNEST ANTHONY JAWORSKI'S STORY begins in the small town of Jasło, located in southeastern Poland, where his parents, Henry Jaworski and Mary Frances Jzyk, met and married. The town of 10,000 was annexed by Austria in the late 1700s and returned to Poland at the end of World War I in 1918. Henry and Mary's birth certificates reflect that they were born in Austria.

After their marriage, in response to persuasive recruiters for the Berkshire County mills, Henry and Mary immigrated to the United States in 1897. Mary's sister probably accompanied the young couple. Henry became employed at the Berkshire Hathaway mill in the spinning and spooling room, and they settled into a pleasant, if hardworking, way of life in the Berkshires.

The couple's first child was born in 1898; they would have

eight children in total. Ernest Anthony Jaworski, their last child, was born on February 22, 1914. One twin died shortly after childbirth, another son died as a young child, but the other six children, two girls and four boys, were all born at home and would thrive and reach adulthood.

The couple belonged to the Polish National Church (PNC); after settling in Adams, they attended St. Mary's Polish National Church. The PNC had split off from the Roman Catholic Church in 1897 over disputes about beliefs, although Mary would reconcile her concerns and convert to Catholicism before she passed away.

Mary, who spoke little English, was a busy homemaker and maintained a flower and expansive vegetable garden with cherry, plum, and peach trees. She canned her produce in the fall and stored it in a cold cellar. The family rarely needed to buy vegetables.

It was a busy household, with most children attending Hoosac Street Elementary School. Ernest entered Adams High School in 1927 and quickly excelled in most sports, becoming a star athlete. He was a guard on the Hurricanes basketball team and played first base for its baseball team. In 1930, Ernest, now called Ernie by everyone, was named All-Tournament Guard while winning the state basketball tournament held at the University of Massachusetts. In addition to athletics, he was a Pro Merito honor student, worked on the yearbook staff, and was chosen to deliver the "class prophecy" at graduation in 1931. At one point, Ernie briefly joined the Civilian Conservation Corps, looking for extra income to help support the family. He used his brother Cy's ID to join since he was underage.

During his high school summers, Ernie played basketball in the boys' division of the Saint Stanislaus Athletic Club. In the Mill Street gymnasium, he first met Alodia Modzelewski, who played basketball on the girls' team.

In 1931, Ernie was accepted at the University of Massachusetts and given a farewell party hosted by the St. Stan's girls' athletic team. While at UMass, he co-captained the basketball team, played left guard, and was a member of its 1933-34 undefeated varsity team, the only undefeated UMass team in its history. He also played baseball and was an active member of Kappa Epsilon Fraternity. He graduated in 1935 with a bachelor's degree in education.

After graduating, Ernie received an appointment to the C.T. Plunkett Junior High School in Adams to serve as a science and geography instructor for the eighth grade. Not long afterward, he was promoted to the position of ninth-grade science teacher. He remained deeply involved in the sports program, coaching the junior varsity basketball team, all the while attending summer courses at Columbia University in New York and receiving his Master of Science degree.

It was during this time that Henry, Ernie's dad, passed away in 1939 from stomach cancer.

In 1940, Ernie dipped his toe into local politics: he ran and won Precinct Two's three-year committee member position, not realizing his term would be interrupted by World War II and never completed.

Ernie had continued his relationship all this time with Alodia, who had received her nursing degree and moved to New York, perhaps another reason he chose to study in the summers at Columbia. The romance blossomed, and the couple became engaged in 1941. Alodia's only stipulation was that Jay, her nickname for Ernie, needed to convert to Catholicism before she would marry him.

In 1942, as World War II escalated, Ernie enlisted and received a pre-induction physical exam in February. *The Transcript* noted on February 19 that he concluded his duties as science instructor at C.T. Plunkett Junior High, and at his farewell party was "…presented with a purse of money from his faculty associates and the basketball association…pupils of the school also presented him with a gift of cigarettes."

Another news article in early March 1942 noted: "Ernest Jaworski Now Awaits Service Call: recently enlisted in the chemical warfare division of the armed forces awaiting a call to duty which he expects will come any time…" and later that month, "Ernest Jaworski

Leaves for Service Today" (3-31-1942). He was twenty-eight years old.

After basic training in April 1942, PFC Ernest Jaworski was assigned with 200 other soldiers to Battery D, 2nd Antiaircraft Replacement Training Center at Fort Eustis, Virginia.

Antiaircraft Artillery in WWII

EARLY IN WORLD WAR II, the Antiaircraft Command was established and separated from what was formerly known as the Coastal Artillery Corps. Realizing the approaching demand, over 100 antiaircraft battalions were created and staffed, along with numerous training bases for their crews, including Fort Eustis.

In addition to Ernie's eight weeks of basic training, antiaircraft artillery training lasted fourteen weeks. Working closely with infantry forces also required weeks of gunnery training at air and ground targets. Ernie would be assigned to a 40mm gun crew and receive two weeks of training devoted explicitly to the 40mm gun. The men enjoyed shooting at targets towed by C-47 cargo planes.

During the war, antiaircraft units were credited with destroying over 5,000 enemy aircraft, representing 25% of all downed enemy planes. But early on, the shooting down of friendly planes was of grave concern. Much effort was made to lower the amount of fratricide, and the trainees were taught to distinguish the painted aircraft noses, or to use radar if possible and recognize the signs of friendly aircraft, such as rocking their wings. Training also included repeated use of flashcards to distinguish Allied aircraft models.

While in training, Ernie, now a Catholic, received a furlough and wedded Alodia on June 20, 1942, at St. Clement Mary Church in New York City, where she was supervising at Foundling Hospital and working as a private duty nurse. Stanley, Ernie's brother, came to serve as his best man.

Their time together was brief, and Ernie returned on June 30 to complete antiaircraft training. During this period, Ernie was promoted to corporal and, on October 1, honorably discharged from the Army to accept an appointment as a 2nd lieutenant on October 2, 1942, in the US Army's Officer Corps.

The stunning young couple in their wedding attire. (Courtesy of Jaworski family)

Now an automatic weapons officer, Ernie was assigned as gun crew leader to the 451st Antiaircraft Automatic Weapons Battalion based at Camp Stewart, Georgia.

The "fighting" 451st Battalion was organized into four batteries, A through D. Each battery was led by a captain responsible for approximately eighty soldiers. Within the battery were four platoons; Ernie led a platoon in C Battery.

The battery had between four and eight Swedish-designed

Bofors 40mm antiaircraft guns and several .50-caliber machine guns mounted on vehicles. The Bofors' crew size was four to six soldiers. The battalion also had a headquarters group, including motor transport, communications, medical, and supply groups.

The 451st was designated a "mobile" battalion, which meant that it transported its guns and troops supporting army infantry in the field. The battalion's strength varied from 500 to 600 soldiers.

The Bofors 40mm Antiaircraft Gun

ERNIE'S CREW BECAME EXPERTS in World War II's most widely used antiaircraft weapon, the Bofors. The gun used by most Allied forces was manufactured in Chrysler plants across the United States. It was capable of firing 120 two-pound explosive shells per minute. With a seven-foot-long barrel, its ammunition reached enemy planes as high as 23,000 feet.

The 10,000-pound gun and its supplies were towed by a 2½-ton truck; when necessary, it could be fired from its carriage, but to increase accuracy, more often it was disconnected, its wheels retracted, and the gun lowered on four legs with supporting pads.

Throughout World War II, antiaircraft units were modified from merely in-place defensive weapons protecting ports and airfields to being used offensively in direct support of maneuvering ground troops, which required Ernie and his crews to operate much closer to the front lines. At one point, when enemy aircraft threats had been reduced, the Bofors, firing anti-tank rounds, would be used as a direct-fire weapon against tanks and bunkers.

Ernie and his battery continued to train at Camp Stewart until they left by train to Camp Kilmer, New Jersey, in preparation for deployment. They stayed in bleak two-story, coal-heated barracks for a few days and were given liberty in New York City before departing. During this time, Ernie would get one of his last chances to talk with Alodia.

On March 5, 1943, the 451st Antiaircraft Battalion boarded trains to Pier #13 at Staten Island, New York, and boarded the SS *Mexico Victory*. This "Victory" troopship was a replacement for the earlier "Liberty" ships as the Victory ships were faster and had a larger capacity than the Liberty ships. U-Boats hunting American merchant ships hastened this change. The ship was under a strict blackout, and for the next two weeks, the men weathered a rough voyage and poor meals, no one realizing they were bound for Africa. There was heightened alert aboard the vessel, and depth charges were frequently dropped to thwart any nearby enemy submarines.

Arriving in Casablanca, on March 18, 1943, in what was then French Morocco, the 451st joined the US 5th Army. Ernie and his battery hiked for miles before bivouacking in tents in the desert, waiting to pick up their 40-millimeter guns and vehicles.

Ernie in the field, North Africa. (Courtesy of Jaworski family)

After being outfitted, the 451st left Morocco for Algeria, traveling first to Oran, then just 25 miles farther to the lovely port city of Arzew for weeks of intensive invasion training, requiring repeated entering and exiting of landing craft with their 40mm guns and then conducting mock attacks on pill boxes. At one point, Ernie's battery was assigned to guard General Patton's headquarters in Mostaganem, Algeria, placing its guns directly on top of his bunker.

In what would be last-minute preparations, the battery leaders were sent to an invasion tactics school in August. The 451st, now attached to the 5th Army under General Mark Clark, left Algiers, landing on September 16, 1944 (D-Day +7) on the western beaches of Salerno, Italy, as part of Operation Avalanche, the first American unit to invade the European mainland. While traveling to Salerno, the battalion learned of Italy's surrender to the Allies on September 8. With Italy out of the war, it would be expected that their landing would be unopposed. It was not.

The 5th Army's divisions landed without any preparatory bombardment, hoping for the element of surprise. The Germans were aware, waiting, and held the advantage of the terrain. Fighting across a broad front, General Clark's army faced strong German forces, including the 3rd Panzergrenadier, the 26th and 16th Panzer, and the Hermann Goering Divisions. In addition to the strong enemy forces, the Army faced purposefully destroyed bridges, enemy roadblocks, and countless anti-tank and anti-personnel mines.

The 5th repelled numerous enemy counterattacks as the battle seesawed. At one point, consideration was given to evacuating the beachhead, but it was evaluated to be too difficult while constantly under fire.

Although the Italians had surrendered, the Germans conducted numerous air attacks on the landing ships and beaches, barely missing the stern of Ernie's ship. Because the beach was still being contested, the men remained on board for three days, generating smoke day and night to obscure themselves from German aircraft.

Finally, on the third day, barges helped the battery offload their guns and vehicles. While coming ashore, they came under fire and used their automatic weapons with armor-piercing rounds to destroy two German tanks and bring buildings and snipers under fire. Once on land, Ernie's battery repelled repeated attacks by the German Air Force (Luftwaffe) on massed beach targets and resupply boats.

Once the beach was secure, they moved with haste, proceeding inland to protect bridges and road junctions while suppressing enemy aircraft attacks. In the distance, they could briefly see smoke rising from Mount Vesuvius.

The 451st supported the advancing infantry as they moved up

the Italian peninsula. Conditions were miserable. They were often on the move in the rain, navigating muddy roads in freezing conditions. Every new move required them to dig holes for their gun pits and put up camouflage netting. Subjected as they were to frequent German artillery fire, they followed blackout regulations, with fires prohibited, sleeping with wet blankets in damp tents. There were no hot meals, just C rations.

Despite the conditions, the 451st and its 40mm cannons reduced enemy bombings, securing the skies, and the Germans began a slow retreat. The 5th Army could now advance, entering Naples on October 1, 1943. The 451st helped secure the harbor by fighting off German *Junkers*. The two-person *Junkers*, also known as "Stuka," were considered the backbone of the German air force, most effective as a dive bomber and ground-attack aircraft.

The 451st continued to follow the 5th Army as it neared the Volturno River, effectively placing southern Italy in Allied hands. Ernie's battery was ordered to protect the pontoon bridges from air attack as their soldiers advanced across the river. At one point, infantry units were attacked by German fighters who just missed the bridge, trying to avoid the withering fire of the 451st. The batteries were credited with shooting down eleven enemy aircraft.

During November and December 1943, Ernie's battery continued to advance with the ground troops, always on the move, protecting the skies. German shelling continued for days, knocking out some of the unit's trucks and guns and killing and wounding artillerymen. Many remember having their Thanksgiving meal while standing in mud up to their knees.

In December, the unit returned to the outskirts of Naples for rest, resupply, and waterproofing their vehicles. They began practicing beach landings from LSTs (Landing Ship, Tanks), large ships used for amphibious landings. The antiaircraft units supporting the Salerno invasion, including Ernie's platoon, were credited with shooting down over 400 enemy planes.

There was little rest before the 451st took part in Operation Shingle, the Allied invasion of Nettuno/Anzio, Italy, in early January 1944. (From 1940 to 1945 Nettuno and nearby Anzio were a single municipality.)

Landing under heavy enemy air attacks and beach fire, losses were immediate, and Ernie's battery had 29 trucks destroyed, with numerous soldiers killed and wounded. Once their 40mm guns were set up, the battery shot down 8 out of 20 enemy planes who themselves were trying to destroy Allied guns. The intense response and constant pressure from the 451st caused many German pilots to drop their bombs in the water or abandon their attacks.

On January 29, Anzio Harbor was attacked by 60 German aircraft. The 451st destroyed 38 enemy planes.

Once the beachhead was secure, Ernie's battery slowly advanced, but initially became stuck in fields that were flooded by the Nazis, who'd opened dams as they retreated. Proceeding was difficult; Ernie's unit was constantly shelled while battling the attacking Luftwaffe.

February 1944 found the 451st just twenty-five miles from Rome, slightly behind the front line, protecting a battery of American howitzers. Under almost constant attack from artillery and bombing, the unit witnessed three American B-17s being shot down by German antiaircraft guns. During a seven-day running battle, the 451st accounted for downing another 25 enemy aircraft.

In the middle of March, a German artillery barrage destroyed a number of Ernie's battery trailers and trucks. It also hit a mobile kitchen, shredding many nearby tents and wounding many soldiers.

The 451st advanced through devastated areas where destroyed tanks littered the roads, as did the bodies of American and German soldiers, lying where they fell with full backpacks still on. In early May 1944, their battalion commander was killed by a land mine.

As the Allies prepared to liberate Rome, 1st Lieutenant Jaworski received orders to return home after completing fifteen months overseas, in order to attend Officers Special Basic Course for additional infantry/command training.

With his successful completion of the course on January 17, 1945, Lieutenant Jaworski was promoted to captain in the Coast Artillery Corps. In his absence, the 5th Army continued to fight through Italy, and in May 1945, they linked with the 7th Army. Shortly afterward, the war in Europe was over.

The recently promoted Captain Jaworski. (Courtesy of Jaworski family)

Less than a year later, after serving at Camp Wheeler (Georgia) at the Infantry Training Replacement Center, Captain Jaworski, who started his military service as a private, was honorably discharged from active duty on January 2, 1946, at the Separation Center in Camp Gordon, Georgia.

After returning home to a delighted Alodia, Ernie returned to teaching as a science and mathematics instructor at Adams High School and transferred to the Army National Guard. On January 2, 1947, Ernie was named commanding officer when Company M, 104th Infantry, Massachusetts National Guard of Adams, was reactivated and federalized. Ernie was credited with a significant improvement in readiness.

He also devoted himself to the students at the high school, evident in the class of 1950 yearbook, dedicated to Ernie with the following insert: "…To Ernest Jaworski, our class advisor, we dedicate this yearbook of memories. May this dedication to you show, in a small way, our appreciation of your loyal and generous guidance."

Ernie continued to be involved in sports. He managed athletics at the high school and became a member of the "Old Timers" group, where he and other former star athletes challenged the Adams High Varsity Basketball Team in an annual holiday Alumni game. He was also in a men's adult baseball league and a member of Berkshire County Football and Basketball Officials Association in order to referee basketball and football games.

In the summer of 1952, Ernie worked temporarily as a clerk at the South Adams Savings Bank. He was attracted to the work, and joined full-time in 1952, relinquishing his teaching position. Ernie eventually became the bank's assistant treasurer.

Also, in 1953, Ernie was promoted to major in the National Guard as commemorated in *The Transcript* of May 5, 1952: "Tribute to Captain Jaworski, CO Company M, celebrating his transfer to 3rd Battalion headquarters as executive officer with a promotion pending." The article noted that 100 people were at the celebration

Ernie, right, making an out on third base. (Courtesy of Jaworski family)

and that in 1950, Company M "attained a superior rating for inspection and that this rating was the highest ever received by any unit in the regiment." Ernie was lauded, described as an "excellent soldier, a perfect gentleman, a good dad, and a wonderful husband."

During this time, Ernie and Alodia, known now to everyone as Alice, were busy raising three girls, and while he worked at the bank and commanded Company M, Alice worked for the Board of Health and as a school nurse for St. Stanislaus and Notre Dame.

The family often visited Ernie's mom on North Summer Street, where she lived with some of her adult children. The home was the center of family activities. Mary, called *Babciu* (grandmother in Polish), occupied the second floor, and her grandchildren fondly remember running up to visit, opening her cupboard drawer and cutting a thick slice of *chleb* (rye bread), then smothering it with *masło* (butter). Most times, a loaf was purchased daily at the Polish bakery on Hoosac Street by Uncle Johnny, who lived in the house.

The girls and Babciu, who spoke only Polish, communicated through endless games of the card game War. Mary passed away in 1956, seventeen years after her husband's death. On her deathbed, she converted to Catholicism and was buried next to her husband in Bellevue Cemetery.

The girls remember vacationing in Canada, swimming at local ponds, and many nights after work, they'd pile into the family sedan and, on the way to Babciu's, stop at Owcharski's convenience store for ice cream. One memory that stands out was when Ernie picked up the girls in an Army Jeep and brought them to the National Guard firing range off East Road to watch his company fire their weapons.

Ernie seldom talked about the war, although when asked about having three daughters, he was glad to say, "That's good they will never have to go to war."

In addition to working at the bank and serving in the Guard, Ernie enjoyed playing Whist with Alice and their neighbors, and they never missed the Wednesday-night Perry Como show. Ernie also tended a vegetable garden on a family plot of land and enjoyed planting a flower he found beautiful: one he'd seen a lot of in Italy, the Calla lily.

In March 1957, Major Ernest Jaworski was given a four-month leave of absence from the bank when he was selected to attend the

US Army Advanced Infantry School at Fort Benning, Georgia. He completed the course on August 2, 1957, but while at the base, he became seriously ill, and it was determined that he had advanced stomach cancer.

Sadly, his condition worsened, and Ernie succumbed to cancer shortly after returning home on August 26, 1957, at age forty-three. Alice and their three young daughters were grief-stricken at the sudden loss of Ernie, this calm, quiet man with a kind disposition. The funeral was held at Saint Stanislaus Church, and Ernie was buried at Bellevue Cemetery with full military honors.

Ernie was remembered as a devoted teacher, an involved citizen, a most respected soldier, a sports enthusiast, and most importantly as a person dedicated to his family. Sadly, his life ended early, although he contributed mightily to many others along the way, a fitting tribute to this citizen soldier.

Raymond W. Kelly
Truck Driver
100th Infantry Division

He had already survived over 150 sustained days in combat, and yet, under the most intense artillery, mortar, and small arms fire, he continued to deliver critical ammunition, grenades, and K rations to his battalion's soldiers. Any number of times, he picked up his rifle and helped to fight off counterattacks. The war had been over for eight days when Raymond headed out to bring much-needed water to a company of soldiers. There was a clunking noise in the back of his truck, then an explosion and silence.

TRAGEDY STRUCK EARLY IN Raymond Walter Kelly's life. Raymond was born in Brooklyn on March 11, 1922, to Edward Joseph Thomas Kelly, son of an Irish immigrant, and Jean Thersa (Gunn), a native New Yorker, but in a few short years, he would be an orphan.

Raymond's dad, a laborer and a devoted Mason, died in 1925 of unknown causes when Raymond was three years old. Just four years later, his mom died in 1929, for reasons lost to history, leaving their five young children, four boys and a girl. Initially, the five children were placed with a friend, Ada, who lived on the second floor of a three-story tenement walk-up on 8th Street in Manhattan. At some point, the children were separated; some were sent to live at another friend's house, although Raymond and several brothers remained with Ada. The boys grew up playing with neighborhood kids on the street outside the tenement.

Raymond's most treasured toy was a pink, high-bounce

Spaldeen ball that the kids used to play stickball or any other conceivable game. Few had any manufactured toys, so hours were filled with improvised baseball and the popular local version of tag called Ringolevio, where two teams captured other players, "jailed" them, and tried to free them, inspiring shouts of "Olly olly oxen free."

Raymond attended local public schools and, around home, showed a knack for fixing things, which led him to transfer and finish high school at Western Union Vocational School in New York. During high school, he met and dated a neighborhood girl, and their best times were at Coney Island, walking the boardwalk, swimming at the beach, and trying to decide whether to ride the Wonder Wheel, a 150-foot-tall Ferris wheel, or the Cyclone roller coaster.

After graduation, Raymond, anxious to find employment, accepted a position in Dalton, Massachusetts, with Sawyer, Regan, and Company, a textile mill that manufactured fancy woolen suits and overcoats. Although not unionized, the plant paid a prevailing union wage, and the hourly pay was a strong attraction for Raymond to move in the late 1930s. He worked on the overcoat line as a filling carrier and occasionally as a driver, bringing products to the company's local retail store. He rented a small apartment on River Street in Dalton.

At work, Raymond, called "Kelly" by most friends, met and became close friends with Robert "Bob" Mack. They worked many hours side-by-side in the same department at Sawyer Regan.

Bob was dating a girl from Adams named Frances Siatkowski, and he introduced Kelly to her sister Josephine, whom everyone called "Jo." The attractions flourished, and the young foursome could often be found dancing on the weekend at the St. Stanislaus Hall or the Cartier Club in Adams.

Before long, the two couples were engaged, and Bob, Frances, Raymond, and Josephine were married in a double ceremony on August 12, 1942, at St. Stanislaus Church in Adams, Massachusetts. A write-up in the local newspaper noted that Raymond was employed at Sawyer, Regan and Company, and that his bride worked as a battery hand in the weave shop of No. 1 Berkshire Mill. The two couples honeymooned together, traveling to Montreal, Canada. Upon their return, Raymond and Josephine lived in Dalton.

America was accelerating its war footing by this point. Raymond and his three brothers were soon called up to serve in the military. During this time, his sister Maria would serve in her own way; she became a nun, joined the Sisters of Mercy, and took the name Sister Agnes. In early December 1942, Raymond was drafted, and after passing his physical, he was sent by train to Fort Devens for basic training. Soldiers were required to serve as long as the government needed them, but no longer than six months after the war's end. Josephine, having no idea how long this would be, moved back home to live with her parents on their East Hoosac Street farm.

The next thirteen weeks would be an adjustment for Raymond. The first few weeks included orientation, haircuts, aptitude testing, and the issuance of uniforms, which were too big for Raymond's 5'6" 140-pound frame; tailoring was not available for raw recruits. He also received some toiletries and a mess kit before being assigned to a barracks.

His company was marched everywhere, and their daily routine included calisthenics, close-order drills, and classes on military customs and courtesy. Drill instructors would dog every recruit's every move and use tough sanctions on the newcomers for the slightest infractions. Raymond received his share of kitchen duties and challenging physical punishments. He enjoyed the rifle range and qualified as a marksman.

Based on his aptitude tests and past experiences, Raymond received the military occupational specialty of 745, Truck Driver. After completing his basic training, Raymond was given orders to report to Fort Bragg (now Fort Liberty), North Carolina, having been assigned to the 100th Infantry Division. After the briefest of furloughs, he reported to base and began his classification training as a truck driver. He spent hours learning about the Army's vehicles and studying maintenance in the classroom. It was at Fort Bragg that he would spend considerable time learning about and driving the Army's 2½-ton 6X6 truck.

These trucks, built by General Motors Corporation (GMC), were noted for their ability to navigate in the worst terrain and weather and became known as "the workhorse of the Army." In later years, General Eisenhower was quoted as calling it "one of the six most vital" US vehicles to win the war. Months later, Raymond would be using the 6X6 to transport men, supplies, and the wounded as his unit fought its way through France and Germany.

Raymond Kelly in dress uniform. (Courtesy of Kelly family)

Raymond spent additional months of training at Fort Jackson, South Carolina, where Jo had a chance to visit him. Before he headed abroad, he and Jo would have two children: Joanna, born in 1943, and Patricia, born in 1944.

Raymond's division, the 100th Infantry (Century) Division, was initially activated in 1918, then reconstituted in 1942 to include the 397th, 398th, and 399th Regiments. Raymond was assigned to the 399th. Each regiment had approximately 3,000 soldiers.

The division's other groups included field artillery, engineers, medical units, quartermaster corps, and Military Police. The 100th was part of the VI Corps and belonged to the 7th Army.

At the end of September 1944, the regiment moved by train from Fort Bragg to Camp Kilmer in New Jersey, their embarkation point. Raymond, known now to everyone as Kelly, snagged a one-day pass to New York. He took the subway to see his family and then returned to the city. He enjoyed walking along Fifth Avenue, marveling at the number of skyscrapers, and stopped by Times Square, filled with servicemen. The day ended quickly, and after a few beers, he reported back to his barracks that night.

On the morning of October 6, 1944, the regiment was conveyed to Pier 82 on 42nd Street and boarded the USAT *George Washington*. The ocean liner was built in 1908 and was one of the largest steamships in existence. Affectionately called "the *Washington*," the fashionable eight-deck passenger ship accommodated 3,000 people divided between 1st, 2nd, or 3rd class (steerage). Due to the urgent need, it was converted to transport soldiers to Europe in World Wars I and II. The ship would hold all three battalions of the 399th Regiment.

One historical footnote about the *Washington* was well known: On April 14, 1912, the ship passed a huge iceberg and radioed a warning to all nearby ships. The next day, the *Washington* received a radio message that the *Titanic*, which had acknowledged receiving the warning, had struck an iceberg in the same location where it had been reported.

Kelly's voyage was a cold, brisk two-week trip amidst a flotilla of Navy escort ships. The men kept occupied with lifeboat and air-raid drills and cleaning their weapons, mostly M1 rifles, daily due to the salty air. Between drills and weapons cleaning, they would occupy themselves with ongoing stud poker games. Below the main deck, men slept in bunks stacked four-high, just inches from the next man. Kelly and his squad decided to sleep on deck in their overcoats to avoid the closeness and foul air; the evening views were often beautiful.

During the day, Kelly had his share of additional duties, such as working on the chow line, cleaning heads (latrines), and swabbing the deck. He showered in salty water with sudsless soap, never feeling quite clean. The salty water reminded him of swimming in the ocean at Coney Island.

On October 20, 1944, Kelly and his regiment arrived in Marseille, France. When the *Washington* anchored, the soldiers clambered over the side and slowly climbed down cargo nets with their full packs and rifles onto a landing ship that ferried them to the beach. When the ramp came down, they were able to walk to shore in about a foot of water.

The unit quickly assembled and hiked in the rain to a staging area ten miles from town, where they assembled their pup tents in the mud. There, the regiment set up latrines, field mess tents, and showers for the days they were there. Kelly and his friend Carl Brown, known as "Brownie," were lucky to snag one-day passes to Marseille. They walked the city, had a meal and some wine at a local café, watched the lovely French girls stroll past, and then reported back to their unit that night.

Once the regiment's trucks were delivered, the unit was on the move, and Kelly's work began. Departing the staging area, his 2½-ton truck, called a *deuce and a half* or a *six-by-six* because six wheels powered the truck, was loaded with soldiers sitting on wooden benches in the back, and so began their trip to the front lines.

As they traveled through France, the men could see the war coming closer, observing burnt-out tank hulks, smashed trucks, bombed-out houses—and, as they neared the front, they passed a row of dead GIs by the road in bloodied white body bags that had once served as their mattress covers. The chatter in the back of the truck ceased.

That night they dug in to 3-man foxholes, dozing to the sounds of artillery.

By November 1, Kelly's regiment was on the front line, having relieved the gaunt 45th Army Division. Now, in the daunting Vosges Mountains, the regiment faced dug-in German soldiers and began taking its first casualties. After overcoming German positions and a hail of artillery fire, St. Remy would be one of the first towns liberated by the regiment—but not without a number of casualties.

A pattern for Kelly began: daily firefights, followed by delivering supplies to his unit under fire, evacuating the wounded, and returning to the front. The unit was always moving forward through small villages and towns, pushing the Germans ahead of them, never quite sure when a massive firefight would erupt.

During these intense battles, Kelly and the other drivers were called to fight alongside the infantry squads. They participated in duels using the M1 rifles, .30-caliber machine guns, and BARs (Browning Automatic Rifles) to counter German machine guns, burp guns, and rapid-fire machine pistols they called "Schmeissers."

Among Kelly's personal items is a German lighter from the war. (Courtesy of Kelly family)

The front-line soldiers dug in every night, often sleeping with damp blankets in water-filled foxholes. Kelly, a bit more fortunate, slept in his truck when he wasn't transporting or resupplying troops as the regiment pushed the retreating Germans across France.

Either by truck or, more often, on foot, the regiment moved across France, often in rain or snow. It was said that the winter of 1944-45 was the coldest in Europe for forty years, with temperatures often well below freezing.

The months of November and December found the regiment on the offensive, with casualties mounting by the day. Green replacements were shuttled to the front by Kelly, who was always on the alert for tank mines.

He would drive for countless miles, bypassing piles of rubble that were once houses and swerving to avoid dead livestock along the road, sometimes on their back with legs sticking straight up in the air. An especially grim sight for Kelly (and for replacement troops riding along) would be the dead American soldiers dragged back to the roadside to be brought to Graves Registration before their trip to a local cemetery. When casualties were high and ambulances overloaded, sometimes the bodies would be put in the back of his truck to be carried to the rear.

After the regiment liberated the small town of Lemberg, they were withdrawn several miles from the front and put in reserve. They could now sleep in commandeered or abandoned houses, have a chance for a shower, and get their mail. During this respite, they heard about a large German offensive north of them in the Ardennes, which would soon become known as the Battle of the Bulge.

After the brief rest in December, the regiment continued to move forward, fighting through the wooded area near Bitche, France, and facing bunkers on the Maginot Line. At this point, there was a pause in the action as many resources were redeployed to counter the Germans at the Battle of the Bulge.

Quickly returning to action in early January 1945, the regiment passed through and liberated a number of small towns, including Bertrichamps, Le Clairupt, Raon l'Etape, and Saint Blaise-Moyenmoutier. It was at Moyenmoutier that Kelly and Brownie had a chance to sleep in a hotel.

Returning to action, and after fighting off numerous counterattacks, the regiment finally liberated the town of Bitche in March 1945.

As the regiment entered Germany in late March, it was moving constantly through destroyed towns, stopping to fight remnants of the German Army, passing thousands of displaced persons, and collecting hundreds of surrendering German soldiers. They crossed the Rhine River in late March 1945 and found themselves celebrating Easter Mass on Sunday, April 1, 1945, in a bombed-out church.

Kelly's regiment reached Stuttgart, Germany, in late April. After 163 days of combat, it was put in reserve to rest. As the war's end neared, the men began area patrolling and assuming occupational duties. Kelly's mail caught up with him. He had frequently been writing and receiving mail from Jo and from his childhood girlfriend in Brooklyn.

On May 5, 1945, the division was notified to stop firing on

enemy troops unless fired upon first; "unconditional surrender" terms were reached between the 7th Army and the Germans on May 6. Kelly heard the announcement played over radios every fifteen minutes to ensure the Germans (as well as the Americans) understood hostilities had ceased.

Right after the ceasefire, Kelly was nominated for his second award, the Bronze Star, for meritorious action from November 11, 1944, through May 4, 1945. His commanding officer told him that both awards were for the countless times he courageously resupplied his unit under relentless enemy fire. The captain declared that during critical battles and counterattacks, even with his truck riddled with shrapnel and windshield blown out, Kelly always delivered critical ammunition.

THE UNITED STATES OF AMERICA

TO ALL WHO SHALL SEE THESE PRESENTS, GREETING: THIS IS TO CERTIFY THAT THE PRESIDENT OF THE UNITED STATES OF AMERICA AUTHORIZED BY EXECUTIVE ORDER, 24 AUGUST 1962 HAS AWARDED

THE BRONZE STAR MEDAL

TO PRIVATE FIRST CLASS RAYMOND W. KELLY
HEADQUARTERS COMPANY, 2D BATTALION, 399TH INFANTRY REGIMENT

FOR meritorious achievement in active ground combat against the enemy, effective 23 November 1944, with the 100th Infantry Division in France. Private First Class Kelly's exemplary performance of duty in active ground combat was in keeping with the finest traditions of military service and reflects great credit upon himself, his unit, and the Army of the United States.

GIVEN UNDER MY HAND IN THE CITY OF WASHINGTON
THIS 13TH DAY OF MARCH 2024

THE ADJUTANT GENERAL
U.S. Army Human Resources Command
Fort Knox, Kentucky 40122-5408

SECRETARY OF THE ARMY

Kelly's Bronze Star certificate, recently requested by his daughter Patricia. (Courtesy of Kelly family)

About a week later, after the Armistice, Kelly was on a water run for a company of soldiers. It was May 18 and he was by himself; Brownie wasn't available to ride shotgun. Suddenly the truck was attacked by a German army straggler, or perhaps a die-hard Nazi SS trooper, who threw a grenade into his truck, igniting several others and critically wounding Kelly. The grenade shredded his left leg and peppered his entire left side with shrapnel.

Medics found Kelly semi-conscious and carried him to the Battalion Aid Station, where his clothes were cut away. He was then given a shot of morphine, the bleeding was slowed, and his wound was dusted with sulfa powder and bandaged. Before being moved, he was also given a tetanus shot and several pints of plasma to replace the loss of blood and avoid shock.

Once stabilized, he was taken with three others on a bumpy ambulance ride to a clearing station in Germany, where his friend Carl Brown was able to visit him. The same day, Kelly was forwarded quickly to a General Hospital in Nancy, France, where x-rays showed that the wounds to Kelly's left leg were quite grievous. His leg was amputated. Numerous grenade fragments were also removed from the left side of his body. He was dosed daily with penicillin to prevent infection and received his first infusion of whole blood. Doctors would frequently sniff his heavily bandaged leg, smelling for infection and the dreaded possibility of gangrene.

The Second General Hospital in Nancy was about 150 miles from where Kelly was wounded. The pre-World War I complex had been liberated from the Germans in September 1944, upgraded, and in full operation by January 1945—just in time to receive patients from across the battlefields, including the Battle of the Bulge.

The 1500-bed hospital had a large staff that manned extra surgical and medical wards. The vast facility, much like a stateside hospital, had electricity, central heating, its own blood bank, and an X-ray department.

When Kelly awakened, a nurse, Simone, brought him his first full meal and offered him one of her cigarettes, a Lucky Strike. After weeks of treatment and several more operations, Kelly was air-evacuated to England from France in an Air Transport Command Plane, a four-engine Douglas C-54 filled with other wounded soldiers.

At home, the newspaper article on June 15, 1945, was headlined, "Raymond Kelly Loses Left Leg" and followed with the subtitle, "Amputation Necessary Following a Grenade Explosion - Now in France." The article quotes Kelly as saying, "A bunch of hand grenades blew up in my truck, and I got so much shrapnel in my left leg that they had to amputate it. Now you can see why the War's all over for me and why I'll be home for good."

After more procedures and recovery time in England, Kelly was flown to the United States, arriving on July 31, 1945. It had been over two months since he was wounded. After checking in at Thompson General Hospital in Atlantic City, New Jersey, Kelly was given a 40-day furlough.

On September 21, 1945, after spending time at home with Jo and the girls, he returned to Thompson General for another operation and sent Brownie a letter saying, "I'll be shipped to Walter Reed in Washington, DC. They can't fit me for a leg here; it's cut too high up."

In the Fall of 1945, Kelly was transferred to Walter Reed Hospital, one of the two major medical centers that could fit veterans with prostheses. Kelly was initially fitted with a temporary prosthesis, participated in therapy sessions, and then had a permanent fitting weeks later. He learned to walk with a new gait but had to rely on his crutches. Jo visited him several times, and once, unknown to the family, his old girlfriend from Brooklyn also visited.

December 7, 1946, five years to the day after the infamous Japanese attack on Pearl Harbor, Kelly received an Honorable Discharge under disability conditions. Not long after, on January 20, 1946, Kelly reported to Brownie that he was back in at Walter Reed for another operation. The war had been over for eight months, and Kelly was still being treated.

His service record shows that Kelly earned two Bronze Star Medals and was also entitled to wear the Combat Infantryman's

Badge, a Good Conduct Medal, a European–African–Middle Eastern Campaign Medal, the World War II Victory Medal, and an American Campaign Medal. His Purple Heart was not listed on his discharge papers, so one of his daughters later requested the medal.

All in all, the 100th (Century) Division had participated in the Rhineland, Alsace-Ardennes, and Central Europe campaigns and captured over 13,000 Germans. The price had been high, suffering over 800 killed-in-action and 3,500 wounded, with 1,000 more missing in action or prisoners of war.

Raymond Kelly returned to Adams in the spring of 1946, delighted to be home finally with Jo and their two daughters. They rented a first-floor apartment on Crotteau Street in Adams. He was still recovering from his operations, and even though his leg seemed to always be sore and the prosthesis a nuisance, he didn't lose his sense of humor. Jo helped by wrapping old diapers around the crutch under his arm to help with soreness.

Unable to find work right away, he assisted at his mother-in-law's small store on East Hoosac Street. He helped stock and sell eggs, bread, butter, soda, seltzer water, and ice cream from her tall cooler. Jo drove him to ongoing medical appointments in her mom's two-door Ford coupe.

Raymond, Jo, and their children enjoying a sunny picnic, adjusting to postwar life. (Courtesy of Kelly family)

Kelly stayed in touch with Carl Brown, who settled in Maine, and the family visited Brownie and his wife Irene in summertime.

A year or so after he returned home, with his leg still causing pain, Kelly left Adams. He returned to New York, and he and Jo eventually separated. Both remarried. Kelly married his childhood sweetheart, with whom he had stayed in touch throughout the years. They went on to have two daughters together.

Kelly found work at the Raritan Arsenal in New Jersey, working in its mammoth warehouse and helping to track repair orders. At the time, the arsenal repaired motorized assemblies for military units. Privately, in his off hours, he repaired and sold watches.

In Adams, Jo and their daughters moved back to her parents' farm on East Hoosac Street and remained there until she remarried. She and the girls continued to visit Brownie and Irene every summer in Maine, and the Browns would visit them in Adams.

With his leg still bothering him, Kelly and his wife moved to San Antonio, Texas, where he found work at Fort Sam Houston in the PX selling stationery and pens. Shortly after their arrival, some of the remaining shrapnel in his leg caused gangrene to set in, and Kelly underwent another operation with more of his leg amputated.

Once recovered, he and his family moved back to New Jersey, where his health continued to decline. As his mobility decreased, Kelly read a lot, especially mysteries, and enjoyed listening to "his" Red Sox on the radio with a beer and his bulldog Gui curled up by his feet.

Sadly, in June 1955, at the age of thirty-three, Raymond Kelly passed away, leaving his wife and four daughters. Years later, some of the girls discovered each other, met, and talked about their dad and moms, recounting family history. One of the daughters named them "the Kelly Girls," an acknowledgment that kept his memory in their hearts.

After surviving many days of ground combat and earning two Bronze Stars, Raymond Kelly was buried with full military honors at the Beverly National Cemetery in New Jersey.

One of his daughters noted that even though "his wounds followed him without much relief, he was always upbeat, smiling, happy, and had something good to say about everybody." Though he died far too soon, it was a tremendous final tribute to Kelly, the soldier who would move heaven and earth to make sure everybody had what they needed.

William S. Linscott
Rifleman
10th Mountain Division

After a night and a morning of artillery and mortar barrages, it had become deathly quiet, with the exception of occasional machine gun and rifle fire in the valley. Bill was relieved to have a break in the action. They were on the backside of the ridge and should be out of sight of the German observers. It was the right time to get out of their wet, two-man foxholes, grab a smoke, and eat some K rations. Suddenly, a deafening explosion rended the silence. A high explosive tree-burst mortar round hit the group, raining shrapnel down on them. All was chaos for a few moments. It soon became clear that everyone in range was grievously wounded—but only one was killed, and it was Bill's closest friend.

WILLIAM STERLING LINSCOTT, a future member of the 10th Mountain Division, was born to Donald A. and Ruth (Thompson) Linscott on May 3, 1925. The family resided on Orchard Street in Adams, Massachusetts.

Donald, born in Argyle, Illinois, in 1899, moved to Adams as a child and attended Adams High School. After working at a local bank, he founded what became the Thompson & Linscott Insurance Agency in 1925. Located on the second floor of the Adams Savings building, his office was adjacent to that of Sheriff John J. Thompson, a veteran of the Spanish-American War. Sheriff Thompson would become a partner in the Linscott Insurance Agency, and it is thought that Donald met Ruth Thompson, the Sheriff's daughter, while working there. Donald and Ruth had two sons, Donald Jr. and William.

In 1934, as skiing became popular in the United States, the 107th Savoy, Massachusetts, Civilian Conservation Corps began constructing a ski trail down the face of Mount Greylock that would become known as the Thunderbolt. Thirty young men, with 300 pounds of dynamite over four months, would carve a two-mile expert ski trail on the face of the mountain. It's remarkable that no one was injured in the process.

Skiing the Thunderbolt, named after a rollercoaster at Revere Beach, Massachusetts, caught on quickly, and the first race was held in 1935. Locally, Donald Linscott Sr. helped organize and became president of the Thunderbolt Ski Club.

William, known to all as Bill, attended Liberty Street Elementary School and C.T. Plunkett Junior High. He also attended the First Congregational Church with his family and was a junior choir member. He and his brother Donald played in tennis matches, competing against each other, and in summertime they attended Camp Sunrise, the Boy Scout site in nearby Otis, Massachusetts. In the summer of 1933, the local paper noted that the boys attended Coach Fox's Day Camp to learn the fundamentals of baseball and improve their swimming skills.

At a young age, both boys became enamored with skiing, and their parents purchased them the one-year-guaranteed Griswold skis for $22.50 from Art Simmons, a local furniture store owner. Bill was on the slopes at the age of ten. By the time he was a teenager, he and his friends would rush home from school or factories to make one steep climb and then ski down the Thunderbolt before darkness, negotiating the almost two-mile run, traversing sections known as the Big Bend, Needle's Eye, and the Big Schuss, making a tight S turn and then a drop, headed toward their finish line.

In 1939, at age thirteen, Bill was one of the fifty-nine skiers from twelve clubs participating in the Massachusetts Downhill race. In one of the time trials, he finished twelfth, a respectable showing for a youngster.

As a member of the Thunderbolt Ski Club, Bill continued to

hone his skills and, in early 1941, was part of a four-man team that entered the US Eastern Amateur Ski Association's combined downhill and slalom race (*Transcript,* 2-14-41) "to be run tomorrow and Sunday.... on Taft Trail, Cannon Mountain, Franconia, N.H."

His biggest win came in March 1942, at sixteen, wearing bib number 11. Bill, at this point an Adams High School sophomore, won the Massachusetts Downhill Championship Race on the Thunderbolt Trail, winning the Governor's Cup. He placed 1st out of 32 skiers.

Bill's trophy cup still holds special meaning for his daughters. (Courtesy of Linscott family)

At the end of his sophomore year, Bill's parents decided to transfer him and his brother to Vermont Academy in Saxtons River, Vermont. The parents thought that without local distractions, the boys could better concentrate on their studies. It was a move that caused little anxiety for either boy, exiled as they were into the middle of ski country. Both boys quickly joined the school's ski team and began competing.

At the end of Bill's junior year, he returned home and worked briefly at L.L. Brown Paper Company. With the world engaged in a global conflict, he responded to a *Transcript* news article titled "Mountain Troops Seek Recruits" (June 22, 1943). The article mentions getting applications from Art Simmons and also from Bill's dad, both members of the National Ski Association authorized to help with recruiting. The article notes that those selected "are sent directly from the induction center to Camp Hale, Pando, Colorado, right in the heart of the Rocky Mountains for their basic and advanced training." Near Leadville, Colorado, the Pando Valley sat at a 9,250-foot elevation, meant to acclimatize the recruits. At the time, the Army sought experienced skiers from colleges and ski clubs.

Bill's application and three letters of recommendation testifying to his mountaineering and ski skills were quickly approved, and in July, he passed his physical and entered the Army on August 9, 1943. A *Transcript* news article of the same date noted the men "left Adams by bus for North Adams where they boarded the 9:27 a.m. Boston & Maine train for Fort Devens." By the end of the war, the small town of Adams, Massachusetts, would have provided the highest number of men per capita in the 10th Mountain Division than any other town in the United States.

After a brief stop at Fort Devens, the volunteers traveled five days by train to Camp Hale. The camp was a small city, carved from nothing. It encompassed more than 50,000 acres of training grounds with ski runs, barracks, mess halls, stables, and a movie theater. It was here that the 10th Mountain Division was activated in 1943. The division would comprise three regiments—the 85th, 86th, and 87th—and attached artillery battalions. Each regiment also featured a pack mule company.

Adams would send 20 young men to serve in the division, though Bill would be the only one assigned to the 85th Regiment. Instructors from the National Ski Patrol would train the 10th Mountain soldiers.

Training began in earnest at Camp Hale and the Cooper Ski Area. The men would train under the harshest conditions. High in the Rocky Mountains, the area often received twelve feet of snow, and temperatures could hit 30 below zero Fahrenheit.

Their regimen consisted of almost daily forced marches, mountain climbs, and ski and rock-climbing training. When out overnight, the troopers often laid their skis parallel on the snow and threw their sleeping bags on top to catch a few hours of sleep.

In late March 1944, with below-zero temperatures, the division left the warmth of their huts on skis and snowshoes with pack animals for four weeks in the open, an exercise known as the D-Series maneuvers. It was one of the most grueling tests an Army division would be subjected to.

With the upcoming battles in Europe, regiments would practice outflanking and ambushing the enemy, attacking fortified bunkers under fire, rappelling down cliffs, and evacuating the battlefield of the wounded. It would be a long, damp time of snow and cold, allowing for little sleep or food out in the open. They conducted tactics on skis or snowshoes in sometimes waist-deep snow.

Bill, left, and his brother Don, happy to have survived the D-Series at Camp Hale, Colorado. (Courtesy of Linscott family)

The men hiked miles between exercises wearing 90-pound packs containing a tent, sleeping bag, K rations, extra clothing, and rifle. At its completion, the Division's Commanding General said there were no fatalities, only several hundred cases of frostbite, and 300 other injuries, like broken bones and sprains. The arduous training prepared the 10th for the extreme conditions they would

Bill's rudimentary ski "skins" could be attached under the skis to provide traction for uphill trekking. (Courtesy of Linscott family)

face in the Italian mountains.

In November 1944, near the completion of their training, the 10th Mountain soldiers were given their soon-to-be-fabled insignia, an arched tab with the word "Mountain" sewn over a crossed bayonet patch.

Once, later and in the presence of his daughters, Bill reflected on these times. He recounted how the men learned to create snow caves to live in, then roll a ball of snow in front to conceal themselves from the enemy. He remembered when he was back at base camp, skipping a training class, getting caught by an officer, and having two days of KP duty ("kitchen police"). Despite this infraction, Bill was quickly promoted to Private First Class in December 1943. *The Transcript* noted that "...the advancement (in rank) is regarded as a decided tribute to Pvt. Linscott."

Mountain training continued into 1944. In June, the division was abruptly moved to Camp Swift near Austin, Texas, for maneuvers in much different weather. Forced marches were now conducted in 100-degree weather and dusty terrain.

After months in Texas, the division returned to Camp Hale. It departed in late December 1944 for Camp Patrick Henry in Virginia and would sail from nearby Hampton Roads, Virginia, bound for Europe. After nine days at sea onboard the USS *West Point* (formerly the luxury liner SS *America*), weathering dismal rain squalls, they docked at Naples, Italy.

With little delay, Bill's regiment was loaded on LCIs (Landing Craft Infantry) and, following the Italian coastline northward, landed near Pisa, where they slept in a field. They gathered equipment, supplies, and ammunition the following day and moved 75 miles to the front lines, high in the Apennines. So would begin over one hundred days of combat.

Combat and reconnaissance patrols started almost immediately, and Bill's company was ordered to capture prisoners, find paths through minefields, and make contact with the Germans to test their strength. Captives and casualties accumulated quickly. Some of the division's first casualties were soldiers shot by friendly outposts. Patrolling was difficult, as it meant climbing icy, steep terrain, often laboriously carving steps into the crusted snow, all the while watching for anti-personnel mines.

In mid-February, Bill's regiment took part in Operation Encore, directed to seize a series of mountain peaks in the Apennine range that were vigorously defended by Germans intent on preventing Allied forces from advancing into Europe. Riva Ridge and Mount Belvedere were two of the most prominent peaks to be captured. If the battalions could push the Germans off them, the Allies would control the high ground and be able to observe German activity all the way to the Po Valley, miles away.

The 86th Regiment assaulted Riva Ridge. The unit, with a number of Adams soldiers, scaled the rock face under cover of darkness, ordered to use just bayonets and grenades. They surprised portions of the 232nd German division and captured the ridge.

The next day, Bill's battalion assaulted Mount Belvedere and Monte della Torraccia while supported by P-47 fighter bombers. After negotiating mines, booby traps, artillery, and machine gun fire, the peaks were secured, with many counterattacks repelled, but with heavy losses. Bill would witness numerous pack mules coming down the mountainside with dead GIs lashed over their saddles. Bill's 2nd Battalion lost men: 24 were killed in action and 76 were wounded, just on February 21.

The 2nd Battalion was relieved on February 24 and sent to Camp Tizzoro for baths, rest, and much-needed replacements. It was a short reprieve from the fighting; the regiment was back on the front lines just days later for a lengthy fight to capture Monte della Spe, which was wrested from the Germans after three days in early March 1945. The capture of Monte della Spe cut off supplies to the Germans, which drew fire, literally; even after its capture, enemy artillery fire at the location remained fierce. Bill remembered a number of close calls and one time recounted to his daughters a memory of lying in a stream with the water pouring in and out of his shirt front while bullets flew overhead.

Bill's company remained in defensive positions under fire for three more weeks, sending out many recon, combat, and observation patrols. During this time, American and German dead had begun littering the mountain paths; they were retrieved with extreme caution as the enemy had begun booby trapping bodies, trying to kill souvenir hunters or grave registration soldiers retrieving American dead.

The 2nd Battalion was sent to a rest center on March 21 for four days and then returned to the front in the rain and darkness, again initiating platoon-size combat patrols seeking enemy contact and prisoners. The 1st and 2nd Battalions continued to hold the high ground on the rearward side of Monte della Spe while under heavy enemy artillery fire. In March, the battalion captured 150 German soldiers.

The men dug two-man foxholes on the rear side of Monte della Castellana, out of view of the Germans, and, where possible, placed sandbags or logs over the top to protect from shrapnel. (In tree-burst mortars, the shell itself would be set up to explode tree-high, showering the soldiers below with shrapnel. Mortars or other types of artillery used this kind of round to inflict maximum casualties.) Conditions, in general, were miserable. It was rainy, wet, and cold, with little to eat other than K rations. One soldier always remained awake on watch, a safer but lonely existence. The smallest of movements usually drew enemy fire.

The three infantry companies continued to send out high-risk night patrols trying to avoid numerous mines and booby traps.

Usually, the edge of a minefield was identified by finding a dead body lying over a freshly blown hole. Caution was the utmost priority since mines often had two trip wires, one at the foot and another at chest level.

On April 1, 1945, Easter Sunday, as the shelling had fallen off, Bill and several other soldiers slipped out of their foxholes in the early afternoon to enjoy a quick smoke, some chow, and a rare moment of quiet conversation. Suddenly, the enemy launched a surprise tree-burst mortar barrage that caught the men in the open. They were all hit. Pvt. Shapley Haines, Bill's friend, was killed (see *History of the 85th Mountain Infantry January 4, 1945-May 31, 1945*), and everyone else was wounded. "Haines killed. Linscott injured" read the report, reprinted in a memoir by another member of the unit, titled *See Naples and Die—A World War II Memoir* (page 170). Bill recalls Shapley being hit in the head and falling back into his foxhole.

Bill resting on a ration box, enjoying a meal. (Courtesy of Linscott family)

They all suffered wounds from shrapnel and wood splinters from a nearby tree. Medics triaged the men and stripped them of their gear, then stretcher-bearers brought them down the mountain. Bill was hit in his right side and elbow. In a letter dated April 2 to his parents, he hoped to notify them before they received the oft-dreaded Western Union gram: "Bill said, 'I wrote to you yesterday, but I think the letter was blown to bits. I've got a small wound in my left side and elbow. It shouldn't take long to heal. They've got me so tightly strapped that I can't bend at all.' The letter did reach his parents before Western Union" (*Transcript,* 4-11-45).

Once he reached the battalion aid station, Bill was evacuated by train to an Army hospital in Naples, Italy, over five hundred miles away. He would spend the next several months in the hospital recovering from his wounds. As an aside, it is likely that the group had been hit by a high explosive shell from the standard German infantry mortar (8-cm *Granatwerfer* 34), very similar to the US 81mm mortar. The German mortar launched 7.7-pound high explosive rounds that provided devastating airbursts.

Two weeks after Bill was wounded, Lt. Robert Dole, a future United States Senator and presidential candidate, was assigned to a sister company as a replacement officer. On April 14, while leading a platoon to attack a hillside machine gun nest, a wounded Dole dragged a crippled runner out of the line of fire and was himself hit by an explosive bullet, maiming his right arm and eventually requiring many operations and three years in recovery.

Also, on April 14, while Bill's regiment continued to fight through the mountains, Private John Magrath, fighting on a nearby hill with Company G, would assail a number of German machine gun nests and be posthumously awarded the Medal of Honor, the 10th Mountain's first and only soldier to receive the nation's highest military honor.

After recovering in Naples, Bill rejoined his battalion as it advanced into the Po Valley. They crossed the Po River in assault boats, continued fighting through small towns and villages, and reached Lake Garda at the foot of the Alps as German resistance began to wane. The regiment was in Italy at the end of April. The men started hearing rumors by May 2 that the war may be ending. As Bill later recalled to his daughters, he was in a cabin near Lake Garda when soldiers began shooting their guns off all over, even into the ceiling, and he thought surely someone would get killed.

The division moved on to Austria when the Germans unilaterally surrendered on May 8, 1945. The 10th continued to send out patrols with interpreters, collecting and disarming prisoners. Over 15,000 Germans would surrender to the 10th Mountain Division.

In 114 days of combat, the 10th lost 992 soldiers killed in action and had 4,154 wounded. Few other divisions lost so many soldiers in such a short period. Almost every Adams mountaineer sustained wounds, and one was killed.

Bill left Europe with the 85th Regiment on July 30, 1945, and arrived in New York ten days later, on August 10. The regiment of over 3,000 soldiers arrived aboard the USS *Marine Fox* after serving eight months overseas. While on board, the announcement was made of the atomic bomb being dropped on Japan. The news raised the men's morale since many had been training for the final assault on Japan.

On August 10, 1945, *The Transcript* noted, "William Linscott Back in Country.... Pvt. 1st Class William S. Linscott....is aboard the USS 'Marine Fox' scheduled to arrive in New York today." Four days later, a *Transcript* headline read: "Eight Ski Troop Members Now Home—Spending Furloughs in Adams after Overseas Service."

On November 30, 1945, the 10th Mountain Division was officially inactivated. During his service, Bill had earned the Purple Heart, a Victory Medal, a Good Conduct Medal, a European–African–Middle Eastern Campaign Ribbon, and an American Theater Campaign Ribbon, and he was honorably discharged in Massachusetts on February 3, 1946, at Fort Devens Separation Center.

Bill's family had moved while he was away and would later joke with friends that they purposefully did not tell him their new address.

Following his release from active duty, Bill became one of the area's first certified ski instructors and taught at Bromley Mountain Ski Area for five years. He worked at varied jobs in the summers, for a while at the Forest Park Country Club and one summer at the local Berkshire Mills with his brother Donald, "...painting, puttying, and repairing all the windows on the No. 3 mill. We worked on a scaffold and every morning would cover our faces with Vaseline so we wouldn't have to wash the paint off at night," Bill recalled in an interview with Paul Clermont's news article, "Life's People" (January 31, 1986).

During the late 1940s, Bill met a pretty young lady, Patricia Gillery, at the Dale Carnegie course "How to Win Friends and Influence People." Patricia had moved from Maine to work as a medical technologist at the North Adams and Adams hospitals. It was about that time, after the couple had become engaged, that Bill decided to accept his dad's suggestion of working with him in the insurance business. He would assume the role of office manager until his dad retired in 1965.

On November 24, 1951, Bill and Patricia were married at St. Mark's Episcopal Church. After a wedding trip to Maine, the couple settled in Adams and had two daughters, Robin and Heather. It's interesting to note that for years after their marriage, the couple would still find wooden splinters erupting from Bill's scarred left side, a reminder of his close call in the mountains of Italy.

Like many other 10th Mountain veterans returning home, Bill quickly became engaged in local ski activities and was elected President of the Thunderbolt Ski Club, with Patricia serving as its secretary and treasurer.

In addition to their ski outings, the club established a membership club at the minimal cost of three dollars per year that sponsored youth skiing and instruction at the Forest Park Country Club. The ski club installed a 300-foot tow rope and lighting on poles at the country club's 6th hole, offering skiing and instruction two or three nights a week and occasionally on Sunday. Over the years, the club was credited with introducing skiing to over 3,000 youths.

Bill and his buddies, many former 10th Mountaineers and obvious ski enthusiasts, once tobogganed a car engine to the foot of Greylock and set up a tow 500 yards up the Thunderbolt Trail for recreational skiers. Across the country, returning 10th Mountaineers were igniting interest in skiing. Some became instructors, some began operating ski schools or opened ski areas, and others found success and satisfaction writing for and publishing ski magazines. In 1984, Bill was honored by the Berkshire Hills Conference with a "Man of the Year" award for his ongoing contributions to the sport of skiing.

In 1985, Bill and other mountaineers traveled back to Italy to participate in ceremonies marking the 40th anniversary of the end of the war. They were hosted by villagers who gladly celebrated the servicemen that freed them from Nazi occupation.

During this visit, a group of Bill's friends went for a hike up the mountain to walk former battlefields and see if they could find their old foxholes. On the way back down the mountain, they stopped to talk to a farmer's wife and noticed an old canteen cup on the shelf in her chicken coop. The men passed the cup around, and when one of them turned it over, much to their surprise they found *Linscott* scratched on the bottom. Later that same night, Bill's 10th Mountain buddies presented him with the canteen cup, but not before chiding him for losing government property. He often reflected on the emotional moment because it was such a magical thing to happen. He later donated the cup to the 10th Mountain Museum in Denver, Colorado, where it can be seen today.

Bill's daughters remember their father as always ready for an adventure. It might be grabbing their skates and heading to the pond at the top of Mount Greylock, where the weather was colder and the ice thicker, or heading to Cheshire Lake for skating, sometimes making their mom nervous about the thickness of the ice, or lack thereof. Other times, on a beautiful day, Bill would rouse the family for a hike or, after a night's magical snow, to ski on splendid new powder. Any day was a good day when the family could ski the Thunderbolt.

Another adventure with Dad was a fishing trip to Cheshire Lake, borrowing a leaky boat, which the girls needed to keep bailing to stay afloat. As was custom then, no one had a life jacket, and the girls loved it. They always knew that when mom played golf on Thursday nights, they would be bass fishing somewhere.

Then there were the family tent-camping trips with Dad driving their black Country Squire Ford station wagon, pulling a packed 14-foot boat for two-week fishing trips to Maine or to Lake Champlain or St. Catherine National Park in Vermont.

Bill's outgoing ways and friendly nature had him deeply involved in the Adams community. In addition to serving as the President of the Ski Club, he was a Director of the Chamber of Commerce, the President of the Adams Insurance Agents Association, and an active member in the Elks, Lions, American Legion, and Veterans of Foreign Wars.

In 2000, Bill was honored for a half-century of dedication to the Salvation Army. He worked as the chairman and welfare secretary, and in a *Transcript* news article dated January 11, 2000, a representative stated that Bill was a "truly caring volunteer, willing to go beyond the call of duty to make sure people in town had what they needed...a volunteer *par excellence*."

He was again honored in 2000 at the 27th Annual Hathaway Christmas Dinner at Hoosac Valley High School. As part of the state's Operation Recognition, Bill and another veteran who had left Adams to serve in World War II were presented once and for all with their high school diplomas.

Bill and Patricia continued attending 10th Mountain reunions, sometimes bringing their daughters to meet the men Bill had soldiered with many years ago. At one reunion, the girls remember meeting German mountaineers who had fought against the 10th Mountain. They shared a love for mountains and skiing and were putting the past behind them.

Later in life, Bill and Patricia purchased a home on West Road where they could view Mount Greylock directly from their kitchen and living room windows. After almost forty years in the insurance business, Bill retired in the 1990s and continued to stay involved in community activities, with a particular interest in outdoor activities on the Thunderbolt.

When he passed away in 2001, Bill Linscott was accorded full military honors by the 10th Mountain Division, including an honor guard. Especially poignant was the eulogy given by a fellow

10th Mountaineer, Jeddie Brooks from Adams, who, like Bill, had answered his country's call so many years ago.

The Thunderbolt tradition carries on today with the Thunderbolt Ski Runners Club, an organization that includes Heather and Robin, who are following in their dad's footsteps, helping to preserve and upkeep the legacy of the fabled ski trail and skiing on it whenever they get a chance.

Narcheeso Massaconi
Radar Operator
752nd Antiaircraft Battalion

"Among Americans serving on Iwo Jima Island,
uncommon valor was a common virtue."
—Admiral Chester W. Nimitz

The soft, black, coarse sand shifted every time he moved; it was hard to get his footing and even more difficult to dig a foxhole. He was a radar operator for an antiaircraft gun, but with the high casualty rate, he had been impressed into duty as an infantryman. He had trained in the fine art of signals intelligence, but now he knew only the incessant firing from Nambu machine guns. It seemed to cover every inch of the beach and promised certain death if he lifted his head. To Cheeso, it appeared that his shallow, two-man foxhole would also be his grave.

AT OVER ONE HUNDRED years old, Narcheeso "Cheeso" Massaconi is one of the survivors of the long and arduous battle of Iwo Jima and resides today in his hometown of Cheshire, Massachusetts. Born at home on October 9, 1922, the baby was named Narcheeso by his mother, a name described by the family as Italian for Charles. Pietro and Rosina (Pasini) Massaconi, Cheeso's parents, were themselves born in northern Italy in the late 1800s. They married, then immigrated through Ellis Island, reaching the United States in 1914.

The family initially moved to Lee, Massachusetts, but resettled in Cheshire. Pietro worked many years as a laborer on construction jobs, then at the local General Electric Company, and spent much time working on the family's 85 acres that Pietro had bought with his brother. Rosina was a homemaker to the family's large passel of children, five girls and four boys (one of whom died shortly after birth). Their grandchildren remember hearing Rosina reading the newspaper aloud to Pietro, who spoke some English but could not read or write.

Cheeso's family lived on the farm for about ten years, from when he was a young boy until his teenage years. The farm had a horse and three milking cows. In a recent conversation from his home, Cheeso recalled that "Mom always had 100 chickens on hand," as well as hogs for sausages and a considerable vegetable garden.

"We were well fed," said Cheeso, describing a bounty of corn, potatoes, tomatoes, peppers, and turnips, and extensive canning efforts supervised by Rosina. For additional money, the family sold milk and cheese. Sadly, Cheeso's uncle sold the farm at one point and absconded with all the money. His father's name was not on the deed, and the family was forced to move.

Cheeso attended grammar school in Cheshire and fondly remembers getting a group of sixth-grade Cheshire boys together to play a nearby Adams middle-school football team. His group only had three or four helmets between them and were up against a much stronger and better equipped team. Cheshire won 18 to 0, and Cheeso scored all three touchdowns.

As a young child, he loved baseball, hunting, fishing, and trapping. Trapping added to the family's income, with muskrat pelts bringing in four dollars each, the occasional beaver $35, or a choice mink skin $18. He regularly checked on his many traps, approximately one hundred of them, at Cheshire Lake and Reservoir and around nearby streams from Pittsfield to Adams, all the while trying to closely observe trapping laws such as placing traps so many feet from a beaver's den or ensuring those traps had jaws at least five inches.

Cheeso attended Adams High School and quit at fifteen, just

several weeks short of his sixteenth birthday. The principal made every effort to get him to go back to school because he was under age, but it was so close to his birthday that the principal finally gave up his efforts.

When he quit school in late 1937, Cheeso began working forty hours a week at Berkshire Mills as a second-shift spinning machine tender, earning twelve dollars a week, replacing the spinning bobbins as quickly as possible. In 1938, he started at General Electric as a stock chaser.

In late 1942, he received his draft notice and underwent a physical at the induction center in Springfield, Massachusetts. Rosina, Cheeso's mom, pleaded with him to accept a deferment because his two brothers were already in the armed forces and his dad needed help. If he really must enlist, she asked that he wait until after Christmas.

Cheeso complied with his mother's holiday wishes but felt strongly that his country needed him and entered active duty on January 8, 1943. His thirteen-week boot camp passed quickly at Fort Eustis in Virginia. After completing basic training in May, he was sent directly to Schofield Barracks on the Hawaiian island of Oahu and was assigned to the newly formed Headquarters Battery 752nd AAA (Antiaircraft) Gun Battalion as a radar operator. The battalion's logo shows a shield with a missile, lightning rods, and the motto *Keepers of the Gate*.

Early picture of Cheeso, after arriving in Hawaii. (Courtesy of Cheeso Massaconi and family)

While preparing for the possibility of another attack on

Pearl Harbor by the Japanese, the battalion assigned Cheeso's company to remove 5.25 antiaircraft guns and fire control equipment from sunken warships in the nearby harbor. The guns were craned to land and remounted on fixed concrete bases in a diamond formation. Cheeso received his rudimentary radar training from an officer aboard one of the warships. He still remembers enjoying Navy cooking—much better than Army rations.

Hawaii wasn't always the paradise it might have appeared. Liberty was often spent at one of the jam-packed bars on Hotel Street in downtown Honolulu or on the beach. Sadly, several of Cheeso's close friends drowned while playing around in the rough surf. He usually avoided the beach, except for some occasional oyster digging, because the bright sun and hot weather seemed to cause debilitating headaches. An Army doctor offered the opportunity for him to return to the States. He declined, saying, "I'm staying in the service until the war's end, win or lose."

Cheeso, left, with his army buddy Tommy Porcello on maneuvers in Hawaii. (Courtesy of Cheeso Massaconi and family)

In fall of 1944, Cheeso's group received the Army's 120mm antiaircraft guns with the M-10 director and radar. Not long after, in early 1945, his antiaircraft unit was sent to Eniwetok Atoll (today known as *Enewetak)* in the Marshall Islands and then to Saipan, arriving on February 6, 1945, months after the atoll had been technically secured. In a January 2020 interview with *CapeNews.net* featuring Cheeso as their Veterans Spotlight, he explained, "I was on radar patrol tracking enemy planes. Our planes would take off with bombs to hit Japan…they'd rise slow, then drop close to the water, shudder, then go back up. [I'll] never forget [when a] plane coming back from a mission…dropped right in the water and exploded…oil and gas burned for two hours…lost 12 young guys."

With minimal enemy air activity, Cheeso and his four-man anti-aircraft crew received M1 rifles, became infantrymen, and patrolled for months, ferreting out remaining enemy soldiers. He noted that "the Japanese always came at us at night."

Initially, they lived in foxholes (and later two-man pup tents) and, at night, manned three-person guard posts, often intercepting Japanese soldiers sneaking through their lines seeking water or food. His months on the island involved frequent skirmishes with enemy stragglers. Japanese resistance continued until December 1, 1945, three months after the official surrender of Japan, when the last hold outs (among them Captain Oda, known as "The Fox," and his band of men) surrendered.

While Cheeso's unit was mopping up on Saipan, one of the war's fiercest battles took place on an island seven hundred miles north, Iwo Jima. Nicknamed "Sulphur Island," Iwo Jima was a rocky, hilly, and barren volcanic island with the dormant 550-foot Mount Suribachi anchoring its southern end. Black sand covered the beaches below; little grew on this piece of soft volcanic rock with an area of just eight square miles.

From February 19 to March 26, 1945, tens of thousands of Marines and soldiers fought to wrest the island from over 20,000 Japanese soldiers. Their tactical goal was to capture Iwo Jima's three airfields and use them to launch B-29 bomber air attacks on Japan, only 600 miles away.

American forces faced a deeply entrenched enemy who had months to prepare for this battle on an island close to their homeland.

Over the preceding months, Japan had sent its best mining engineers to develop a system of interconnected blockhouses, caves, bunkers, ramparts, and communication centers. It is estimated that over eleven miles of concealed tunnels hid artillery pieces, mortars, and antiaircraft guns. Some bunkers had up to seven levels underground.

The Japanese used their weaponry to rain down precise artillery, mortar, and machine gun fire as Marine units landed on both sides of Mount Suribachi. The US forces' amphibious vehicles, called LVTs (Landing Vehicle Tracked), were easy targets for the enemy's guns.

America would go on to suffer more than 26,000 casualties on Iwo Jima, including over 7,000 dead, mostly Marines, in a 36-day bloodbath that resulted in over 17,000 enemy troops being destroyed, with 3,000 remaining to be killed or captured by the soldiers who relieved the Marines. That would be Cheeso's unit, the 752nd Gun Battalion.

Cheeso's unit landed on Iwo Jima at the base of Mount Suribachi on or around April 11, 1945. He remembers watching the bombardment as their ship approached the island and saying to a friend, "It's lit up like the Fourth of July."

With little need for their antiaircraft artillery (the Japanese air force had already been decimated by American carrier planes), Cheeso and his fellow soldiers again became infantrymen. His unit was attached to the 147th Army regiment, assigned to "mop up" the thousands of enemy stragglers. For the next three months, using bayonets, bullets, grenades, flame throwers, and satchel charges, they would slog across the island, digging out Japanese pockets of resistance.

Cheeso describes it as simply "hell." He recalls, "There were no trees, it was hot, the ground was steaming, and we had no water unless the Seabees brought it to us. They would bring in ten-gallon cans, and we could refill our canteens." The island had a noxious smell like rotten eggs (sulfur), and the steep terrain was soft black ash (volcanic residue), making digging foxholes easier but also becoming sticky when it rained.

His unit quickly set up, under fire, a two/three-man foxhole-buddy system. They rotated who would sleep, but Cheeso readily admits he was usually too scared to sleep. Often the enemy fire was so intense that "the men would defecate in their helmets and throw the shit out of the foxholes rather than expose themselves."

Cheeso also recalled, "After leaving Pearl Harbor, there were no more showers. We washed our hands and faces with water from our helmet (liner removed). We didn't notice our smell. We all smelled the same."

The food situation was no better. Army K rations were the order of the day. Cheeso said that he and his men were "always hungry and thirsty."

They tried hunting down Japanese stragglers in daytime, but the Japanese would probe their lines at night throwing grenades and were skilled at infiltrating. The situation was fraught with danger, and Cheeso was almost killed when a sniper barely missed him. The bullet whizzed by his head.

Shortly after their arrival, his unit cautioned a nearby platoon of soldiers not to use tents but to dig foxholes because it was so dangerous aboveground. Cheeso said, "We warned them how dangerous it was…the Japanese staged a sneak attack one night and went right down the line, throwing grenades into the tents…one by one. It killed everyone...it was sad."

He said the fighting was vicious. Neither side took many prisoners; usually, it was a fight to the death. Several times, small groups of enemy soldiers would give themselves up after killing Americans and running out of ammunition; often, they were shown no quarter and cut down.

Cheeso and his squad would trudge across the island for months, finding, killing, or capturing Japanese "holdouts" who had opted not to surrender and continued fighting, with no provisions. They were often caught leaving their warrens for food and especially water. Cheeso accepted the surrender of a Japanese officer clothed only in a loincloth and passed him off to others. He never heard what became of the prisoner.

In April, his unit captured the largest number of prisoners at one time during the entire battle for Iwo Jima. Over 70 Japanese soldiers surrendered and emerged from a hundred-foot-deep underground hospital. His unit's patrols and ambushes were credited with killing over 900 Japanese in April, another 252 in May, and 17 in June.

As the island became more secure, he had the chance to visit the grave of John Basilone, a Marine hero who earned the Congressional Medal of Honor on Guadalcanal. Basilone had been slain on the first day of the invasion of Iwo Jima while leading his men who were attacking enemy blockhouses. There are differences of opinion on whether mortar shrapnel or small arms fire killed him. Basilone was posthumously decorated for his gallant actions on Iwo Jima with the Navy Cross, the nation's second-highest military honor. Cheeso's friend Tommy from New Jersey took a picture of Cheeso kneeling by Basilone's grave.

A much cherished photograph of Cheeso paying tribute to a fallen hero. (Courtesy of Cheeso Massaconi and family)

In 1948, the government started moving the remains of thousands of Marines and soldiers buried on Iwo Jima to a final resting place in the United States, according to their families' wishes. John Basilone now rests in Arlington National Cemetery.

After months on the island, Cheeso was offered a ride up Mount Suribachi. He quickly declined, and recalls saying, "I have had enough of this island. I just want to go home." Shortly afterward, he returned to Saipan, received new winter uniforms and the necessary inoculations, and headed home, departing by ship for the United States in November 1945.

(NOTE: The American casualty rate for the battle of Iwo Jima was almost 30% of the total committed force. Rifle battalions involved in hand-to-hand combat suffered close to a 75% casualty rate. The last Japanese holdouts did not surrender until 1949, three and a half years after the end of the war.)

Cheeso was honorably discharged in late November at Fort Devens in Massachusetts. In his two years and six months of foreign service, he had earned the Asiatic–Pacific Theater Campaign Medal with battle stars, the Army's Good Conduct Medal, and Victory Medal. During his processing, he was offered a promotion from corporal to sergeant if he would reenlist. He recalls telling them, "No, keep your stripes."

Just days after an on-base Thanksgiving dinner, his family picked Cheeso up and brought him home to Cheshire, Massachusetts, where like so many others, he was anxious to resume his civilian life.

Cheeso returned to his job at General Electric's transformer division, working dispatching materials. He resumed his outdoor passions of trapping, hunting, and fishing. On weekends and holidays, you could find Cheeso in his waders, fishing trout streams and local brooks. In the winter, he would be ice-fishing on Cheshire, Pontoosuc, and Onota Lakes for perch, largemouth bass, pickerel, and pike.

He was an avid hunter and, for many years, hunted rabbits with his favorite Beagles. Then in later years, he pursued pheasants on state lands with his Brittany Spaniels. As a left-handed shooter, he was unerringly accurate with his 16-gauge shotgun.

In 1950, home from the war for five years, he met Joan Bondini at a local function and was smitten by the younger woman's zest for life. They soon married and would have six children—four boys and two girls—over thirteen years. Their personalities meshed nicely.

They were both hard workers and kind, although their children agreed that mom was the stricter disciplinarian.

The family lived in a two-story, four-bedroom house Cheeso built in the early 1950s, where he continues to live today. The gray, vinyl-sided house with blue shutters sits on an acre and a half of land and still has a sizeable garden. Cheeso continued at General Electric for decades before retiring as a dispatcher in 1962. He described General Electric as "the best place on the planet to work."

As the children were growing up, it would be his habit to come home from work each day at 3:30 p.m., eat supper with the family, and work in his garden until dark. He fed his family and shared the large harvest with neighbors. There were always plenty of tomatoes, peppers, string beans, cucumbers, and radishes for everyone. He would also give his neighbors seedlings to start their gardens. Cheeso and Joan spent hours canning tomatoes, peppers, and green beans.

Not one for idle moments, Cheeso made dandelion and cherry wine in the house's cellar. The children would pick dandelions and bring them to the cellar to place in large crocks to be concocted with yeast, water, and other ingredients. He would purchase cherries from the supermarket for the cherry wine. When appropriately strained and aged, the final bottled product would be sealed with Cheeso's capping machine.

Cheeso played baseball early in life and, after returning from the war, he played until his forties. He initially played hardball and was an outfielder/backup catcher. He describes himself as "a hard-to-strike-out batter…not a home-run hitter, mainly singles and doubles."

As a starting player with the Pittsfield Tyler Aces, Cheeso played in tournaments throughout Berkshire County and in other states. He fondly remembers his best game in the late 1940s. It was at a tournament in Wichita, Kansas, when his championship New England team had earned a spot at Nationals, and he faced Bob Grim, a soon-to-be Yankee pitcher. Cheeso said, "I had four-for-four hits off of him and the winning hit in that game."

Later, a local team asked him to play fast-pitch softball where, as a center fielder, he backed up the infield and enjoyed depriving the other team of hits by catching their fly balls. Cheeso was elected to the Berkshire County UNICO Baseball and Softball Hall of Fame.

With a large family and one paycheck, vacations in their blueish Ford station wagon often meant modest trips to Mountain Park, visiting relatives or friends, and enjoying picnics or local clambakes. There was always the well-attended Fourth of July party at their house.

Later in life, he and Joan attended several Army reunions, mainly in the Midwest and California, although their trips grew less frequent as his comrades passed away. They also returned to Italy several times for extended periods, visiting family and friends. Cheeso and Joan shared a rich and devoted life together for over sixty-five years until her passing in 2017.

Cheeso continued to hunt and fish well into his 90s. His favorite times have been hunting deer with his sons and other relatives. He hunted on nearby Mount Greylock, in Vermont, and, for several years, leased a cabin in New York State. In Vermont and New York, as the law allowed, he used his .308 Remington Woodmaster rifle, and in Massachusetts, he used his 16-gauge shotgun, exchanging his shotgun barrel to hunt small game for a special slug barrel for deer hunting. (His wife's only rule for the often-successful hunters was "no mud in the house." She was adamant that the mud-splattered hunters access the cellar around the back of the house.)

These days, Cheeso spends much of his time in his cozy garage (or "man cave"), surrounded by his most poignant memories. There is a beautifully mounted deer head, a turkey, and a trout, just some of the souvenirs of an outdoorsman's life. Pictures on the wall memorialize family, hunting excursions, and baseball teams. He greatly admires Joe DiMaggio, his favorite player, and the New York Yankees. His get-away area also includes a TV and hot coffee.

He still enjoys a taste of wine at supper, and his favorite meal is hot deer stew over cornmeal polenta, which his son makes for him three times a year. His son, grandson, and others help as Cheeso's mobility is limited. They visit often and cook him a pancake and sausage breakfast or help their centenarian dad with shaving and the occasional "buzzcut," joking that he looks like he is back in the Army.

Cheeso walks with a cane and can still get upstairs to his second-story bedroom. Everyone describes him as kind-hearted, thrifty, and a hard worker. He continued to work in his beloved garden until his late 90s. His memory remains sharp, especially when talking about Iwo Jima. In the January 2020 *CapeNews.net* interview, he shared a wealth of memories with Wayne Soares, a noted veterans' supporter:

Even when recounting war memories, Cheeso keeps a smile on his face. (Courtesy of the author, 2023)

"There wasn't a battle like it," Cheeso told Soares. "In Europe, you always knew where the enemy was and who you were fighting…not at Iwo Jima…you never knew where the enemy was…the Japanese attacked when you were the most vulnerable. The Japanese had big guns in the tunnels on Mount Suribachi that came out on tracks. They unloaded on us [and] we were sitting ducks. I was no hero…I was too scared even to eat. [W]e worried about staying alive.…If you wanted to die, you got out of your foxhole at night."

When reflecting on his time in the service, Cheeso went on to say, "I loved my country and wanted to do what's right…and we did okay…although I can still see my mother crying, saying, 'You no go…stay home and help the family'." In the end, he was able to do both—do what's right *and* return home to his mom, marry, and help raise a new generation. No doubt his mother would be pleased to know her Cheeso is still going strong and thriving, now into his second century.

ALFRED H. NEVEU
RIFLEMAN
79TH INFANTRY DIVISION

The bedraggled, sodden soldiers of Company I, after almost 100 days of relentless combat, were ordered to clear Forêt de Parroy, a vast network of natural wooded defenses in eastern France near the German border, heavily guarded by some of Germany's best infantry, supported by artillery, mortars, and tanks. The eleven-day battle would be under the most miserable, bone-chilling conditions: constant rain, bitter cold, and a quagmire of mud. Vigilance would be extreme with the possibility of the enemy behind every tree…and casualties would be high for Al Neveu's company.

ALFRED WAS BORN ON November 18, 1924, to French Canadian parents, Adolphe and Mary (Mousseau) Neveu. His parents had married in 1904 and gone on to have ten children: five daughters and four surviving sons. Adolphe was a millwright/carpenter with the local mills. Mary was a homemaker.

Tragically, Mary died during the birth of her tenth child, Edward Eugene, in June 1927, and Edward followed a short time later. Alfred, now the caboose in the family, was two and a half when his mom died and quickly became everyone's favorite child. Everyone called him Al.

Adolphe remarried about a year after his wife's death to Laura Guyette, a single woman who would graciously help him raise the nine children. The marriage would last twenty-two years until her unexpected death in 1950.

As the youngest, Alfred was said to be his father's favorite. When chores got to him, his dad often indulged him, saying, "Go play baseball." Alfred loved a good pick-up game and, at one point, is thought to have played on a number of local teams.

As he got older, Al worked with his brothers and sisters in the family's small greenhouse business. His dad had constructed the hothouse in their backyard and the family grew and sold vegetables to the neighborhood. Each child took responsibility for different customers. Every few days during the growing season, each child would fill a basket with fresh produce and go door-to-door in assigned neighborhoods selling the veggies. What money they collected was put in a large coffee can to help the family.

Al attended Renfrew Elementary School, C.T. Plunkett Middle, and Adams High School. He worked long hours as a teenager at Berkshire Fine Spinning, a cotton textile mill on Hoosac Street in Adams, to help the family's finances.

In 1934, when Al was ten, the Savoy, Massachusetts, Civilian Conservation Corps spent months carving a two-mile-long trail on the steep east slope of Greylock Mountain. It would be called the Thunderbolt. It wasn't long before his older brother was skiing down it, often dragging his younger brother Al with him.

After school, the boys would climb the mountain with wooden skis on their backs or drag them in the snow and then have an exhilarating, minutes-long ride back to the bottom. Early on, having little skiing finesse, they would flop in the snow if they needed to stop or to avoid partially cut stumps.

As the sport grew in popularity, a furniture store owner, Art Simmons, assisted local boys by creating a ski section in his store and selling equipment on credit or at a discount. In the 1930s, money was scarce, and Art's generous terms were greatly appreciated. Skiers of the era often used the popular seven-foot Griswold hickory skis. It is said that some skiers would take advantage of the ski company's one-year guarantee and after a hard winter's use "accidentally" break a tip and receive a new pair.

After the attack on Pearl Harbor on December 7, 1941, the United States declared War on Japan and Germany, and during the following months approximately 20 Adams men volunteered for the 87th Regiment of the 10th Mountain Division. All of the applicants were accomplished skiers, and the men were considered one of the largest groups of skiers to volunteer from a single small town. Al was in this group. He was eighteen.

Early photo of Al in his dress uniform. (Courtesy of Neveu family)

After submitting reference letters, Al received his approval in early 1943 to join the mountain troopers. Not long after, he departed to Camp Hale, Colorado, where he began his basic training. It was arduous and grueling at higher elevations and bone-chillingly cold. They often trained in foul weather, wearing their skis or snowshoes, and were heavily ladened with rucksacks full of equipment and M1 rifles.

Living in tents and thin wooden barracks heated only by small coal burning stoves caused considerable illness among the troopers. Most recovered, but Al developed rheumatic fever; after hospitalization, he was offered and declined a medical discharge. He felt he needed to do his part in the war against tyranny.

The Army reassigned Al to the 79th Infantry Division. The division was formed in 1917 during World War I. It was noted for its participation in the Meuse-Argonne offensive. In 1918, infantry divisions were asked to submit an insignia design. Having battled in the Lorraine sector of France, they chose the blue and white Croix de Lorraine. Henceforth their soldiers would be known as "Lorrainers" and wear the blue and white cross on their left shoulder.

In June 1942, the 79th Division had preliminary training and boot camp at Camp Pickett, Virginia (now Fort Barfoot), and then more training in Camp Blanding, Florida, with field exercises in Tennessee and Arizona. In December 1943, Alfred joined the division at Camp Phillips in Kansas for field training in winter conditions.

Their training was completed four months later, and the Lorrainers reported to Camp Myles Standish, Massachusetts, for embarkation. The division arrived in Liverpool, England, in mid-April and was billeted in Cheshire. At this point, training was focused on amphibious landings, and many days featured wet, bedraggled men struggling back to their tents or Quonset huts.

Al was now assigned to Company I, 3rd Battalion of the 313th Regiment.

Shortly after D-Day, the division was moved to Falmouth/Southampton, preparing to sail for France. The 79th Division was part of a corps assigned the job of seizing the city of Cherbourg. Alfred waded ashore at Utah Beach on June 7 (D-Day + 1), ahead of the main body of the division.

The landing was Al's first close brush with death. His vanguard had come under intermittent shelling and bombing. On a wooden Higgins Boat landing craft with a driver nervous from the nearby shelling, Al was dropped off early, in shoulder-high water. Stepping into an unforeseen shell hole ladened with 70 pounds of equipment, he almost drowned.

In re-telling the story to his granddaughter, Al explained, "two men next to me saw it, and helped me out of the hole, where I would have drowned." Then what Al saw next, he told his granddaughter, "was awful. There were dead GIs everywhere." The beach, while tentatively secure, was littered with destroyed vehicles, dead German soldiers, and crashed plywood gliders with rows of dead paratroopers lined up beside them. This was no time for reflection: Within moments, the 3rd Battalion would suffer its first casualties.

The Battle for Cherbourg

THE 313TH HAD BEEN assigned to spearhead a drive toward the heavily defended city of Cherbourg. Over the next twelve days, as the unit proceeded throughout the Cherbourg peninsula, it was faced with countless hedgerows; those centuries-old mounds of dirt, stone, and underbrush that defined the borders of farmers' fields also provided concealment for deadly German tanks, machine gun nests, concrete bunkers, and numerous enemy infantry. It was a new type of fighting, conquering one field at a time, almost like a game of checkers. Initially, hidden German anti-tank guns decimated American tanks.

At one point, the Americans creatively modified tanks to become tank dozers, adept at breaking up the hedgerows so infantry could proceed.

In early June 1944, as the 313th Regiment approached the hilly outer edge of Cherbourg, it continued to repel vicious counter-attacks. The first line of the German defense was concrete pillboxes/bunkers between four and five feet thick, armed with machine guns and 88mm artillery pieces. The bunkers were built with firing ports level with the ground supported by adjacent riflemen and mortars. The approaches were lined with minefields and barbed wire. Therefore, the whole defense was linked, allowing communication through camouflaged trenches and tunnels.

Faced with this daunting defense, Alfred's regiment was accompanied by a talented tank and engineering battalion that initially blasted through the hedgerows and used explosives to help destroy bunkers.

In combat now over two weeks, the bearded, dirty men were tired and carried just what they needed for the ongoing assault:

grenades in their pockets, a canteen, shovel, rifle, ammunition, knife, and a bayonet. Most had long ago lost or dropped their blankets to lighten their load and slept uncovered and cold in wet foxholes.

Al spent the morning of June 14 with his unit patrolling the city's outskirts and then engaging the Germans in furious fighting. During the battle, the Germans had artillery on the high ground, and the 313th was heavily shelled.

Later that day, while patrolling, Al and his unit came under heavy fire from 88 airbursts out of one of Cherbourg's last major defenses, Fort du Roule. As Al later related to his granddaughter, "I was standing next to a tree when a shell hit that tree. It got me in the back and neck, so I had some pieces sticking out all over me. They sent me to the first aid station, and I was there about two days. While I was there my regiment had moved. They told me there was no transportation, so I had to get back the best way I could."

In Al's absence, the three regiments of the division had continued their attack on Cherbourg, and his battalion had reached its initial objective, although communications with the division had been cut by enemy fire. Company I suffered heavy casualties during this fight. After a brief respite, the 313th resumed its attack on June 24, and Al's 3rd Battalion approached Cherbourg from the east under heavy artillery fire.

When the 313th eventually entered Cherbourg, they found the town deserted and seriously damaged. The men noticed that every window in the city had broken from bombardment concussions, and many window openings had been bricked up to serve as firing ports for machine guns. As the division took control, it captured over 6,000 prisoners from four different German infantry divisions, under the occasional sniper fire.

As Al recounted to his granddaughter, "During the fight for Cherbourg, I was with a supply sergeant in a foxhole. I said to him that I had to go back about a mile to get some supplies and ammunition. He said he would be waiting in the hole, and when I got back [Germans] had shelled the area right next to the hole. The poor guy...just his feet were sticking out of the hole." Much later in his life, when recounting the story to family, Al said he "never got over that image and often felt guilty that I stayed alive when he and many others died."

Without much rest, the 313th was back in the fray in early July, working with tank units to break through the highly defended and dangerous hedgerows. The fights were ongoing as Company I fought across France, almost always under mortar or artillery fire.

During one of these skirmishes, Al, now a scout and messenger, was ordered to carry a message to an adjacent rifle company. The assignment was extraordinarily dangerous since he needed to cross an open field under enemy fire. Thinking quickly, he laid on his belly between nearby railroad tracks, his small frame hugging the ground to deliver the message while shrapnel and bullets snapped overhead. He escaped serious injury once more.

Al and his platoon were patrolling constantly, often trying to anticipate ambushes. During one skirmish when he saw bushes moving to his right, he sprayed the bushes with his BAR (Browning Automatic Rifle) and when he moved through the area, he saw the young German soldier he had killed. That image would haunt him for days.

The division fought on through towns and villages in places like "Bloody Hill," La Haye-du-Puits, and Lessay, incurring heavy casualties. Its first eleven days in combat recorded almost 3,000 killed or wounded. At one point, the 313th became motorized as it pushed through the city of Le Mans and, after so many more fights, eventually arrived in Paris in August 1944.

In late August, the 79th moved into Belgium with the 313th in the vanguard, fighting through villages and towns and securing bridges. The division captured thousands of prisoners, numerous weapons, and enemy motor vehicles. With enemy vehicles as part of their convoy, the division became concerned that fighters from either side might bomb their group. In one of the strange twists of war, it was decided to let the Germans operate their mobile anti-aircraft guns to shoot down any approaching German planes.

After five days of almost continuous action, the division saw its first overseas USO show featuring Bing Crosby, one of America's favorite singers. Troops from the 313th constructed a platform in the center of a large green field and placed anti-aircraft guns around it to safeguard the troupe (and troops) from aerial attack. More soldiers were also placed on the perimeter to protect the unit from surprise attacks. There were two performances; Al and the 313th attended the first one at 2:00 p.m. on September 18. The second show that night was interrupted when troops were called to the front.

Bing Crosby show near Avrainville, France, September 17, 1944

The Bing Crosby show makes the papers; Al is in the crowd, back right. (Courtesy of Neveu family)

Following the show, the entire 313th was ordered back to the front. The Germans continued to fight doggedly as they retreated across France, trying to delay the division's progress. In late September 1944, the 313th moved from Lunéville, France, with directions to push the Germans out of the Forêt de Parroy and its acres of heavily forested woods. They were up against the dug-in 15th and 113th Panzer divisions. (Hitler had fought in the same forested area in World War I and commanded it to be defended at all costs.)

After eleven miserable days of rain, mud, and intense combat against entrenched infantry, tanks, and artillery, and often only able to travel on rutted, water-filled roads, the 313th could push through the woods. The company suffered heavy casualties with 60 men wounded or killed, and their dead were not easily retrievable, scattered as they were about the wooded quagmire. The intense battle resulted in 2,000 casualties for the 79th, more than any other battle to date.

By this time, the 200 soldiers originally in Al's Company I had only 50 of its original troopers. It was now being refilled with replacements. Many of Al's close friends had been killed or wounded and he wasn't inclined to make new acquaintances. It was too hard losing friends.

While patrolling, Al and his squad were approached by a frenetic French woman who said her husband, a resistance member, had been summarily shot by the Germans, and she wanted his patrol to try and save him. Willing to help, Al and another soldier commandeered a vehicle, sped to the nearby location, and treated the man's serious wound. Al and his comrade brought the man back to his home and then moved on, uncertain whether or not he would survive.

There was no rest for the Lorrainers. They fought on, subject to torrents of small arms and artillery fire in almost continuous rain. The bedraggled men were close to exhaustion.

The town of Emberménil was their next objective. Al's regiment, assisted by two others, captured the town and then was ordered to capture some nearby hills. The night of October 13, 1944, his company moved into position, ready to assault a stone farmhouse. Men nervously took cover behind a stone wall and waited for a signal to commence their early-morning assault.

Upon the signal, Company I climbed over the wall and began to move on the farmhouse. Al was carrying his BAR, with bandoliers of ammunition slung across his chest. Tanks accompanied the soldiers, which meant that the Germans could hear their approach and quickly greeted them with a fusillade of machine gun, artillery, and mortar fire.

The action was violent and quick. The tank near Al was hit and the crew killed. The soldier to his left was shot and a German 88 artillery shell landed near Al, imbedding shrapnel in his spine, chest, and thigh.

As he related to his granddaughter, "A shell hit, and I passed out. I had got it right through the side." Crawling to a nearby foxhole, he drank from an abandoned German canteen and ate some food scattered about, while waiting for help. Al continued: "Two medics saw me and picked me up. One under each arm. All of sudden, the shells started coming again. They dropped me on the ground, and I passed out again."

Finally, the medics were able to carry him the rest of the way to a combat aid station. In one of the oddities of war, Doctor Rosenthal from his hometown looked at his dog tags and recognized his name before anesthetizing Al and removing the shell fragments from his body. The extensive surgical efforts left Al with a large hole in his hip and numerous stitches.

The next day, Dr. Rosenthal visited his recovering patient and explained his wounds which in addition to being caused by shrapnel may have included being gunshot. The doctor hypothesized that the demolished bandolier Al had been wearing across his chest may have saved his life, protecting his chest from additional shrapnel.

Rosenthal said that he would be headed home in a week and would contact Al's mother and father to tell them he was okay. His generous care and personal concern lifted Al's morale.

Shortly afterwards, Al was airlifted to a hospital in Italy for more surgery.

Back home in Adams, his stepmom, Laura, received a Western Union Telegram dated October 27 that reported her stepson had been wounded.

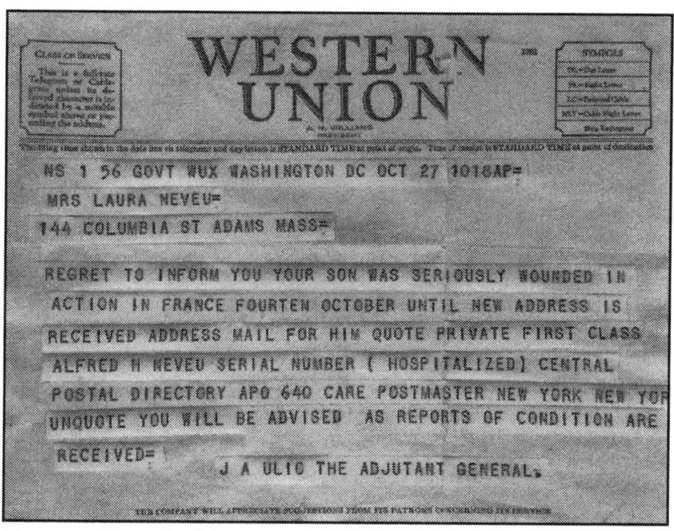

WESTERN UNION

NS 1 56 GOVT WUX WASHINGTON DC OCT 27 1018AP=

MRS LAURA NEVEU=

144 COLUMBIA ST ADAMS MASS=

REGRET TO INFORM YOU YOUR SON WAS SERIOUSLY WOUNDED IN ACTION IN FRANCE FOURTEN OCTOBER UNTIL NEW ADDRESS IS RECEIVED ADDRESS MAIL FOR HIM QUOTE PRIVATE FIRST CLASS ALFRED H NEVEU SERIAL NUMBER (HOSPITALIZED) CENTRAL POSTAL DIRECTORY APO 640 CARE POSTMASTER NEW YORK NEW YOR UNQUOTE YOU WILL BE ADVISED AS REPORTS OF CONDITION ARE RECEIVED=

J A ULIO THE ADJUTANT GENERAL.

(Courtesy of Neveu family)

While recovering, Al learned that one of his letters had reached home and somehow in return correspondence, the nurse on his wing told him that his older brother, who had been wounded in Italy with the 10th Mountain Division, was recovering in a nearby hospital ship in the Naples harbor.

Determined to see his brother, who was confined to the ship, Al, though still recovering from his wounds and with no transportation available, walked several miles on crutches to see him.

Their reunion was announced in a *Transcript* newspaper piece on February 17, 1945: "Adams Brothers Meet in Italy…S/Sgt Bernard Neveu…and his brother Pvt. 1st Class Alfred Neveu had an enjoyable five-hour reunion recently at a hospital…."

While the visit went well, Al's stitches had torn, and a serious infection developed. Not long after returning, he was operated on again to repair the damage and deal with his infection. In his words to his granddaughter, "...my stomach was swollen and blown up from blood poisoning…. The doctor took one look at me and brought me to the operating room. The doctor scraped my hip. So, he put a drain in my stomach."

After recovering, Al was medically evacuated with stops in

Dakar, North Africa, the Azores, Florida and then to Camp Edwards in Massachusetts where he was honorably discharged in July 1945.

His yearlong odyssey of overseas service was quite a tale. The twenty-one-year-old had survived serious shrapnel wounds, infections, and fevers as well as many close calls in the field.

For his years of service, Al was awarded the prestigious Combat Infantrymen's Badge, the Bronze Star Medal, and two Purple Hearts in addition to his campaign medals.

Postscript: The 79th Division would continue to fight on without Al and received a Presidential Unit Citation for its heroics entering Germany. When the War with Germany ended on May 8, 1945, the soldiers collected and disarmed prisoners, assisted thousands of displaced persons, and helped with administration in the war-torn areas. In the late summer of 1945, the Lorrainers participated in an eight-week training program in preparation for redeployment to the Pacific in anticipation of invading Japan. Fortunately, the Japanese surrendered on August 14, 1945, and the troops started processing for their return to the United States.

Al Neveu, back home on leave. (Courtesy of Neveu family)

When Al was on medical furlough in April 1945, he had met Elizabeth Brice from North Adams. They fell in love, married in October 1946, and made their home at 129 Glen Avenue, North Adams. Al and Elizabeth lived with her parents in the two-story duplex. With a large porch and expansive yard populated with greenhouses, a chicken coop, and a rabbit's hutch, it was the perfect place to raise their five children.

Al, particularly good with numbers, completed math, geometry, engineering, and mechanical drafting courses and was employed for many years as a draftsman in GE's Pittsfield Transformer Division. He also worked at James Hunter Machine Company and was known for creating technical drawings for their textile machinery. He would retire from Hunter in the late 1980s.

After their five children were born, Elizabeth, the valedictorian of her high school class, entered college. She graduated 1961 magna cum laude from North Adams State College with a degree in education and taught at Johnson Elementary School for many years. She was a highly accomplished pianist and in addition to English spoke three languages: German, French, and Latin.

It was an idyllic life. The family's meals were every night at 5:00 p.m., and Elizabeth or Grandma summoned the kids from the neighborhood with a school bell. Often in the summertime, Al would cook the evening meal in the backyard on a Coleman stove, with the family converging on two picnic tables. Al made some of the best hamburgers, usually accompanied by several dozen ears of corn from their garden.

Their camping trips were memorable. Packed together in their baby-blue Ford station wagon, with kids spaced strategically and a rooftop rack piled high and covered with a tarp, the nine would sally forth to Acadia Park in Maine, Lake George in New York, or Cape Cod. They also camped along the Mohawk Trail.

Equipped with coolers, a large wall tent, and the three-burner Coleman, it wouldn't take long to set up camp and erect a tarp over their eating area. The kids slept on the ground, and Mom and Dad had cots. His son describes it as "Fantastic times, the best of memories."

When camping and swimming at the beach, the kids would notice Dad's scars from the war. He had numerous shrapnel marks on his chest and a jaw-dropping fist-size hole in his hip. When his wound had become infected after visiting his brother in Naples, the surgeons had scraped it out, creating a deep fissure. He seldom talked about his war experiences, although Al occasionally suffered from nightmares and often thought of the man in his foxhole who did not survive.

When not working in his vegetable garden or doing home maintenance, Al enjoyed trout fishing with kids on the Deerfield River and oil painting, taking as his subjects the lovely New England landscapes and flowers. Trips downtown would find him enjoying a meal at Jack's Hot Dog Stand on Eagle Street in North Adams.

Al was described by his son as a "very smart, soft-spoken, dedicated family man, who was a hard worker, incredibly funny, and loved a good joke. He never once complained about his service or injuries." When asked about his combat experience, Al would typically reply, "It was terrible. You don't want to hear about it," or "What I did was nothing special. We had a job to do, and we did it. Others had it worse, much worse."

Another one of America's World War II heroes died peacefully at home on February 16, 2005. Al was eighty years old. The daring Thunderbolt skier of long ago was at rest.

BERNARD J. ST. JOHN
FIGHTER PILOT
VT-18 BOMBER SQUADRON

This red-headed, teenaged, bread-truck driver from Adams would become an unflappable naval aviator and participate in one of World War II's largest naval battles. He dodged a blizzard of bullets to attack the largest battleship in the world and indirectly sank a huge Japanese cruiser, placing him squarely in America's pantheon of heroes. His Navy Cross citation reads, "Boldly flying through intense antiaircraft fire to press home a low-level attack on a Battleship Task Force, Lieutenant, Junior Grade, (then Ensign) St. John succeeded in scoring a direct hit on a cruiser which later sank and although his plane was damaged, made a safe return to base."

BERNARD JOSEPH ST. JOHN'S story begins with his birth at the W.B. Plunkett Hospital in Adams, Massachusetts, on August 17, 1921. His parents were Edmund and Veronica (Gavin) St. John, who married in 1919 and had three sons and two daughters.

Edmund was also born in Adams. He played on its high school football team and served in the Army during WWI, spending eleven months in France with Company B, 116th field signal battalion, as a first sergeant. The family lived on Orchard Street, and Edmund ran an electrical contractor business for twenty-five years out of his shop on Summer Street. At one point, Edmund was also commander of the local American Legion.

Bernard (called "Ben") was a member of the class of 1939 at Adams High School and became involved in many activities. He was in the senior class play, on the ski team, and in speech, arts, and science clubs. At one point, he found time to manage the baseball team. Yet, he maintained his greatest focus on music. A prominent school band and orchestra member, Ben performed at a number of concerts; evidently, as a high school junior, he played an impressive French horn solo in the Andante from *Concerto in F, Opus 8* by Strauss (*Transcript,* 5-25-1938). He participated in orchestras from North Adams, Pittsfield, and Williams College. In his senior year, he also served as an assistant conductor in several concerts.

Over the years, Ben took part in many of Adams' musical productions, displaying his magnificent tenor voice. In minstrel shows, he had singing solos augmented by his dancing, and the local newspaper noted the audience greatly appreciated him. Ben also joined the St. Thomas Church Choir.

For spending money, Ben worked as a journeyman electrician for his dad, wiring row houses in Adams. His employment was brief when he was found to have connected one house to the next-door neighbor's electric meter.

While still in high school, he and his brother Edmund became bakery route drivers for Renton Baking Company in North Adams. They bought their trucks and worked on commission delivering door-to-door bread, cakes, and cinnamon rolls.

Once, he and Edmund had a long-distance delivery to Albany, New York, and the two teenagers were caught in the vicious 1938 hurricane. It was the most savage hurricane to hit New England in the twentieth century, killing over six hundred people and devastating highways, homes, and bridges. It took the young men several days to navigate flooded areas and return home.

The boys operated their bread trucks until late 1941, but after the attack on Pearl Harbor, both decided to join the military. Having heard tales from his dad about World War I and life in the trenches, Ben knew he did not want to be drafted into the Army. He hoped to become a naval aviator.

After passing the entrance test, and with his parents' permission, he sold his bread truck and was sworn into the Navy on July 17, 1942, beginning active duty in November.

Cadet St. John's first stop was an eight-week civilian pilot training under naval jurisdiction at Williston Academy in January, then a month of preparatory flight training at Williams College. Then he was transferred to US Navy Pre-Flight training school at Chapel Hill, North Carolina, for three months of instruction in the essentials of naval service, military drill, physical conditioning, and survival training.

The new aviator in dress whites, showing his wings. (Courtesy of St. John family)

Ben traveled to the Naval Air Station in Glenview, Illinois, for three more months of flight training before heading to Corpus Christi, the world's largest naval aviation training center, for additional flight schooling.

He began flying the Navy's AT-6, single-engine advanced flight trainer. It was at his last stage of training when Ben almost washed out of flight school. He would get queasy with high overhead maneuvers, especially performing loops. But his instructors liked his grit. The lead instructor took him up in the air and said he would do loops until Ben no longer got sick. The continuous inversions seemed to cure him, and he retched no more.

With that challenge behind him, Ben was commissioned an Ensign on March 1, 1944, and upon graduation, was awarded his gold Navy Aviator's Wings.

After a furlough, reported *The Transcript*, he headed to Fort Lauderdale, Florida, "for specialized operational training" (3-4-44).

The Naval Station Fort Lauderdale (NASFL) trained pilots and crews on the Grumman Avenger torpedo bomber, a forty-foot plane with a fifty-foot wingspan that was conceived in the late 1930s, with the first prototype flown in August 1941. (Ironically, Grumman's ceremony to open a new Avenger manufacturing plant occurred on December 7, 1941—the same day as the attack on Pearl Harbor.)

Once his training on the Avenger was completed, Ben returned to Naval Air Station Glendale for Carrier Qualifications. This consisted of landing and taking off from a simulated stationary flight deck. After weeks of "carrier" landings, he traveled to San Diego and was sent to Hawaii as an Avenger replacement pilot.

The TBF-1C Grumman Avenger

THE AVENGER BECAME THE most widely used torpedo bomber of World War II, with more than 9,000 manufactured. The single-engine plane was one of the heaviest of its time, weighing 15,000 pounds, with a 14-cylinder engine that could generate 1900 horsepower. It possessed wings that would fold hydraulically and rest against the side of the aircraft, shrinking its fifty-foot wingspan to sixteen feet for more compact storage on a crowded flight deck.

The Avenger, sometimes nicknamed the "turkey," was rugged and tough to shoot down, and while the controls were a little stiff, its powerful radio, thousand-mile range, and 30,000-foot ceiling were its best characteristics. It was painted a camouflage blue-gray with a distinctive national insignia: a white star in a circle on both sides of its wings and fuselage.

Ben would pilot the bomber from up front, handling the instrumentation and two .50-caliber wing machine guns. His cramped quarters featured an armored bulkhead that separated him from the plane's other two crew members, the turret gunner and radioman/bombardier. He operated the only set of flight controls, and no one else could access his seat.

His turret gunner was right behind him under a bubble canopy, facing rearward, and operated another .50-caliber machine gun. Protected by an armored shield and a piece of ballistic glass, the machine gun had an interrupter mechanism to ensure it would not shoot off the plane's tail. The gunner had an awkward climb in when entering the aircraft from below.

A later photograph of Ben and his crew flying in San Diego clearly shows Ben at the controls. (Courtesy of St. John family)

The radio operator sat in a lower-level crew compartment behind the bomb bay in an area described by the Pearl Harbor Aviation Museum as "the cheap seats that were noisy, smelly, and claustrophobic" (12-26-2017). His only connection to the pilot was an electric intercom. This critical position managed the plane's radar, navigation, and weapons systems. The radio operator, using radar, would direct the pilot to the target, calling out altitude and distance while arming bombs. He lacked the armor the pilot and turret gunner had, although he operated a .30-caliber machine gun when the plane was under attack.

All three wore a one-piece khaki coverall and a parachute harness. The two crewmen entered through the starboard hatch, and the pilot climbed on the wing and lowered himself into the cockpit.

The Avenger was a difficult plane for crew members to exit in an emergency. Their parachutes were too bulky to wear during flight, and each crew member needed to climb out of his area before attaching a chute to his harness. All too often, the pilot was the only crew member to survive when the plane got into trouble.

The bomb bay, depending on the mission, would hold a Mark 13 torpedo with 600 pounds of explosives in its warhead, a single 2000-pound bomb, four 500-pound bombs, or depth charges.

The Avenger would approach its target low and fast. Often flying just a few hundred feet above the water at high speed, the pilot was constantly "jinking" his controls, causing the aircraft to weave from side to side and hopefully avoid antiaircraft fire. The torpedo would be released when the plane was within 1500 yards of its target, and then the pilot would abruptly turn the aircraft away, staying low until far away from the enemy's guns.

Avengers were also used as bombers to hit land-based targets such as parked aircraft, airfields, or oil tanks. On those missions, extreme caution needed to be used when dropping 2000 pounds of explosives. The pilots were trained not to release their bombs from lower than 2000 feet; during one strike on an enemy oil field, a friend of Ben's released a bomb at 800 feet, and the ensuing explosion blew the tail end off his plane, killing him and his crew members. Ben helped pack the man's footlocker to be sent home to his family. It was a sobering reminder of the dangers of their occupation.

Some noted Avenger aviators included President George H. W. Bush, who, as a pilot, was shot down on a bombing run and rescued by a submarine, although both of his crewmates died. The actor Paul Newman flew as a turret gunner on an Avenger. He had wanted to be a pilot but was color-blind.

On a curious note: The Avenger is rather famous for a mysterious, well documented event in US naval history. On December 5, 1945, five US Navy Avengers disappeared on a routine training mission (dubbed Flight 19) that took off in clear weather from Ft. Lauderdale Naval Air Station. They were scheduled to fly over the Florida Keys and drop their training payload at an area called Hen and Chicken Shoals. The planes and their fourteen crewmen maintained some radio contact and were heard to say that their compasses were malfunctioning, and they were low on fuel. Other radio signals triangulated them just north of the Bahamas, far from Bermuda, before they disappeared, likely due to fuel shortage. Sadly, a rescue aircraft searching for the five Avengers also disappeared that same night. Presumed to have crashed, neither the plane nor its thirteen-man crew were ever found. Theories for the loss of all six planes ranged from alien abductions to the Bermuda Triangle, but the likeliest scenarios, though more mundane, are usually correct.

After training and transfer to Hawaii, Ben was assigned to *Intrepid* Aircraft Carrier CV11, an Essex class ship, as a replacement pilot. He reported to Torpedo Squadron 18 on the *Intrepid* in early August 1944. Ben was flown to the *Intrepid* as a passenger on an Avenger because he was considered too new and untested to be trusted with an aircraft at that point.

Landing on the *Intrepid*'s deck was never easy, especially on high seas with the ship heaving. Ensuring the tail hook caught the arresting wire was critical to avoid a crash or, even worse, going over the side into the ocean many stories below. Exhausted pilots and shot-up planes made the whole perilous process more difficult.

In one of the unusual occurrences of war, the *Intrepid* was at that point commanded by another resident of Adams, Massachusetts: Captain (later Vice Admiral) Joseph F. Bolger. Captain Bolger, a World War I veteran, was also a torpedo bomber aviator. Bolger was awarded two Navy Crosses for his heroics during World War II. On several occasions upon meeting Ensign St. John, the Captain acknowledged their Adams connection and asked about local events.

In early August 1944, Ben was assigned to Squadron VT-18 (18th bomber squadron) as a pilot flying a Grumman TBF Avenger torpedo bomber. He became the squadron's newest and most junior member. The squadron was nicknamed the "Carrier Clowns," with an emblem created by a crew member with a barking seal balancing an antiship mine, a zebra, and ordnance on its nose—as if to say, it's all part of a "circus act."

The *Intrepid,* nicknamed "the Fighting I" and once described as "the nation's most shot-at carrier," was commissioned in the summer of 1943. The ship, with its 2600 men, was also home to about one hundred aircraft. As part of the Navy's 3rd Fleet and Task Force 38.2, the *Intrepid* would support the invasion of the Philippine Islands, with the goal of destroying enemy naval and air forces.

During Ben's time aboard the *Intrepid*, his squadron focused on targets in the Philippines, Formosa, and Okinawa.

The *Intrepid* carried three groups of planes: a torpedo squadron flying Avenger aircraft; Helldiver bombers; and a squadron of fighters known as Hellcats. On missions, fighters would launch first (to get in position to protect the other launching groups), then dive bombers, and finally torpedo planes. Each group assembled above the *Intrepid*, then flew in vee formation several thousand feet apart, toward the target. Fighters always flew at the highest altitude to protect the bombers.

The order of attack was usually Hellcat fighters spraying enemy shipping with machine gun fire to distract the antiaircraft crews, then dive bombers unloading their bombs, all the while torpedo bombers would be jockeying at about 900 feet above sea level to assume a glide path to launch their torpedoes.

Shortly after Ben's arrival on the *Intrepid*, she left on her second war cruise. Ben took his first combat flight in September 1944. As junior crew, he was often selected for the monotonous job of submarine sweeps, patrolling and scouting or sowing mines. Over the next three months, Ben would fly 23 combat missions and survive several harrowing incidents.

VT-18 had its own ready room where pilots were briefed and debriefed. It also served as a lounge, and in the more tranquil moments of shipboard life, pilots wrote letters, drank, played cards, read magazines, or conducted fierce ping pong tournaments. Ben, a teetotaler, gave his alcohol allocation to other crew members. He found it a useful way for a junior pilot to make friends.

In mid-October 1944, VT-18 was assigned the mission of bombing a seaplane base in northern Formosa (as Japan called the island of Taiwan when they were the occupying force), with the goal of destroying its hangers, warehouses, ramps, and oil tanks. As the formation approached the target, the planes were buffeted by Japanese radar-controlled antiaircraft fire. As a member of Strike 2, Able Ben, as he was known, maintained his focus and was credited with destroying two oil tanks.

Once the mission was completed, Japanese fighters repeatedly attacked the group. Ben's plane was hit and his electrical system knocked out, leaving him without radio communications or navigation. The formation leader took evasive action, leading the group into the clouds as they tried to shake off the fastest enemy fighters. Ben became separated from the group; using only his instruments, he returned to the carrier just before running out of fuel.

As he approached the *Intrepid*, Ben realized his IFF (Identification Friend or Foe) system was not working and became concerned that he would not be identified as a friendly. Ben remembered the landing protocol of flying 360 degrees around the task force, and on this day, he had the good fortune of turning right on his approach (turns right and left on certain days were another requirement). His mates were gladdened to see him. They had thought he was lost at sea.

Ben received an Air Medal for his actions: "St. John bombed oil drums, was attacked by fighters, became separated from his squadron, and eventually made it back to the *Intrepid*. He received an Air Medal for these actions" (*iBerkshires.com* 11-10-2019).

During later missions, the Avengers experimented with dropping bags of aluminum strips of chaff (called "windows") to confuse Japanese radar. It worked, with the flak exploding behind the planes.

On October 24, 1945, Ben participated in the 2nd Battle of the Philippine Sea, one of the largest naval battles in history. With three other Avenger pilots as part of Strike 2 Charlie, he would be approaching a huge Japanese task force comprised of five battleships, with numerous cruisers and destroyers deployed around the battleships to protect them. All twenty-eight vessels possessed radar-controlled antiaircraft artillery.

Only four Avengers were available for the mission, and five aviators. Ben won a coin toss and manned a bomber. The attack on the Japanese task force was made by dive bombers, fighters, and Avenger Torpedo bombers who, as they approached the armada from 12,000 feet, quickly came under intense, multicolored antiaircraft fire. (The Japanese Navy used explosions of varied colors to help judge and adjust the accuracy of their antiaircraft fire.)

First, the Hellcat fighters sprayed the enemy ships lengthwise to try and suppress the antiaircraft fire. While this was occurring, the pilots noted the huge battleships in the center of the formation, only later to find out they were called the *Musashi* and *Yamamoto*, the largest warships in the world.

Ben lined his plane up on the *Musashi*. He faced a huge ship bristling with over 100 antiaircraft guns, countless machine guns, nine 18-inch deck guns, and a 16-inch armored hull below the water line. The behemoth was as tall as a sixteen-story building.

He descended, seeking the right height and angle to launch his only torpedo, constantly "jinking" his controls and swerving his plane to avoid antiaircraft fire. Ben launched the armed torpedo from 2000 feet. Braving this torrent of fire, his torpedo went slightly astern of the *Musashi* and sank a Mogami-class cruiser behind it.

Other Avengers crippled the *Musashi*, and it sank within days, resulting in a loss of over 1,000 Japanese sailors.

Ben's hometown newspaper noted on September 22, 1945, "Bernard St. John gets Navy Cross." The now twenty-four-year-old Lieutenant JG (junior grade) St. John was awarded the Navy Cross "for knifing through a heavy curtain of antiaircraft fire at a low altitude to score a direct hit that sank a large Japanese cruiser during a furious air battle over Leyte Gulf last October."

THE SECRETARY OF THE NAVY
WASHINGTON

The President of the United States takes pleasure in presenting the NAVY CROSS to

LIEUTENANT, JUNIOR GRADE, BERNARD JOSEPH ST. JOHN
UNITED STATES NAVAL RESERVE

for service as set forth in the following

CITATION:

"For extraordinary heroism as Pilot of a Torpedo Plane in Torpedo Squadron EIGHTEEN, in action against enemy Japanese forces during the Battle for Leyte Gulf on October 24, 1944. Boldly flying through intense antiaircraft fire to press home a low-level attack on a Battleship Task Force, Lieutenant, Junior Grade, (then Ensign) St. John succeeded in scoring a direct hit on a cruiser which later sank and, although his plane was damaged, made a safe return to base. By his outstanding airmanship, courage and devotion to duty, Lieutenant, Junior Grade, St. John contributed to the infliction of costly damage upon the enemy and upheld the highest traditions of the United States Naval Service."

For the President,

James Forrestal

Secretary of the Navy

Ben's Navy Cross citation. (Courtesy of St. John family)

When he returned home, the Navy Cross was presented to Ben at the US Naval Air Station in San Diego, California. He also received an official citation from Vice Admiral Marc Mitscher praising him for his "coolness, courage, and skill for making the hazardous mission in a carrier-based Avenger torpedo plane."

His missions weren't over yet. In November, VT-18 attacked Clark Airfield in the Philippines in an ongoing effort to suppress Japanese air power. Multiple Avengers dropped thousands of pounds of bombs, seriously damaging the runway. The accompanying Hellcat fighters protected the bombers and shot down 12 enemy airplanes.

After one of the Philippine missions, Ben's group of Avengers returned to the *Intrepid* in the late afternoon while the ship was enduring a ferocious squall. The carrier was unwilling to alter its course away from the squall to receive the returning bombers because it had been warned of an enemy aerial attack. With darkness setting in, and the group low on fuel, the flight leader decided an instrument landing on the *Intrepid*'s one-hundred-foot-wide flight deck was too risky, and the group made a water landing.

Ben was the last to ditch his plane, and it sank in less than a minute. Luckily, he had repeatedly rehearsed with his crew a change in protocol on how they would exit the bomber in a water landing. Ben would open the canopy and exit on the plane's right side (instead of the left) and help the gunner out, then the radio man would exit on the left side, dragging out the life raft. Ben had made the alteration due to the fear of the plane buckling when it hit the water and wanted to ensure everyone exited rapidly.

The crew evacuated safely, inflated their life raft, and climbed aboard. They had ditched their plane close to friendly forces and were picked up by a PT boat the next morning. That day VT-18 lost six Avengers, but the eighteen men all survived.

In one of his final combat missions, on November 25, 1944, Ben and his crew launched at 12:44 p.m., and less than ten minutes later, *kamikazes* attacked the *Intrepid.* As he joined his squadron above, Ben saw the first *kamikaze* hit *Intrepid*'s flight deck. Minutes later, a second *kamikaze* hit, blowing a massive hole in the flight deck, killing or injuring over one hundred sailors. This was not the ship's first *kamikaze* attack, but it was the most devastating.

Ben's flight group continued with their mission. Their landing strip was obscured, so they had no way to help those still on the *Intrepid.* The group was headed to attack three Japanese minelayers. Only two enemy ships were found, and Ben, the last plane in the formation, dropped low, attacked one minelayer (running fore and aft), and dropped four 500-pound bombs on it. He achieved a direct hit, and the minelayer broke in two, sinking almost immediately. His gunner yelled, "We got it!" The crew could see the flames rise 1500 feet in the air. Ben would earn the Distinguished Flying Cross for his actions.

The remarkable photograph captured by a crewman, showing the direct hit. (Courtesy of St. John family)

In the meantime, the *Intrepid*'s flight deck, hit by the two *kamikazes*, was ablaze. The pilots were diverted to land in the Philippines. From there, they flew to Peleliu, and Ulithi, then returned to the *Intrepid*, which would be ordered to Hawaii for repairs. The work needed was too extensive, and the ship was sent back to the United States in December 1944.

Ben, a veteran of actions over Palau, the Philippines, Formosa, and Okinawa, had by this point "executed 23 combat missions totaling 100 hours of flight time" (*iBerkshires.com* 11-10-2019). Fifteen pilots from VT-18 were awarded Navy Crosses, the nation's second-highest military honor, for their wartime actions.

"Ensign Bernard J. St. John…spending a 30-day leave in Adams...is credited with torpedoing a Japanese heavy cruiser…as part of Naval Air Group 18. In 80 days of concentrated combat action…the group destroyed or damaged 557 Japanese planes in the air and on the ground, sank 69 ships, probably 27 others, and damaged 88. The torpedo group of which he is a member is nicknamed the 'Circus Clowns'" (*Transcript,* 12-30-44).

After his return home, Ben met and married Grace Tagarelli in California. Grace was from the Bronx and had been an officer in the Navy Nurses Corps. After a monthlong, whirlwind romance, they married at the Sacred Heart Church in Coronado, California, in August 1945. While on their honeymoon, they learned that Hiroshima had been bombed. Not long after, in September 1945, Ben was honorably discharged from the Navy.

The two were eager to get on with their lives. Ben attended the University of Cincinnati, received a Bachelor of Engineering degree, and passed the State Board of Engineering exam. He soon began work as an electrical engineer with Republic Aviation Corporation in Farmingdale, New York.

After a short time, Ben accepted a job as an electrical engineer with Grumman Aircraft Engineering Corporation, working in an area he appreciated, fighter aircraft. He was engaged with weapons system design and troubleshooting on a number of warplane styles, most notably Grumman's F-14 Tomcat.

In subsequent years, Ben and Grace's family grew to five children, and they enjoyed vacation trips in the family car, a large-finned Chrysler sedan. Ben often put the top down in the red convertible, listening and singing along to John Philip Sousa's lively martial music.

Later in life, he and Grace enjoyed traveling throughout the United States, Europe, Egypt, Singapore, Japan, and the Caribbean. Ben golfed, but he was the first to admit he wasn't that good.

After retiring from Grumman, Ben took on the caretaker role for his beloved wife, Grace, until her passing in 2001.

His children and grandchildren describe him as an extrovert, optimistic and cheerful. He was "fun to be around, had a hardy laugh, and could be a joker." One family member remembers when Ben had a pacemaker installed late in life, the hospital said a battery would last ten years, and he responded, "You better give me two of them."

He was also an avid swimmer, could "float on his back like a fish," and frequently went to YMCA for water aerobics. He liked taking pictures with his camera, but the family often joked that, inevitably, his thumb would be on the lens.

Ben didn't speak much about the war, but he was proud of his service in both the Navy and with Grumman. He wore his Navy Cross lapel pin on his sport coat, had a large picture on his wall of him flying an Avenger during a training run, and displayed his award plaques from Grumman.

In March 1974, the *Intrepid* was decommissioned and, in 1982, it became part of the *Intrepid* Sea, Air & Space Museum located at Pier 86 in New York City. It is now designated as a National Historic Landmark. During its life, it earned five battle stars and a Presidential Unit Citation.

Above, Ben poses with the Grumman Avenger on the *Intrepid* (courtesy of St. John family). At left, the USS *Intrepid* patch (courtesy of the author).

Ben visited the *Intrepid* several times at its permanent dock in the Hudson River, on the west side of Manhattan. He participated in an oral history project at the museum (open to visitors and worth a listen) and has a designated "Seat of Honor" in its Lutnick Theater memorializing his service aboard "the Fighting I."

Ben passed away in 2016 at the age of ninety-five, sharp to the end…the sound of taps wafting over his final flight. He and Grace are buried on Long Island at the Queen of All Saints Cemetery in Central Islip, New York—just under fifty miles east of the ship that carried him so far, through submarine-plagued waters, across distant oceans, and back safely to land, to live out a long life—and to know happiness.

Frank J. Wotkowicz
Bombardier
321st Medium Bomber Group

As they approached the target, the planes flew into a blizzard of antiaircraft fire. Loaded with thousand-pound bombs and hundreds of gallons of aviation fuel, these thirty-six low-flying bombers suddenly became targets themselves as flak began to shred their planes. Frank, the lead bombardier, was crammed into a plexiglass bubble in his plane's nose, with a front-row seat to the steel gauntlet. His plane was hit almost immediately.

FRANK WAS THE SON of Joseph and Julia Wotkowicz, who emigrated from Poland around 1900. Joseph worked in the coal mines in Pennsylvania before moving to Chicopee, Massachusetts, where he met and married Julia. That same year, the young couple moved to Adams, Massachusetts, and opened a bakery shop on Hoosac Street. Later, they opened a hosiery plant in the same building with the capability of producing 300 pairs of hosiery a week. The business closed during the Great Depression, and Joseph became a night watchman at Berkshire Mill #3 before retiring.

Julia, a homemaker for a family of eight children, four girls and four boys, was an active member of the family's church, Saint Stanislaus Kostka, and was involved in the Polish Women's Club and the PTA. Joseph and Julia felt honored to have one of their daughters, Mary, serve as a religious Sister of Providence for many years.

When Joseph emigrated, his name was spelled *Wołkowicz*, with the lowercase *l* having an accent line through it. At some point, for convenience, the line melded with the L, becoming a T, now spelled *Wotkowicz.*

Frank Joseph Wotkowicz, the family's seventh child, was born at home on May 30, 1916, Memorial Day. Frank and all his brothers were given the middle name of Joseph, a tradition and tribute to their father.

As a youth, he attended Saint Stanislaus Kostka and C.T. Plunkett Junior High schools. Early pictures of Frank show him happily skiing, snowplow style, on his wooden skis. Even though busy with home chores, he still found time to belong to St. Stan's Boy Scout Troop #41 and earned the required number of merit badges to attain the rank of First Class. Frank also enjoyed sports. He was a strong batter and played left field for Troop 41's baseball team; in the fall, he was a guard on the troop's basketball team.

Frank, a serious student, often with perfect attendance, played varsity baseball for Adams High School and graduated in 1934. On the weekends, when not working, he golfed with his friends.

In this original photograph of the Adams High men who lettered in sports, Frank is on the second row, second from the right, wearing a light sweater. (Courtesy of Wotkowicz family)

Not long after graduation, he joined the local Civilian Conservation Corps (CCC); records list him as a construction laborer and, at one point, a supervisor. It is presumed he worked on forestry projects and may have helped put the finishing touches on the historic Thunderbolt Trail. He kept five dollars from his $30 monthly pay and sent the rest home to his mom.

Shortly after leaving the CCC, Frank found employment with the Sprague Electric Company, working as a machine operator involved in the precision work of manufacturing compressors and condensers. In 1937, he joined the Adams National Guard unit, Company M of the 104th Infantry, and would remain with both until World War II began.

Within Company M, Frank quickly assumed the responsibilities of company clerk and was promoted to corporal. A state inspection of supplies and ordnance lauded him, confirming that the items were "properly taken care of" (*Transcript,* 4-2-40).

After three weeks of training in the summer of 1940, Company M was inducted into federal service in January 1941, and the unit spent the following year in further training at Camp Edwards. At some point, Frank was promoted to Staff Sergeant.

While undergoing infantry training, Frank had applied to the Army Air Corps. He was accepted, designated an Aviation Cadet, and transferred to the Air Corps in December 1942. His first assignment was eight weeks of pre-flight training, then he attended twelve weeks at bombardier school, where his successful completion earned him silver bombardier wings and promotion to 2nd Lieutenant in June 1943.

New bombardiers showing dedication to their craft (Frank, far left). (Courtesy of Wotkowicz family and *The Transcript*)

Later in life, Frank shared with his daughter that he was the only non-degreed person in officer and bombardier training. At a disadvantage, he would study late into the night in the latrine since it was the only area permitted to have a light.

His training continued, and a *Transcript* news article from June 1943 reports that Frank has been sent to "Carlsbad Army Airfield, Carlsbad, N.M., for a course on dead reckoning navigation. He thus began his second step in his intensive training to become a 'double threat'...able to direct a plane to its objective, drop the bombs, and pilot the course homeward." After successfully completing the six-week course, Frank was designated a bombardier and radar observer.

In July, Frank was assigned to the 309th Bombardment Group at the Columbia Air Base in Columbia, South Carolina, and would fly almost daily for the next five months to practice his new-found skills. In December 1943, he was transferred to Morrison Field in Florida. The field was activated in January 1942 and served as a departure site for air crews headed to war.

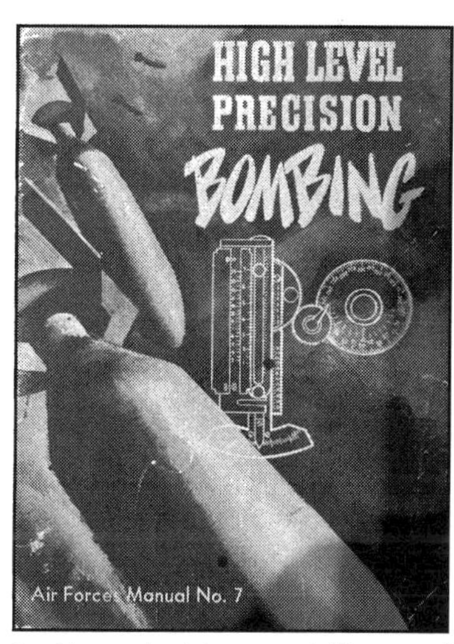

Frank's actual training manual. (Courtesy of Wotkowicz family)

The Ferrying Division, which would soon transport Frank overseas, transported thousands of planes and fliers to bases near the front—often via the South Atlantic air ferry route that would have a series of stops before landing in Africa or Europe. The Ferrying Division, as part of the Air Transport Command, included the famous Women Air Force Service Pilots (WASP). The women pilots would ferry aircraft from manufacturing plants to where they were needed for transport overseas. At one point, it was decided to ferry the planes under their own power versus shipping them overseas.

Frank arrived in late January 1944 and was assigned as a bombardier/navigator to the 321st Bombardment Group (Medium), activated in June 1942 and part of the 12th Air Force. His group was composed of four squadrons of B-25 Mitchell bombers: 445th, 446th, 447th, and 448th. Frank was in the 446th. Its planes could be identified by a Roman numeral II on their tailfins and a red stripe at the top of their tails.

Congressional Medal of Honor winner General James "Jimmy" Doolittle was the first to command the 12th Air Force. His bold, long-distance attack on Japan, only four months after the attack on Pearl Harbor, using 16 B-25 Mitchell bombers from the decks of aircraft carriers, was considered a morale boost for the United States. The renowned attack had introduced the rugged B-25 to the American public.

The aircrews on that heroic mission knew it was a one-way trip as they did not have enough fuel to return to the carriers. Many bailed out over China, and most reached safety with the help of Chinese guerrillas. Seven of the eighty crew members were executed by the Japanese, and others died from crash landings.

The B-25 Bomber

MOST AIRMEN PREFERRED THE compact B-25 Mitchell bomber for its ease of handling over its larger sister and the higher-flying B-17 bomber. It was named after Major General William "Billy" Mitchell, known as the "Father of the United States Air Force." Mitchell had been a highly decorated Army officer and aggressive advocate for air power. He was awarded a posthumous Congressional Gold Medal and was one of the few people to have a military aircraft named after him.

The rugged and reliable 20,000-pound bomber primarily supported ground troops. The three-wheeled aircraft had twin vertical tails that provided better control, and its profile made it difficult to attack from the rear. The crew of five—pilot, co-pilot, bombardier, navigator/radio operator, and gunner—operated out of its 54-foot-long aluminum capsule with a 67-foot wingspan. Powered by two 14-cylinder 1700 horsepower engines, the B-25 traveled 300 miles per hour and had a range of 1300 miles, often operating at 15,000 feet. It carried 3,000 pounds of bombs released through its two nine-foot bomb bay doors.

Compared to the B-17, the plane and its crew of five airmen were lightly armed with three .30-caliber machine guns.

Records indicate that shortly after Frank arrived at an airbase in Italy, the 321st Bomber Group had a tragic day, losing eight bombers on one mission. The German Luftwaffe shot down five, and three crashed due to weather. This was Frank's ominous introduction to aerial warfare. Most B-25 squadrons had only eight to twelve bombers.

Not long after Frank's arrival, the 321st Bombardment Group moved from Gaudo, Italy, to operate out of Solenzara Air Base on the island of Corsica. Corsica, one of the larger islands in the Mediterranean, is located 100 miles from France and 50 miles from Italy, making it a strategically important airfield in supporting the war effort. After Corsica was freed from German occupiers in 1943, the 12th Air Force engineers constructed an all-weather field using pierced steel planking for runways. They erected hundreds of tents that housed the flyers and maintenance crews.

During the war, Corsica would support 17 airfields along its eastern coast, and Solenzara was the furthest south of the airfields. So many airmen were stationed there that the aircrews began calling it the USS *Corsica*. This would be Frank's home during his seventy B-25 missions.

Living conditions offered minimal amenities with tents and coal stoves for sleeping. Entertainment was limited to playing cards, writing letters, drinking at a nearby café, or spending nights at the Phoenix Hotel, a rest home for crews.

During the spring of 1944, Frank and the 321st were busy providing daily support for the upcoming D-Day landings and the invasion of southern France. Their targets would be enemy ground troops and anything that supported them. They would bomb marshaling yards, rail lines, bridges, roads, troop concentrations, and harbors in France, Sicily, Italy, Bulgaria, Yugoslavia, and Greece.

Ready for flight with his headset and parachute. (Courtesy of Wotkowicz family)

Records indicate that the crews flew almost daily. At times, there would be several days of respite between flights. As the bombardier, Frank would be in the plexiglass nose of the plane, right in front of and below the pilots. There was a crawlway from the pilots' seats to the bombardier's position; with two overhead handrails, he would pull himself on his back on a smooth aluminum floor to his position.

With the high rate of crashes, either from mechanical issues, battle damage, or lack of fuel, Frank and his crew often practiced emergency and ditching procedures. Exiting quickly was often a matter of life or death. If the plane's pilot thought ditching might be necessary, he notified the crew and radioed base. Frank and the crew knew the drill and their assigned activities well. Once the plane landed on land or water, they were able to evacuate the aircraft in less than a minute, sometimes in 30 seconds.

Frank was decorated with his first Air Medal several months after his arrival. The citation read:

> *Air Medal Award—March 19, 1944: While flying lead ship of the second box of six planes in an attack upon the marshaling yards at Avezzano, Italy, Lieut. Wotkowicz observed that his leader had mistaken a road junction for the target and led the formation on a bomb run over the junction. Immediately sighting the assigned target, Lieut. Wotkowicz directed his*

> *pilot on the proper course, and with all his bombardiers releasing upon his signal, his flight blocked the main choke point and cut the central railroad line into the marshaling yards. His outstanding professional skill in combat reflects great credit upon himself and the Armed Forces of the United States.*

While on another mission, again as the lead bombardier, Frank's second Air Medal Citation read:

> *May 25, 1944: ...while flying in an attack on a Todi, Italy, road bridge, the high degree of skill with which Lt. Wotkowicz dropped his bomb enabled the formation to register 100% bombing accuracy....*

During Frank's tour of duty, he would receive seven individual Air Medals for conspicuous heroism.

During May and June 1944, the 12th Air Force flew over 70,000 sorties and was credited with destroying over 6,000 enemy transport vehicles. Frank's reputation for accuracy became well-known during this period, and he was chosen to become the lead bombardier on most missions.

Army Air Force Command, desiring better bombing results, introduced a "combat box" formation, a densely packed group of bombers, with its best bombardiers in the lead, and instead of everyone using the coveted Norden bombsight, only the lead bombardiers would use it. All other planes would drop their bombs when the lead bomber did—and this significantly improved accuracy.

The Norden bombsight was a highly classified wartime secret. All bombardiers were required to protect it with their lives and had to swear to disable it with their pistol if downed behind enemy lines. When returning to base, the bombsights were removed from planes and kept in a guarded, secured area where they could undergo maintenance and calibration. Later in life, Frank seldom talked about the war, but he did repeat the oft-told comment that with the bombsight, "you could hit a pickle barrel at 5,000 feet." While a slight exaggeration, his reputation grew as an accurate bombardier, and the sight added to his accuracy.

In May, after sustained days in the air, Frank and his crew were given an eight-day rest and flew to Egypt and Palestine. Photos from their "milk run" mission show Frank visiting the Garden of Gethsemane in Palestine and various mosques and temples in Cairo. One image stands out, a picture of him atop a camel with the pyramids and a sphinx in the background.

Frank piloting a different type of craft, one less responsive to his directions. (Courtesy of Wotkowicz family)

Back in action, Frank continued to lead his bomber group and was decorated for actions on June 8, 1944, receiving his first award of the Distinguished Flying Cross.

His records indicate that from his arrival in late January until

June 8, 1944, Frank had already been on fifty missions. In June, he was promoted to 1st Lieutenant.

In the summer of 1944, Frank's unit achieved its 450th Combat Mission, as reported by *The Transcript*: "…The attack was against a heavily fortified, vital railroad bridge being used by the Germans to resupply their troops. Lieut. Wotkowicz was the lead bombardier" (8-26-44).

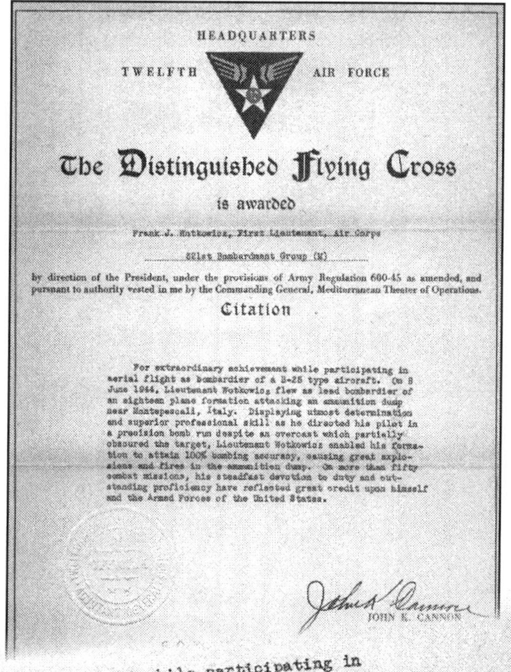

HEADQUARTERS

TWELFTH AIR FORCE

The Distinguished Flying Cross

is awarded

Frank J. Wotkowicz, First Lieutenant, Air Corps

321st Bombardment Group (M)

by direction of the President, under the provisions of Army Regulation 600-45 as amended, and pursuant to authority vested in me by the Commanding General, Mediterranean Theater of Operations.

Citation

For extraordinary achievement while participating in aerial flight as bombardier of a B-25 type aircraft. On 8 June 1944, Lieutenant Wotkowicz flew as lead bombardier of an eighteen plane formation attacking an ammunition dump near Montepescali, Italy. Displaying utmost determination and superior professional skill as he directed his pilot in a precision bomb run despite an overcast which partially obscured the target, Lieutenant Wotkowicz enabled his formation to attain 100% bombing accuracy, causing great explosions and fires in the ammunition dump. On more than fifty combat missions, his steadfast devotion to duty and outstanding proficiency have reflected great credit upon himself and the Armed Forces of the United States.

JOHN K. CANNON
Major General, USA
Commanding

G. O. No. 131, 15 August 1944

Frank's first Flying Cross Award, August 1944. (Courtesy of Wotkowicz family)

In August 1944, in support of the invasion of southern France, Frank's squadron was alerted for what the aircrews realize will be one of their most perilous missions. They were ordered to attack warships anchored in the harbor of Toulon, France. The 321st had been picked because it boasted the best record for bombing accuracy, placing over 90% of its bombs within the target area. But Toulon would be different: The harbor was protected by 88 heavy antiaircraft guns and the remnants of the French Fleet. Reconnaissance photos showed a battleship, cruiser, destroyer, and submarine in the harbor, all considered a threat to nearby allies.

Frank's 446th squadron would lead the mission, with Frank as lead bomber. He knew this mission (#498, code name DRYBEEF) would be different. His plane was usually loaded with six 500-pound bombs; this time, he watched the ground crew load three 1000-pound armor-piercing and general-purpose bombs on his B-25.

Usually, a mission of this nature was assigned to high-altitude heavy bombers to reduce the number of casualties. The Air Force command decided that the urgency of the threat called for low-altitude precision bombing and was willing to risk sacrificing some aircrews.

On August 18, 1944, Frank's bomber, leading thirty-six planes, took off at 11:00 a.m. and negotiated the flight from Corsica. Due to hazardous weather, they used dead reckoning to reach their target. Several other bombing groups had turned back due to the weather. Squadron 321, flying at an altitude of 13,000 feet, considered dangerously low and vulnerable to antiaircraft guns, approached the target and employed "windows" (clouds of aluminum chaff to distract German radar). Still, the flak was intense, and barrages of flak tracked planes on their run into the target and also leaving the target.

Almost immediately, Frank's bomber was hit by "heavy antiaircraft fire scoring a direct hit upon his aircraft, seriously damaging the plane" (*Transcript*, undated). Colonel Smith, the plane's pilot and the attack group's leader, acutely aware of the damage but focusing on the mission, steadied the gravely damaged plane, and despite its condition, Frank continued plotting the bomb drop.

Bombs were dropped around noon, and the group had eight direct hits on the battleship *Strasbourg*; the heavy cruiser was also hit, and the submarine sank. Quickly turning around, they faced heavy squalls on the return home and had to fly low (1,000 feet) to avoid the weather. Pilots worried about being shot at by the nearby Allied fleet fired flares and used radio channels to let everyone know of their presence. Emergency landings were scattered over three airfields because of the low, overcast weather and damaged bombers. Twenty-seven of the thirty-six planes on the mission were damaged, and eighteen aircrew members were wounded. But no planes were lost.

Frank, for his heroics as the lead bombardier of the group, received his second Distinguished Flying Cross. The citation read:

> *Frank J. Wotkowicz, First Lieutenant, 446th Bomb Group, 321st Bomb Sq., AAF. For extraordinary achievement while participating in aerial flight as bombardier of a B-25 aircraft. On August 18, 1944, Lt. Wotkowicz flew as a flight bombardier of a large formation attacking enemy warships in the harbor at Toulon, France. Upon approach to the target, direct hits from intense antiaircraft fire heavily damaged his airplane. Despite the crippled condition of his plane, Lt. Wotkowicz displaying superior professional skill, directed his pilot on a perfect run over the objective, thereby enabling his bombers to score direct hits contributing to the destruction of one battleship, a cruiser, and a submarine. On more than sixty combat missions, his outstanding proficiency and steadfast devotion to duty have reflected great credit upon himself and the Armed Forces of the United States.*

Officials described the action as one of the most destructive attacks ever carried out by a group of medium bombers. His hometown newspaper noted, "Lieut. Wotkowicz…engaged in action over the big French naval base of Toulon describe the flak sent by the

Germans 'the worst since Anzio'" (*Transcript,* 8-19-44). His unit would be awarded the Presidential Unit Citation.

Another *Transcript* news article dated 9-23-1944 wrote, "The terrible firepower of these formidable naval units constituted a serious threat to the west flank of the Allied invasion forces. Photo made by a reconnaissance plane the day following the attack showed the 702-foot battleship gutted, burning, and completely disabled, the cruiser over on its side and the submarine sunk…. the B-25 Mitchell group contributed greatly to the success of the landing operation."

With little rest, the following day, the bombing group was sent on another assignment, achieving its 500th mission by smashing a bridge at Montélimar, France, with 100% bombing accuracy reported. Frank was done. Amazingly, he had survived his missions while being in the exposed position of bombardier and often in the lead plane. Survival rates for bomber aircrews in World War II were less than 50%, and the bombardier's location in the plane's nose would be the position most impacted by flak.

Just before heading home, Frank received a certificate authenticating his flight service from the 321st Bombardment Group. It read, "…1st Lt. Frank J. Wotkowicz, while a member of this command, has completed seventy (70) combat missions in a B-25 aircraft. He has been accredited with sixty-two and a half sorties and flown two hundred and twenty-nine hours and thirty minutes in combat…. four of the above missions as a bombardier leading the group, eighteen as a bombardier leading a flight, thirty-nine as a bombardier leading an element, and nine as a bombardier on the wing."

All in all, the 12th Air Force, including Frank's squadron, was credited with flying over 400,000 sorties and destroying 2800 enemy aircraft while losing 2600 of their planes during World War II. Fifty-five thousand airmen were killed in the war.

Frank returned home in October 1944 and, after a three-week leave, reported to Fort Devens for reassignment. During his last year in service, he served as a bombardier instructor and radar instructor at airfields in Texas and California.

When honorably discharged in November 1945 at Westover Airfield, his decorations would include two Distinguished Flying Crosses, seven Air Medals, a European–African–Middle Eastern Campaign Medal (three stars), an American Defense Service Medal, a WWII Victory Medal, and a Distinguished Unit Badge. The Air Medals were awarded from May 21 to August 27, 1944, for actions in Avezzano, Viterbo, Ostiglia, Borgoforte, Feltre, and Torreberretti, Italy.

Frank returned to work as a machinist at the Sprague Electric Company and resided in his father's large white stucco house at 9 Hoosac Street in Adams, just down the street from his church, Saint Stanislaus Kostka. It is presumed that is where he met the attractive Lottie Frances Wysocki at one of the numerous after-war GI weddings. Within one year of his discharge, the couple married in August 1946 and honeymooned at Lake Champlain and different sites in Canada.

Upon returning home, they moved from 9 Hoosac Street (known to the family as the "stucco" house) to the two-story apartment house behind it, also owned by Frank's father. In his spare time, Frank and his brothers would become the family's maintenance crew for both buildings, painting, mowing the lawns, doing minor repairs, and collecting the rent.

Initially, he and Lottie both worked at Sprague Electric Company. As their five daughters began to arrive, she became a homemaker with involvement in St. Stan's Rosary Sodality and the Polish Women's Club. As the family grew, the five girls plus mom and dad, would vie for time and space in their one small bathroom. The benefit of their location was that living just down the street from Saint Stanislaus Elementary School allowed the girls to come home for lunch.

Frank's birthday on May 30, Memorial Day, was always a big family celebration. Together, the family would watch the town's parade from the stucco house's front porch, then Frank would visit the family cemetery plot on Maple Street, and everyone would have a backyard charcoal-grilled cookout.

On the weekend and some temperate nights, Frank and the girls, hanging from ladders tied together, would often pick fruit, including pears, apples, and cherries from their backyard or apricots and plums from the trees at the nearby stucco house. Then, there were always vegetables to gather from Uncle Stanley's large garden. Lottie was often busy canning their harvest.

In 1957, Frank's father Joseph passed away after a good long life spent in the Berkshires. Julia followed him in 1970; both were buried in the Maple Street Cemetery.

With one wage earner, the family's vacations were limited to several short visits to Hampton, New Hampshire, and Orchard, Maine, beaches. Their most memorable tradition was Sunday picnics. With everyone packed into the family's blue Chevrolet station wagon, they would travel to the nearby ponds and parks, sometimes cooking hot dogs and hamburgers, but more often reheating Lottie's baked chicken, *golumpki*, and *pierogi*.

Frank's return to Sprague meant commuting and carpooling with his lady passengers, co-workers who otherwise would not have transportation. He picked them up and dropped them off at their homes around Adams. Seldom missing work or staying late for overtime, he was a dependable ride and always wanted to be home in time for the 5:30 p.m. family dinner.

Dinner was a quiet affair, typically with a foundation of meat and potatoes. Sometimes, careers were discussed with the girls. It was an "understanding" that Dad and Mom thought college should be in everyone's plans. Frank was a strong proponent of teaching careers. Frank would emphasize the job's stability, the chance for ongoing learning, and summers off. What could be better? All five daughters graduated from college, and most would work in teaching.

After the girls were grown, their mom returned to work. Anytime she worked overtime, the girls were fairly certain that they would be eating Dad's favorite meal for supper: hot dogs and Campbell's beans.

Frank loved walking to the local library to read newspapers and magazines. Frequently, with a daughter or friend in tow, he would head there on weekends and leisurely update himself on current events. After his retirement in 1981, Frank visited the library almost every day.

Frank was a Town Meeting Member for many years, always appearing in a jacket and tie, representing his precinct with distinction. He also served as a committee man for St. Stanislaus Boy Scout Troop #56 and occasionally bowled with team #3 on the East Hoosac League.

Frank liked to watch sports on Sunday afternoons. It could be the Boston Red Sox, the Celtics, or a football game. In the evening, he would relax in his easy chair, often tuned in to the *Wall $treet Week with Louis Rukeyser* show on PBS from 7:00 to 8:00 p.m. He enjoyed Rukeyser's financial updates.

On weekends, Frank and Lottie often walked the "square," leaving their home, walking down Hoosac to Summer Street, then onto Center Street, Park Street, and returning to Hoosac.

Their almost fifty-year marriage would come to an end when Lottie passed away in 1995, then Frank less than a year later. They were buried together in the Saint Stanislaus cemetery.

Frank will always be remembered as a quiet, reserved thinker with a thirst for knowledge. His girls pay tribute to him through their memories: "he was loyal, patriotic, and devoted to his wife, family, grandchildren, country, and of course his carpool."

The serious-looking man with black-rimmed glasses, normally sequestered with his newspapers and magazines, was soon missed at the Adams Free Library, and realizing how much enjoyment he had there, the Wotkowicz family made a book donation to the Adams Library in honor of Frank and Lottie.

North Adams, Massachusetts

Abbott D. Abbott
Infantry Officer
36th Texas Infantry Division

The landing craft's ramp slammed down, and 2nd Lieutenant Abbott's heavy weapons platoon ran across the beach under what was described as "light artillery and machine gun fire," which sounds somewhat benign until considering the open beach, the deep sand, the soldiers' wobbly sea legs. There, facing them, were German infantry and tanks from the 16th Panzer Division. Stakes were high. Quickly and without hesitation, setting aside his M1 carbine, Abbott grabbed a bazooka and set off for the closest tank.

THE STORY OF ABBOTT Demetrius began many years earlier and not under the last name of Abbott. In approximately 1915, John Demetrius Aboud and his bride Mary Haddad emigrated from Syria to the United States via Ellis Island. Both were glad to leave the oppressiveness of the Turkish regime that had controlled their country.

Both John and Mary were Christians, and Mary, a determined young woman, had a fish tattooed on her forearm, a symbol of her faith that she did not hide.

Upon their entrance into the United States, John gave his name to the authorities as "Aboud," and they responded, "You must mean Abbott. That's more of an American name,"...and just like that, the change was made.

The couple moved to East Main Street in North Adams, Massachusetts, settling in a large two-story white house with a wraparound veranda. John opened several neighborhood "fruit and variety stores" in various parts of the city, one right across the street from the young couple's home.

John and Mary would go on to have seven children, four boys and three girls. Abbott was born in 1919, and they gave him the middle name Demetrius as a tribute to his father. Nine years later, a great calamity occurred when John died at age fifty-one, leaving his wife to manage the stores. Abbott D. Abbott, the middle child, was now a boy without a father. Mary ran the stores for a while but, speaking little English, found it a challenge juggling the business alongside trying to raise her children.

Early on, Mary nicknamed Abbott "Booty," presumedly a derivative of Aboud, and it was quickly adopted by his family, friends, and schoolmates. Booty and his siblings helped run the store on East Main Street until it closed shortly after John's death. Abbott attended Houghton Elementary School with his siblings, helped his mom, who doted on him, and occasionally worked on his uncle Gabriel's farm on Florida Mountain. Mary ensured the large family was punctual about attending evening meals at home and Sunday Mass at Saint Francis Church.

In helping to support the family, Abbott and his brothers brought home any money they earned when not working at the store. The boys had a lucrative (and hospitable) business of lugging jugs up to the Western Summit on the Mohawk Trail and selling water to tourists whose cars had overheated.

Abbott's special responsibility was fermenting apple cider in the home's basement. On more than one occasion, he was cautioned when trying to hurry the process by sticking a red-hot poker into the vat. Abbott and his siblings loved their mother's cooking, especially her stuffed grape leaves known as *dolmas* or *dolmades*, a derivative of a Turkish word meaning "to be filled." The kids would gather grape leaves from a hillside, and Mary would add rice, ground beef, and herbs and cook the leaves. Her children quickly devoured the tasty rolls. They also loved her homemade pita bread.

Abbott attended Drury High School and did not play sports

because of an injured arm, although he was known as the go-to guy for sports statistics on almost any professional player or team. After graduating in 1937 with a healed arm, he played semi-professional football as a running back. An unfortunate kick in the face resulted in sutures, almost eliminating his right eyebrow.

Just before graduation, in April 1937, Abbott enlisted in the North Adams National Guard unit Company K of the 104th Infantry Regiment, 26th Yankee Division, and was quickly promoted to corporal. With rumors of war approaching, the guard unit was federalized (made part of the regular Army) in January 1941, and he was promoted to sergeant shortly afterward. He would remain an enlisted man until his commissioning as a 2nd lieutenant in January 1943.

Company K's training began in earnest once war had been declared on Japan (December 8, 1941) and Germany (December 11, 1941). In February 1942, the unit moved to Camp Blanding, Florida, and from there, spent the months of July and August on maneuvers in the Carolinas.

After returning to Camp Edwards, Massachusetts, and Fort Dix, New Jersey, training had taken on a new urgency, and Company K focused on small unit tactics, marksmanship, and physical conditioning. Each soldier qualified with the M1 rifle and became familiar with .30- and .50-caliber machine guns, the Browning Automatic Rifle (BAR), and anti-tank guns. Training would continue through March 1943.

In late 1942, Abbott was recommended to attend Infantry Officer Candidate School at Fort Benning, Georgia. After weeks of rigorous training and classroom activity, he was commissioned a 2nd lieutenant.

Shortly after graduation, Abbott was assigned to the storied 36th Texas Division that sported a distinctive T shoulder patch, sometimes known as "T patchers." The President had federalized the unit on November 25, 1940, and its soldiers were mainly from Texas or nearby Oklahoma.

The 36th Division—nicknamed the Texas Army—had been

Early promotion photo of Lieutenant Abbott. (Courtesy of Abbott family)

formed just after the United States entered WWI and was now composed of National Guard units. Their ancestry was easily traced back to Texas Volunteer Guard and the Texas Militia, even to periods before the Alamo.

The Texas Army had three infantry regiments (141st, 142nd, and 143rd), each with three infantry battalions. Each battalion had four companies and various supporting units such as headquarters, quartermaster, artillery, medical, and engineering, bringing the division's total number of soldiers to 16,000 men.

Abbott's assignment to the 36th brought him back to Fort Edwards for more training, and there he was assigned to the 141st Regiment as a heavy weapons platoon leader with the 3rd Battalion's Company M. Heavy weapons platoons such as Abbott's supported infantry companies with machine guns, mortars, and anti-tank weapons.

After several months of training, the 36th was ordered to North Africa, and the soldiers were entrained to New York Harbor for embarkation and departure on April 2, 1944. Five huge transports, containing the entire 36th Division, would soon join a large convoy protected by seven destroyers, the battleship *Arkansas*, and other warships. The convoy's biggest threat was German submarines, and the warships used their anti-aircraft guns and daily depth charges to ensure preparedness.

The 36th arrived in Oran, Algeria, on April 16 and moved eighty miles south to Magenta for more maneuvers and tactical exercises. The division also practiced landing exercises in Arzew, a small nearby port city. There would be no combat in Africa for the division…but it wasn't far away.

After months of training, the 36th was assigned to participate in Operation Avalanche, the invasion of Italy at the port city of Salerno. There was some skepticism by the General Staff as to whether the unblooded division could be the first Americans to land and fight on the mainland of Europe. Still, their intense amphibious preparations convinced leadership to make use of the division.

The Texas Army left Oran by ship on September 5, 1943, headed to Salerno only to learn en route that Italy had surrendered to the Allied forces on September 8. The soldiers, first anticipating they would face Italian and German divisions, now began to think their landing might be a cakewalk.

It was not to be. On September 9, 1943, 2nd Lieutenant Abbott and his weapons platoon disembarked from a landing craft and waded ashore at Salerno. The shore had been divided into four sectors (red, green, yellow, and blue). The 141st Regiment landed on beaches designated blue and yellow.

It was thought they would surprise enemy forces, so no naval or aerial bombardment was planned before landing. This failed. The Germans had artillery and machine guns zeroed in on the landing zones, backed up by eight German divisions that included several Panzer Corps. The 16th Panzer Corps was waiting to meet the 141st.

The Germans were determined to deprive the Allies of a beachhead, and the German response was ferocious. The 141st ran into trouble almost immediately. Units established a tenuous beach hold under nearly continuous artillery and small arms fire.

On the day of the landing, September 9, Abbott displayed his first heroics recorded on Official Army General Orders No. 251, Approved by Major General Dahlquist. The order states:

Action

*Abbott D. Abbott, First Lieutenant (then 2nd Lieutenant), 141st Infantry Regiment, for gallantry in action on September 9, 1943, in the vicinity of **** (censored) Italy. As platoon*

> *leader of a heavy machine gun platoon Lieutenant Abbott was instructed to support the 3rd Battalion in the fighting on the strategic beachhead during the invasion of Italy. The Battalion advanced against stiff enemy resistance and under heavy mortar and artillery shelling until the friendly troops were pinned down by the direct fire from several enemy tanks and the hostile infantry. Lieutenant Abbott immediately seized a bazooka and, leaving his covered position, pressed forward to an exposed location where he could direct fire on the hostile tanks. Engaging the enemy singlehandedly, he took careful aim and fired his bazooka, seriously damaging one of the tanks. When the tanks had withdrawn under heavy naval fire, he again exposed himself to the intense, rapid enemy fire to organize all the riflemen near him and, supported by a heavy machine gun section, valiantly led a firefight against the hostile force, directing the men with such skill and accuracy that the enemy infantry was forced to withdraw.*

The General Order would result in Abbott's first award of the Silver Star.

The landing was contested for days, and six German divisions counterattacked on September 12, determined to push the Allied forces back into the sea. At one point, the 141st Regiment was cut off, suffered numerous casualties, and many of its soldiers were captured. Eventually, American and British forces took the surrounding heights, eliminating the enemy's artillery and mortar fire.

With this, the Italian Campaign began, and Allied forces struggled up the Italian "boot."

The division's cost had been high, with several hundred soldiers killed, over 800 wounded, and 700 missing in action, presumed captured. As Abbott and his weapons platoon trudged out of Salerno, they passed by German POWs digging sixty-foot-long trenches for the American dead. All soldiers wore two dog tags. When killed in action, one was placed in the shroud-wrapped body and the other on the rough cross over the grave.

The 36th would continue up the Italian peninsula, fighting and capturing towns along the way. Often conditions were abysmal. They were climbing and fighting over mountains against an entrenched enemy. American and German bodies were strewn along the mountain paths. The men became rain-soaked and cold. Trench foot was a common ailment. If lucky, they would sleep in two-person pup tents heated by an open can of gas; if unlucky, on the stony ground. Pack mules were used to evacuate the wounded and, on their return trip, would bring replacements and supplies. When it was too difficult for even the mules to reach them, resupply was done by hand.

In December 1943, when continuing to fight through small villages and towns, Abbott was wounded and awarded the Purple Heart "for wounds received in action at Mount Rotundo, Italy, on December 5, 1943," as described by Army correspondence. He was also promoted to 1st Lieutenant. In late December, General Walker, Division Commander, visited Abbott's regiment and decorated many soldiers. Presumedly, this is when Abbott officially received his Silver Star.

In December, Ernie Pyle, a famous war correspondent known for his personal, relatable soldier interviews, visited the 36th and wrote one of his most famous newspaper columns of World War II, titled "The Death of Captain Waskow," a 143rd Regiment leader who was killed in action. The story is based on Waskow's devotion to his country and men. Eventually, Pyle went to serve in the Pacific Theater, where he was killed by Japanese machine gun fire in April 1944 on a small island northwest of Okinawa.

In late January 1944, Abbott's 141st Regiment and the 143rd were ordered to ford the Rapido River. It would be a disaster. Platoons of men were ordered to cross minefields under artillery bombardment while carrying 400-pound boats and try to traverse a swiftly flowing river. The boats were shredded before they could cross, the gunfire was intense from the riverbank on the other side, and hundreds were killed or drowned. The effort was repeated a second time, with the same disastrous results. Abbott's regiment and the 143rd were decimated, with over 150 killed, over 1,000 wounded, and 900 missing in action (presumed and hopefully captured). The division had lost almost two full regiments. Abbott was one of the survivors.

In February 1944, Abbott was wounded a second time and released after several weeks in the hospital with an official medical record stating: "diagnosis, wound penetrating multiple, moderate, back, bilateral."

His regiment continued to have vicious skirmishes in the towns of San Pietro, Avellino, Mount La Difensa, Maggiore, and Sammucro. In June 1944, four months after the disastrous Rapido River debacle, the 36th had great tactical success in surprising and routing the German Army at Velletri. Abbott's 141st acted as a blocking force. He was again in the "thick" of the action.

June found Abbott listed as the commanding officer of Company M, one of the first units to enter Rome. They were ordered not to stop and drive straight through the city, in hot pursuit of the retreating German Army.

In the early morning of August 1944, after entering France, Abbott's unit was approaching the town of Montélimar, on the Rhone north of Avignon, when the enemy opened fire, and he sprang into action. The General Order issued at the time aptly describes his action:

> *ABBOTT D. ABBOTT, Captain (then First Lieutenant), 141st Infantry Regiment, for gallantry in action on August 28, 1944, in France. The 3rd Battalion, 141st Infantry Regiment, was assigned the mission of attacking enemy defenses on a strategically important hill in a well-defended town. Lieutenant Abbott advanced across an exposed valley toward the objective with the assault company supported by a platoon of heavy machine guns. As the attackers approached*

> *the town, the enemy suddenly opened fire, sweeping the valley with machine guns and rifle fire and blasting it with an artillery and mortar barrage. The assault company, depleted by heavy casualties, was split into small units by fire from interlacing enemy final protective fires. A second company advanced on the left flank, and when the company commander was wounded, it also became disorganized. Aware of the necessity for immediate, aggressive action Lieutenant Abbott put his machine gun platoon into action and engaged the enemy in an intense firefight. Then moving fearlessly from one shell-shattered house to another, he contacted the scattered rifle elements and began reorganizing the men. He finally managed to assemble a group of almost platoon strength in one place. When higher headquarters ordered the companies to withdraw, Lieutenant Abbott used his machine guns to lay down a base of fire and valiantly led the riflemen in a series of local counterattacks, remaining on the hill until all the men had withdrawn to safety and all the casualties had been evacuated. Lieutenant Abbott was painfully wounded while withdrawing from his exposed position....*
>
> *His heroism exemplifies the finest traditions of the Armed Forces of the United States.*

In the two hours of fighting, Company M had dozens of soldiers killed and wounded and was credited with capturing eighty prisoners. For his heroic leadership, he was awarded a second Silver Star and the French *Croix De Guerre* (*Transcript,* 6-29-45). Abbott was evacuated to the 45th General Hospital, US Army, for surgery and recovery.

Back with his unit in September 1944, promoted to Captain, Abbott assumed the position of Battalion Executive Officer, managing "rear installations, which include the aid station, motor pool, and supply dumps." Abbott was cited as follows: "He displayed great ability in supervising the necessary large carrying parties needed to hand-carry all supplies to the distant positions far up into the mountains. The wise planning of supply and evacuation routes on the part of Captain Abbott made it possible for the troops to gain their objectives." This was not unlike the work he and his siblings had done decades earlier on the Mohawk Trail, providing crucial supplies to needy travelers.

The action continued, and on October 9, Abbott was wounded a third time in a forward battalion command post near the town of Herpelmont, France. His wound was treated in the field.

Abbott's war continued and he was again cited, as follows: "His high courage was shown on the night of November 20, 1944, in the vicinity of Gerbrepal, France, when he led a carrying party through a large minefield. Capt. Abbott had not had the time for prior reconnaissance. Nevertheless, he fearlessly led his party through the minefield to the front-line troops, thus ensuring the resupply of the Battalion." (This was part of his recommendation for future promotion to Major.)

Finally, after months of almost continuous fighting, the 36th Division was placed in a relief role and entered Germany. The unit returned to action briefly in April 1945 to root out diehard SS troops and assist at recently discovered concentration camps. Abbott and his soldiers were shocked at the condition of captives and at the mounds of the dead.

In May 1945, members of the 36th Division took Hermann Goering into custody. He was the second most powerful person in Germany at this time, and the Chief of the Luftwaffe. Goering surrendered, both himself and his family. After over a 200-day trial in Nuremberg, Germany, he was convicted of atrocities and sentenced to death. Not wanting to be hanged, Goering committed suicide after his appeal to be shot was rejected. After witnesses observed the body, his cremated ashes were thrown into a river.

Abbott was taken offline and placed in command of the non-commissioned officer's school in Ebenhofen, Germany. At that time, he officially received his second Silver Star (with Oak Leaf

Cluster) for his actions the previous August and the *Croix de Guerre* from France.

With the 36th Division, he participated in five campaigns in the European Theatre during World War II: Naples-Goggia, Rome-Arno, Southern France, Rhineland, and Central Europe. The 36th suffered 26,000 casualties from Salerno to Austria (with 5700 KIAs) and was credited with capturing 175,000 prisoners.

PROPOSED CITATION

CROIX DE GUERRE

ABBOTT D. ABBOTT, 0-1309153, Captain, Infantry, 141st Infantry Regiment, for extraordinary heroism in action on 28 August 1944, in the vicinity of MONTELIMAR, FRANCE.

On the morning of 26 August 1944, the Third Battalion, 141st Infantry, was ordered to attack a hill and the town of CLEARIE in the vicinity of MONTELIMAR, FRANCE. Captain ABBOTT, as Commanding Officer of Company "M", 141st Infantry, moved across the valley with the attacking company towards this objective with one platoon of heavy machine guns. Intense small arms, mortar and artillery fire was encountered as the assault company approached the objective, forcing the men to take whatever cover was available. The company was split into small units by interlacing enemy machine gun fire. As a second attacking company moved in on the left flank of the first company, its company commander was wounded and the company was similarly split up by the heavy enemy fire.

Constantly exposing himself to enemy fire, Captain ABBOTT placed his heavy machine guns in positions where they could engage the opposing forces. He re-organized the two scattered rifle companies by moving from house to house, directing the men to routes of withdrawal so that they could reach an area where they could once again assemble.

- 1 -

RESTRICTED

The proposed citation for Abbott's *Croix de Guerre*. (Courtesy of Abbott family)

After the war, the 36th existed until 1968 but saw no further military action. As an aside, in 1950, Audie Murphy, a Texan native and the most decorated soldier of World War II, joined the 36th to help promote the Texas National Guard. Notably, many of the battles he fought in northern Italy and southern France were the same as Abbott's.

Abbott was transferred to the replacement depot in Thionville, France, and began his journey home. Shortly after he arrived in the United States, he was discharged from the Army and returned to North Adams. In February 1946, he married the former Josephine Monahan and accepted a position at her father's company, Monahan Iron & Steel, on Ashland Street. Over the years, the Abbotts had three sons. His wife Josephine was a woman of great talent: As a member of the Drury band, she played the clarinet at Herbert Hoover's 1929 Inauguration.

Not long after returning home, in 1947 Abbott rejoined Company K as its commander and remained with the unit until he decided to return to active duty in 1951. It must have been satisfying for Abbott, who served as a corporal four years earlier, to command his old unit now.

Around this same time, in 1950, Abbott generously donated six acres of land inherited from his uncle Gabriel to the Town of Florida for their new schoolhouse. The school, currently still in existence, is called the Gabriel Abbott Memorial School, and has continued the legacy of the Abbott name in the community.

For the next sixteen years until his retirement in 1967, Abbott attended a number of highly regarded Army schools and served in some prominent positions. He graduated from the Army's Language School, taking courses in Turkish during the day and listening to records at night. Abbott also completed the Army's four-month Intelligence course and the Army's rigorous six-month Infantry School.

Over his career, he served two one-year tours, without his family, as an advisor to the Turkish Army along the Russian border, helping to strengthen Turkish cavalry regiments. Then he served another tour in Germany during the Cold War as an intelligence agent reporting on Russian and East German troop movements.

His family did accompany him to Berlin, and their youngest child was born there. The older boys attended American-run schools and closely followed the rules; any misbehavior was reported to their father's commanding officer. The boys and their mom traveled to Switzerland, Italy, and France. Usually, Abbott did not accompany them, explaining to Josephine, "I saw enough of Europe during the war." When it was available, the boys swam in the 1936 Olympic pool located in the British sector of Berlin. At the pool, the boys noticed their dad's shrapnel-scarred back.

The family's highlight of their German tour of duty was attending the 1958 World's Fair in Brussels. Abbott and the boys viewed the Fair the day before it opened when they snuck through a hedge. They saw the Atomium, a 335-foot-tall stainless-steel structure that served as the Fair's centerpiece dedicated to science. The boys also remembered IBM's room-size computer and the Russian Sputnik model.

Back in the United States, Abbott served at different forts, often as an infantry intelligence and a supply officer. He was promoted to major when serving at Fort Holabird in Maryland. While on the intelligence staff, he escorted visiting Turkish Generals and acted as their interpreter.

Back in the Berkshires, Major Abbott (left) congratulates a fellow officer on his transfer to Korea. (Courtesy of Abbott family and *The Transcript*)

In 1962, Abbott was promoted to Lieutenant Colonel and, after completing his second tour of duty in Turkey, became the Army Advisor to all National Guard units in Western Massachusetts, directed to improve mobilization readiness and combat effectiveness. Serving in this capacity during the mid-sixties, he was often called upon to notify families of their soldiers' death in Vietnam.

In August 1963, author Harold L. Bond, a professor from Dartmouth College, wrote about his experiences as an officer with the 141st Regiment, and included mentions of Lieutenant Abbott. The book is titled *Return to Cassino—A Memoir of the Fight for Rome.* Shortly after its publication, Harold sent Abbott a letter telling him that he had used fictitious names for all the officers mentioned in the book and that Lieutenant Allen was modeled after Abbott, called a man who "represented the quiet courage that made us possible to win."

In portions of the book, Bond refers to Allen/Abbott as "a second lieutenant in charge of one of our machine gun platoons…the finest junior officer I knew in the war…. He had shown such skill and bravery in the fighting at Salerno that a petition for his promotion to commissioned rank had been sent in after the division had been in combat less than a month…. Of all the men I have known, Allen was the one I most enjoyed knowing. His honesty and courage were combined with a simple modesty. He had a genuine affection for his soldiers…."

Retiring in 1967 with twenty years of military service, Lieutenant Colonel Abbott and his family moved to Longmeadow, Massachusetts, where he used his organizational background to skillfully manage a real estate company in Springfield.

Abbott, always a sports fan of the Red Sox, now had time to attend Fenway Park games with his boys. He was also able to pursue his favorite hobby of playing bridge and joined the Longmeadow/Springfield Bridge Club. Abbott played in many bridge tournaments throughout the United States, earning the coveted title of *Life Master.*

During this time, the family, including Abbott, purchased the Bennington Hotel and a small restaurant. The hotel became the epicenter for extended family Christmases and the always accompanying bridge games.

During the later years of his life, Abbott experienced heart difficulties. While attending a bridge tournament in upstate New York, he decided to watch a Monday football game between the Buffalo Bills and the New York Jets. While at the game, he was stricken with a massive heart attack and, to the shock of everyone, died instantly.

Abbot was fifty-six. In the words of his son, "He liked being around people, but once he put his uniform on, he was 'regular' Army, had expectations of those soldiers who reported to him, and was by the book."

This native of North Adams, given over to the maelstrom of World War II, was one of few men to receive two battlefield promotions within four months, rising from 2nd Lieutenant to Captain. His gallantry was acknowledged by the Silver Star (twice), three Purple Hearts for his wounds, and the coveted *Croix De Guerre*, among his many other decorations.

Abbott now rests peacefully in the family plot in Southview Cemetery.

William F. Beattie & Madeline E. (Smith) Beattie
Reconnaissance Technician, *308th Bombardment Group*
Combat Nurse, *314th General/Evacuation Hospital*

During the war, they were stationed 1500 miles apart, Madeline "Maddie" Evelyn Smith in Manila and William "Bill" Floyd Beattie in Kunming, China. Bill was with the 308th Bombardment Group, making harrowing flights through narrow Himalayan passes to record and process combat films. Maddie served as a psychiatric charge nurse caring for hundreds of ill soldiers suffering from mental and physical diseases. Bill and Maddie would leave their combat areas, return home a month apart, and meet, providentially, several months later.

Corporal William Floyd Beattie

WILLIAM FLOYD BEATTIE WAS born in North Adams, Massachusetts, on October 25, 1921, to William Roy and Bessie Josephine (Lent) Beattie, both North Adams natives. At birth, William was given the middle name Floyd from his maternal grandfather.

His father, William Roy Beattie, was born in the late 1800s. He attended local schools and served first as an enlisted man and then as a Second Lieutenant in the US Army during World War I. Records show that during his five years of service, he was attached to the 11th Cavalry in the Pacific Northwest, patrolling Yellowstone National Park before there was a Park Service, and then with the country's emerging Air Corps, supervising the harvesting of timber for *aero planes*, as they were called at that time.

Returning home, the elder William began a long career in the printing business, working as a foreman for Byam Printing in North Adams, Sun Printing in Pittsfield, and back in North Adams at Excelsior Printing in his last years before retirement. Active in local government, William Roy Beattie served as City Councilor, was a member of the Board of Appeals and Warden for Ward 10, and, after retiring in 1958, volunteered as a Red Cross driver.

Bessie Josephine Lent, born in the 1890s, was a 1910 graduate of Drury Academy and clerked for the Boston & Albany Railroad and the First National Bank of North Adams. She met William Roy Beattie, and they married in 1920 at the Methodist Episcopal Church; they would have three children, two boys and a girl, with William Floyd as the oldest. In 1966, Bessie was chosen as "Woman of the Year" by the Women's Society. In 1975, she passed away and was buried in Maple Street Cemetery in Adams, connected to it by her Quaker background.

William Roy passed away four years later and would donate his body to medical research.

Growing up, their son William Floyd, now called Bill by everyone, enjoyed photography and hiking. He took his treasured Brownie box camera everywhere, snapping pictures and then returning home to develop them in his basement. His interests leaned toward the arts; he enjoyed drawing and playing stringed instruments, especially the violin.

As a teenager, he liked to hike portions of the Long Trail, which begins at the Massachusetts-Vermont border and runs to Canada. Often, his hikes included fishing for trout in the backwoods streams.

Bill attended Drury High School, and the 1940 yearbook notes that he is a "Wit, in ... the finest sense in the world." In his junior and senior years, he joined the school choir, the photography and music clubs, and the track team. His career desire was to be a commercial photographer. Upon graduation, he found employment at the James Hunter Machine Company working in the foundry, cleaning and pouring red-hot lead into molds. It was a hot, oppressive, sticky environment.

Bill, after working several years at Hunter Machine, volunteered for service with the Army Air Force and enlisted in October 1942. He traveled to Greensboro, North Carolina, to one of the twelve Army Air Force Training Centers dedicated to recruit basic training. After just eight weeks, they'd be prepared to deploy for war, either in Europe or the Pacific.

His first few days entailed undergoing testing, haircuts, a general orientation, basic hygiene lessons, issuance of uniforms, and inoculations. The remainder of his time on the 600-acre reservation included weapons training, drills, military customs, instruction on chemical warfare (including wearing a gas mask), first aid, and one hour of physical exercise. His unit would repeatedly run the Center's challenging obstacle course under their instructors' stern scrutiny and commands. As a boost of encouragement along the course, the instructors had posted pictures of Adolf Hitler and Benito Mussolini.

His recruit mental tests revealed an aptitude for photography, and the military's demand for technical skills may have slightly shortened his basic training. Bill's photo hobby as a teenager translated to classification as a photo laboratory technician. Ironically, he did not work in his specialty until he was overseas.

Upon graduation, Bill was transferred to the newly constructed Turner Army Airfield near Albany, Georgia. The Airfield Training Command had three freshly poured concrete runways, numerous hangers, and training facilities. The Command trained Army Air Force navigators, air crews from France and Britain, and other support personnel.

Bill spent a little over a year at Turner Airfield, and his greatest enjoyment was taking what is known as "hops"—free passages on military planes to see different areas of the country and, in the process, accumulate flying time. During this period, he became familiar with the B-25 Mitchell bomber and its aerial photography capabilities. As a Private First Class, he was assigned some of the more boring duties of the guard: what seemed like endless K.P. in the mess hall and working as a fireman stoking furnaces.

In letters home, Bill described one of his early flight experiences:

> *We were up at 10,000 feet the other day doing power stalls in a B-25. What happens, the pilot climbs the plane at a steep angle then cuts the throttles way down. Immediately the nose drops, and we drop quite a way then the pilot gives the ship full throttle and hauls back on the stick and we level off or climb again. It was the first time I ever was up in a 25 when the pilot was trying stalls, so it was quite a thrill. It seems as though your stomach is left up a couple of hundred feet. It's fun, though. I didn't wear my chute when we first went up but after the pilot started that stuff it didn't take long for me to climb into it.*

In a follow-up letter to his parents, he says, "I'm still getting flying time in, mostly on a B-25. At present, I've got around 20½ hours. That's not bad considering the fact that we have to bum those rides." The Training Command allowed airmen interested in flying or those who had never flown to be given rides while navigators were being trained.

One day, on a "hop," much to Bill's delight, the pilot of an AT-10, an Army Air Force training aircraft, let Bill take over the controls and even let him take the plane into a dive. It was an exhilarating day.

In one of his many letters home, Bill noted seeing a large number of German P.O.W.s march onto the base and presumed they would be put to work in the area's pecan farms. Bill wrote home frequently, often populating his letters with funny caricatures that showed him being sick at sea or flying airplanes.

In April 1944, Bill was briefly transferred back to Greensboro, North Carolina, where his appendix ruptured; in serious condition after a misdiagnosis, he was hospitalized for thirty-six days. When he returned to full duty, stints of guard duty begin, with more K.P., inspections, and a trip to the rifle range where they slept in tents and fought swarms of mosquitos, all for pre-deployment readiness.

In August 1944, his unit entrained to New York for deployment. Letters from this time became censored, with sections cut out that did not comply with the military's censorship guidelines.

In September 1944, Bill's letters say he was "aboard a ship somewhere in the Atlantic…and I don't know if I have my sea legs yet." He mentions the transport ship was "quite crowded" below deck, but "every other night we are allowed to sleep up on the deck." Portions of this letter are censored.

It appears Bill was on the USS *General T.H. Bliss*, headed for Karachi, India (now Pakistan). There, he was assigned to the 14th Air Force's 308th Bombardment Group, working with the Headquarters photography section. From Karachi, Bill traveled to Assam, India, and took a flight to Kunming, China, which would serve as his home base.

PFC Beattie, left, in India posing with another member of his unit. (Courtesy of Beattie family)

The following 14 months were spent flying between Assam and Kunming, working in processing labs at both bases. The Fourteenth Air Force was activated on March 5, 1943, and was based in Kunming, China. The Chinese Air Task Force (CTAF), formerly part of the Flying Tigers, was merged into the newly activated 14th Air Force. The 14th Air Groups included squadrons of B-25 and B-24 bombers and P-40 and P-51 Mustang fighters.

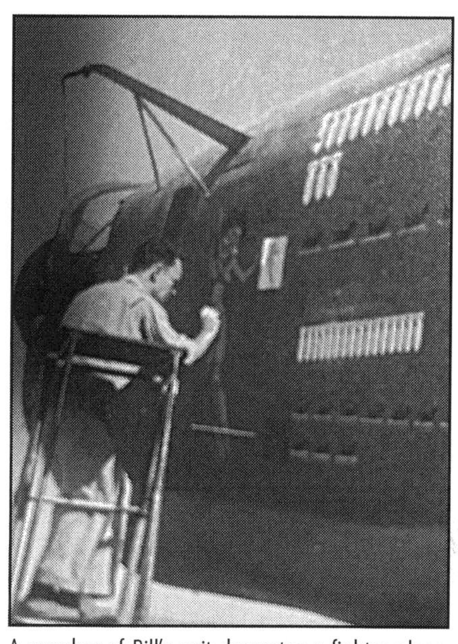
A member of Bill's unit decorates a fighter plane. (Courtesy of Beattie family)

Bill's unit, the 308th Bombardment Group, would fly B-24 bombers. The 308th's insignia was a thundercloud with three lightning flashes and three bombs pointing downward with the motto *Non Sibi, Sed Aliis*—"Not for Self, But for Others." The group operated from Chinese bases until late in the war when it moved to India, then, in December 1945, returned to the United States, where it was inactivated in January 1946.

Upon arrival at Kunming, Bill's on-the-job training included becoming familiar with the cameras used for photo reconnaissance. He learned to remove heavy cameras from planes or, in some cases, simply retrieve the film to be processed. He would also experience the laborious process of developing military film.

Bill spent hours using motorized winding and unwinding mechanisms, spooling and unspooling 25-foot-long film rolls, each with 5 X 5-inch images. The spools were placed in development solutions and then dried, creating negatives that would be converted into pictures. Each photo must be labeled, identifying the organization, location, date, and time in the lower right-hand corner. The processing was done entirely in the dark.

His group developed thousands of feet of films from its bombers, both B-24 and 25, and their fighters.

Bill's photos of the 308th bombing runs, which supported Chinese ground forces, reveal bomb damage to enemy airfields, docks, refineries, and supply yards located in Indochina, Burma, and the East and South China Seas. Due to its valiant efforts, the 308th received two Distinguished Unit Citations.

In one of his early letters home, Bill wrote that he was "finally doing the work I want to do."

Bill's work required him to travel between India and China, weaving through the dangerous Himalayan mountains, a section known as "Aluminum Alley" for the number of frequent crashes and the planes' aluminum remnants that could be seen strewn on the mountainsides. Weaving through the mountains, the crews faced three different air masses producing violent winds that made travel especially dangerous over what was called "the Hump" by crewmen.

During one of the flights at a high altitude, the bomber Bill was on began to stall, and the pilot told the oxygen-masked crew that they might have to bail out. After some tense minutes, the pilot got the engine running smoothly, which saved the day. The trips were not all precarious. In another of Bill's letters home, he recounted how on one flight he brought along his pet monkey, Edna (named after his aunt), and at 22,000 feet when she started to pass out, he shared his oxygen mask with her for a while. Just before he passed out, he would reclaim it to breathe. "We kept that up most of the trip…" and both primates landed safely with no side effects.

Bill was usually on a B-25 bomber during these trips and learned a great deal about aerial photography. Most cameras operated electronically, and the 308th used the popular K-24 camera manufactured by the Eastman Kodak Company of Rochester, New York. The camera's 178-millimeter lens was effective at high altitudes and began shooting when the bomb bay doors opened. The camera verified a bomber's position over the target when a bomb was released and then assessed the damage.

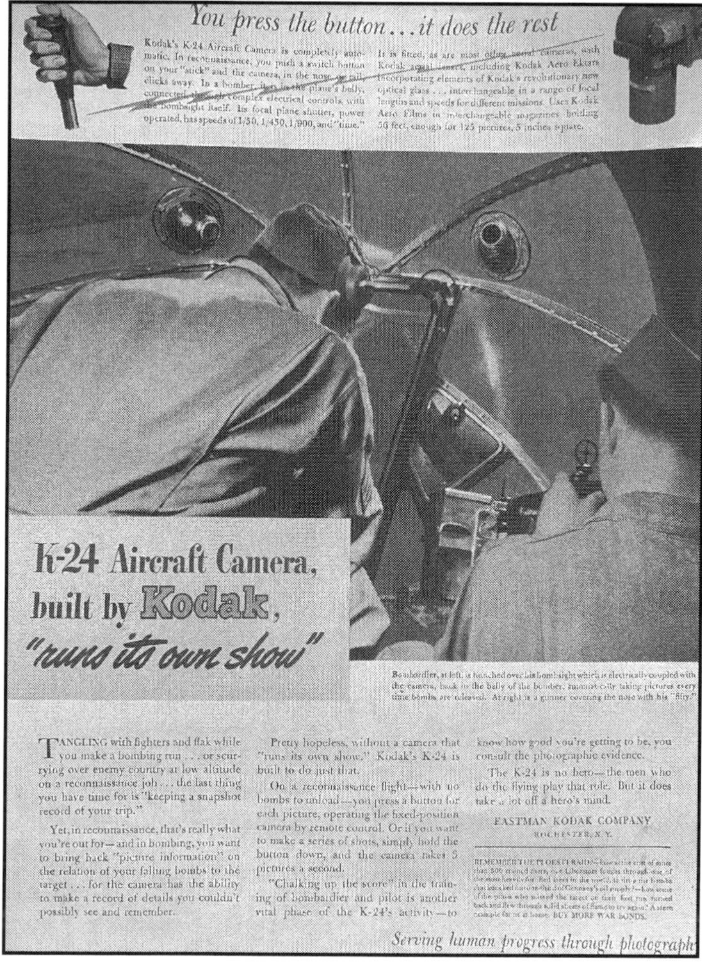

Eastman Kodak advertisement in *LIFE* magazine lauding their K-24 reconnaissance camera. (Courtesy of the author and *LIFE* magazine)

When flights landed, Bill or one of his team would collect the film or camera, place it in the group's Jeep, nicknamed "Shutterbug," and return to their wooden shanty for development. The team had development shacks in India and Kunming, China. The developed film was important; it would let Command know whether the target had been hit, how effectively, and whether it needed to be targeted again.

When not working, the crew lived initially in tents and then wooden barracks. They enjoyed going to town, especially in India, where their money, exchanged into rupees, bought them excellent meals. In China, Bill roamed around the countryside taking photos of the native people, and his letters reported that he struggled using chopsticks.

2nd Lieutenant Madeline Evelyn Smith (Beattie)

HUNDREDS OF MILES FROM North Adams in Calais, Maine, near the St. Croix River and next to the Canadian border, Madeline Evelyn Smith was born on November 3, 1921, the fourth child of Eben and Cora (Glidden) Smith. Just one week earlier, Madeline's future husband William Beattie had been born in North Adams.

Eben and Cora had five children altogether, two boys and three girls. Eben was a self-sufficient dairy farmer, logger, and the owner of a gristmill and sawmill. Cora was a homemaker; both she and Eben hailed from early Maine settlers who preceded its 1820 statehood.

Madeline was always active. She had a long list of farm chores to complete, and when those were finished, she would often fish with her dad. She attended local schools and graduated from Calais High School in 1939. An excellent student, Maddie was also an outstanding athlete, captaining the women's basketball team, where she played as a guard, and the women's softball team.

After graduation, she attended the Lawrence General School of Nursing in Lawrence, Massachusetts, graduating with her nursing degree in 1942. She remained there for the next two and a half years, gaining experience as a floor nurse.

In the first days of 1945, Maddie volunteered for the Army Nursing Corps, passed her physical, was inducted on January 29, and began active duty on February 14, 1945.

The Corps had been created in 1901, and its nurses served heroically and tirelessly in World War I. It wasn't until after the start of World War II that nurses, once they had completed basic training, were given an officer's commissioned status of 2nd Lieutenant. In 1944, when nurses were granted full officer status, they also qualified for retirement packages, equal pay, and dependent allowances.

The Corps would transition from 1,000 nurses at the beginning of World War II to 59,000 by the time hostilities ceased in 1945. During the war years, nurses served in every theater of operations worldwide.

Maddie spent her first weeks in the service undergoing basic training at Fort Devens, Massachusetts. She took classes in military customs and courtesies, was trained to march in formation, and learned basic sanitation and ward management, coupled with the use of camouflage and gas masks. The nurse candidates also learned map reading and defensive measures against air, chemical, and mechanized attacks. To keep up morale and physical fitness, they participated in daily calisthenics.

Madeline, left, with a friend on the doorstep of her parents' home in Calais, Maine, before she goes overseas. (Courtesy of Beattie family.

As the war progressed, the need became clear for nurses specializing in psychiatric care. Often, the military struggled to realize the necessity of caring for those service members not physically ill or bedridden, yet one out of every twelve hospital admissions required psychiatric assistance. In response to this great need, the Surgeon General developed a twelve-week program to train nurses in care and medication for such patients.

Once 2nd Lieutenant Smith completed her basic training, she likely attended an abbreviated psychiatric course offered at Cushing General Hospital in Framingham, Massachusetts. Its content included hours of lectures on psychiatry and neurology, and students spent between five and eight hours daily on clinical duty.

After the briefest of furloughs, Maddie was assigned to the 314th General/Evacuation Hospital on the recently liberated Clark Air Force base in the Philippines. She, other nurses, and some technicians embarked from the United States by boat in April 1945. When the transport ship arrived in Manila Bay in May 1945, the nurses were transferred to a landing craft to be shuttled to shore.

The boat's commander instructed the nurses to stay low because they would come under sniper fire. His cautions rang true when bullets pinged off the craft's side as they approached the shore. Maddie experienced a quick realization that her life was about to change significantly. Manila, just sixty miles away from Clark Airfield, had only two months earlier been liberated after months of vicious fighting that destroyed the city. Enemy activity would continue on the island until the end of the war in August 1945.

With her experience and training, Maddie was assigned as a charge nurse to the 314th General Hospital's neuropsychiatric section. She and her staff cared for patients in the sixty-eight beds in the psychiatric ward, nowhere near enough to accommodate all the soldiers, so extra cots usually spilled over into other wards. While the charge nurse's office was separate and locked when not in use, the wards were open for serious cases that would respond to treatment.

Diagnoses were often non-specific and related to the person's proximity to battle. Acute psychiatric patients were usually evacuated by ship or plane as soon as possible. When necessary, sedation and restraints were used. Often, sodium pentothal, an anesthesia popularized to be a form of truth serum, also had efficacy as an anti-anxiety medication, and was used to treat the most serious patients.

Psychiatric treatment was rudimentary by today's standards, although somewhat helpful. In addition to encouraging

Madeline's medical books used during her time in the Philippines. (Courtesy of Beattie family)

patients to discuss their anxieties, hospitals also had success with simple distractions including recreational activities, reading, games, building tables or shelves, and painting. Often, treatment was complicated by physical illnesses and tropical diseases like typhus, dengue fever, and dysentery.

The psychiatric technicians, mostly untrained enlisted men, gradually adapted to their roles and provided a sympathetic ear for patients to vent about their combat experiences, essentially talk therapy. These conversations allowed technicians to furnish Maddie with observations of the patient's eating, sleeping, and social disturbances.

The nurses lived in guarded barracks close to the hospital, guarded for several reasons: in case of enemy activity (there were still hundreds of Japanese stragglers) and to preclude any amorous intentions by local soldiers. Later in life, Maddie told her son that she often heard overhead the departure and return of squadrons of B-17s who were completing their missions, a reminder of the daily stresses felt by all combatants. Although the nurses worked under hot and humid conditions, the General Hospital differed from most field hospitals because it had electricity and running water.

Maddie and her group were busy seven days a week helping and processing the numerous soldiers. The liberation of the Philippines resulted in over 200,000 casualties, over half from non-battle reasons. Many would find their way to the General Hospital and Maddie's psych ward. Clark Hospital would be the last stop for those soldiers needing advanced treatment and evacuation; for others less injured, it might mean a return to the front lines.

The Army psychiatric nurses working closely with soldiers were generally considered to be some of the most adaptable, understanding, and versatile officers in the Nursing Corps. Many of Maddie's patients affectionately called her "Sarge" even though she was a Second Lieutenant. In appreciation of his care, one of her patients gave her a stick of Beeman's gum in the wrapper, which she never opened and held as a keepsake until she passed away many decades later.

Postwar Life Begins

CORPORAL WILLIAM BEATTIE, AFTER serving almost fifteen months overseas, returned by ship to the United States, arriving in late December 1945, and was honorably discharged at the Fort Devens Separation Center just days later, December 31, 1945.

Bill participated in the India–Burma Air Offensive and Japan–China Western Pacific campaigns, earning the Distinguished Unit Badge with one oak leaf cluster, Good Conduct Medal, Asia Pacific Theater Campaign Ribbon, American Theater Campaign Ribbon, and Victory Medal.

Maddie, who had an opportunity to fly home, was asked by her elderly mother to travel by ship since her mother worried about the safety of airplanes. Obediently, Maddie returned to the states aboard the USS *Hope*, a hospital ship with, ironically, a history of being attacked by submarines, bombers, and *kamikazes*. Luckily, with the war over, the ship and its many patients encountered only a tropical typhoon before arriving in San Francisco in late January 1946.

Maddie traveled by train across the United States and was honorably discharged at the Fort Dix Separation Center on March 5, 1946. By participating in the Luzon, Philippine Campaign, she earned the Asiatic Pacific Campaign Medal, Philippine Liberation Medal, and Victory Medal.

After separating from the Army, Maddie returned to work at Lawrence General Hospital, where she met Bill, who was visiting an aunt and uncle living in the area. After several dates, with Bill living in North Adams, the couple began long-distance dating. On September 23, 1947, with Bill's brother as the best man, they were married at First Methodist Church in Methuen, Massachusetts.

Maddie and Bill would move to the Berkshires, initially renting a downstairs apartment in a brick house along Route 2 in Williamstown and then moving to North Adams. The couple would have two children, William and Rose Alice.

Maddie worked as a registered nurse, often caring privately for prominent local families. She also worked many years and retired from the Sweet Brook Nursing Home in Williamstown. Bill spent almost twenty years at the Sprague Electric Company as a photo lab technician and later as a color mixer for the Excelsior Print Company.

Bill's early enthusiasm for music carried into adulthood. He continued tinkering with string instruments and, for some time, was the bass player with the five-man Richmond Train Blue Grass Band, which played occasionally at the local Heritage Park. One time, Bill, Maddie, and the kids had the opportunity to listen to Dave Brubeck, a famous jazz musician, and his Quartet play at Williams College.

Music played a large part in the Beattie family's life. Maddie, a gifted singer, was a member of the Methodist Church's Choir, the Sweet Adeline Chorus, and Bill sang with a barbershop quartet, the Berkshire Hillsman Barber Shop Chorus.

Family vacations included two weeks in Calais, Maine, visiting

Maddie's parents. She, her dad, and Bill often fished while the kids enjoyed roaming about the farm. On several return trips, Bill drove a Studebaker recently purchased from Maddie's brother, who owned a dealership in Maine.

Locally, the family enjoyed the outdoors, hiking around Mount Greylock, picnicking, and swimming at the cold North Pond in Florida, Massachusetts. Several times, they spent a weekend at Cape Cod and Niagara Falls.

Early in their lives together, Bill and Madeline enjoyed trout fishing and hiking with the kids in Rowe, Massachusetts. The farm girl and town boy spent a lot of time together gardening and tending their fruit trees. Maddie was known for making great squash pies and Scottish shortbread. In her spare time, she sewed costumes for the Sweet Adelines.

Bill enjoyed reading about and visiting local historical sites. He continued to draw cartoons and loved tinkering in the basement. It's where he retreated to use his bandsaw and lathe, creating bird houses, chairs, and even a go-cart for his son. At times, it also served as his darkroom.

Bill and Maddie would be married forty-nine years when he passed away in 1996; Maddie lived another thirteen years until 2009. They were buried with his Quaker grandparents in Maple Street Cemetery.

The patriotic couple proudly answered their country's call during World War II. Maddie deployed to the Philippines, secure in her role as a caring, efficient, get-things-done leader of a psychiatric ward, while Bill traveled through dangerous air space between China and India to ensure the development of high-quality reconnaissance films. They were a couple certainly "with courage and honor," but also with intelligence and ingenuity. They were among the best of the Berkshires and surely made their neighbors proud.

JAMES G. GARVIE, JR.
RIFLEMAN SCOUT
712TH TANK BATTALION

He joined Company B in October 1944, three months after their first day of combat. Jim was a replacement on the scout/reconnaissance platoon destined to fight for the next eight months. His platoon was tasked with leading the 712th tank battalion, nicknamed "The Armored Fist of the 90th," from village to village across France and Germany, relentlessly pushing the enemy out, and serving as the advance team across minefields, through unsecured towns, and once into a concentration camp. As Jim soon discovered, the job of a scout was mentally arduous and physically perilous, as they were at constant risk of stumbling upon the enemy.

MINNIE (LECLAIR) AND JAMES Glen Garvie were the proud parents of a healthy baby boy born on May 2, 1911, in Charlemont, Massachusetts. They promptly named him James Garvie, Jr. He would be the first of three boys born to the couple. He was soon to be known as Jimmy, and later in adulthood, as Jim.

James, the father, a coal miner, emigrated from Glasgow, Scotland, near the turn of the 19th century and eventually met and married Minnie, a Charlemont native. Not long after Jimmy's birth, they moved to North Adams, attracted by its growing population and opportunities.

James' actual last name was Glengarvie. He was from the "glens" (valleys) in Scotland; traditionally, the word was attached to your last name. When James Sr. arrived in the United States with his two brothers, their family name was divided by the immigration clerk: Glen became a middle name and Garvie a last name.

James Sr. quickly found custodial work at the brand-new Drury High School and would work there for twenty-nine years from its construction in 1916 until his retirement due to illness in 1945. Minnie was a homemaker and was kept busy with their three sons, Jimmy, Joseph, and Gordon. As they grew up, neighbors would often distinguish between them by saying that Jimmy was the nice-mannered Garvie boy, Joseph was the talker and mischievous one, and Gordon was the handsome one.

The family lived on East Quincy Street, and Jimmy and his siblings attended Houghton Elementary School, where he received his eighth-grade diploma. The family regularly attended the First Baptist Church on Monument Square at the bottom of their hill.

As a youth, Jimmy would help his dad with his hobby of raising and racing homing pigeons. James Sr. belonged to the North Adams Homing Pigeon Club and was a race committee member. His son would help him band birds before the races, and then James Sr. would compute race times.

His prized pigeon *Blue Cheek* was a frequent winner in the group's fall races. On one race from Fonda, New York, to North Adams, an air distance of 67 miles, she placed first, averaging 1,367 yards per minute. The birds did remarkably well, flying through inclement weather and avoiding sparrow hawks and unthinking hunters. In some races, the birds found their way home after flying over 500 miles in a single day. Local news articles often mentioned James Sr. as a local expert willing to share his knowledge with newcomers.

In his teen years, Jimmy loved to fish and would often be seen walking or bicycling to his favorite haunts on the Hoosic River or at Mauserts Pond in nearby Clarksburg. He was always searching for trout, perch, or bullhead. Surprisingly, during one of his forays he met a young girl there who also liked to fish. Her name was Yvonne Martelle. Though she lived in Clarksburg, she had attended

St. Joseph's Elementary School in North Adams. It was only a short time before they were fishing partners.

Their special spot to meet was Sunnyside, a local gathering place in Clarksburg with a bar and grill next to the north branch of the Hoosic River, where they could fish and swim. Sadly, their teenage romance broke up. Years later, Yvonne married someone else and had three children, all born in the mid-1930s. That marriage did not last, however.

She reconnected with Jim, who had always loved her. Almost as if in a fairy-tale, Jim married Yvonne Martelle Leary on April 29, 1939, and adopted her three young children. He and Yvonne would go on to have two daughters, one born just before the outbreak of World War II and one just afterward.

Initially, the family lived in the second-floor apartment at his parents' house on East Quincy Street while Jim grew his house-painting business. Shortly after his mother died in 1942, the family moved to Liberty Street, where they would remain until after the war. When Jim's dad passed away in 1949, he was buried in Southview Cemetery with Minnie.

With World War II well in its third year of American involvement, Jim was drafted, and on March 16, 1944, the local newspaper's headline read, "Many Youngsters See Army Dads Off—February Army Quota Leaves Today." The article noted that one volunteer had nine children. Families said their teary but proud goodbyes at the railroad depot.

After his induction at Fort Devens, Massachusetts, but before his basic training began in March, Jim and Yvonne, with their four children, went to a recording studio in downtown North Adams where they made several 78-format records, keepsakes so they could listen to Jim's voice while he was gone.

Jim began basic training at Camp Croft, South Carolina, in February 1944. The 13-week course centered around instilling Army discipline and included weapons training with the M1 and Browning Automatic Rifles, close-order drill, surviving exposure at the camp's gas chamber, and improving physical strength by repeatedly running the obstacle course.

After additional training at Fort Meade, Maryland, Jim departed in late August 1944 on a troop ship bound for England. After several weeks of waiting in England, he sailed for France, arriving in October 1944 at a replacement depot. He was quickly assigned as a scout to the 712th Tank Battalion, one of the seventy separate tank battalions in the United States Army. The scout unit had the use of four Jeeps and one M2 half-track, an armored scout car with normal wheels in front for easier steering and tracks in back to propel the vehicle across mud or snow.

Scout platoons were charged with providing early warning to tank and infantry units, often guarding their flanks and, in many cases, forging ahead, maintaining pressure on the enemy while reconnoitering safe avenues of approach, routes or river crossings. They were also tasked with identifying enemy obstacles—most notoriously, land mines.

Long before Jim arrived, the 712th had been activated in September 1943 at Fort Benning, Georgia, and had armor training at Fort Knox, Kentucky. After months of training, the entire battalion left Boston on the SS *Exchequer*, ending up in England for more pre-D-Day training. After combining exercises with infantry units, nighttime tactical maneuvers, and more firing of the tank's weapons, the unit departed Weymouth, England, landing on Utah Beach on June 28, 1944, three weeks after D-Day.

Combat for the 712th began on July 3, 1944, and almost immediately, the battalion was assigned to support the 90th Infantry Division (nicknamed the Tough 'Ombres to represent their recruitment zone: T for Texas and O for Oklahoma). As they proceeded inland, they passed by crashed American gliders with dead paratroopers still inside, a dark caution that training was over. The unit faced the enemy and adjusted to fighting through hedgerows. The combat was bitter. Half of their tanks were knocked out by the end of their first two days.

Replacement tanks were quickly offloaded from LSTs, and the

unit began its advance through towns and villages, always in support of one of the regiments belonging to the 90th Infantry Division (357th, 358th, or 359th). So began 311 days of combat.

The 712th Tank Battalion had four tank companies (A, B, C, and D), a headquarters and service company, one antitank platoon, and one scout platoon. Each company had three platoons of tanks; with five tanks to a platoon, fifteen to a company, this totaled over 60 tanks in the battalion. Jim was assigned to the battalion's scout platoon, supporting Company B.

Jim, as a scout, would learn much about tanks, namely their battalion's 60 plus M4 Sherman tanks, considered medium tanks and the backbone of support for infantry forces. Each tank weighed 30 tons and had firepower supplied by one 75mm cannon, two .30-caliber guns, and one .50-caliber machine gun.

Each M4 had a five-person crew that included a driver, a co-driver that also operated a .30-caliber machine gun, a loader, a gunner, and a commander. In Company B, 1st Platoon's five tanks were numbered 1 through 5, 2nd Platoon's 6 through 10, and 3rd Platoon's 11 through 15.

The mass-produced, easy-to-maintain tanks had nine-cylinder engines that allowed speeds up to 30 miles per hour and a 120-mile range thanks to its 200-gallon gas tank. The tank was 19 feet long, almost 9 feet wide, and 9 feet tall. It had four hatches: three on top and one on the bottom.

Its three-inch-deep, angled, cast steel front made the Sherman equal to Germany's Panzer III and IV tanks that the Allies faced early on. The Sherman's 75mm cannons were less effective against the larger Panther and Tiger Tanks, although they could score a kill from the flank or rear. Later in the war, the Shermans would sport a high-velocity 76mm cannon that was effective head-on against German heavy armor. Each tank carried 90 rounds of cannon ammunition.

For added protection against heavier enemy tanks, Sherman crews often added sandbags on top of their tanks, extra tank tracks, and even logs for increased protection. After some testing that proved enemy tank cannons blew away the sandbags and still penetrated the armor, General Patton forbade their use…but crews kept using them.

In addition to the larger Panther and Tiger tanks, dangers to the Sherman included the highly accurate German 88mm antitank gun and Teller mines. The Sherman was also vulnerable to the Panzerfaust, a powerful, single-shot, shoulder-fired antitank weapon.

Just before Jim joined the 712th in October 1944, the unit had a raging battle at Mairy, France, and destroyed most of the German 106th Panzer Brigade, earning the nickname "The Armored Fist."

In October, Jim and his reconnaissance platoon began advancing into enemy territory searching for the unit's best and safest approaches to towns and bridges, always on the lookout for ambushes, snipers, and Panzerfaust men. Jim worked closely with the 357th Infantry Regiment. The scouts would serve many other functions, involved in helping resupply units, search for missing soldiers, and sometimes—Jim's most distasteful task—climbing into demolished tanks and collecting dog tags from the remnants or ashes of incinerated men.

Upon his arrival, Jim was involved in the three-week siege of the City of Metz, supporting the infantry trying to capture several key forts around the city. Company B's M4 Sherman spent day after day blasting at massive concrete bunkers. Sometimes, firing from under 200 yards at the four-foot, reinforced walls, it took up to five or more rounds of cannon fire to penetrate the walls sufficiently to allow a soldier to insert an explosive charge.

During a pause in the fighting, Jim saw the Germans wave a red flag, indicating a desire to collect their wounded. The flag was honored, and the German medics and stretcher-bearers came out to collect wounded men. Afterward, when Company B's medics were collecting wounded American soldiers, a German sniper killed one of the medics. The Shermans used their cannons to blast the sniper out of his tree…but any further trust had been destroyed, utterly.

During the fighting, Jim often slept outside in his Jeep or on the ground, often sharing their C or K rations with nearby tankers, warming the food on highly valued Coleman burners. As the fighting slowed down, before moving out to the next town, he joined a group of inventive tankers that had converted large metal buckets into stoves, lining the bottom with inches of dirt soaked in gasoline, and cooking potatoes and vegetables filched from a nearby farm. The same innovative group later fished for large brown trout with grenades and seemed very successful.

In July and August, the scout platoon manned several roadblocks and captured many German prisoners, but not without being strafed by three German fighters. Jim jumped into the nearest foxhole during the aerial attack, not realizing the retreating enemy forces had booby-trapped it. He noticed a thin wire across the edge of the hole, and when he cautiously uncovered it, he found the wire attached to a German "potato masher" grenade. Gently exiting the foxhole, he warned the other scouts and threw a short log into the hole, exploding the grenade.

For the following weeks, Jim and his squad continued along at the forefront as their unit passed through many small towns and villages; some encounters required a fight with rear-guard German units or even meant repelling strong counterattacks. They were almost always under enemy artillery shelling.

In November 1944, they prepared to cross the Moselle River with the 359th Regiment and helped company tanks navigate the heavy minefields. Three were damaged by Teller mines and put out of action. Jim's platoon sergeant stepped on a mine and lost a foot, as did the reconnaissance lieutenant who tried to rescue him. Finally, a tank commander and another scout ran into the field and carried both men out, but not before the scout set off another mine, receiving a severe leg injury and further injuring the sergeant and lieutenant they were carrying. The reconnaissance group pulled back briefly to evacuate its wounded.

At the same time, the 359th engaged a horse-drawn convoy

of enemy artillery, destroying vehicles, killing several dozen of the enemy, and taking seventeen prisoners; luckily, in the process, they repatriated a captured American medic POW who was in one of the vehicles. The event remained vivid in Jim's mind because of the screaming horses that needed to be finished off.

By the end of November, Company B was on high ground overlooking the Saar River. In early December, the scout platoon helped the assault team by manning six .50-caliber machine guns, firing on enemy pillboxes across the river. They received heavy enemy fire from small arms, artillery, and mortars. One of the machine guns was knocked out; presumedly, it was at this point that Jim and another soldier were slightly wounded. The company medic put sulfanilamide powder on the wounds to prevent bacterial infection, then stitched and bandaged them. Jim returned to battle the next day.

Company B continued to support the 359th Regiment as it crossed the river and began attacking dozens of enemy pillboxes. The tankers often fired their cannons at the point-blank range of 100 yards, forcing the enemy to button down their firing apertures to withstand the fusillade. Finally, a determined soldier would have to approach, placing a C-2 explosive charge on the bunker's door, thus killing, wounding, or capturing its occupants. The 76mm cannon on the M4 Sherman was considered superior to the 75mm for penetrating bunkers. Its high-velocity armor-piercing (AP) shells, followed by heavy explosive (HE) rounds, often penetrated bunkers. If this didn't work, few bunkers would then survive a C-2 explosive charge placed by an infantryman.

As they continued to pass through villages, one of the scout platoon's Jeeps hit a mine. Three were killed and one wounded. Conditions continued to worsen with cold weather setting in, followed by heavy snows, and the roads became icy, with tanks slipping and spinning off them. The tanks had now been whitewashed to blend in with local conditions.

In early January 1945, the 712th pulled back across the Saar

River when it received emergency orders to proceed northward to help blunt a surprise attack by Germany in what became one of the largest battles of World War II, known as the Battle of the Bulge. A "bulge" evident on the map indicated where enemy forces had pushed back the Allies, indenting their defensive lines.

Led by Jim and the scouts, Company B traveled day and night cross-country on miles of treacherous, icy mountain roads. As they approached the battle, they began to see burnt-out vehicles and dead American soldiers all over the road. The tankers frequently stopped to move the frozen bodies out of the road, but in some cases, under fire, they had little choice but to roll over them. The cold was so severe that ice formed inside the tanks, and blowtorches were needed to warm up engines. Luckily, the tank's engine oil had been changed from 30-weight viscosity to the lighter 10-weight oil.

By January 9, 1945, the 712th Tank Battalion had arrived in the Ardennes region, which encompassed parts of France, Luxembourg, and Belgium, though much of the combat occurred in Belgium. They soon engaged the enemy. On the first day of the attack, their battalion commander was killed by artillery. Continuing to fight across snow-covered ridges, Company B suffered heavy losses in tanks and men. For weeks, the fight continued with men in slippery, cold tanks as M4 Shermans came up against Mark V Panzers, slugging it out in forests and fields.

The fighting was vicious. On one attack in mid-January, Company B knocked out eight Mark V tanks and six self-propelled guns and captured 150 prisoners, all in the face of numerous counterattacks.

By the end of January, the "bulge" had been eliminated, and territory was regained. Company B tanks passed through the devastated St. Vith with Jim and the scouts out front looking for alternative routes to the muddy, almost impassable roads. After continuous fighting for 25 days, Company B received 69 replacements for its dead and wounded.

In February, the battalion had earned a break for much-needed rest. Soldiers received hot showers and warm meals, and tanks received much-needed maintenance. Tank engines were repaired or replaced.

Jim and the scouts stayed busy uncovering minefields and calling in engineers to disable them. The small unit also captured groups of discouraged German soldiers who had determined that the war was in its final throes. At one point, the scout platoon shot a German motorcyclist carrying a complete set of enemy withdrawal plans; they quickly passed the plans up the line to headquarters.

The fast-moving scouts had been sleeping in their Jeeps or on the ground for months. As they progressed through Germany, accommodations improved, and they found themselves stretching out in relative leisure inside semi-demolished structures, barns, hay lofts, or deserted homes at night. K rations were still the meal of the day.

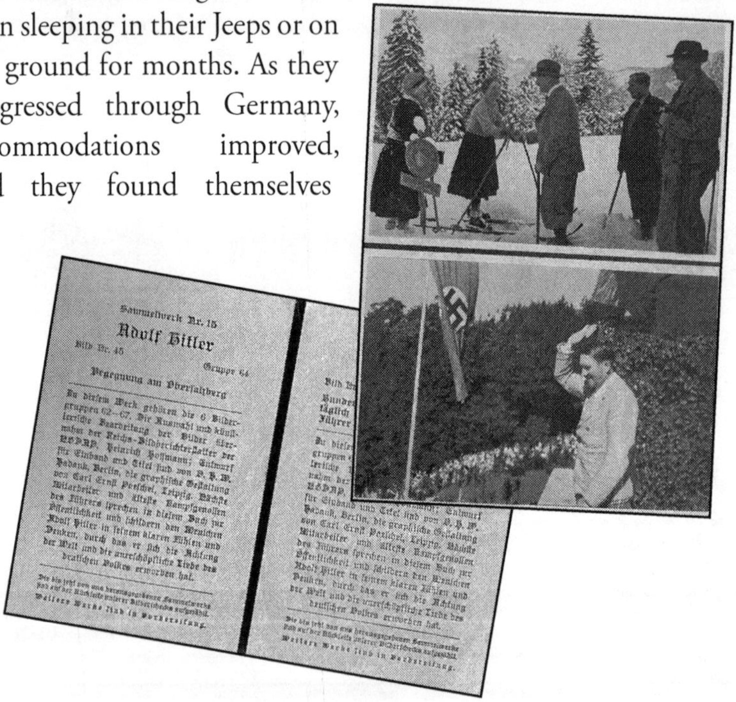

Promotional Hitler postcards that Jim picked up while moving through the various villages. (Courtesy of Garvie family)

In March 1945, Company B was back in action, crossing the

Rhine River and passing quickly through towns, sometimes moving so fast that German units came into the towns, not realizing Americans already occupied them.

The battalion continued to destroy pillboxes and enemy equipment. It began capturing thousands of soldiers and many artillery pieces, mortars, and even cars and motorcycles, often working under mortar and artillery fire as the Germans were forced to retreat.

The drawing of Rosemary, preserved over all these years. (Courtesy of Garvie family)

The tanks pushed through roadblocks, bypassing abandoned enemy equipment as resistance lessened. The tankers begin using prisoners of war for the dangerous work of clearing minefields. One of the prisoners that Jim got to know was a family man and an artist. After some effort at communicating, Jim located some sketch pencils, gave the prisoner a photo of his daughter Rosemary that he carried in his wallet, and the soldier drew a picture of her and signed it. Jim carried the sketch with him for the remainder of the war.

In April 1945, passing through the German town of Merkers, elements of the 712th supporting the 358th Infantry Regiment discovered a gigantic salt mine used by the Nazis to store an immense amount of wealth they had stolen. The unit retrieved over 100 tons of gold bullion, millions of dollars in American, French, and German currencies, and 200 masterpiece paintings and other highly valued art pieces. The mine's elevator had allowed the stolen goods to be stored 600 feet underground in over three miles of tunnels. The 712th guards helped retrieve them, and Companies C and D saw Generals Eisenhower, Bradley, and Patton inspect the recovered art.

The pace picked up, in pursuit of the retreating Germans. If towns displayed white flags, commanders met with the mayor and established regulations concerning curfew and weapons possession; if it was late in the day, they would also find houses to sleep in. If a town did not display white flags, it was approached with caution. Often, after soldiers firing three or four tank rounds down the main street, the citizenry would comply with orders.

Also, in April, the 712th participated in the liberation of the Flossenbürg death camp and the 1500 prisoners remaining alive. The scouts, even after seeing so much combat, could hardly comprehend the piles of bodies waiting to be incinerated and the unfathomable heaps of eyeglasses and shoes that had belonged to so many victims. These Americans, all part of the 90th Division, became known as the "Liberators of Flossenbürg."

War in Europe ended the following month, with Victory in Europe (VE) Day being declared on May 8, 1945. The 712th Tank Battalion's companies were at this time in Czechoslovakia enjoying a well-deserved rest. The men slept inside repaired Nazi barracks, ate at mess halls, and in their free time, swam, fished, and even did a bit of sightseeing. At one point, some 712th soldiers created a band called the "Downbeats" and published a newsletter called *Tank-Tracks*.

In mid-September 1945, four months after War in Europe ended, the 712th was moved by train to an area near Marseilles, where on October 15 they boarded the S.S. *George Washington* and arrived in New York on October 26. They were transported to Camp Joyce Kilmer, where former tank operators began to be discharged and headed home by train, plane, or bus.

The North Adams newspaper on October 27 announced: "Due at New York City- Pvt 1st Class James G. Garvie Jr., husband of Mrs. Yvonne Garvie of 92 Liberty Street, was due to arrive yesterday at New York City aboard the S.S. *George Washington*...Garvie entered the service in February 1944 and went overseas the following October."

Jim was honorably discharged on October 30, 1945, shortly after his arrival at the Separation Center in Fort Dix, New Jersey. In his twenty months of service, he spent eight months of direct

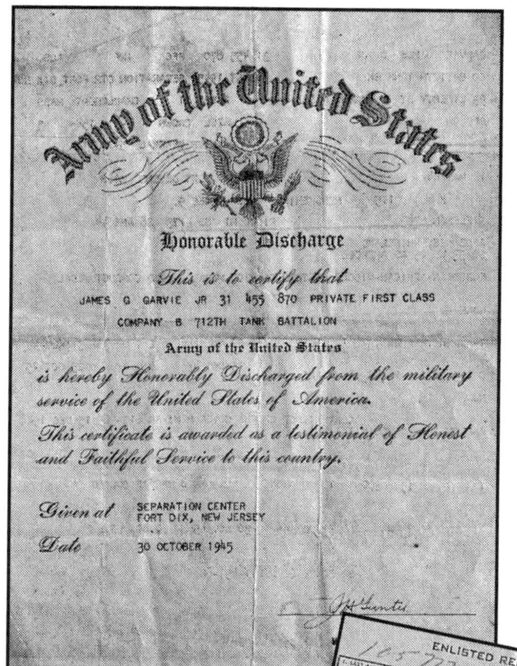

Army of the United States

Honorable Discharge

This is to certify that

JAMES G GARVIE JR 31 455 870 PRIVATE FIRST CLASS

COMPANY B 712TH TANK BATTALION

Army of the United States

is hereby Honorably Discharged from the military service of the United States of America.

This certificate is awarded as a testimonial of Honest and Faithful Service to this country.

Given at SEPARATION CENTER FORT DIX, NEW JERSEY

Date 30 OCTOBER 1945

and almost continuous combat with the 712th.

Delighted to be home and see Yvonne and the children, Jim returned to the work he knew best: painting, and started a company with a friend, J. Blondin. Their business, Blondin and Garvey, specialized in washing walls, woodwork, and ceilings.

ENLISTED RECORD AND REPORT OF SEPARATION
HONORABLE DISCHARGE

GARVIE JAMES G JR — 31 455 870 — PFC — INF — AUS
CO B 712TH TANK BN — 30 OCT 1945 — SEPARATION CTR FORT DIX NJ
93 LIBERTY ST N ADAMS MASS — 2 MAY 11 — CHARLEMONT MASS
SEE 9 — HAZEL BROWN 5-5 158 5
PAINTER GENERAL 5-27.010
16 MAY 44 — 16 MAR 44 — FORT DEVENS MASS
115 BERSKSHIRE MASS — SEE 9
RIFLEMAN 745 — RIFLE M1 SS 173 28 APR 44
ARDENNES, RHINELAND
GO 33 WD 45 AS AMENDED
EUROPEAN-AFRICAN-MIDDLE EASTERN SERVICE MEDAL, GOOD CONDUCT MEDAL
NONE
15APR44 15APR44 15APR44 NONE
0 5 11 1 2 4 PFC — 22 AUG 44 ETO 31 AUG 44
NONE — 15 OCT 45 USA 25 OCT 45
AR RR 1-1 (DEMOBILIZATION) CONVENIENCE OF THE GOVERNMENT AR 615-365 15 DEC 1944
NONE
1 7 15 300 — NONE — 8 0 0
X — J HARRIS COL FD
31 OCT 45 30 NOV 45 7.40 X
LAPEL BUTTON ISSUED
ASR SCORE (2 SEP 1945)-82
James G. Garvie — J E WHITE JR CAPT AC

Jim, known for his generosity, would accept whatever the customer could afford as payment. When he came home, Jim would tell Yvonne he had accepted less and that it was okay, they "would get by." She would gently admonish him, reminding him he also had a family to feed.

Jim's honorable discharge papers. (Courtesy of Garvie family)

Not long after returning from the war, Jim and Yvonne bought a house on Frederick Street in North Adams where they would raise their family. As the children grew up, Jim found work at Arnold Print Works as a crane operator and then a silk screener, and Yvonne found employment as a roller with the Sprague Electric Company.

Jim and Yvonne would continue to go fishing together, as they had when they first met, but now they involved their five children. Every summer, the couple would take the family on a two-week fishing expedition to Lake Champlain near Burlington, Vermont. Their white Plymouth Valiant would tow the family's rowboat packed with supplies for their campsite. A large two-room canvas tent would serve as their home while they fished daily for the evening meal.

Family photo taken in front of Drury High School, just after Jim returns home. (Courtesy of Garvie family)

At home, they would take the kids fishing for trout, bullhead, and perch at local rivers and ponds. These forays almost always included a friendly competition between mom and dad on who caught the most or landed the largest specimen.

The entire family helped manage the bait box, kept filled with worms and night crawlers in the backyard. The kids would bring out coffee grounds and collect leaves to nourish the bait and often went on nighttime flashlight hunts with Dad to capture more crawlers.

Jim and Yvonne were also avid Red Sox fans. They relished evenings sitting together at the kitchen table smoking Viceroys, playing Rummy, and listening to night baseball games on the transistor radio. If the Sox were losing, Jim would get out of his chair and walk around it three times for good luck. With the advent of black-and-white TV, the couple also enjoyed watching candle-pin bowling on Saturday mornings and knew the statistics of their favorite bowlers. Whenever the National Anthem was played on TV, Jim would stand, place his hand on his heart, and gently sing along with the commentator.

He seldom talked about the war, other than the fact that he participated in the Battle of the Bulge. He did mention the German soldier-artist he guarded and that he spent several nights in one of Hitler's houses, although he never identified which one. He occasionally said that he had "walked—or ridden—through most of Germany." Almost daily, he would sing his favorite song, "If You're Only a Soldier Boy," to his children and grandchildren, who often harmonized with him.

Jim, a gentle, loving family man and patriot, was diagnosed with Alzheimer's dementia and, as the deadly disease progressed, he was admitted to the Veterans Hospital in Albany, New York, where Yvonne and the children frequently visited him.

Jim passed away on August 26, 1972. He was one of the 1,200 valiant men, including those first to the war and their replacements, who served with the 712th Tank Battalion as it fought in five major campaigns across Europe, Germany, and Belgium, a tremendous feat for which they earned five Unit Citations for meritorious service. As a scout, the bravest of men, Jim had to go first so others could later follow. And so it was in death, as in life.

Robert T. Leitch
Navigator
447th Bombardment Group

Bob was anxiously looking forward to his first mission. As his bomber, the "Barbara Jane," approached her target, the plane right in front of them exploded. Bob's handwritten note read, "On my first mission, the B-17 in front of us blew up near the target area, two chutes were seen." Ten airmen fly on a B-17, and though it was a hopeful sign that some were able to parachute out, their landing would bring a new set of challenges. It was a harsh introduction to his new world and the beginning of what seemed like a daunting goal, surviving death's constant presence while achieving the Army Air Force's 30-mission requirement.

ROBERT THEODORE LEITCH WAS born on February 16, 1924, to Arthur L. and Helen (Dziok) Leitch at Plunkett Memorial Hospital in Adams, Massachusetts. His middle name is a tribute to his Uncle Teddy. Robert would be the middle son, born between brothers Arthur and Ralph.

W.B. Plunkett Memorial Hospital was relatively new when Robert was born. Built in 1918, the hospital served the local community for fifty-five years until its closure in 1973. It had been named for William B. Plunkett, the President of Berkshire Cotton Manufacturing Co. The Plunketts were a family of local textile industrialists who were friends of President William McKinley and known for their generosity throughout the Berkshires. It was a community hospital open to everyone. In 2000, the hospital was converted to condominiums for seniors. A Folklore & Haunted

Location Guide reports that unidentified spirits still roam the old hospital today.

Robert's father, Arthur, was of Scottish heritage, and a long-time employee of General Electric as a highly skilled machinist and toolmaker. Sadly, he died suddenly from a heart attack at age 52.

Of Polish ancestry, Helen lived a long life, passing away at 97. Early in life, she had worked as a bobbin tender at one of the local mills and, after Arthur's death, was employed at Woolworth's on Park Street and the well-known Miss Adams Diner.

Growing up, Robert (known to all as Bob) and his older brother were close, mischievous, and always involved in some caper. They attended Hoosac Street Elementary School, and many a day after school, they would stop at the Polish Bakery to pick up rye bread for ten cents to eat on their walk home.

His mom fretted when she heard of his daredevil antics, whether it was diving from the highest rocks at Tophet Brook or the tower at Anthony's Pond. In his quieter moments, he enjoyed playing marbles and collecting baseball cards. He hunted and fished the local brooks, usually with Arthur and his best friend, Leonard.

Bob attended Adams High School and, by all measures, was a serious and ambitious student. He enjoyed mathematics, which would play a role later in military service. He was often on the school's honor roll and perfect attendance list. After school and in the summers, he worked as a clerk/salesman at Schiff's Clothing Store on Summer Street, sometimes modeling clothes during the store's special events. One of his more mundane tasks was shoveling water out of the store after the 1936 Great Flood.

As he became accustomed to dressing up, he continued this habit when attending high school. Although sometimes heckled by jeans-wearing students, he enjoyed donning a dress shirt, slacks, tie, and jacket to attend school.

Robert played the banjo as a member of the school's orchestra. Together with the Glee Club, the school's chorus and band performed at several well-regarded concerts. The orchestra itself performed the

Strauss waltzes "East of Suez (Intermezzo Orientale)," and "Petite Suite de Ballet," and also the Russian sailors' dance from "Red Poppy" (*Transcript,* 4-18-41).

When he graduated from Adams High School in June 1943 alongside 115 other students, the ceremony took on a somber note, with twenty-two young men in attendance having been inducted into the military just the day before. The class of 1943 was graduating amid World War II.

Bob underwent a military physical the same month as graduation, was inducted shortly afterward, and headed to eight weeks of basic training at the Army Air Force (AAF) Basic Training Center located in Greensboro, North Carolina. His daily regimen included military customs and courtesies, daily drills, and strengthening physical activities. Testing revealed a high math aptitude, and the Army classified him as a pre-aviation cadet. Once basic was completed, the Army sent Bob to the University of Cincinnati for eight additional weeks of training.

From there, Bob was ordered to Ellington Field in Texas for eight weeks of pre-flight instruction at the San Antonio Aviation Cadet Center (SAACC).

In February 1944, continuing to excel, Bob was transferred to San Marcos, Texas, for eighteen weeks of advanced navigator training. *The Transcript* reported that he was "One of 17 Massachusetts members in a new class of aviation cadets and students assigned to the Army Air Forces Navigation School at San Marcos, Texas, for an advanced course in aerial navigation. Upon completion of the course, the members will qualify for the silver wings of the aerial navigator and be commissioned as a second lieutenant" (2-12-44).

The rigorous training involved many complex subjects, including celestial navigation and dead reckoning. Each candidate was required to have 100 hours in local and long-distance navigation to graduate.

Ellington Field had expanded in 1940 to train tens of thousands of AAF recruits, resulting in six 8-inch-thick concrete runways and taxi aprons, boasting that it had the largest piece of cement in the United States. The complex also had five control towers, two huge steel hangers for storing and maintaining aircraft, five mess halls, and seventy-four two-story cadet barracks. The aviation cadets flew one of the 350 single-engine trainers on site.

Bob, shortly after qualifying as a radar navigator. (Courtesy of Leitch family)

Bob graduated and received his silver wings. Before going overseas, he had several weeks of additional Instructor Navigator Training in Boca Raton, Florida, and then completed a stint with the Replacement Training Unit (RTU) on a B-17 at MacDill Field in Tampa, Florida. He also served briefly at Langley Field in Virginia. Bob was now qualified as a radar/navigator crew member.

The B-17 (heavy) bomber introduced in the late 1930s became the Army Air Force's workhorse during World War II. Known as the "Flying Fortress," the aluminum cylinder-shaped plane weighed 65,000 pounds and cost Boeing $250,000 to build. It was powered by four 1200-horsepower Wright engines and carried up to 8,000 pounds of bombs. The plane sported thirteen .50-caliber machine guns for protection and could cruise at 160 miles per hour, although on the attack it could reach speeds of over 300 miles per hour. The vaunted plane had a 100-foot wingspan, was 75 feet wide, and 19 feet tall. Inside, it had cramped quarters and the narrowest of passageways for the ten-man crew to negotiate.

Bob flew with his crew from Langley Field to Manchester, New Hampshire, then to Labrador, Canada, with stops in Greenland and Scotland before landing in England. He ended up, finally, at Royal

Air Force Base Rattlesden (Airfield Station-126), in the county of Suffolk on England's eastern coast. Built in 1942, it was like dozens of other bases across the English countryside, with three intersecting runways, control towers, and simple metal huts built to house B-17 crews. Crew accommodations were minimal, with concrete or dirt floors, bunks lining the walls, and a coal-burning metal stove in the hut's center that kept no one warm.

He had been assigned as a radar operator-navigator with the 709th Bomb Squadron, 447th Bombardment Group. The 709th was one of four squadrons (708th, 709th, 710th, and 711th) in the group and flew between twelve and eighteen B-17G bombers.

The 447th flew its first missions out of Rattlesden on Christmas Eve 1943. During the war, the 447th flew 257 missions out of the airfield and achieved one of the best bombing accuracy records, often placing their bombs within 1,000 feet of the target. It came at a cost: the 447th lost 97 aircraft and hundreds of crew members.

The biggest enemies of the Flying Fortress were German flak guns known as eighty-eights (the millimeter size of its shells) and enemy fighters. The German 88s, with a ten-man crew, fired 12 to 15 high-explosive rounds a minute. The nine pounds of explosives created a wall of shrapnel for the planes to pass through. The Messerschmitt Bf-109 and the Focke-Wulf 190, two of the best fighters in World War II, were the backbone of the German Air Force (*Luftwaffe*), both fast, maneuverable, and deadly interceptors of bomber squadrons.

Bob's position was located in the nose of the plane, sharing the cramped space with a bombardier. They would have a limited view, provided by a plexiglass nose cone. Working off a small table with his navigator's map and plotting charts, Bob would continuously plot the plane's location as it proceeded to the target and then helped get the plane home. He also maintained the mission log that recorded when they reached the intended target and the coordinates of enemy activity. His location in the aircraft and the plexiglass cone provided a scary ringside seat to countless puffs of black anti-aircraft shells exploding, planes being hit, and some parachutes opening. Too often, there were many fewer than 10.

He was in front of and slightly below the plane's pilots, with whom he would talk most of the flight. When not busy navigating, Bob used a nearby .50-caliber machine gun to ward off enemy fighters. The bone-chilling cold was omnipresent; the crew wore their long johns and flight overalls over wool pants and shirts and donned fleece-lined boots, pants, and jackets, but nothing seemed to overcome the minus 55-degree temperatures. Fortunately for their appendages, their gloves and socks were also plugged into the plane's electrical system.

Their mission routinely started with an early morning breakfast, a briefing on primary and secondary targets, a Jeep ride to their plane, and then takeoff, first assembling overhead and then heading toward the objective. Fog was a persistent problem in England as the formation assembled with bombers; because they'd gather 100 feet apart, midair collisions were a constant concern.

Bob's position as a navigator allowed him to make contemporaneous notes, an absolute treasure to later historians. He described a typical morning:

> *Some missions, takeoff was fogged in—were only able to see the side of the runway—took off in runway direction—then climbed in a set pattern until getting over clouds at probably 3500 feet. Fighter support would be picked up at the coast because of gas—we would get another group of fighters at the target area. Our loads were so heavy on one occasion the pilot took three trips to get up speed before getting lift off.*
>
> *Flights started by forming squadron, Group, Wings, Division—all had assigned times along the coast into Europe to get all lined up—if two minutes off, two groups would be in the same space.*

Though takeoff and assembly were tightly timed, portions of

the often eight-hour flights would be boring, often giving the crew far too much time to ponder all the patches in their aluminum cylinder from previous missions.

The Allies took shifts: United States planes bombed targets during daylight; the British bombed at night.

Bob's first mission was on October 2, 1944; the target was Kassel, Germany, the headquarters of the German High Command and combat tank production facilities. He and his crew were most likely given the "tail-end Charlie" spot until they had more experience. Bob's notes from that day focus on the B-17 that exploded in front of his plane, with only two crew members able to escape, only two chutes floating down. Overall, the 8th Air Force considered the mission a success. Bob's crew would change planes during their missions depending on which B-17s were serviceable, so they had to be adaptable and comfortable in different aircraft. He was often in the Barbara Jane and the Leading Lady.

Bob and the crew in front of the *Barbara Jane*; he is on the far right of the second row. (Courtesy of Leitch family)

His notes from the first mission also say:

> *The experienced crew I flew with on my first mission had trouble on their next and last mission. They were all shot up coming thru Ruhr Valley and having trouble. British Spitfires (a fighter plane) helped by shooting at the flak towers so the American plane would not get shot down—the British lost one Spitfire.*

The crew was assigned to bomb shipyards, airfields, railroads, sub-pens, tank production facilities, refineries, and any industrial complex that supported the Nazi war machine. Five days later, on his fifth mission, Bob navigated his B-17 over Merseburg, near Leipzig, Germany, a high-value target whose refinery was critical to Hitler's war machine. This mission awarded Bob his first Air Medal, which he received in November. Depending on the theater of war, Air Medals were awarded after a certain number of sorties. In Bob's case, it was after his fifth perilous mission.

The citation read: "For meritorious achievement while participating in heavy bombardment missions in the air offensive against the enemy over Continental Europe. The courage, coolness, and skill distinguished by Leitch on these occasions reflect great credit upon himself and the Armed Forces of the United States" (*Transcript,* 11-13-44).

His notes say:

> *On the mission to Mersberg [sic] where the German synthetic oil was made, our crew chief counted holes in the plane—over 200—the area had 2000 88s shooting at us—on two occasions, they shot down 30 B17s in one day.*

In November, another navigator in the adjacent 711th squadron, 2nd Lieutenant Robert "Bob" Femoyer, was cited for extraordinary heroism when he successfully navigated a crippled B-17 back to

Rattlesden Airfield. After receiving terrible flak wounds to his back and body, he refused medical treatment and guided his crippled plane home. He died shortly after landing, and received the Medal of Honor.

Bob Leitch probably knew Bob Femoyer and had raided the same site, Merseburg. Many at the time called the assignment the "Dreaded Merseburg." It was thought to be better protected than Berlin.

When back on base, Bob had the experience of hearing and seeing German buzz bombs fly over. The 27-foot bombs (a version of an early cruise missile) emitted an engine buzzing noise and carried 1800-pound warheads. The deadly missile, usually flying 3,000 feet at 300 miles per hour, devastated cities and killed over 6,000 English civilians. The threat would be eliminated only after Allied troops landed in France and destroyed their launch sites.

Bob's missions continued; some were daily, others with four or five days of rest in between. On one mission, the plane's tire was shot off, and when landing, they skidded off the runway into a field. As he gained experience (and a solid reputation), Bob would serve as the lead navigator/radar for his squadron and group on many of

Relieved to be safely on the ground, Bob, in the light colored flight suit, is seen here laughing. (Courtesy of Leitch family)

his thirty missions. Being up front in large formations is a dangerous spot often targeted by enemy aircraft to disrupt bombing efforts. In his notes, he wrote, *we knew where the German guns were—so a good navigator would change course to stay away from them.*

On one of his last flights in early April 1945 near Kiel, Germany, the crew caught sight of a Messerschmitt Me 262, the world's first jet-powered fighter. Its speed of 540 miles an hour was 100 miles an hour faster than the United States' fastest, the 51-Mustang fighter. There was no tracking it as it sped by in a blur. Fortunately, the jet was introduced near the end of World War II, and only 300 of them saw combat. Germany was in the midst of a final assault by the Allies on its production facilities and was suffering from a lack of pilots.

While the crew's target sites were generally in Germany, their last flight on April 15, 1945, was in France. Bob's B-17, Leading Lady, was part of a massive 1000-plane bombing raid near the city of Royan, in an area called the Royan Pocket where thousands of enemy soldiers had refused to surrender. His plane was selected to lead the mission, which involved his squadron's first use of napalm bombs. The bombs created what was described as a "blazing furnace" on the ground, leading to the enemy's capitulation. His notes say, *napalm bomb used for the first time on mission with 30-foot arming wires to assure clearance of plane.*

On an earlier mission, he wrote,

> *We were on the bomb runs with about 2 or 3 minutes to go—when looking up—we were looking into the bomb bay of one of the high squadron planes that was out of position—a call got him moved—what would be worst [sic] than being knocked down by one of your own planes—it had happened [before]. B-17 bomber formations had squadron planes in the lead and other planes following in higher and lower altitudes to provide all-around protection against enemy fighters.*

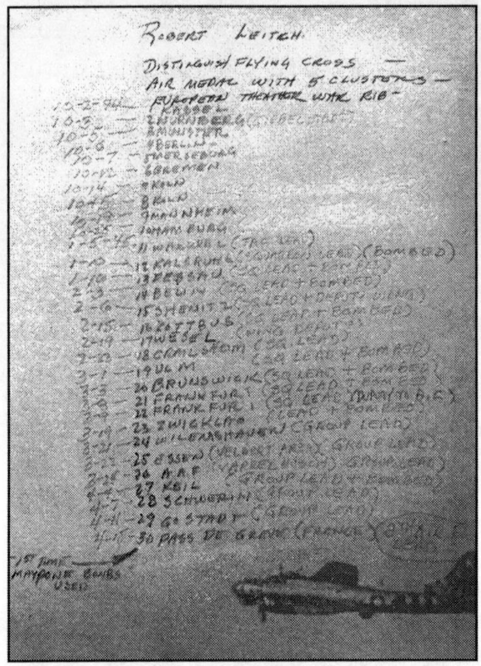

Bob's handwritten notes showing dates and places of all thirty missions. (Courtesy of Leitch family)

On April 15, 1945, Bob reached his 30th mission and qualified to return to the United States. He considers himself lucky. US Bomber Commands had an extremely high casualty rate, losing over 55,000 crewmen, an estimated 44% death rate.

Bob was also recognized for leading his squadron into battle and received the Distinguished Flying Cross. The citation read, "Lieut. Leitch demonstrated exceptional proficiency and extraordinary achievement in navigating to the assigned targets in devastating attacks against industries at Dessau, Frankfurt, and Zwickau, Germany, despite anti-aircraft fire on every mission. The courageous devotion to duty and expert navigational techniques displayed by Lieut. Leitch, on these occasions, reflects the highest credit on himself and the Army Air Forces" (*Transcript*, 7-19-45).

He arrived in the United States in late May 1945 and was granted a 30-day leave as reported in the local newspaper: "Robert T. Leitch Visits in Adams.... During his tour of duty, Lieut. Leitch made nine bomb runs through complete cloud coverage. He was a lead radar navigator-bombardier and, in that position, led many types of formations, including the 8th Air Force on one of its 1,300 plane raids" (*Transcript*, 5-29-45).

Bob was honorably discharged at Fort Devens in October 1945. Not long after his return home, while on furlough, Bob met

Ellen Schwab at Simon's Soda Shop, a popular youth hangout on Park Street. Ellen worked at an insurance agency above the store. The uniformed, bemedaled, handsome young man made a lasting impression. After dating for months, they became engaged, and they married on July 27, 1946, at St. Thomas Church in Adams. When teased about the whirlwind romance, Ellen would say, "It must have been the uniform!"

Bob was selected as a General Electric drafting trainee in January 1946. After completing his apprenticeship, he worked at G.E. for his entire career, retiring as Manager of the Power Transformer Drafting Department. Ellen, who is still alive, worked as an accountant most of her life before retiring as the treasurer for the Charles H. McCann Technical School.

The couple had two sons, Robert and James, and lived on North Summer Street in Adams. When they first purchased the home, it needed repair, and Bob quickly became embroiled in its renovation, which included all the mechanical systems. One son remembers him recounting that the first winter they lived in the house right after his brother was born, "there would be frost on the nail heads of the interior walls" as they had only a parlor stove for heat.

He didn't talk much about the war. He mentioned they often returned from missions with their plane riddled with holes so that "it looked like Swiss cheese." On missions, "bullets would fly through the fuselage within inches" of him.

With his outgoing and sunny personality, he always kept himself busy. Bob loved gardening, both vegetables and flowers. He enjoyed harvesting the fruit from his yard's apple, pear, and cherry trees. Bob was known for making the best sauerkraut in large crocks in the basement, which Ellen would can for winter.

Another of his hobbies was making homemade root beer soda. It was a family affair involving sanitizing bottles, siphoning the mix out of a huge kettle into bottles, and capping the bottles with a hand press. The bottles would get stacked next to a radiator to ferment.

Sometimes, at night, the boys would hear a bottle explode.

One of his biggest projects was designing and building a vacation cabin on a lot in Windsor, Massachusetts. Building this getaway close to Windsor Pond would take almost a decade. It took years to cut down trees, remove stumps, and dig out the long driveway by hand to access the construction location. Bob worked with hand saws and axes, sometimes burning out the stumps. He also hand-dug and installed the well and septic system.

The foundation was also dug out by hand, with concrete mixed and poured by hand into 55-gallon drums. The cabin's lumber was salvaged by dismantling local barns. Nails were pulled from the lumber for reuse, and any broken lumber was trimmed. His son James still remembers melting snow off the roof in the springtime and mixing it with concrete. Every trip to the camp required a trunk full of rocks to repair the soft spots in the driveway.

The two-story structure had a first-floor kitchen, living room, and porch with a wood stove for heat, and the second floor was a huge sleeping alcove with six or seven beds.

This labor of love would be used for years as a vacation spot for the family. Bob would always spend his two weeks of summer vacation at the camp with his family and then commute to G.E. for the rest of the summer while they remained to enjoy it.

Bob's love of the outdoors didn't go away in winter; family could find him in Windsor, trudging his way up to shovel snow off the cabin's roof, and there was always wood to chop. He and his boys used their rowboat to fish for catfish and trout, and the whole family would go on blueberry-picking excursions. Bob also hunted deer with his son in Windsor and nearby Savoy.

When not at the camp, the family would vacation in upstate New York, visiting Lake George and the Catskill Mountains in the family's late model Chevy Impala, "the one with wings and backup lights that looked like eyes," remembered his son.

His family describes Bob as having an upbeat personality, hardworking, and outgoing, although at times serious. In his military pictures, it's easy to pick out the thin, six-foot two-inch crewman who is usually smiling.

Bob's military separation papers state, "He flew as a navigator a total of 625 hours, 231 of which were combat hours comprising a total of 30 combat missions....was the lead radar and bombardier for 20 combat missions. Received the following awards: Distinguished Flying Cross, Air Medal with 4 Oak Leaf Clusters, European–African–Middle Eastern Service Medal with 2 Battle Stars, and 1 overseas service bar for nine months overseas."

In Bob's words, *During wars such as WWII, you should be afraid—could be afraid...[But] I don't remember being afraid—the reason [being] I was so busy during the mission I didn't have time for it.*

He and the many Allied aircrews based in England would be the epitome of heroism: day-after-day donning heavy flight gear, climbing aboard patched-up planes, and flying hundreds of miles across unfriendly Channel waters into the teeth of heavy enemy resistance, knowing there was but a 50% chance of survival. This Berkshire boy beat the odds and, lucky for us, lived to tell about it.

RENO L. MASELLI
RIFLEMAN
147TH INFANTRY REGIMENT

Reno's regiment landed on a bomb-devastated atoll, ordered to clear the island of the few remaining enemy soldiers. A mopping-up operation began with little resistance. Then what they found were thousands of Japanese soldiers entrenched in sophisticated, deep, concrete bunkers, many willing to fight to their death, and so commenced a months-long slog of killing or capturing enemy soldiers and neutralizing the island. In one narrow valley, Reno and his foxhole buddy were under fire for three days, unable to move, only periodically peeking out of their shallow foxhole…until one of them was hit in the head by a sniper.

RENO MASELLI'S PARENTS, LIKE many others, immigrated to the United States from northern Italy at the turn of the nineteenth century. His father, Modesto, arrived in 1902, and his mom, Elide Domenchi, came in 1907. They met at Saint Anthony's Church in North Adams, Massachusetts, and were married there on December 22, 1913.

For the first five years of their marriage, they lived and found work in a little village twenty miles away called Mountain Mills, a borough of Wilmington, Vermont. The area employed hundreds of newly arrived immigrants to cut trees, create railroad beds, and lay track for a narrow-gauge railroad running from Massachusetts to Vermont. Modesto was a laborer for the Hoot-Toot-and-Whistle railroad.

Elide, a hard worker in her own right, operated a disciplined, profitable boarding house for laborers and lumberjacks.

While they were there, the New England Power Company began a hydroelectric project and built a reservoir that would eventually harness the Deerfield River and create Lake Whitingham, one of Vermont's largest bodies of water. During this effort, three cemeteries were moved, and the settlement of Mountain Mills ceased to exist; its boarding house, store, post office, and several nearby brothels were forever submerged underwater.

Returning to the North Adams–Clarksburg area, Modesto worked at Arnold Print Works and also as a furnace fireman at the local Paramount Theater. During their time in Vermont, the couple had started a family, and once in Clarksburg, Elide would initially remain home to raise their four boys and a girl.

Over time, both Modesto and Elide would become employed by the Sprague Electric Company working piecework positions, assembling capacitors, and earning a little less than ten dollars per week for 5½ days of work. Elide served as an outspoken union representative, and the two stayed at Sprague until their retirement.

Their fourth child, Reno, was born at their home in Clarksburg on January 12, 1925. He and his siblings attended Clarksburg Elementary School. It was a loving household, with their father Modesto having a quiet, calm, and easygoing temperament and their mother Elide having quite the opposite; she was boisterous, self-assured, and outspoken.

Early in life, Reno seemed predisposed to music. He often reached up to play the keys on his mother's organ. It wasn't long before he started private lessons at age ten, costing $1.50 per hour, and traveling to Pittsfield several times a week. He soon began forming local bands with other musical kids nearby.

During high school, he worked odd jobs as a laborer; at one point, he cemented shanks to the insoles of shoes for Gale Shoe Manufacturing Company. He remained at Drury High School until his sophomore/junior year (1941). For five months before entering the service, he was employed at the Norad Knitting Mill as a bobbin boy. On this fast-paced job, he was responsible for filling and changing bobbins on fifteen looms.

He received his draft notice and decided to enlist in the Army. Inducted into service on May 19, 1943, he began active duty on June 2, 1943, when he traveled by train to Pittsfield, Massachusetts, the furthest he had been away from home, then on to Camp Wheeler in Macon, Georgia.

The sprawling Army base was used as a training camp for recruits destined to serve as replacements for combat casualties. In an oral history recorded by his son-in-law, Reno describes the thirteen weeks of basic, rising at 6:00 a.m. and often training until 9:00 p.m. in hot and humid Georgia weather. He talks about tough drill sergeants and an obstacle course, crawling through it with live machine gun fire overhead. It was where he first threw a hand grenade and was drilled on the use of the M1 rifle, the BAR, the bazooka, and the flamethrower.

In the oral history, he describes the hardest part of the thirteen weeks as a 25-mile forced march with rifles and full packs weighing at least 35 pounds. When liberty was available, he noted how the Georgia bartenders always served Southerners first and made the likely Northerners wait. His New England accent put him in this category. He attributed the obvious disdain to leftover Civil War sentiments.

Reno as a recent basic training graduate, proudly wearing his marksmanship badge. (Courtesy of Maselli family)

He also related a time when he headed into town on a local bus and gave up his seat to an elderly black woman. The bus driver, who was armed with a pistol, immediately stopped the bus, told the woman to get to the back where she belonged, and then strongly cautioned Reno never to do that again.

After basic training, Reno had a brief fourteen-day home furlough and then traveled by troop train across the country, reporting to Camp Stoneman at Pittsburg, California, for embarkation. He remembers in his oral history that the trip across the country was surprisingly fun, with a bunch of young guys just acting up.

Camp Stoneman was the largest troop staging area on the West Coast for those deploying during World War II. In just three years, from 1942 to 1945, over 1,000,000 men would deploy from there. Reno arrived at Camp Stoneman in the fall of 1943, a year after it had opened.

The 2800-acre camp could house and feed 20,000 troops awaiting deployment and also served as a POW stockade for German and Italian prisoners. The camp was often described as "a city unto itself" with over 300 barracks, numerous mess halls, a post office, a library, a stockade, basketball courts, and boxing rings. At the time, it was one of the largest call centers in the United States, containing 75 phone booths with operators handling 2,000 calls daily.

Reno would be on site for only four or five days of processing that included medical exams, inoculations, fitting for eyeglasses, preparation of wills, and any final dental work in one of the 45 dental chairs running continuously eighteen hours a day.

Reno's equipment would be checked as well, especially the two most essential items to an infantryman: his M1 rifle and his shoes. Soldiers would also be routed through last-minute classes on how to abandon ship and how to administer first aid. There was a palpable urgency to get these needed replacements overseas.

The men were trucked to wharves for their departure and passed under a sign that read, "Through these portals pass the best damn soldiers in the world." An hours-long ferry ride then delivered the troops to piers in San Francisco.

In his recorded oral history, Reno remembers getting on a boat near Oakland, California, looking up as they passed under the

Golden Gate Bridge, and wondering if he would ever see it again, reflecting that many did not return home alive to do so.

He left the United States on December 10, 1943, spending over twenty days on the packed, humid troop ship, often below deck. Everyone on the ship was a replacement. They tried to get topside whenever possible, but most of their time was limited to playing cards, telling stories, and reading paperbacks. This would be the beginning of a two-year combat odyssey.

On Christmas Eve, 1943, Reno arrived overseas and, a short time later, was assigned to the 147th Infantry Regiment and transported with the 3rd Battalion aboard the USS *George O. Squier* to Noumea, New Caledonia, arriving in February 1944. It was his first real chance to disembark, a new landscape for a young man who until recently had never left the Berkshires. He found the island beautiful and picturesque, a first impression that stayed with him. The island was relatively safe; it had been secured months before, becoming the central South Pacific Fleet base for the US Navy. On New Caledonia, Reno, as a casualty replacement, said goodbye to his friends, some he had known since leaving North Adams. As with most replacements, it took him some time to make new friends and be accepted by his new unit, who were likely mourning the losses that brought him there in the first place.

THE 147TH INFANTRY

THE 147TH INFANTRY REGIMENT was part of the 37th "Buckeye" Division, an Ohio National Guard unit, with a history of service extending back to the Civil War, including participation in several major World War I battles.

During World War II, the 147th Regiment was detached from its division, a strategic choice that meant the 147th spent almost its entire combat duty supporting the Marines by fighting and mopping up thousands of entrenched enemy soldiers on islands after the

Marines departed. The regiment spent so much time with other military branches that they became known as the "lost regiment" or the "Gypsies of the Pacific."

The 147th Regiment consisted of three battalions totaling over 100 officers and 2700 enlisted men. In addition to a headquarters unit, each battalion had four 200-man companies. The 1st Battalion had companies A, B, C, and D; the 2nd with E, F, G, and H; and the 3rd Battalion (Reno's) had Company I as well as J, K, and L.

These several thousand young men would fight in some of the Pacific's most brutal battles, often in the shadow of the US Marines and Navy. Though categorized as mop-up or garrison troops, they would instead find themselves thrown into direct combat with the enemy. The 147th saw its first combat on Guadalcanal. In January and February 1942, Company I, which would soon be Reno's company, served as a blocking force cutting off Japanese escape routes, allowing other Marine and Army units to secure the island.

The 147th Regiment patch, whose motto, *Cargoneek Guyoxim*, is a Chippewa phrase meaning Always Ready. (Courtesy of Maselli family)

On New Caledonia, Reno and his battalion established themselves at Camp Stevens on the western coast and continued to take small-arms weapons and hand-to-hand combat training. (In 1853, Napoleon III had claimed the remote location of New Caledonia for the French government where it became a penal colony incarcerating thousands of convicts and political prisoners.)

In Reno's oral history, he comments on New Caledonia's beauty, lauding its picturesque landscapes and beaches. He notes that the natives are friendly and that many of the adults have stained teeth.

At the time, a local custom was to chew betel, which darkened teeth and was believed to make them firmer. Reno was probably meeting members of the close-knit, indigenous Kanek tribe dominated by family-based clans. They were first documented in western history by the British explorer Captain Cook in 1774; the tribe itself had undergone horrible subjugation by slavers who carried them off to other islands for brutal plantation work.

After several months, the 147th stopped in New Guinea, off the coast of Australia, and some of its units would conduct brief mopping-up operations for the few Japanese holdouts. Reno noted his company received training at this time from Australian soldiers (he called them Aussies) who were noted for their expertise in jungle warfare, and the unit learned camouflaging and patrolling techniques.

On April 11, 1944, Reno's unit was ordered to occupy the island of Emirau, about 200 miles away from New Guinea, and relieve the invasion troops. The 147th was charged to perform garrison duties and help the Seabees construct an airfield. As part of the 3rd Marine Division, the 147th Regiment would provide tactical relief and security during the construction. It also became Reno's initiation into combat.

One of the few surviving photographs of Reno in the field. (Courtesy of Maselli family)

The small island (several miles long and less than one mile across) was a thicket of jungle with muddy and often impassible roads. As the Seabees worked, the 3rd Battalion guarded them, with Reno's company conducting combat patrols and ambushes. He noted how the local people "helped us find the Japanese holdouts." For his unit, camp was primitive, first in damp, mildewed tents with muddy floors, then, eventually, rough wood-hewed buildings replaced the tents. Showers were infrequent and often taken during a rainstorm or in the nearby ocean.

Other units of the 147th conducted enemy-clearing operations on the islands of Saipan and Tinian. When relieved, the entire regiment returned to Camp Bailey in Noumea, New Caledonia, in July 1944 aboard the Dutch vessel *Brastagi*. They would remain there for almost six months for additional training, resupply, and to receive replacements. The regiment surgeon noted that 85% of the unit had experienced a bout with malaria in 1944. Reno is thought to have contracted malaria while moving between different islands.

In September, the 147th was combined with an artillery unit designated a Regimental Combat Team. For the following months, the men would see intensified training on jungle warfare and small unit patrolling, but now training was expanded to include amphibious landing techniques and rope ladders.

In February 1945, the regiment learned that the Marines had landed on Iwo Jima, waiting to know whether this would be their next assignment. In early March 1945, Reno's 3rd Battalion boarded the USS *Alkaid*, and shortly after departure, the troops were told that Iwo Jima would be their next stop. They were ordered to provide garrison support and mop up the few hundred remaining enemy soldiers. (The number of holdouts was vastly underestimated.)

While on board, the men started their days with briefings and then turned to sharpening bayonets, cleaning their rifles, and filling ammunition belts with clean bullets. They wrote letters, played cards, and read.

In late March 1945, they landed on the secured Purple beach. Reno's battalion would be assigned to patrol the southern third of the island. The volcanic island, with its large swath of sulfur fields, had a distinct odor and was particularly hot. Turning over the wrong rock might produce a shaft of steam, potentially scalding a soldier. There was no island drinking water; it was brought to land from the ships, and to further add to the misery index, wind blew nearly all the time, bringing with it fine black sand that covered the men and fouled their weapons.

As soon as they landed, Reno and his company started conducting daylight patrols, nighttime ambushes, and cave assaults while providing round-the-clock security for the island's air bases. Even though the island had been "pacified" when the initial assault force of Marines had come through, there were still thousands of enemy soldiers on the island. Battles with the holdouts were bitter and savage, and often meant rooting out a well-supplied, cave-hidden enemy; the Americans resorted to using grenades, flamethrowers, gasoline, and explosives. Sometimes, interpreters and recent captives were successful in getting Japanese soldiers to surrender.

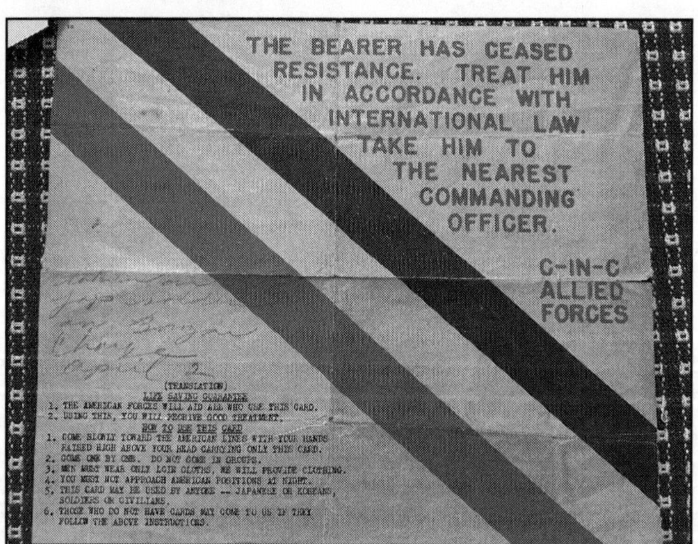

THE BEARER HAS CEASED RESISTANCE. TREAT HIM IN ACCORDANCE WITH INTERNATIONAL LAW. TAKE HIM TO THE NEAREST COMMANDING OFFICER.

C-IN-C ALLIED FORCES

(TRANSLATION)

LIFE SAVING GUARANTEE

1. THE AMERICAN FORCES WILL AID ALL WHO USE THIS CARD.
2. USING THIS, YOU WILL RECEIVE GOOD TREATMENT.

HOW TO USE THIS CARD

1. COME SLOWLY TOWARD THE AMERICAN LINES WITH YOUR HANDS RAISED HIGH ABOVE YOUR HEAD CARRYING ONLY THIS CARD.
2. COME ONE BY ONE. DO NOT COME IN GROUPS.
3. MEN MUST WEAR ONLY LOIN CLOTHS, WE WILL PROVIDE CLOTHING.
4. YOU MUST NOT APPROACH AMERICAN POSITIONS AT NIGHT.
5. THIS CARD MAY BE USED BY ANYONE -- JAPANESE OR KOREANS, SOLDIERS OR CIVILIANS.
6. THOSE WHO DO NOT HAVE CARDS MAY COME TO US IF THEY FOLLOW THE ABOVE INSTRUCTIONS.

A surrender pass. Handwriting on the pass, presumably Reno's, indicates that it was "taken from Jap soldier on *Banzai* charge, April 2." (Courtesy of Maselli family)

The danger was omnipresent, and in late March, 300 Japanese, in a surprise *banzai* charge, killed over fifty airmen, soldiers, and

Marines. Some number of the American casualties had their throats cut while sleeping.

Reno would be out all day on patrol, often carrying a Browning Automatic Rifle (BAR), then return to his lines for evening chow (cold and dried C or K rations), and then go out on a nighttime ambush with machine guns and flares. There was no talking or smoking when lying in wait, and half the twelve-man squad would be on a two-hour sleeping rotation. Many surviving Japanese traveled at night in search of food and fell into American ambushes.

Almost all their time on Iwo Jima, the men slept in foxholes. The holes were difficult to dig in the collapsing ashy soil; where it wasn't ash, it was rocky. Often, the men dug a shallow two-man foxhole and built a parapet of rocks for a defensive berm. Reno relates that his unit "had a lot of casualties, and I don't care to go into that." Still, he was "thankful I am still alive." He mentioned one time a bomb went off nearby and "blinded soldiers for life."

One enemy they could neither plan for nor outwit were the flies. They were everywhere, always on the men's food, flying in swarms around the many dead bodies. Large, feasting maggots were so numerous they appeared like white sheets moving over the bodies of friend and foe alike.

Some of Reno's worst experiences occurred on Iwo Jima. He and his best friend, Eddie from Detroit, were pinned down in a foxhole by a torrent of artillery and gunfire, unable to safely raise their heads. After hours of being fired upon, they began taking turns looking up to see whether it was possible to advance. At one point, Eddie said he would take Reno's turn, telling Reno he was willing to take the risk and besides, he was an orphan, while Reno had a family waiting at home.

The next time Eddie peeked out, he was shot in the forehead by a sniper located in a cave several hundred yards away. Trapped in the foxhole, Reno would remain there for several days, sharing it with his lifeless friend, unable to clean the blood and gore off himself. The event would bother Reno for the rest of his life, and he would come close to breaking down whenever he recounted it.

In all likelihood, the sniper that killed Eddie was using an Arisaka-Type 97 sniper rifle outfitted with a 2.5x-powered scope. The bolt action gun was reliable, deadly up to hundreds of yards, and fired a smokeless cartridge, making it nearly impossible to spot and return fire.

Finally, Reno trudged on with his platoon, performing the perilous job of clearing bunkers. Not many days after Eddie's death, Reno was behind another friend who was operating a flamethrower when that man was killed. The platoon commander shouted at Reno to pick up the flamethrower and give the nearby bunker a "squirt." Reno pulled the trigger and sprayed the cave.

Within seconds, screaming and hollering came from the bunker as enemy soldiers poured out of it, all of them on fire. Reno and his squad moved on to the next bunker while the lieutenant dispatched those who were mortally burned.

The tedious task of attacking and penetrating thirteen miles of underground bunkers continued for weeks. The soldiers used grenades, flamethrowers, Bangalore torpedoes, and, as a last resort, pumped in hundreds of gallons of flammable salt water mixed with gasoline and oil. This nightmarish work would take its toll on Reno's company.

The 147th Regiment, using force or interpreters, killed and captured the remaining Japanese soldiers. After almost seventy days of battle, the regiment was credited with capturing hundreds of enemy soldiers and killing 1600. The total did not include an unknown number who were sealed in caves with explosives.

Once secure, the island's airfield became a haven for disabled B-29 bombers able to land on their way home from bombing Japan, saving hundreds of crewmembers' lives.

On August 15, 1945, President Harry Truman announced that Japan had surrendered, and the 147th made a final sweep of Iwo Jima, scouring it for any remaining holdouts; no enemy were found, and the regiment was relieved of duty (also, surely, relieved to be done). Reno and his battalion boarded the USS *Alcoa Polaris* in early September 1945, bound for Okinawa.

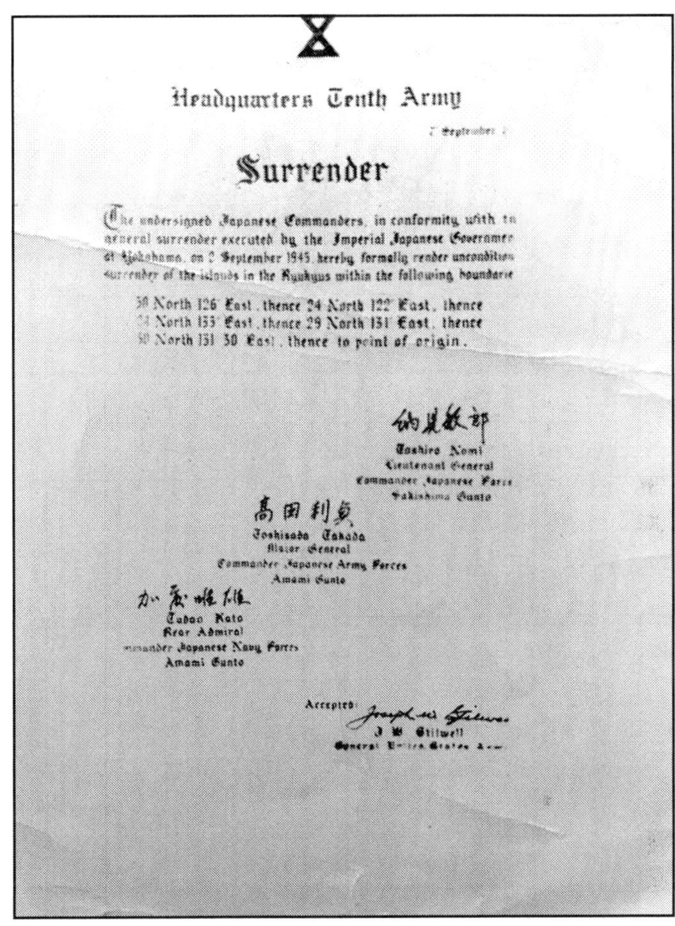

Headquarters Tenth Army

September

Surrender

The undersigned Japanese Commanders, in conformity with the general surrender executed by the Imperial Japanese Government at Yokohama, on 2 September 1945, hereby formally render unconditional surrender of the islands in the Ryukyus within the following boundaries:

30 North 126 East, thence 24 North 122 East, thence
24 North 133 East, thence 29 North 131 East, thence
30 North 131 30 East, thence to point of origin.

Toshiro Nomi
Lieutenant General
Commander Japanese Forces
Sakishima Gunto

Toshisada Takada
Major General
Commander Japanese Army Forces
Amami Gunto

Tadao Kato
Rear Admiral
Commander Japanese Navy Forces
Amami Gunto

Accepted: Joseph W. Stilwell
J. W. Stilwell
General United States Army

Japanese certificate, signed by three Japanese generals, surrendering unconditionally to General Stilwell. (Courtesy of Maselli family)

The news of the surrender was received with celebration. The 147th had been assigned to General Joseph "Vinegar Joe" Stillwell's 10th Army Division, which was scheduled to participate in Operation Olympic, the invasion of a heavily fortified Japan, which would have been, as the name suggests, a herculean effort.

Upon the unit's arrival in Okinawa, Reno and his company were busy again trying to convince any remaining holdouts to surrender, gathering prisoners, and collecting weapons. At one point, a Japanese battalion of 800 armed soldiers appeared on the hill above Reno's company of fewer than 200 strong. Although the battalion had agreed to surrender, there was some trepidation when the large armed formation led by a colonel proceeded down the hill, unsure if this wasn't a trick and a chance for one last *banzai* charge. A US Army officer instructed them to stop, line up, and drop their weapons at their feet. The soldiers complied with his order, weapons were collected, and the Japanese colonel presented his sword to Reno's company commander.

In a lighter moment, while on the island, Reno caught a baby monkey and named him "Toto." To lure the monkey closer, Reno had drilled a hole in a coconut and filled it with a dollop of rice. When the creature put its hand into the coconut and wouldn't let the rice go, it became immobile, unable to climb a tree with the heavy coconut but unwilling to release the treat. Reno pursued and caught him. Toto was his buddy for the rest of his time in Okinawa. Initially, Reno hoped he could bring the pet home, but his request was denied, and the companion was left behind.

Reno's experiences didn't end with the surrender of the island's occupiers. When he was guarding Japanese prisoners in a barbed wire compound, someone spoke out in perfect English, "Hey buddy, you got a cigarette?" It was a Japanese American man who'd been educated in the United States, visited Japan when War broke out, and was drafted into the Japanese Army. He got his smokes.

Another time, when guarding a long procession of prisoners, a screaming Ryukyuan man (an Okinawa native) ran by Reno, apparently recognizing a Japanese lieutenant who had tortured him, and before he could be stopped, he had gashed the officer's windpipe, killing him almost immediately. When he was finally detained, the man's body showed evidence of past torture, with long slash marks on his back. The soldiers let him go.

After Reno's twenty-four months overseas, his regiment returned to the United States and was inactivated in Seattle, Washington, on Christmas Day 1945.

Over the course of World War II, the 147th fought at Guadalcanal,

Saipan, Tinian, Iwo Jima, and Okinawa. No other Army unit fought in these battles. Reno's decorations included the Bronze Star, a Good Conduct Medal, the Asiatic–Pacific Campaign Medal, an American Campaign Medal, the WWII Victory Medal, and a Combat Infantryman Badge.

Upon arriving in the United States, Reno took a train across the country, where he was honorably discharged at the Separation Center at Fort Devens, Massachusetts, on January 19, 1946.

Next was a train ride home to be united with his family. As his train approached the depot, Reno later told a close friend how embarrassed he was of his reduced physical condition, how worried he felt about meeting his parents at the station. Initially, Reno was reluctant to get off the train; his fears were well founded when his parents did not immediately recognize their 135-pound son, emaciated and with a yellow cast to his body. Reno would later attribute his yellow skin color to taking the antimalarial pills of the era, Atabrine, which was known to cause yellowing of the skin and eyes but fortunately did not result in true jaundice or liver injury. No matter his condition, the reunion was joyful, and many tears were shed.

He quickly started looking for a job. His mother surprised him with a small nest egg to get him started: a bank book she'd maintained in his absence, containing all his poker winnings from overseas card games. He had sent the money home to support his family and never expected to get it back. Reno found a job at Arnold Print Works and soon became fond of a girl he met at a dance, a date arranged by his cousin. After a brief courtship, he and JoAnn Cariddi were married on April 3, 1948, at Saint Anthony of Padua Church in North Adams.

One day, Reno had a surprise visit from a buddy he had served with on Iwo Jima. During a lull in the fighting, the men had discovered a US $5 bill on a dead Japanese soldier. The bill had been cut in half by machine gun fire, and the men each kept a half, resolving to meet up again if they survived. In 1948, Reno's father showed up at a local ballgame Reno was watching and said a friend was waiting at the house. Surprisingly, it was his buddy, now living in Worcester, Massachusetts. They spent hours reminiscing, and as his friend was leaving, Reno asked if he still had his half of the bill. He pulled it out of his wallet to match Reno's. They'd made it.

Reno worked for a while at General Electric and then in the custom order room at Waverly Products. After a layoff at Waverly, he found a secure position with the North Adams school system in building maintenance, where he worked until retirement in 1983. At times, serving as a union steward on Local 204 of the American Federation of State, County, and Municipal Employees, he would aid in negotiating contracts with the City of North Adams. At one point, Reno returned to Drury High School and completed the requirements for his diploma.

JoAnn worked in her family's business, Cariddi Sales, a wholesaler distributor of toys and sports equipment, and managed their quickly growing family of four daughters and a son. She was active at Saint Anthony's, was involved in organizing high school reunions, and was known for baking beautiful wedding cakes for relatives.

Reno had always been part of an ensemble in his younger years and, at one point, had his own "orchestra" that he called the Melody Boys. In 1946, right after returning from the war, Reno founded a band called The Aladdins. Initially featured as the Aladdin Trio, Reno played his accordion, accompanied by a guitarist and a drummer.

The band often played Saturdays at weddings and in the evening at restaurants such as Sunnyside, Twin Brooks, and the Fireside Lounge. The band eventually expanded to include vocalists, a banjo player, and a pianist on keyboard.

The band enjoyed a resurgence in the 1980s, and Reno's friend Tommy Leonesio joined up, bringing his accordion. In one 1999 interview with *The Transcript,* Leonesio said, "We play Polish, Italian, and French music. We're from the big band era, and that's our style." The band of mostly retirees gave thousands of performances, as often as three or four times a week.

The Aladdins became renowned for their volunteer gigs as well;

they'd bring smiles to the faces of music lovers at church bazaars, nursing homes, senior centers, colleges, and the annual American Legion Christmas Dinner. Sometimes described as the "rock stars" of the Berkshires, their generosity was recognized when in 1999 the band was awarded the Rosasco Humanitarian Award, named after Judge Rosasco, a North Adams jurist known for his community service and care for others.

Every summer, the family of seven packed their silver 1960 Plymouth Fury station wagon with its big fins and looked forward to their summer cottage vacation at Hampton Beach. Loaded with foodstuffs and clothing, they would happily head off on the four-hour trip. Later in life, Reno and JoAnn would vacation at the Jersey shore.

For an interest other than music, Reno decided to learn how to upholster furniture. He attended a local class, and, from then on, upholstered and reconditioned furniture for his family until his eyesight began to fail.

Family dinners with the children usually began at 5:00 p.m. Even with seven people, there was little conversation; Reno encouraged everyone to listen to the local news on WMNB radio. Reno and JoAnn would often encourage their children to dream big and seek higher education. All five would go to college.

In later years, Reno and JoAnn started a tradition of Friday night family suppers at their house with the children and grandchildren. Usually, after supper, everyone was entertained with some excellent accordion music. Reno's son recalls the quiet joy of having a Budweiser with his dad and reflecting on life. As he aged, this quiet, modest man would reflect on the positive things that occurred while he was in the Army, such as hanging out with his buddies, playing cards, going on liberty, and looking for souvenirs. Drafted at 18 and a half years old and just six months later finding himself in a foxhole fighting for his life, Reno understood his great fortune. He told his son, "The heroes were the ones that didn't come home."

In early 2000, Reno and members of his family visited the

World War II memorial in Washington, DC. His son remembers being upgraded to first class, a special accommodation for Reno's service, then having a mid-flight drink with his dad who acknowledged in a reflective moment, "The best thing that ever happened to me was your mother." During the early years of their marriage, JoAnn had helped Reno deal with his recurring bouts of malaria and fearsome nightmares.

Even with declining eyesight, Reno continued to play his accordion at picnics and gatherings and would play just weeks before his passing. Reno passed away in 2011, and JoAnn followed nine years later. They rest now in Southview Cemetery in North Adams, buried next to Reno's dad and mom and his brother Milio and his wife. All are greatly missed by their families, and Reno is remembered as a true American hero.

ROBERT B. NICHOLS
GUNNER
USS *MISSOURI*

The plane's dull red "meatball" insignia was easily distinguishable. The anti-aircraft crew had been tracking and firing at the Japanese kamikaze *as it sped toward them at over 300 miles per hour; now, only fractions of seconds remained before certain impact. The crew continued pouring 20-millimeter rounds into the plane, knocking off one of its wings, hoping to adjust its trajectory...but it kept coming, hitting the ship just 70 yards from the crew.*

ROBERT'S LIFE BEGAN IN Ballston Spa, New York, where he was born on January 26, 1926, under the name Robert Henry Williams. Some unknown calamitous event caused his parents to place him and his siblings in an orphanage when he was barely a toddler. It was there that Joseph and Delia (Robarge) Nichols, both from North Adams, found him. (Other families adopted his siblings, although his new parents ensured they stayed in contact with each other.)

The Nichols family brought Robert home to North Adams in 1928 when he was two years old (*Transcript,* 4-5-2006), to be welcomed by the rest of their children, two girls, and a boy. They lived at one point on Center Street, and also River Street, and Joseph, skilled with his hands, presumedly worked at the local mills, while Delia was both a homemaker and a long-term Sprague Electric Company employee at their Brown Street plant.

The children attended Brayton Elementary School. As a young adolescent and tall for his age, Robert found a job helping deliver large blocks of ice to surrounding towns. He attended Drury High School for one year and then dropped out to help support the family. At fifteen, he found a job at Berkshire Fine Spinning, one of the local textile mills, as a "cloth boy."

Robert was assigned many low-level tasks, ranging from sweeping and moving cloth racks from room to room, to the fast-paced job of doffing (removing full spindles/bobbins and replacing them with empty ones). He worked six days a week, usually eight to eleven hours a day, all for less than ten dollars.

In 1943, when the country was at the height of war and Robert was seventeen years of age, he talked to his mom about enlisting in the Navy. He complied with her request that he delay his entry and remain home for Christmas. Once his eighteenth birthday arrived on January 26, 1944, Robert received his draft notice and officially entered the Navy on March 17, 1944.

Just before entering the service, on February 23, 1944, he had gone to Probate Court alongside his adoptive parents and officially changed his name to Robert Bruno Nichols. Some presume it was his affinity to Joseph and Delia, so that his future military records would reflect their name, and perhaps this was a less bureaucratic process at eighteen than it would have been as a minor. At the time, he also adopted as his middle name that of his brother-in-law, Bruno.

The young recruit, getting ready to ship out. (Courtesy of Nichols family)

Robert served his basic training at Sampson Naval Training Station (NTS) in upstate New York. Arriving by train, he was immediately immersed in a jam-packed program, reduced due to war demands from sixteen weeks to eight. Over 400,000 recruits were trained at Sampson during the war years.

Early morning reveilles, platoon drills, and numerous classes were the routine of his day. The instructors covered military history, mathematics, mechanical skills, and most importantly, naval vernacular: floors became decks, walls became bulkheads, stairways became ladderways, and bathrooms became heads. Your left side was port, your right side was starboard. And off you go!

During training, Robert earned $50 a month. Upon graduation, he was promoted to Seaman 2nd class. His next duty station was to be the Naval Training Station (NTS) at Newport, Rhode Island. He learned he had been assigned to the USS *Missouri* as a 20-millimeter gunner. His training focused primarily on the 20-millimeter Oerlikon cannon. Over the following weeks, he spent countless hours disassembling and reassembling the weapon until he could almost do it blindfolded. Every time it was fired, he would take it apart, clean and lubricate it, and then reassemble it. The practice he enjoyed the most was live-firing at a sleeve target towed by an airplane over the nearby Atlantic Ocean. Piloting the tow-plane must have been a high-stress assignment.

USS *MISSOURI*

HIS SHIP, THE USS *Missouri*-BB-63, was launched in late January 1944, christened by Margaret Truman, the daughter of then-Senator Harry Truman, Democrat of Missouri. The BB-63 designation indicated she was the 63rd battleship authorized for naval service and had a crew of 189 officers, 2700 enlisted men.

The warship, nicknamed *The Mighty Mo*, weighed 57,000 tons, and measured 880 feet long by 108 feet wide. Her eight boilers produced steam that drove four giant propellers, helping the ship attain speeds of almost 40 miles per hour (33 knots). The camouflage colors were painted dull black, light, and darker gray.

Mighty Mo bristled with weaponry. Each of her three huge turrets sported three 16" guns, twenty dual 5" guns, twenty quad 40mm mounts, and more than fifty 20mm Oerlikon cannons, which were Robert's assigned weapon.

The Oerlikon, a short-range anti-aircraft gun, was popular for its ease of use, rate of fire, and durability. It would run dirty, wet, frozen, or covered with blood or salt water. The gun could accurately fire at most 450 seven-inch rounds a minute almost one mile away. It usually had a crew of four sailors, and every 200 rounds one member would be assigned to change the barrel using asbestos gloves.

Unfortunately, 20-millimeter Oerlikons were also used with great success by Japanese Zeros (fighter planes) and the Japanese Navy. The enemy would use the same cannons to fire at US Navy airplanes.

Once Robert's training was complete at NTS Rhode Island, he joined the USS *Missouri* as one of her original crew members in Norfolk, Virginia. Robert was always proud of being a "plank owner," defined as a crew member at the time of initial commission. He told *The Transcript*, "I'm what they call a plank owner; I was on the ship when it was commissioned [in June 1944]…" (4-5-2006).

Right away, the warship headed out to sea for a Caribbean "shakedown cruise" in July, with stops in Trinidad and Puerto Rico. This was a demanding time for the crew, with repeated shipboard drills preparing for battle. There was ongoing gunnery practice, especially with the 16" guns, to ensure no damage could be done to the ship once she got into action.

In addition to gunnery training, shipboard life included standing four-hour watches as well as ongoing scraping and repainting some portion of the ship. Robert's section would often find themselves holystoning (removing the paint) from the wooden deck before repainting. Using broomsticks with gritty stones attached or scrubbing on their knees with slabs of stone, salt water, and sand, they would strip the wooden deck down to bare wood and then repaint it.

Free time could involve listening to the ship's band, watching a USO show, enjoying a movie on the ship's fantail, writing letters, reading, or participating in one of the ever-present card games.

Bob's sleeping quarters, main deck portside near turret 3. (Courtesy of Nichols family)

When the shakedown cruise was completed, the USS *Missouri* left Norfolk for the Pacific in November 1944, with stops in San Francisco and Hawaii before joining Task Force 58, comprised of 118 warships assigned to support the Iwo Jima invasion. During the invasion, *Missouri*'s duty was to protect the aircraft carriers with its anti-aircraft guns. The warship recorded her first kill, downing a Japanese twin-engine bomber (known as a Helen). The plane was hit by an explosive round from their five-inch gun and blew apart.

In late March and early April 1945, the USS *Missouri* assisted in the invasion of Okinawa, using her 16-inch guns to bombard and destroy enemy concentrations, bunkers, fuel depots, and other targets of opportunity. Each of the 68-foot 16-inch guns weighed over 200,000 pounds and fired two rounds a minute. The guns, operated by a crew of 79 sailors, could accurately fire a 2700-pound projectile (weight of a Volkswagen) at a target twenty-four miles distant and land within a hundred yards of its target.

While shelling was happening, Robert and his gun crew were manning a 20-millimeter Oerlikon machine gun on the ship's starboard side. The *Missouri* was protected by over twenty of these guns on each side of the huge warship. Robert was assigned to gun number 49.

He would be harnessed to the gun with a waist belt, a safety precaution because the gun was so close to the ship's edge. One seaman was swept overboard during daily drills but luckily retrieved by a nearby destroyer. The anti-aircraft gun was mounted on a fixed pedestal that could freely rotate and featured shoulder supports for the crew member firing the gun. An essential set of blocking cams ensured the gun would not traverse too far left or right into areas covered by other guns. The cams, when correctly set, would stop the gun from firing. Later in life, Robert mentioned to an American Legion member that the ship's maintenance crew would override these safety settings and modify the elevation cams to be able to depress the guns enough to shoot at low-flying enemy planes.

Bob at his gun station, in an original photo treasured by his family. (Courtesy of Nichols family)

The 20-millimeter Oerlikons were the ship's short-range weapons. The crews knew it was time to hit the deck when the guns opened up on an incoming plane.

In late March 1945, the *Missouri* began participating in *Operation Iceberg*, the invasion of Okinawa, firing at shore targets and destroying ammunition dumps, large gun emplacements, and

A *kamikaze*, upper left, prepares to crash into the USS *Missouri*. (Courtesy of Nichols family)

barracks. The ships were on high alert for the new threat of Japan's Special Attack Corps: *kamikazes*.

The USS *Missouri*'s first *kamikaze* attack occurred on April 11 when one of these suicidal warplanes, a Mitsubishi A6M Zero, hit the *Missouri*'s starboard hull about 70 feet from Robert's gun station. He remembers seeing the "red zero on the wing just before it hit." The crew's firing diverted it from the superstructure, and it did only minor damage other than causing a gasoline fire. Luckily, its bomb did not explode, and most of the plane fell into the sea.

One of the plane's aluminum wings, some other wreckage, and half of the pilot's body fell on *Missouri*'s deck. The wing and part of the bloody Plexiglas canopy were eventually cut up for souvenirs. Robert brought home pieces of both.

At the captain's orders, the Japanese pilot's mutilated body was buried at sea with military honors, much to the chagrin of some of the sailors.

For most of April, *Missouri*'s crew was at general quarters, and for good reason. On April 16,

The piece of windshield and fuselage parts from a *kamikaze* that crashed on the *Missouri* April 11, 1945, seventy feet from Bob Nichols who collected the parts. (Courtesy of Nichols family)

another *kamikaze* attacked the ship's stern and exploded in the ship's wake, damaging a crane on the fantail and wounding two sailors. It came so close that Robert's group was told to seek shelter under one of the turrets. When the enemy plane exploded, the pilot was thrown high in the air, his parachute was deployed, and he gently floated down into the ocean, shredded by shrapnel. The crew watched him sink.

After successfully completing the Okinawa invasion during the summer of 1945, the USS *Missouri* shelled Japanese home islands, destroying steel and iron works, industrial targets, and any other manufacturing sites supporting Japan's war effort. The men were hoping that the rumors of war's end were true.

In August word reached the ship about the atomic bombing of Hiroshima and Nagasaki and shortly afterwards that the forty-four-month war with Japan was over. The USS *Missouri* had the great honor of being selected to host the surrender ceremonies in Tokyo Bay. It is said that President Harry Truman (formerly Senator Truman) dictated that the ceremony would take place on the *Missouri* and in the center of Tokyo Bay as a definitive sign to the Japanese of their defeat.

The *Missouri* purposefully anchored close to where Commodore Matthew Perry had landed ninety-two years previously (in 1854) when "opening" Japan to the outside world, rekindling in the words of the State Department, "regular trade and discourse." The flag displayed on the *Missouri* was from Commodore Perry's ship and had been flown in from the Naval Academy for the ceremony.

The Navy flotilla accompanying the *Missouri* was on high alert, anticipating a fanatical attack by remnants of the Japanese Navy. Combat air patrols and anti-aircraft guns covering the sky on VJ (Victory over Japan) Day on August 15, 1945, had shot down thirty-eight enemy planes.

At his gun station, Robert heard a male voice on the loudspeaker announcing the end of the war by saying, "The war is over; if any Japanese planes come over, shoot them down in a friendly manner."

Robert acknowledges the "friendly fire" comment was more like a joke, but "we did not trust them" (*Berkshire Record* 9-6-2013).

The official surrender and treaty-signing occurred on September 2, 1945. The 2700-plus ship's crew knew the day's significance, and black-and-white pictures show its decks are mobbed. The eleven-man Japanese delegation came aboard around 9:00 a.m. to face an array of American generals and admirals. It is said when the Japanese delegation came aboard, they needed to walk through a preselected honorary gauntlet of enlisted men, all chosen for their height of six feet or taller, a humbling experience for the smaller Japanese.

A view of the ship's fantail, with Bob's 20mm Oerlikons in the foreground, left center. (Courtesy of Nichols family)

Robert was on watch from 8:00 a.m. to noon that day, manning a quad 40-millimeter gun on the fantail during the ceremonies. "If I were any farther away, I would have been in the ocean," he told *The Berkshire Eagle* in 2015.

He did see dignitaries boarding and exiting the ship. He saw Generals MacArthur and Wainwright and Admiral Halsey: "I could hear some of the ceremony over the loudspeakers. I can still hear Gen. (Douglas) MacArthur saying in his stern voice, '*These proceedings are over.*'"

General MacArthur, the Japanese Foreign Minister, and the

General of its Army were the principal signatories of the peace document. Few knew that the Japanese general opposed the surrender but was ordered by Emperor Hirohito to sign the document.

The surrender ceremony included both sides signing two documents, one in English and the other in Japanese. General MacArthur's aide had found one-hundred-year-old parchment paper at a monastery in Manila to be used for the surrender document. Two copies were signed, and the entire meeting took less than 30 minutes.

Moments after the signing at MacArthur's signal, hundreds of B-29 bombers and fighters flew overhead, helping to remind the Japanese that further resistance was hopeless. Nichols said, "The sky over Tokyo Bay was full of planes. You could hardly see the sky. All I could think was, *I'm going home, and I'm still alive*" (*Transcript,* 4-5-2006). The nearby ocean was also filled with American warships.

The signing had occurred on a mess table covered with green cloth. As an afterthought, the *Missouri* skipper decided to recover the table for posterity, only to find out the cooks had already retrieved it for noon chow, and it was mixed below deck with dozens of other tables. The green cloth is preserved at the Naval Academy Museum in Annapolis.

Not long after the ceremony, to the sailors' delight, the *Missouri* headed home, with stops in Guam, Pearl Harbor, and the Panama Canal. While the crew enjoyed the local sights, the *Missouri* barely fit through the canal, brushing against its walls and chipping off pieces of concrete. Robert kept some of the pieces as souvenirs.

Arriving in New York City in October 1945, the ship participated in Navy Day Fleet Review and then returned to Norfolk, Virginia, where many sailors were discharged. Robert remained with the ship to complete his active duty.

In early 1946, Robert was part of the ship's goodwill tour throughout the Mediterranean, visiting other nations "showing the flag" of this special warship. At one point, the *Missouri* was given the responsibility of returning to Istanbul the remains of the Turkish Ambassador to the United States. Another time, the ship transported

President Truman and his family back from South America. During this goodwill tour, Robert and his crewmates participated in an audience with Pope Pius XII in Rome.

First Class Seaman Robert Nichols was honorably discharged on May 13, 1946, and entitled to wear the World War II Victory Medal, American Theater Medal, and the Asiatic–Pacific Theater Medal with three battle stars.

The USS *Missouri* would actively participate in the Korean War and then be decommissioned in 1955. The *Mighty Mo* was reactivated in 1986; her weapons systems were upgraded to include Tomahawk missiles, and then the warship participated in the early part of Operation Desert Storm (the Gulf War). The *Missouri* was decommissioned for the final time in 1992. In 1998, the *Missouri* was transferred to the Memorial Association in Hawaii to be moored at Ford Island facing the USS *Arizona*. The two great ships symbolize the beginning and end of World War II.

Despite all of his world travels, one of Robert's biggest thrills was meeting Bela Lugosi on his way home to North Adams. He successfully requested Bela's penciled autograph on a notebook and treasured it for the rest of his life. Bela was well known for playing in numerous horror films and is best remembered for playing Count Dracula in the 1931 horror film *Dracula*. Robert's children would tease him and question the authenticity of the faint autograph later in life.

Once home, Robert worked in a textile mill for a while, drove a truck, and then worked nights at Arnold Print Works, usually doing handyman jobs during the day. He purchased his first car, a 1937 two-door black Chevy with a hood ornament of a woman he called "the flying lady." Jokingly, he wrapped some bits of cloth around the lady, properly outfitting her in the summer and winter.

During this time, he met Nancy Anne Tanguay at a youth picnic. They dated for a number of months and married in October 1949. Nancy and Robert went on to have a son, two daughters, and a wonderful sixty-eight-year marriage.

The family lived in a gray duplex with black shutters on the upper end of Beaver Street, almost to the Clarksburg line. Using his handyman skills, Robert built a large playhouse complete with windows, doors, flower boxes, shutters, and cots for sleeping. The playhouse also had an intercom connected to the family's kitchen so the kids could be called when it was time to eat. The house was awarded the prestigious "Golden Hammer" commendation by *Mechanix Illustrated* and was also featured in the magazine.

Robert was later hired by the James Hunter Machine Company (subsequently, Morrison Berkshire) as a technician. He would travel and fix textile machinery all over the United States, eventually retiring from Morrison Berkshire in 1991. Nancy retired after working years for Adams Supermarkets.

With both parents working, and Robert often having two jobs, vacations were usually limited to day-trips. They'd go to Story Town, Frontier Land, or the North Pole in nearby New York or a picnic at the Fishpond in North Adams. The family's 1955 green Chevy station wagon was used for many trips to the outdoor movies; with pre-made popcorn and a mattress in the back, the kids could watch the first show, but had to go to sleep before the second movie began.

Sundays were family time with the stores closed. The Nichols family often visited other family members, went on rides, and had picnics. Riding around in their dad's yellow Rambler convertible with the top down was also a treat. Robert enjoyed music and taught himself to play the accordion and played it on birthdays.

Over the years, he enjoyed bird and deer hunting with his son and fishing for trout in the Deerfield River. He bowled but, admittedly, was not a great bowler. He loved photography and always had his 35-millimeter Canon with him. He took hundreds of photos of his family and of the beautiful landscape in and around North Adams. He was serious enough about his hobby to set up a darkroom in the basement.

Robert's daughter described him as "A people person: he enjoyed people, was a good listener, and could talk to anyone. Sometimes [he] might go to the corner market for milk and be gone an hour chatting with someone he met."

He became an active member of the local VFW, American Legion, and the USS *Missouri* Association. He and Nancy traveled to a number of USS *Missouri* reunions. Robert was proud of his time in the Navy and serving on the famous warship. For years, he had a three-foot plastic replica of the *Missouri* displayed on the radiator cover in his living room. Later, after the kids left home, he converted a bedroom to a den and moved his computer and the replica there with other war and work remembrances. He displayed pieces of the *kamikaze* shot down so many years previously and a piece of its windshield with a speck of blood on it. Central to the room was a large wall map with tacks identifying all the places he had traveled in the Navy and for work.

Bob in North Adams, reflecting on his Navy days. (Courtesy of Nichols family)

As the years passed, when well into his nineties, Robert was honored for his service when he was asked to participate in a flag ceremony at a Boston College game. Later, he was recognized as the guest of honor at a Bruins alumni game in his hometown.

Robert, his son, and his daughter planned to attend the 75th USS *Missouri* reunion when COVID struck, and the event was delayed. Before a rescheduled reunion, Robert passed away on April 2, 2020. He is buried at Southview Cemetery in North Adams, next to Nancy, who had preceded him in death in 2017.

This humble and kind man was justifiably proud of his years of navy service. Robert Bruno Nichols of little North Adams was more than just a brave Seaman: He was a plank owner on one of the United States' last great battleships, the *Mighty Mo*, which was credited with shooting down eleven enemy planes, hosting the VJ peace treaty, even enjoying a second life as a recommissioned warship. And Robert had an exceptional ringside seat to all the action.

HENRY ST. PIERRE

PARATROOPER

101ST AIRBORNE

Henry St. Pierre participated in, and survived, three of World War II's major battles. Parachuting into France on D-Day, he was wounded, then recovered in England in time to parachute into Holland as part of Operation Market Garden. Within weeks, he was quickly trucked as part of a relief force to the Battle of the Bulge in Belgium. While helping the besieged forces at Bastogne, at times in hand-to-hand combat, he was captured and remained in a prisoner-of-war camp until the war's end.

HENRY ST. PIERRE WAS the eighth child among eight sons and six daughters born at home to the large French Catholic family of Jean Baptiste and Edmire (Landry) St. Pierre. Two other children died shortly after birth.

Henry's dad, Jean, a native of Canada, was born in Québec in 1878 and immigrated to the United States as a young man in the late 1890s. Edmire, born in 1883 in St. Valentin, Québec, immigrated to the United States as a little girl. Both families attended Notre Dame Church in North Adams, where it is presumed they met. They eventually were married at the church on October 13, 1902.

Their children were born over a period of 22 years, from 1903 to 1925. Interestingly, in the French Canadian tradition, all the boys were named Joseph (after Saint Joseph) and all the girls Marie (after the Blessed Virgin Mary) at baptism. This practice caused some confusion later in life because the temporary baptismal name was entered on their birth certificates and didn't correlate with their actual first names.

The family first lived on Taft Street and moved to Notch Road in the Greylock area around 1931 during the Great Depression. Edmire's brother had purchased an abandoned mansion and let the family reside there. The mansion had belonged to Harry R. Hamer, a local industrialist who had invented the "Hamer Perfect Washing Machine," manufactured on Notch Road near his home. In declining health, at age 46, the well-liked Harry committed suicide "at 1:10 o'clock by shooting himself through the head in the waiting room of the Hoosac Valley street railroad" (*Transcript,* 4-12-02).

Heating and cooking with a wood stove kept the boys busy, requiring cords of wood to be chopped year-round. The large fireplace alone took four-foot logs. The children attended grammar school at a nearby schoolhouse and, shortly after graduating, went to work in the nearby Greylock Mill, bringing home their pay to Mom. Some of the younger children attended Holy Family Grammar School after it was constructed in the late 1920s. All went to work in the mill at a very young age.

On Sunday, the family attended Mass at Holy Family Church. Jean often made two or three trips to church, shuttling kids in his old two-door pickup. Invariably, some children had to walk.

Jean worked the night shift in the weave department at the local Greylock textile mill. At one point, he also was a loom fixer. Night work allowed him to work at his subsistence farm on Notch Road during the day. The St. Pierres had fourteen milking cows and sold milk locally. The family also had a huge garden, and the kids helped Edmire can prodigious amounts of vegetables and fruits for their large family, then sold any extras to the local corner stores.

With fourteen children, Jean and Edmire were always busy clothing the children, repairing shoes, and feeding them. Jean worked at the mill until his late 70s and died in 1958 while picking strawberries from his garden. His wake was held at the family home on Notch Road. His numerous grandchildren remember him smoking a pipe and always taking them back to his rhubarb patch to pick each of them a stalk. (Edmire, who spoke little English, passed away in 1973, fifteen years after Jean.)

Henry was born at home on Taft Street in North Adams, Massachusetts, on October 1, 1914. After finishing eighth grade, he began working at the nearby Greylock Mill in the weave department. It wasn't uncommon to find him working beside other thirteen-year-old children. When not at the mill, he worked on the family's farm.

An early portrait of the young Private St. Pierre. (Courtesy of St. Pierre family)

Four of the St. Pierre sons would serve in World War II. In October 1939, at the age of twenty-five, Henry enlisted in the local National Guard unit. The following summer (1940) the unit trained for three weeks in Potsdam, New York, before being inducted in October 1940 into one year of federal service with a departure date scheduled for early 1941.

"Sober Farewells Given as Berkshire Units Depart for Camp Today," announced *The Transcript* on January 27, 1941: "Company K, 104th Infantry Regiment, 28th Division, leaves for their year of Federal Training at Camp Edwards in Falmouth, Massachusetts. The unit marched from the Ashland Street Armory to the railroad depot in low temperatures and light snowfall.... Company M from Adams occupied the first two coaches, Company K the next two, and Company L from Greenfield the last two coaches. Before leaving, Company M's armorer posted a 'For Rent' sign at the local armory." Camp Edwards would later become a German Prisoner of War Camp, housing up to 2,000 prisoners.

A number of local volunteers were from the Greylock section

of North Adams and enthusiastically supported as noted in the local newspaper: "21 Greylock Club Men Bearing Arms...twenty-one of the original 45 members of the Greylock Community Club are now serving in the armed forces....the club recently sent Christmas packages to all of its members in the service" (*Transcript,* 12-14-42).

Initially assigned to the 104th Parachute Infantry as a mortar crewman, Henry found himself bored when reassigned to the Coastal Artillery in Maine, so he volunteered for the paratroopers. He was sent to Fort Benning, Georgia, to complete a rigorous four-week parachute school. In addition to strenuous physical training and forced marches, the troopers learned to pack their chutes, exit a plane, and handle air-dropped equipment. After several jumps, Henry earned his wings and joined the 502nd Parachute Infantry Regiment, becoming part of the 101st Airborne Division in August 1942.

Henry's paratrooper insignia. This one is often referred to as the "Bat Wings" or the "Widowmaker." (Courtesy of the author)

He was proud to be in the role of a paratrooper, considered one of America's toughest soldiers. Usually, they are the first unit sent into battle, often behind enemy lines. Their task was to take the brunt of enemy counterattacks, hold their ground, and be relieved by large forces after ten to twenty days in direct combat. Then, they regroup, resupply, train replacements, and head to their next battle.

The 502nd Parachute Infantry Regiment (PIR), known as the "Five-Oh-Deuce" or simply the "Deuce," moved its troopers to Fort Bragg (now Fort Liberty), North Carolina, and throughout the rest of 1942 and into 1943, they took part in grueling individual, unit, and divisional training, with travel to Tennessee for additional maneuvers.

When training was complete, the 502nd reported to Camp Shanks in New York and left the United States on September 1, 1943, aboard the SS *Strathnaver*. They were bound for England, stopping first in Newfoundland to repair the ship's water system. The troops finally arrived in the United Kingdom on October 18, 1943.

Stationed in Quonset huts in one of the many villages in Wiltshire County, England, for the next seven months, the 502nd continued training, including 15-to-25-mile forced marches. Ongoing combat exercises were the rule of the day. They trained in chemical warfare, small arms, map reading, and became experts in using German weapons. They also participated in coordinated company and battalion parachute drops during this time.

Not long after arriving in England, Henry unexpectedly ran into his brother Joe. "Two Local Brothers Reunited in England," announced *The Transcript* in December 1943: "Two local brothers… had an unexpected meeting at the American Red Cross club in England…Henry St. Pierre, parachutist, who has been in England a month and a half, and Corporal Joseph St. Pierre who has been in England for seven months…the Director of the club sent Mrs. St. Pierre a note saying the 'boys were in fine physical condition and that the reunion was most happy.'"

On May 5, 1944, *The Transcript* added, "2 Local Parachutists are in Great Britain: Pvt. William Lesure, a rifleman…and Pvt. Henry St. Pierre of the Notch Road, former weaver, who is now an assistant mortar gunner…was trained at Fort Benning, Georgia, parachute school…are waiting with airborne troops…to fight in the final assault against Hitler's strongly fortified Europe."

A month after the news article, Henry's 502nd was standing by at the Membury and Common Green Airfield late on June 5, ready to board C-47 transport planes to participate in one of the largest operations in history, the Normandy Invasion. Henry was part of Operation Neptune, the initial assault phase of the huge Operation Overlord.

Henry and other members of Company F, all with burnt-cork faces, loaded down with gear, got to meet General Eisenhower in a now-famous picture as he sent the troops into battle *(see cover)*.

Henry later told one of his nephews that he "jumped early in the morning on D-Day with my pack and equipment weighing almost as much as I did." At 5'6" tall, the paratrooper weighed less than 140 pounds and, in addition to his standard equipment, was probably parachuting with three mortar rounds strapped to his leg. His equipment likely included, at minimum, an M1 rifle, a .45-caliber pistol, helmet, hand and rifle grenades, entrenching tool, ammunition, rope, first aid kit, tent, and blanket.

His C-47 took off for the one-hour flight over the English Channel, assigned to hit Drop Zone (DZ) A. On the flight over, most of the troopers took their airsick pills, enjoyed a last cigarette, prayed, joked, and even dozed. As the waves of C-47s and gliders approached France, they were subject to a blizzard of anti-aircraft fire. Many planes were hit, and some dropped from the sky, killing all 15 occupants. Two groups of paratroopers from Company A mistakenly jumped into the English Channel and were drowned.

With the heavy enemy fire and the violent rocking of the plane, troopers were glad to exit and responded quickly to the red-ready light and then the green light telling them to jump.

Due to the chaotic air drops, the 502nd parachutists were widely dispersed across the land, and it took hours to get back together. As soon as they reformed the unit, through stiff fighting, they secured two causeways blocking German reinforcements and destroyed a German artillery site.

Once their initial goals were achieved, Henry's battalion was charged with seizing the town of Carentan, a channel for German reinforcements. So far, all the units' efforts continued to focus on stopping any German reinforcements from repelling the Allied beach landings.

Henry's platoon had three rifle squads and his six-man mortar squad. Without the initial availability of heavy artillery, the group relied heavily on Henry's team. The portable 42-pound 60mm mortars provided valuable fire support. His team, who jumped into combat with mortar rounds and retrieved additional air-dropped rounds, fired up to 20 rounds a minute, supporting Company F's advance...although they quickly ran out of ammunition and fought on as infantrymen.

The 502nd, as part of the 101st Airborne, battled for the town of Carentan against enemy bombers, which killed scores of troopers, and artillery, sniper, and machine gun fire. After hand-to-hand combat, the town was captured on June 10, 1944. The small town was by this point a pile of rubble: everywhere the smell of death, German bodies, destroyed equipment, decaying animals, and garbage.

German tanks counterattacked on June 13, 1944, causing the 502nd Battalion to withdraw briefly, and it was during this vicious fighting that Henry was wounded. The Germans finally started withdrawing from Carentan on June 14. The town was secured, and Henry, stabilized by medics, was evacuated to England for medical treatment. The 502nd had succeeded in securing the link to Omaha Beach.

The Transcript on July 8, 1944, read: "Pvt. St. Pierre Wounded in France...according to telegram received by parents...Henry sent a letter to parents saying he was confined to an English hospital...did not describe the extent of his wound...." It is presumed that Henry was wounded by tank shrapnel and took weeks to recover.

In July or August, he rejoined the 502nd, which had returned to England in late June 1944 for rest, refitting, and replacements. Little did Henry know that the 502nd had already been selected to participate in Operation Market Garden, an ambitious operation that involved dropping airborne troops behind enemy lines into the Netherlands. The risky endeavor hoped to split the region in half and open a faster pathway into Germany with the enticing possibility of ending the war within months.

Less than three months after returning from France, Henry's 101st, along with the 82nd Airborne divisions, British paratroopers, and a Polish brigade, prepared for a massive, daring daytime parachute jump into Holland. They aimed to capture bridges and roadways and create a corridor to advance into Germany.

The airborne jump took place on September 17, 1944, a beautiful day. Company F, 502nd Parachute Infantry Regiment troopers were gathered at RAF Greenham Common, the same airbase where they had gathered for their D-Day jump in June.

At about 13:00 hours, the men of Company F left England and headed toward Drop Zone "B," which was close to the small town of Son. With little flak, it was almost a textbook landing. The groups quickly assembled and, within hours, had seized several bridges. Over three days of drops (September 17-19), the division would use hundreds of C-47s and gliders, with 15 men per aircraft, to land 20,000 troops.

In an oddity of war, by chance, a German soldier inspecting one of the 101st shot-down gliders found the battle plans on the corpse of an American soldier who had disobeyed orders, taking them with him. The plans were quickly forwarded to and used by the German high command and found very useful.

Initially, the 101st successfully captured several bridges and two canal crossings. However, stiff resistance began to hamstring the further efforts seriously. Planners had thought the German army in retreat from Normandy would be easily routed and unable to concentrate troops to stop the breakthrough. That wasn't the case; the Germans responded quickly, and the unknown presence of an additional Panzer group doomed Market Garden.

The airborne troops also found seizing narrow roadways difficult, where a small German anti-tank unit could easily disable one vehicle and block the road, setting up a killing zone for the following vehicles. The US troopers would then need bulldozers to push them off the road.

Henry's 2nd Battalion, up against a Panzer brigade fighting around the towns of Veghel and St. Oedenrode, would suffer many casualties. At the end of the three-month battle, the 502nd would take a defensive position near "The Island," a section of land ringed by dikes, while Germans held the high ground across the river.

Market Garden's ultimate objective of capturing the Arnhem Bridge was thwarted, and units began withdrawing. Before evacuating to France to reorganize, the total casualties for the 101st and 82nd divisions were 6,000 paratroopers. The 101st had 3,000 killed, wounded, or missing in action.

Market Garden was an operational failure, meaning the war would continue into 1945. Few records exist of Henry's participation, although news articles confirm his fighting in Holland. (In 1973, millions of military records, including many from World War II, were destroyed in a disastrous fire at the National Personnel Records Center in St. Louis, Missouri.)

With little rest, the 101st quickly resupplied and filled its ranks with replacement troopers, none too soon. Within a month, a staggering German offensive began, and became known as the Battle of the Bulge—a last-gasp attempt to push back the Allied advance and cut supply lines. The December 16 battle included over 400,000 German soldiers, hundreds of Panzer tanks, and thousands of pieces of artillery from three different armies that included thirteen infantry and seven armor divisions.

Initially overwhelmed, American forces retreated and were surrounded in Bastogne, Belgium, becoming a significant obstacle to the advancing 5th Panzer army. Henry's company, as part of the 101st Airborne, was jammed into trucks and rushed overnight. They arrived on December 18 to help secure the northern section of the perimeter around the town.

As Company F troopers approached Bastogne, the sounds of war intensified with booming artillery and machine gun chatter. They faced a scene of intense cold and deep snow. Enemy artillery airbursts became deadly without foxholes, yet the ground was so hard it was almost impossible to chip out one, even with a pickaxe.

When not fighting, the men tried to keep warm and avoid frostbite by tucking their hands in their armpits, shuffling their feet, and, worst of all, continuous walking that prevented sleep. They would sleep two together, wrapped in a tarp or parachute shroud when possible. There was no shaving or brushing of teeth. They stripped warm clothes from the dead.

The battle see-sawed, with Company F constantly patrolling and conducting ambushes. It was close-in combat where little plots of land would change hands during vicious counterattacks. Some troopers began using dead German soldiers, propping them up in foxholes with GI helmets as decoys to be shot first when enemy soldiers infiltrated.

In early January, Company F was frequently attacked; the battalion commander was killed, and forty troopers, including Henry, were captured. Henry later recounted that, at the Bulge, "If there were two of us and one of them, we took them prisoner—then if there were two of us and three of them, they took us prisoner."

Fighting would continue after Henry's capture until General Patton's 4th Armored Division broke through the encirclement. Later, the 101st, including the 502nd, were awarded the Distinguished Unit Citation by General Eisenhower for their actions at Bastogne.

Missing in Action

HENRY ST. PIERRE

Henry St. Pierre Missing in Action

Former Member of Company K, National Guard

IN BELGIUM

Notch Road Private One of Four Brothers in Service —Lost Since Jan. 13— Previously Wounded in France.

An all-too-common headline during the war, another soldier missing in action. (Courtesy of St. Pierre family)

A February 23, 1945, article in *The Transcript* reported the difficult news: "Henry St. Pierre Missing in Action…Pvt Henry St. Pierre…a former member of Company K, has been missing in action in Belgium since January 13 according to a War department telegram received last night by his parents." In April 1945, his parents were officially notified that Henry was a prisoner of the German government.

In the meantime, Henry had been forced to march in the sub-zero cold to Stalag XII A, located in Limburg, Germany, about 160 miles from Bastogne. The trek to Stalag XII A was arduous for the weary troopers who had been relieved of their overcoats and gloves. Stragglers or wounded were left to die from exposure or starvation, or they were shot. The captives slept on frozen ground, were fed crusts of dark brown bread, and drank snow. After the war, a paratrooper from Paterson, New Jersey, visited Henry, whom he credited with saving his life when he needed assistance during the long trek to captivity.

The conditions at Stalag XII A were dire. It was intended to be a transient camp for processing new prisoners of war, so little had been done to upkeep the location. Thousands of men were processed there; as captives would arrive, they would be interrogated and moved elsewhere within weeks, although, for some reason, Henry remained there permanently.

At one point, he was moved from large, crowded "circus-like" tents where they slept back-to-back on the ground to wooden barracks with straw mattresses and a small coal stove for heat. There were no furnishings, and meals were minimal, almost starvation portions of a loaf of bread for breakfast and watered-down soup for the noon and evening meals. Sometimes, they received crackers or a small piece of potato. After such little nutrition, the daily work details drained all the men's strength. Henry recounted to his nephews memories of "building roads throughout Germany with a two-pound hammer."

There was no lighting in the camp, and with stone toilets serving thousands of men, disease was rampant, most prisoners had diarrhea, and there were no medical facilities. Camp rules were severe; prisoners touching the perimeter barbed wire were immediately shot.

Shortly after his arrival, he recalls being interrogated by a German officer. The officer asked if he was German because of his light hair color and blue eyes. Once that question was answered, and Henry refused to answer anymore, he heard a shot outside the room, and the officer indicated his previous interviewee had been shot for not answering questions. Henry still refused and was dragged out of the room. His guard took him to the courtyard and fired a shot into the air, standing in the courtyard where the prisoners were previously questioned.

Henry was not a model prisoner, escaping and being recaptured at least once. Interrogated and refusing to deny his Catholic faith while showing disdain for his captors, his meager rations were cut. Henry remembers being on a work detail cutting grasses by hand, smuggling some of the grass back to his tent, and boiling it on the stove for nourishment. Often at night, he dreamed of and even imagined the smells of his mother's cooking.

In late March 1945, as Allied troops began to approach, the German guards started evacuating the camp, driving prisoners to a rail side and packing 50 to 80 men in a train car with little room to stand and barely able to breathe. Several of the early trains were unknowingly strafed by US planes.

Henry was fortunate and had missed his train ride on April 2 when tanks from the 9th Armored Division broke down the gates and freed the prisoners. Sadly, several tanks ran over what they thought were bundles of rags on the road but were in fact severely malnourished Americans.

In a letter home, Pvt. St. Pierre wrote that if the Americans had not liberated them when they did, it would have been "only a matter of a couple more days" before they would have starved to death (*Transcript,* 4-19-45). Those severely emaciated like Henry were fed, quickly given intravenous fluids, and medicated. He had lost over 50 pounds from his 5'5" 145-pound frame. All the POWs suffered from malnutrition and dysentery, which were the camp's biggest killers.

Stalag XII A was renamed Allied Prisoner Camp No. 2. Food rations were greatly improved to help the recovering men, and the facilities were repaired as they waited for transportation home. The captured German guards were put to work on camp maintenance and some even cooked.

Henry, relieved to be with his mom on Berkshire soil. (Courtesy of St. Pierre family)

Henry departed Europe in late April and arrived home in May to a joyous welcome. He had spent twenty months and five days overseas.

After Henry's capture in January, the 502nd continued to see action as it moved through Germany and, in May, on its final mission, it captured Hitler's Eagles Nest in Berchtesgaden, Germany. Until relieved, the men continued searching for hidden German soldiers and arms and assisting refugees. At the war's end, their summer was spent in Mittersill, Austria, near Salzburg, and then returned to France for transportation home.

Not long after Henry's arrival home on June 13, 1945, *The Transcript* noted, "Former Prisoner of the Nazis Now at Lake Placid, N.Y.: Private 1st Class Henry St. Pierre…recently returned to this country from overseas where he was held as a prisoner of War by the Germans and is stationed at the Army Ground and Service Forces Redistribution Station in Lake Placid, N.Y. While at Lake Placid…. he will be processed for his next assignment."

Henry was discharged on July 26, 1945, at the Fort Devens Separation Center.

Credited with fighting in the battles and campaigns of Normandy, Rhineland, Ardennes, and Central Europe, Henry was decorated with a Distinguished Unit Badge, the American Defense Medal, the European–African–Middle Eastern Campaign Ribbon, the American Theater Campaign Ribbon, A Victory Medal, and the Purple Heart. Henry also qualified retroactively for the POW medal established by Congress in 1985.

Upon his return home, Henry's sister introduced him to Gladys Ruth Foster, a co-worker at Sprague Electric Company. It wasn't long before they were engaged, and they married on September 2, 1946, at Holy Family Church in Greylock. Gladys would leave Sprague and become a homemaker when their two daughters were born.

Henry returned to the mill, but persistent stomach problems never allowed him to work a whole week. At one point, he decided to use his GI Bill benefits and attended a nearby barber school. Upon graduation, he worked at his brother's shop in Williamstown until opening his own business, the Community Barber Shop, on State Road in North Adams. Even at his barber shop, with a partner, where he could establish his own work hours, his health plagued him.

Henry's barber shop remained open for ten or twelve years until his declining health caused him to close it during the 1960s. Not many weeks passed without Henry being taken to the Albany VA Medical Center for severe stomach ailments, likely a long-term effect from the near-starvation and dysentery at the camps. The government classified him as 100% disabled.

Henry, who was a jokester, was well-liked by family and friends. He enjoyed talking about and participating in local politics. When the family got together, Whist or Pitch card games were the main source of entertainment, and either four or three-person cut-throat games engaged everyone. His barber shop kept a heavily used cribbage board for the slow times.

Henry enjoyed spending time with his numerous nieces and nephews and had a special relationship with each of them. Known as the fun guy, he would treat them to new restaurants he had discovered, driving there in his red and white 1955 four-door Pontiac. One nephew remembered him thanking a waitress for assistance in German or what sounded like German; they were always curious if it was some gibberish or just a joke. He also used to talk to his terrier in German, saying *raus*, meaning out. He meant for the dog to get up and go outside.

Once a year, his brother would visit from New Jersey, and it was a cause for celebration. Henry and all his brothers (and sometimes brothers-in-law) would play poker for pennies or match sticks every night. Every night was filled with cards, beer, laughter, and a room full of cigar smoke. Their wives were often grateful when it was over.

Despite ongoing visits to VA medical centers, Henry never complained. He had the gift of gab (as described by one nephew), and he greatly enjoyed the company of family. When at the VA, he would always visit those soldiers he described "as the guys who never came back from the war," meaning former soldiers committed to long-term mental care, usually from shell shock.

This patriotic, determined, decorated paratrooper, at times a jokester, never complained about his wartime experiences or his many hospital visits where he continued to fight the long-term effects of severe malnutrition. In 1974, Henry passed away at the age of fifty-nine and rests peacefully with Gladys, the love of his life, at Eastlawn Cemetery in Williamstown, Massachusetts.

Henry's final resting place. (Courtesy of St. Pierre family)

GEORGE P. TAYLOR
TAIL GUNNER
376TH BOMBARDMENT GROUP

The flak over the refinery was intense. It rocked their plane's frame. Just seconds after the crew released their bombs, two of the plane's four engines were hit, and the aircraft was shredded with shrapnel. Black smoke was everywhere, with two dead engines and a shuddering aircraft. There was no hope, no expectation, of returning to base. Base was hundreds of miles away, and there was no safe place to land the crippled bomber. Suddenly the crew was parachuting. George, in the tail gunner's position, had only seconds to jump, but a panicked waist gunner was blocking the only escape hatch.

GEORGE WAS THE MIDDLE son of seven children (six boys and a girl). He was born in New Bedford, Massachusetts, on December 28, 1925, then, as a toddler, moved with his family to North Adams. All six boys would serve in the military—five in World War II and one in the Korean conflict.

His dad, Hugh Taylor, born in 1894, was a descendant of stouthearted whalers and, after attending local schools, he served as a boatswain on a battleship in the US Navy during World War I. His active-duty service included several perilous trips across the Atlantic. Hugh married Anna Elizabeth Walsh in 1919 and, after settling in North Adams, worked for twenty-five years at North Adams Normal School (now MCLA) as a fireman and custodian.

Born in Boston, Anna Walsh had moved to New Bedford as a child, attended local schools, and worked as a machine operator in textile mills. After arriving in North Adams, she worked for a while at McCraw & Tatro, Inc., a dry goods store on Main Street. Most of all, she was a homemaker to her seven children, who called her Nana. She and Hugh passed away just several years apart and are buried in Southview Cemetery in North Adams, Massachusetts.

The Taylor kids grew up on Gallup Street, and the boys were a rambunctious crew, hosting boxing matches with the neighborhood kids on their front porch. At the cost of a split lip or a black eye, the winner of the fisticuffs would earn a penny. (Though the children were feisty, their home wasn't without discipline. It is said that the banister going upstairs in their two-story house had dings from Nana's near misses with the belt during disciplinary bouts.)

George attended nearby Houghton Elementary School, participating in swimming meets with other grammar schools. He was very competitive in the 50- and 100-yard freestyle and the 50-yard backstroke. It was a useful skill to have. Being a strong swimmer might provide future comfort to a tail gunner flying over huge bodies of water.

George, number 58 on the front right, with Drury High's football team. (Courtesy of Taylor family)

In 1944, George graduated from Drury High School, having played interclass basketball and varsity football during his junior and senior years. *The Transcript* of North Adams noted that George "... held down a regular tackle position with credit on Drury's championship football team a year ago last fall..." (1-24-45). George also worked for *The Transcript* before entering military service his senior year. While still a student, in February 1944, George enlisted in the Army Air Force, then underwent basic training at Westover Airfield. He had additional training in Greensboro, North Carolina, after which he attended gunnery school at Harlingen Field, Texas.

When he graduated from Drury High on Saturday, June 18, 1944, only Aviation Cadet George Paul Taylor and one other serviceman were present at graduation, out of the fourteen members of the class of 1944 who had joined up to serve in the Armed Forces. Parents of the other twelve graduates were presented with their sons' diplomas.

That same month, Pfc. Taylor completed the Army Air Force Flexible Gunnery School and received his silver wings. The training was described by *The Transcript* as "a comprehensive seven-week course in every phase of aerial gunnery warfare [preparing] him for his place in America's stepped-up aerial offensive. Besides learning to use every bit of technology, from camera guns to the deadly .50 Browning, George studied turret manipulation and aircraft recognition. He was required to tear down and assemble weapons while blindfolded. The part he enjoyed the most, and the climax of the course, was firing on towed targets from Liberator bombers under simulated combat conditions" (*Transcript,* 6-10-44).

After further training at Charleston, South Carolina, George departed for his overseas tour on December 10, 1944, arriving in Italy on December 24. Many crews flew their replacement aircraft from the United States, while others arrived by troopship. Presumably, the aircrew he was matched up with in the States took a ship to Italy, but what is documented is that his mom received a brief letter on January 6, 1945, including the words "here I am...." He had arrived at San Pancrazio Airfield, near the southeasternmost tip of Italy (the "heel" of Italy's boot).

George had been assigned to the 514th squadron of the 376th Heavy Bombardment Group, 15th Air Force. The 376th had four squadrons made up of twelve B-24 Liberator bombers each (the 512th, 513th, 514th and 515th), totaling approximately forty-eight aircraft. With over 2,000 personnel per squadron, it was a force of nearly ten thousand men.

All members of the 15th Air Force had been trained and transported to Italy to be closer to its European targets. The enemy could now be bombed daily from both England and Italy. Jimmy Doolittle became the first commander of the 15th and later became the famous Medal of Honor winner who led the first air attack on the Japanese homeland.

The 376th would be focused on destroying enemy aircraft factories, gasoline refinery facilities, railroads, airfields, bridges, and harbors. Their long-range missions were in Italy, France, Germany, Czechoslovakia, Austria, Hungary, and the Balkans.

San Pancrazio Airfield

THE SAN PANCRAZIO AIRFIELD in Apulia was nicknamed "San Pan" by the fliers. The 376 Bombardment Group (nicknamed the *Liberandos*) flew aircraft out of San Pan from November 1943 until VE Day in April 1945.

Living at the airfield was a Spartan experience. One of George's letters described living in a tent and sleeping on a cot. The fliers used discarded oil drums for gasoline heaters. High-octane gasoline or engine oil made the best fuel, although accidental fires were not infrequent. The men showered under a disposable tank made from a fighter's wing that had been hoisted on a seven-foot frame. Its water was warmed only by the sun, which meant cold showers were routine. During the rainy season, muddy, rutted roads were the rule of the day, and photographs show chickens enjoying free range at the base.

The squadrons did have their own barber shops, where local barbers charged ten cents for a haircut and five cents for a shave.

THE PLANE

GEORGE WAS A TAIL gunner on the B-24 Liberator, a name given to it by the British. It was the world's most produced heavy bomber. All 18,500 aircraft were designed with a special 110-foot wing located higher up on the fuselage, allowing for long range and the ability to carry a larger bomb load than the B-17 Flying Fortress. As a trade-off, the Liberator's control was more difficult to handle, the plane had a lower ceiling, and its wing was more susceptible to battle damage than the B-17.

A mile-long assembly line at Ford Motor Company's Willow Run plant in Michigan produced a B-24 every 59 minutes, and 650 monthly. The 60,000-pound aircraft had 1,225,000 parts and cost $297,000 to build. In fact, demand was such that during the height of the war, pilots and crew often slept on nearby cots, waiting for their planes to come off the line.

The plane had a maximum speed of 290 mph at 25,000 feet. The range was determined by bomb load: with a 5,000-pound bomb load (the most common payload being ten 500-pound bombs), the B-24's roundtrip range was 1700 miles. Many missions necessitated roundtrips of over 1,500 miles, bombing targets from an elevation of 18,000 to 25,000 feet, leaving little room for error.

The wings also held the craft's fuel tanks, containing 2400 gallons of fuel, and were very susceptible to being hit and catching fire. The high fuselage-mounted wing made it difficult to survive crash landings; consequently, B-24s were nicknamed the "Flying Coffin." It was not uncommon to see a damaged B-24 fall from the sky with its wings folded like a butterfly. The Liberator also had only one small floor exit near the tail, making it difficult for the flight crew to escape a crippled fuselage.

The B-24 was designed with two central bomb bays that could hold up to 8,000 pounds of bombs in each compartment. The bomb bay doors operated like a roll-top desk retracting into the fuselage. With a full load, the plane's altitude was limited to 25,000 feet, several thousand feet lower than a B-17, making it subject to more intense flak.

This ungainly-looking plane was also called the "Flying Boxcar." It was more complicated to fly and required additional pilot training. With its wing mounted higher on the frame, the plane was dangerous to ditch or belly land since the fuselage tended to break apart.

On top of the other difficulties, the B-24 was prone to leaking aviation fuel and hydraulic fluid, so most crews flew with the bomb bay doors cracked in order to rid the plane of explosive substances. The pilots often prohibited crew members from smoking. B-17 aircrews liked to tease B-24 crews that they were flying the crates the B-17s were shipped in.

Nine or ten crew members manned the B-24s. In the front of the plane, the two pilots were supported by one navigator, a bombardier,

George, on bottom row, second from right, with his ten-man air crew. (Courtesy of Taylor family)

a flight engineer, and a radar/radio operator in the nose and top turrets, followed by the bomb bay area and a nine-inch catwalk to get to the further reaches of the aircraft where the waist (2), ball, and tail gunners were located. The gunners manned ten Browning .50-caliber machine guns with an effective range of 1000 yards.

Flights were usually six to eight hours long, inside a rickety plane that smelled of cordite, cigarette smoke, urine, oil, fuel, and dried blood.

In George's position as a tail gunner, he covered all points behind the craft and had a great view of the following formation and the flak directed at his plane. The lovely view was hampered significantly by his cramped position in a rotating, plexiglass turret. He was constantly searching for enemy aircraft, operating two .50-caliber machine guns.

Over six to eight hours, the crew had to address bodily needs. One additional drawback to George's position was that the ship's crew would urinate into funnels attached to a hose. This hose exited along the side of the bomber. The liquid would flow along the sides of the plane and splashes might find their way into the tail turret through gaps between the turret and the plane. Tail gunners would often threaten crew members if they relieved themselves while the turret was occupied.

George was also listed as a ball turret gunner, requiring him to slip into a retractable plexiglass ball lowered to the underside of the plane, a most difficult position to extract oneself from should the aircraft or electrical system be damaged in battle.

Even moving about the B-24 could be dangerous. Crew members traveling throughout the plane must traverse a 9-inch catwalk in the middle of the bomb bay area. A misstep onto the bomb bay doors would mean a quick ride to the ground.

The Liberators were not pressurized or insulated, so each fighting position was equipped with ports for oxygen, communications, and electrical outlets. The crews wore oxygen masks when flying over 10,000 feet and needed electrically heated flight suits when exposed to freezing temperatures that could reach 50 degrees below zero. The two-piece, electrically wired suit was comprised of a jacket and pants with connected heated gloves and shoes. Frostbite could be seconds away for the careless or wounded.

Some of the B-24's most notable crew members over the course of the war included Joseph P. Kennedy, Jr. (pilot, KIA), actor Walter Matthau (radio man), future US Senator George McGovern (pilot), actor Jimmy Stewart (pilot), future Secretary of the Interior Stewart Udall (waist gunner) and Louis Zamperini, the Olympic runner, (bombardier) brought to life in the celebrated book *Unbroken* by Laura Hillenbrand.

The Enemy

THE THREE MOST SERIOUS dangers during group missions were enemy fighters, anti-aircraft flak, and the weather. Of the enemy fighters, the B-24's aircrew was subject to true peril by the Messerschmitt Bf-109 (Me-109) and the Focke-Wulf (Fw-190), the backbone of the German Luftwaffe.

With its two machine guns and cannon, the Messerschmitt had more aerial kills than any other aircraft in World War II. The Focke-Wulf, introduced after the Messerschmitt Bf-109, was considered a success by Luftwaffe pilots because of its climbing and diving ability, making it a better interceptor against the ever-increasing Allied bomber groups. The powerful, single-engine planes sported two 20mm and two 13mm cannons and could easily reach speeds over 400 miles per hour.

When not contending with enemy fighters, as bombers neared their targets, they were then subject to the oily black puffs of flak from intense barrages of anti-aircraft artillery. The German anti-aircraft guns called eighty-eights (caliber 88mm) were highly accurate, ten-man, crew-served weapons used in batteries of four guns with fire control radar.

The 88 was considered one of the most effective weapons in World War II. They shot 15 to 20 rounds per minute, and their 20-pound high explosive shells were effective to over 26,000 feet, well within the range of Allied raids at 20,000 to 25,000 feet. In 1944, there were over ten thousand 88s in service, most used in Germany as anti-aircraft weapons.

Orientation

NEW CREWS WERE TEMPORARILY split up and spent time flying with more experienced crews. They first had one-on-ones (orientation) with someone holding their job. For George, when he arrived, these orientations occurred just three or four times before he was sent off to fly with his crew.

Flight days were long and strenuous. The 376th Group's practice was to fly three squadrons and stand down the 4th for training, rest, and aircraft maintenance. While missions were not daily, sometimes they came close to that.

The 514th flew six or seven ships to a vee, with one section leading, another to high and right, yet another lower and left, and three vees totaled 18 aircraft, or the squadron. The size of larger group formations with other squadrons was determined by the type of target and its priority. New crews were usually assigned to the rear of the group, in many cases arriving after the German gunners had adjusted their sights, making them very susceptible to flak hits.

During January 1945, George's orientation period, the weather was miserable, and his squadron was grounded most days. A few missions went out, focusing on railyards and steel works in the Vienna area. A number of Liberators and their crew were lost during this "slow" period, often to flak over the target area. It usually took crews months to complete the 35 combat missions required before being relieved…and the odds of them making it unscathed were daunting.

In January, his hometown newspaper noted that George had

been promoted: "George P. Taylor has been promoted to Staff Sergeant in Italy where he is currently serving with an air force unit..." (*Transcript,* 1-23-45).

The seventh of February began like any other preflight day. George's aircrew mates awoke at 4:00 a.m., had breakfast, and then met for a briefing around 6:00 a.m. Trucks carried them to the flight line, and they were in the air and assembled overhead by 9:00 a.m. (Despite the early hour, no one ever skipped shaving: A good fit on the oxygen mask was essential.)

With improved weather, the 514th and George's maiden aircrew was called to assault the heavily defended Moosbierbaum oil refinery near Vienna. Located on the Danube River, it was the last major oil refinery available to the German field forces; consequently, it was heavily defended by flak and enemy aircraft. The Germans used smoke pots in surrounding fields and lit oil tanks on fire, sending up dense clouds of black smoke to obscure the refinery.

Records indicate that George's aircraft was part of two missions that day. His mission was listed as #402, targeting Vienna, with Flight Officer Edward F. McGlynn.

After hours of flying, as they closed on their target, German 88s delivered a torrent of fire, shredding George's formation. After the first few Allied planes dropped their bombs, the German flak gunners adjusted their deadly aim to the following planes in line. The 514th squadron's efforts were reported by the radio operators as a "good bomb run," discounting that four B-24s were destroyed by flak, another was missing due to mechanical problems, and ten others were heavily damaged by anti-aircraft fire with fifty-five crew members missing.

George's plane was hit on the approach to dropping their bombs. The bombardier was able to release the payload, but the concentrated flak had dealt the plane a deadly blow. Two out of four engines were destroyed, flight controls were shredded by shrapnel, and the aircraft began losing altitude quickly. In all likelihood, Flight Officer Edward "Mac" McGlynn had the crew lighten the crippled aircraft by throwing out ammo belts, loose equipment, and anything that might help them stay aloft and return to friendly airspace. It was not to be. The plane was too severely damaged.

Amid the smoke seeping into the plane, while fighting with the damaged controls, McGlynn ordered the crew to bail out while he kept the aircraft straight and level for as long as he could, allowing the men to parachute. The crew snapped on their chutes and left their stations. All the while, the aircraft was shuddering in its death throes. They knew they had only minutes, seconds even, before the plane would be too low to jump.

As George approached the rear escape hatch, other crewmembers crawled to it. Suddenly, a crewmember froze and blocked the hatch, paralyzed as the plane started to corkscrew.

George, thinking fast, pushed him out of the hatch and followed right behind him.

Surprisingly, all ten crew members survived the bailout, including the pilot. Scattered after landing, they found each other, realized they were in Yugoslavia, but were set upon by unfriendly partisans before they could formalize a plan. After some rough treatment, it looked like these partisans were intent on killing the crew. Ironically, at this moment, an SS patrol that had seen the crippled plane crash intervened, and by taking them prisoner saved the men.

Three weeks later, on March 1, George's mom received the Western Union telegram every parent hated to get. It stated, "The Secretary of War desires me to express his deep regret that your son Staff Sergeant George P. Taylor has been reported missing in action since seven February over Yugoslavia. If further details or other information are received, you will be promptly notified. JA Ulio Adjutant General."

A follow-up letter just days later, on March 3, 1945, from the 15th Air Force, advised George's mom that on February 7, while Staff Sergeant Taylor was on a combat mission near Vienna, Austria, "a direct hit by flak damaged two of his plane's engines and it fell from the formation at once. However, the craft continued to fly below the groups until they reached the vicinity of Maribor, Yugoslavia, where it was lost to sight. The bomber was escorted by fighter planes. Should there be a change in George's status (Missing-in-Action), the War Department will notify you at once."

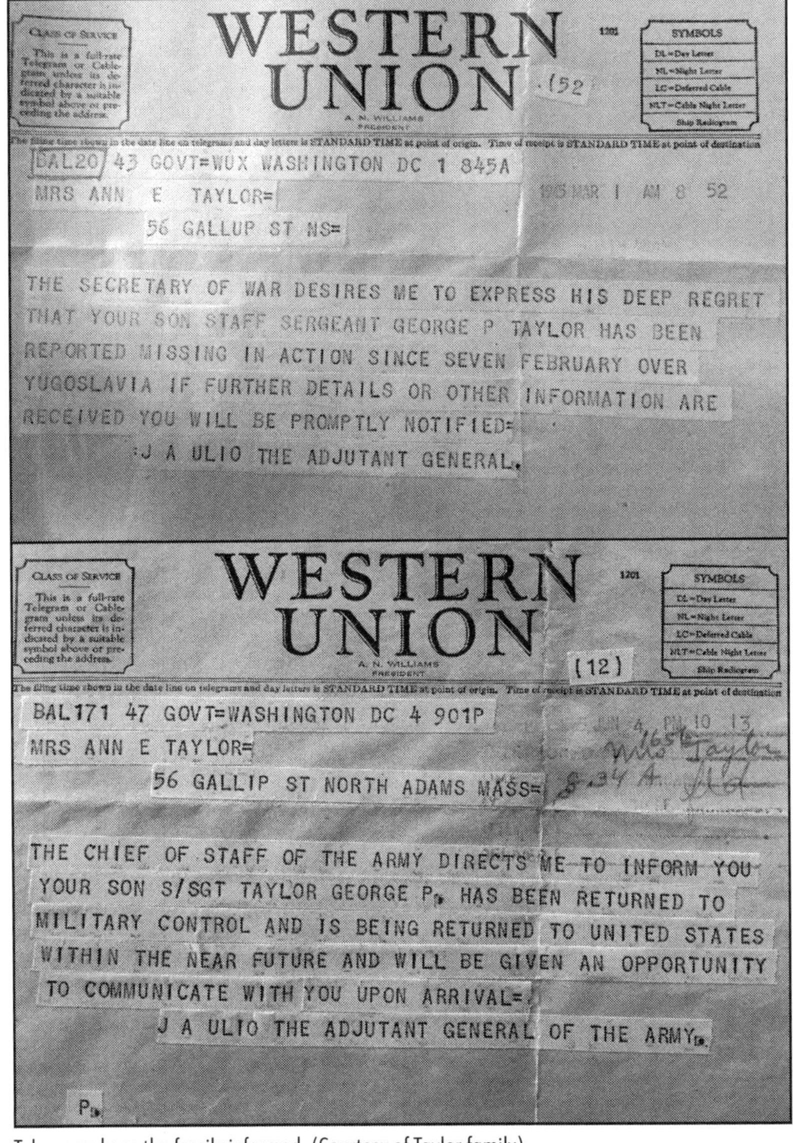

WESTERN UNION

BAL20 43 GOVT=WUX WASHINGTON DC 1 845A

MRS ANN E TAYLOR= 1945 MAR 1 AM 8 52

56 GALLUP ST NS=

THE SECRETARY OF WAR DESIRES ME TO EXPRESS HIS DEEP REGRET THAT YOUR SON STAFF SERGEANT GEORGE P TAYLOR HAS BEEN REPORTED MISSING IN ACTION SINCE SEVEN FEBRUARY OVER YUGOSLAVIA IF FURTHER DETAILS OR OTHER INFORMATION ARE RECEIVED YOU WILL BE PROMPTLY NOTIFIED=

J A ULIO THE ADJUTANT GENERAL.

WESTERN UNION

BAL171 47 GOVT=WASHINGTON DC 4 901P

MRS ANN E TAYLOR=

56 GALLIP ST NORTH ADAMS MASS=

THE CHIEF OF STAFF OF THE ARMY DIRECTS ME TO INFORM YOU YOUR SON S/SGT TAYLOR GEORGE P. HAS BEEN RETURNED TO MILITARY CONTROL AND IS BEING RETURNED TO UNITED STATES WITHIN THE NEAR FUTURE AND WILL BE GIVEN AN OPPORTUNITY TO COMMUNICATE WITH YOU UPON ARRIVAL=

J A ULIO THE ADJUTANT GENERAL OF THE ARMY.

Telegrams keep the family informed. (Courtesy of Taylor family)

Records show the crew's names and positions as follows:

Officers

McGlynn, Edward F. . . . . Pilot
Sliwinski, Walter . . . . Co-pilot
Koehler, Robert J. . . . . Navigator
Wilcox, Robert E. . . . . Bombardier

Enlisted

White, Donald E.. . . . . Engineer
Barrows, Robert S. . . . . Radio Operator
Williams, William C. . . . . Gunner
Waver, Raymond J. . . . . Gunner
Sheuchanko, James. . . . . Top Turret
Taylor, George P. . . . . Ball Turret

(Note: TSgt Alfred Young, who was typically with George's crew, subbed on a different plane that day and escaped captivity.)

With the Germans busy evacuating Yugoslavia, the crew was forced to march back, under guard, to Germany, sleeping along roads or in barns with little food or water. Eventually, they were incarcerated in one of Germany's Stalags. (George's family believes it was Stalag 1XB.) World War II in Europe was in its final stages, and George and his crew experienced the hardships of the Stalag from February until liberated in late April by General George Patton's 3rd Army. It was none too soon; the crew was grossly malnourished due to a lack of food. Three months after George and his crew were shot down, Victory in Europe was declared on May 8, 1945.

Back home, his mom had been persistently sending letters to the War Department requesting more information about her son and the names of the next of kin of the nine other crew members so she could communicate with their families.

In the meantime, George was returning to the United States via plane and boat. Upon his arrival, he recovered from his ordeal at Army Air Forces Convalescent Hospital in Pawling, New York, and during a furlough in June 1945, he was given a welcome home party by his parents and friends (*Transcript,* 6-19-45).

After six months in the European Theater of Operations, he was entitled to wear the European–African–Middle Eastern Theater ribbon with three battle stars, the Victory Medal, a Purple Heart, and a Good Conduct Medal to accompany his Silver Flight Wings. His non-military souvenirs included a German sword, a defused hand grenade, and a staff car flag. Family members still have the sword today.

George, far right, and three of his brothers, happy to be all in the same room again after a long separation. (Courtesy of Taylor family)

George received his honorable discharge from the Army Air Forces Convalescent Hospital at Plattsburgh Barracks, New York (*Transcript,* 12-3-45). As a postscript, George's group, the 376th, was credited with 451 missions over Africa and Italy, destroyed 220 enemy aircraft in aerial combat, and received three Distinguished Unit Citations.

The 15th Air Force lost 3,364 aircraft and had over 21,000 crewmembers killed, wounded, missing in action, or taken prisoner. Most were bomber crewmembers lost while destroying 6300 enemy aircraft in air battles and on the ground. The 15th was also credited with making extraordinary efforts to rescue crewmembers and, over the months, retrieved over 5600 personnel via ship, air rescue, or on foot through enemy lines.

Often pilots named their bombers and decorated the nose of the plane with names, figures, or numbers. The name of George's ship is unknown and lost to time. Usually, one of the aircrew or a ground crew member did the painting. Names ran the gamut, from the Brewery Wagon and Shangri-La to Daisy Mae and Hula-Girl, most frequently involving pictures of beautiful women in various poses.

Thirteen years after the war ended in 1958, British geologists flying over the Libyan desert spotted an aircraft in the dunes. Months later, a search party discovered a B24-Liberator, known as "Lady Be Good" of the 514th (George's Squadron). The plane had disappeared in April 1943 during a bombing mission over Naples, Italy. After an extensive search, the remains of eight airmen were found nearby. The body of the ninth was never retrieved, lost in the vast sands of the desert.

Shortly after his discharge from the Army Air Force, George graduated from General Electric's drafting program and began working in the Ordnance Division. His work as a draftsman and then as an engineer contributed to GE's Polaris Missile program. It was during this time period that George reconnected with Lucille Desnoyers, a friend of his sister who lived on the same street. After months of dating, the young couple wed at Notre Dame Church in North Adams on May 31, 1948.

In the mid-1960s, George accepted a position with IBM, and the family moved to upstate New York. Over the course of his work there, he received patents for his efforts in fiber optics and computer applications.

George and Lucille had two children, Victor and Viola, and the family enjoyed vacationing at a cabin on Lake Saint Catherine in Rutland County, Vermont, where George and his best friend power-boated and taught themselves and their families how to water ski. George bought a blue twenty-five-foot Chris-Craft boat with a white canopy and named it "Lola Baby" after their nickname for Viola. At the time, it was one of the largest boats on the lake.

George also loved to golf, bowl, and watch football. It was an idyllic life, hard earned after a most difficult war. Unexpectedly, George died at the age of forty-nine and was buried in Southview Cemetery in North Adams. Lucille died many years later and is also buried at Southview. He and Lucille parted too early but had many more years together than many of his Air Force compatriots enjoyed with their families.

This hometown boy, a great swimmer, a tackle on his high school football team, and a nascent newspaperman, survived parachuting out of a crippled plane, and saved the life of another crew member in the process. The swirl of war, the nonstop action, could have overwhelmed George Taylor, who was after all just a novice, nineteen and thirty days in. But he reacted admirably, and returned home to soak in all the beauty and adventure the Berkshires could offer. He was a hometown hero, to be sure.

The Taylor family has preserved George's uniform and decorations. (Courtesy of Taylor family)

WILLIAMSTOWN, MASSACHUSETTS

ALBERT BACHAND
MACHINIST MATE
122ND SEABEE BATTALION

Albert and his company macheted their way through the Philippine jungle, looking for a good spot to build a cement operation. Their mission was to support the repair of a nearby runway and provide the concrete to build a naval headquarters. The job was daunting, but the Seabees seemed to work engineering miracles. Acutely aware of the hundreds of remaining stragglers from the defeated Japanese army, men who had little to lose and could appear anywhere, Al kept his Browning Automatic Rifle by his side. During their trek through the jungle, the discovery of rotting corpses constantly reminded them not to let their guard down.

ALBERT BACHAND WAS BORN to French Canadian parents, each of whom immigrated to the United States as a teenager in the 1890s. Joseph Alfred Albert Alphonse Bachand and Mary Albina (Cyr) Bachand had been born in the same year, 1880, just fifteen days apart, in the small Canadian towns of Adamsville and Napierville, both located north of the Vermont border in the Province of Québec. As was the practice in Catholic Canada at the time, male infants were baptized with the first name Joseph and female infants with the name Mary, though in daily life they often went by a middle name, in this case Albert and Albina.

Both families moved south and eventually ended up in North Adams, lured by employment opportunities in the local mills.

Albert and Albina met not long after their arrival. Albert, already working at a local cotton mill, met Albina through friends.

They were married when both reached twenty-two years old, at Notre Dame Church in North Adams on May 12, 1902.

The young marrieds had twelve children between 1903 and 1917, of which seven would survive; five of the children died between birth and three years old. Albert was the couple's tenth child, born on February 8, 1915, in their basement apartment. He was called Al to distinguish from his father Albert, and he grew up with four sisters and two brothers.

Al attended Notre Dame school but was not much of a student. He left in the seventh grade to work in the Hoosac Cotton Mills with his dad to support the family. Bicycling to work at age 14, he swept floors for three dollars per week.

At eighteen years old in 1933, during the depths of the country's Great Depression, he joined the Civilian Conservation Corps (CCC). He was assigned to the 107th Company located in Pittsfield, Massachusetts. A picture of the group shows many young men in a wooden mess hall before heading out to their next work assignment. Al chose to serve two six-month terms, earning $30 a month, and spent most of his time constructing roads and clearing land on Mount Greylock, the highest mountain in Massachusetts.

Returning to the unsatisfying work in the mills triggered his first business endeavor. At nineteen, he coaxed his grandmother into co-signing for a $50 loan to purchase a 1927 REO truck chassis. Al then built a body for the truck and began hauling sand and gravel for fifty cents per cubic yard. When not busy trucking, Al apprenticed himself to a local carpenter and, for fifty cents an hour, helped build the Colonial Shopping Center and the Colonial Village in Williamstown, learning valuable skills in the process.

Al's dad became a naturalized citizen in 1930 at age fifty, and his mom eventually learned to write English, by age eighty. They celebrated their fiftieth wedding anniversary just before Albert passed away in 1953. Albina followed about ten years later and was buried alongside Albert in North Adams' Southview Cemetery.

They did get to see Al start a family, though. He married Beatrice

Champagne in 1937. They bought a small house, and Al, in his spare time, began repairing player pianos in the basement. In addition, he started a small trade, assembling grandfather clock kits, also in the basement. Due to demand, he had to move the operation to a local factory. With several helpers at one point, Al was building 100 clocks a month. This business eventually ended when the supplier of clock parts began making war materiel.

Beatrice and Al in front of their North Adams home, c. 1943. (Courtesy of Bachand family)

Al, the adventure seeker, decided in 1942 at 27 years old to sail a rowboat from the Hoosic River on Eagle Street, North Adams, to the Hudson River in New York. His initial crew of four was reduced to two people due to mishaps: just Al and his brother. On their third attempt, they would successfully navigate the sixty miles of rocks, rapids, dams, waterfalls, and snow in their open, hand-built, 350-pound rowboat.

In the throes of World War II, Al volunteered for the Navy, had a physical in Springfield, and was inducted on July 15, 1943. He was given one week of leave and officially entered the service on July 22, 1943. Al's prior construction experience was quickly, even eagerly, noted; he was assigned to the US Naval Construction Battalion and began his duty with the Seabees, with a nickname derived from its abbreviation, CBs.

SEABEE HISTORY

THE SEABEES WERE ESTABLISHED in 1942 after the US government realized the vast construction and engineering needs required by Allied forces at war worldwide. It was clear that civilians wouldn't be able to fill those needs, especially in a combat environment. Seabees were a unique military service, initially seeking volunteers from trade unions and construction sites, which wanted people skilled at their trades. Broad enlistment rules allowed men to serve up to fifty years old and often bestowed advanced rank for their skills. The Seabees would normally be the highest-paid enlisted men in uniform and often the oldest. Early in the war, their average age was thirty-seven. Notably, the Seabees were also the first fully racially integrated units in World War II.

The bumblebee patch, bringing a little levity to the job. (Courtesy of the author)

Their motto was *Construimus, Batuimus*—"We Build, We Fight"—or the far shorter version, "Can Do," which was cleverly supported by an insignia/patch showing a bumblebee with a sailor's cap and work tools, toting a machine gun.

By late 1942, due to the huge demand for Seabees, the service began taking unskilled civilian workers, sending them through a brief boot camp, then assigning them to Naval Construction Training Centers (NCTCs) and Advance Base Depots (ABDs), where they would be further trained in one of sixty different trades.

In October 1943, the Chief of Naval Operations transferred the 122nd C.B. Battalion to Camp Parks in California, where Al would join his unit of over a thousand men after completing his six-week boot camp.

Camp Parks would serve as a Naval Training and Replacement Center (NTRC) and train tens of thousands of sailors. It was considered the home of the Seabee program. The sprawling facilities included over 1,000 Quonset huts, sixty wooden barracks, numerous classrooms, a bus service, recreation centers, and a hospital. Located east of San Francisco, it was the hub for Seabees deploying to the Pacific and also the welcome center for those returning. The base was decommissioned in 1946 and is now used as an Army Reserve training center.

During November and December 1943, Al received instruction in basic military order, discipline, close-order drills, weapons, and bayonet training from Marine instructors. The seamen were also subjected to rigorous physical exercise, including a vaunted obstacle course. Upon course completion, Al was assigned to the 122nd Seabee Battalion.

A Seabee battalion consisted of a headquarters and four construction companies, each with 1100 officers and enlisted men. Four battalions made up a regiment, and two or more regiments made a brigade. Often, several battalions were assigned to a single building/repair project.

Al in uniform, just prior to heading oversees. (Courtesy of Bachand family)

Al and his battalion continued their learning at Camp Parks, which offered advanced training in sixty building trades, from electricity, carpentry, heavy equipment, machinery, welding, and surveying to pipe fitting and demolitions. Al was assigned a machinist rating, and he asked for additional weapons training with the BAR; the Marine weapons instructors willingly obliged.

The 122nd Battalion received further training at Camp Peary near Williamsburg, Virginia, before heading to Port Hueneme in Southern California for deployment overseas. In February 1944, the battalion boarded the USS *West Point*, a troop transport ship, and weeks later crossed the equator, headed for the Pacific.

A March 28, 1944, *Transcript* article was headlined "In New Guinea - Albert Bachand - Machinist Mate 2nd Class." Days later, on April 1, 1944, his unit operated with the 12th Marine Regiment at Milne Bay, Papua, New Guinea. Over the next eighteen months, the 122nd Battalion spent their days clearing jungles, constructing hundreds of remote bases, and building/repairing airfields, roads, boat docks, canals, storage tanks, hospitals, and thousands of warehouses in New Guinea and the Philippines.

Seabee battalions, including Albert's, built hundreds of Quonset huts to house over 1,000,000 troops. At considerable effort, ten Seabees could erect a 16-foot by 36-foot corrugated metal Quonset hut in a day. They also created pontoon assemblies and box-like structures, in order to assemble them into piers and docks. Ships could now land vast quantities of materiel during amphibious landings that would support troops moving inland.

The Seabees' "Can Do" attitude was pervasive throughout the Corps, especially during airfield construction. Supported by quarries and cement plants, they crushed coral, compacted it, poured cement and asphalt, and installed metal planking in a matter of days, often under severe weather conditions and under fire from enemy snipers and artillery. Tasks that would seem impossible suddenly were possible, like building over 100 PT boat bases, or carving and clearing roads through remote jungles during monsoon season.

During 1944 and 1945, the Seabees constructed nearly 80% of all airfields, barracks, ammunition bunkers, supply depots, and fuel tanks on over 300 islands. A saying became attributed to them: "the difficult we do at once, the impossible takes a little longer." The men

The Seabee camp in New Guinea. (Courtesy of Bachand family)

became noted for their ability to scrounge items, known in the Navy as *cumshawing*, and no effort was spared to complete their projects. (In the annals, there was even a picture of a Seabee-built washing machine powered by a windmill.) General Douglas MacArthur appreciated the Seabees' tremendous contribution to the war effort, saying, "The only problem [we] had with the Seabees was [we] didn't have enough of them."

In the summer of 1944, Al's unit operated out of Hollandia (now Jayapura), a port on the north coast of New Guinea, building facilities, roads, water filtration systems, and barracks. The Seabees were called to repair the Sentani airfields and build a naval base and ammunition dumps. While New Guinea was technically liberated months earlier, hundreds of enemy stragglers were still scattered throughout the area, and sudden, sporadic fighting continued through the fall. Al's BAR was never far from his side. It was not unusual for the Seabees to come across the rotting bodies of dozens of Japanese soldiers and pause to dig burial trenches. It took a decade for some enemy to yield; in 1955, the final four Japanese airmen surrendered at Hollandia.

In December 1944, the 122nd Seabee Battalion left Hollandia by Landing Ship Tank (LST) for Samar, the third largest island in the Philippines. Samar was near the site of several of the war's largest naval battles, the Battle of Leyte Gulf and the Philippine Sea, both victories for Allied forces.

Al brought home a Japanese propaganda leaflet dropped from a plane, intended to discourage Filipino and American forces. (Courtesy of Bachand family)

On land, where the 122nd Seabees were based, the US 6th and 8th Armies continued to fight the Japanese until the end of the war. Al's unit was involved in building a large naval depot and a Naval Air Station, erecting thousands of Quonset hut barracks, medical facilities, airstrips, wooden bridges, and piers.

Living conditions were miserable, with high humidity and temperatures. The men slept in heat-absorbing tents and on wooden pallets draped with mosquito nets to avoid rampant malaria. Eventually, the men would build their own huts and have the luxury of sleeping on cots.

As a petty officer, Al was in charge of the cement operations supporting the Seabees' massive building efforts. He recruited 23 natives from the Waray-Waray people, primarily fishermen and subsistence farmers, to work at the plant. They all spoke the Waray-Waray language and were mostly Catholics with a mixture of ancient beliefs. Earlier, they had served as guides to the Filipino guerillas. The men were especially helpful in warning the Seabees of lingering Japanese soldiers.

In the extreme heat, laundry still has to get done. (Courtesy of Bachand family)

Al and the local workers became close, although most communication was by hand signs. Al would bring food when he visited their simple, thatch-roofed homes; naturally, as a Seabee, he appreciated their construction, using native materials such as bamboo, clay, and palm leaves. The houses were built on stilts two or three feet off the ground, and pigs were penned underneath their bamboo floor. In 1968, when Al traveled to the Philippines, he reunited with one of the workers with whom he had stayed in communication.

Al, center rear, with his local crew, taking a break from making cement. (Courtesy of Bachand family)

Even while in the service, Albert was always looking for business opportunities and created a mail-order business selling photographs of everyday life in the Philippines. He also found time to take courses at the Armed Forces Institute in typing, psychology, and business administration. The Philippines were officially liberated in August 1945. The last Japanese soldier surrendered in 1974.

Just before Albert began heading home, a *Transcript* article noted: "Seabee Albert Bachand Promoted in the Philippines — Machinist Mate 1st Class" (10-9-1945). Al wrote Beatrice a letter just after this, in late October, letting her know he was headed back across the Pacific and would contact her when he landed in San Francisco. Upon arrival, he called home and found out that Beatrice had died at age twenty-seven from a heart ailment. She had been buried already. Devastated and aided by the Red Cross, Al flew directly to New York and took a train to North Adams, where relatives consoled him.

Al was discharged from the Navy at the USN Personnel Separation Center on December 6, 1945; his record book notes that he earned the World War II Victory Medal, Asiatic–Pacific Campaign Medal, Philippine Liberation Medal with one star, and American Campaign Medal.

Dealing with his grief, Al threw himself into countless new business ventures, most of them quite successful. His first was selling Whizzer-brand preassembled motorized bicycles out of a two-stall, stone-block garage behind his home. The first Whizzer bicycle, named "the Pacemaker," looked remarkably similar to today's electric bikes.

Not long after, Al became the area's Indian motorcycle distributor, selling and repairing motorcycles and, in what seems a clever move to support the nascent industry, Al founded the Berkshire Hills Motorcycle Club. Always up for an adventure, as a promotion for Indian motorcycles, Al, using two Indian motorcycles, cruised through forty-eight states in forty-five days, establishing a new record.

During this time, a *Transcript* article dated 12-6-1946 noted that Al enjoyed spelunking with his father-in-law; their experiences were captured in a book called *New England Buried Treasure*. He also promoted and sponsored contestants willing to race down the Hoosic River to the Hudson River in a rowboat, mirroring his accomplishment years prior.

As his businesses flourished, Al set a goal to retire at the age of fifty. To help manage his businesses, he hired Beatrice's younger sister, Theresa, as his secretary. After a while, they realized a mutual attraction, began dating, and were married in 1949, eventually having four daughters.

In the early 1950s, Al began his biggest venture yet, purchasing over 300 acres of farmland along the main highway into Williamstown. At the same time, he founded Contractors' Trailer Company, which converted house trailers into field construction offices he designed.

Al had dreamed of creating an upscale mobile home retirement park and began planning to use the acreage he had purchased to lay out a park. He bought a cement truck and pipe molds for a drainage system. He began constructing roads and setting up individual lots on what would become known at its opening in 1954 as *The Spruces*, a five-star-rated, retirement mobile home community. With land he purchased across the street, he later opened the Country Peddler store. He, Theresa, and their four daughters would go on to live in a home Al built at The Spruces.

Amenities at The Spruces included a concrete pool at the front of the property featuring a windmill with a waterwheel that drew water from a well to fill the pool. He also built a pond on the property, which would serve as a skating rink in the winter and provide paddle-boat fun in the summer. Another popular gathering spot was the community recreation hall, where residents enjoyed shuffleboard, a library, a hobby shop, a laundromat, and a gathering center.

As a public attraction, Al created a giant water display at the pool and called it the Whispering Fountains, featuring over two hundred colored lights and hundreds of water jets that shot water ten stories in the air. The controls were cleverly stored in a rehabbed wooden cabin cruiser permanently located nearby, on shore. The fountains were so popular with residents and tourists that they caused traffic jams and were eventually shut down.

Al was genuinely proud of The Spruces five-star rating, and although residents were responsible for their own property maintenance, he was never shy about reminding someone their lawn needed mowing. (As a sad postscript, in 2012, Hurricane Irene flooded and destroyed the park decades after Al sold it. Today, the two six-foot, one-ton stone lions that Al hired a sculptor to restore are still standing astride and guarding the front entrance. The area, now considered a flood zone, is used as a walking park by the community.)

During this time, Al attended night classes, completed four Dale Carnegie courses, and continued to open, close, and sell businesses. He maintained his goal of retiring at fifty.

In the early 1960s, Al seldom slowed down, well on his way to owning forty different businesses. At one point, he became a real estate broker, a certified pipe fitter, and a licensed painter and rigger, presumably supporting his efforts at The Spruces. He also became involved in selling government surplus goods.

At one point, Al attended the Weber School of Hypnotism and the American Institute of Hypnosis and became a certified hypnotist. News articles indicated that he performed many local demonstrations and went on to say he helped thousands of people in Northern Berkshire to quit smoking, manage pain relief, and achieve weight loss.

During this same time, he established the first Ski-Doo snowmobile dealership in the Berkshires, selling them at The Spruces. He organized and promoted snowmobile races on the back acres of the retirement park and on Mount Greylock. Once, he snowmobiled Senator Edward (Ted) Kennedy to the top of Greylock so the senator could ski down the famous Thunderbolt trail.

Al loved to travel, and family vacations often included his Plymouth station wagon towing a 24-foot travel trailer to campsites in New York State. Fluent in French, he enjoyed taking the family to visit relatives in Québec, Canada. One memorable family trip featured a month-long vacation across the United States in their travel trailer.

In the mid-1960s, at age fifty, Al realized his dream and retired. The celebration took place at The Spruces, with the guest of honor lauding Al's accomplishment as none other than Massachusetts Governor John Volpe, who landed in a helicopter on the lawn near the recreation hall. Governor Volpe, who owned a construction company in the Boston area, had purchased a number of Al's construction trailers over the years, and evidently finding them of high quality, the Governor had appointed Al to the Massachusetts Mobile Home Commission.

In 1964, Al and Theresa separated, divorcing several years later. Al sold The Spruces in 1968 and began his next adventure, traveling the world to see as many countries as possible. Over the next twenty-five years, he visited 160 countries. Al was always methodical, spending three months in preparation and usually two or three months of travel, always with his Konica camera. After returning home, he spent three more months creating vacation slides with a recorded narrative. He enjoyed sharing his travels and presented his slide-narratives to hundreds of organizations.

Never one to forego a business opportunity, in the 1970s, he established the *World Travelogue Company*, created a catalog, and sold prints from his collection, at one point selling slides and videotapes to several film companies.

He continued his travels, often accompanied by his daughters and sometimes their spouses. They took a month-long trip to the British Isles, an Icelandic trip, and a Bermuda cruise. In his later years, the travel slowed, but not before he took a seventy-six-day trip to Africa.

Was Al really retired? Retirement was in the eye of the beholder. In the early 1980s, Al created a business called the Dating Service of

Prestige, a prelude to today's dating apps. He advertised the matchmaking service in local newspapers, marketed to people looking for a partner within fifty miles of Williamstown. Clients were photographed, filled out a preference questionnaire, and chose their own dates from classified registers. Registration cost $150, and individual matches cost $20. Al sold the company several years later.

Locally, Al stayed involved in the community, writing hundreds of "Letters to the Editor" at *The Transcript* and often contributing to the section called *You're getting old if you remember*.... Always a promoter of Berkshire tourism, Al published a book he titled *Tourism in the Northern Berkshire County*. He was also involved in creating the Council on Tourism and coordinated with the local Chamber of Commerce sponsoring bus tours of Berkshire County and southern Vermont.

Al's entire existence was based on daring, hustle, and ingenuity. Although achievement slowed down slightly in the 1990s, his legacy had already been created, beginning as the tenth child of poor French immigrants and fulfilling his dream of retiring, such as it was, at age 50. Al passed away in 2003, a US Navy Seebee to the end. It's clear that much of his success can be attributed to the years in the Seabees, where he learned a broad array of skills in the most difficult and dangerous environments, at the same time finding inspiration in differing cultures. "Can Do" was more than a Seabee motto. It was a life's calling for the Williamstown visionary that was Al Bachand.

Roger J. Dennett
Gunner
409th Bombardment Group

The noise was deafening as the soldiers scrambled out of their tent; seeing a Japanese bomber with its red "meatball" insignia overhead, they realized they were under attack. Using crowbars, the soldiers broke into an armory and armed themselves with brand-new machine guns and rifles, all covered with grease and wrapped in wax paper. Roger ran outside and manned a machine gun, only to find there was no ammunition. Finally, he fired a shot from an Enfield bolt-action rifle before dropping to the ground to avoid withering fire from the scores of attacking planes.

It was a Sunday in early December, just after daybreak, and the torment at Pearl Harbor had only just begun.

ROGER JOSEPH DENNETT WAS born at home in Williamstown, Massachusetts, on Flag Day, June 14, 1921. He was the oldest child of Joseph and Alexina (Laforest) Dennett, who would go on to have four children in all: two boys and two girls.

At one point, Roger's father, from whom he received his middle name, had moved the French-speaking family to Williamstown where he worked as an auto mechanic at B&M Motors. Joseph, a World War I veteran, would become a lifelong member of the newly formed American Legion and, at one point, served as its commander. Eventually, he shifted to custodial work at Berkshire Hall, Williams College, and the National Bank, continuing those duties until retirement.

Roger's mom, Alexina, a Williamstown native, attended local schools and worked many years at Berkshire Fine Spinning Co. of Williamstown, then later in life worked for and retired from Williams College. She was an active member of the American Legion Auxiliary.

When a young child, Roger could only speak French and initially struggled in grammar school. His diminutive size encouraged bullies, but his feistiness quickly ended those thoughts. He also served as a dutiful altar boy at St. Rafael's Church.

Roger helped raise the family's brood of chickens and labored in his mom's large vegetable and flower garden. Alexina was known for and delighted in cultivating African violets.

He attended Williamstown High School and graduated from the school in 1939. The yearbook indicates that his nickname was *Peanut* and he was noted as the *Class Wit*, affirming his relaxed and joking ways. By all accounts, he was fun to be with and always ready with a good joke. Academically, he achieved honors all four years.

After graduation, Roger worked several jobs and held a position in a local bakery until his allergies caused him to leave. During this time, already enamored with planes, he became interested in the newly forming Army Air Corps, enticed by the chance to fly and see the world.

On April 9, 1940, at eighteen years old and less than a year after graduating, Roger enlisted for two years in the Army Air Corps, reporting to Fort Slocum, New York, for his basic training. The fort was an antiquated, almost eighty-year-old former Civil War military installation on Davids Island, just off Westchester County in the far western end of the Long Island Sound. During the Civil War, thousands of wounded Union and Confederate soldiers were treated there. In its early years, it also served as part of the US coastal defense service, sporting artillery batteries.

In WWII, Fort Slocum trained recruits; taught them military courtesy, close order drills, and weapons use; and served as an embarkation point for troops headed overseas. Roger's letters home indicated that the isolated island was a miserable place to be stationed.

This historic postcard illustrates the austere conditions of Fort Slocum. (Courtesy of New Rochelle Public Library Local History Collection)

Broken water pipes meant that his platoon was tasked with lugging salt water from the docks for showers. The men never felt clean, trying to lather up and shower in brackish water. Eventually, the eighty buildings that comprised Fort Slocum were razed, and the Fort closed in 1965. (Davids Island is currently abandoned, plagued by a litany of development obstructions.)

The days were long, with reveille at 5:00 a.m. and taps at 10:00 p.m. In addition to receiving military instruction, the troops would dig ditches, mow lawns, paint old buildings, stand guard duty, and tackle scullery work in the kitchen. Sometimes, the only highlight of Roger's day would be the care packages he received from his mom and sisters, often filled with candy and other treats, which he shared with his buddies.

Fort Slocum's only real advantage was its proximity to New York City. Several times, Roger leapt at the chance to travel into the city. One time in early summer, Roger and another private, both earning less than $30 a month, pooled their money, took a ferry across the Long Island Sound, and traveled by train to Queens to see the 1939 World's Fair. Having little money to spend on activities, the two friends likely stopped by the R.C.A. Pavilion to see the recently introduced five-inch by twelve-inch black-and-white television displays.

He mentioned in one letter home that one of the most memorable events was watching the Aquacade, a synchronized music, dance, and swim event with a floating stage. It's likely he would have seen celebrity swimmers perform, like Johnny Weissmuller, an Olympian and future actor in Tarzan movies, and Gertrude Ederle, the first woman to swim the English Channel, a feat she accomplished in 1926.

Little did he know that he'd be making his own Channel crossing, many times over, in a few short years.

After two months of training, Roger left Fort Slocum on June 8, 1940, for his next assignment: the 10th Air Base Squadron at Hickam Airfield in Hawaii. Departing by ship, his unit first traveled to San Francisco. Upon arrival, he enjoyed a brief liberty, taking the opportunity to visit Chinatown. Reboarding, passing under the newly constructed Golden Gate Bridge, their ship landed in Hawaii thirty days later.

In Hawaii: Roger, far right, with SSgt Curt Davis on left, and Tracy Warner in the middle. Roger kept in touch with Curt his whole life. (Courtesy of Dennett family)

After landing in Hawaii, Roger wrote home, asking his dad to send him civilian clothes. His letters are marked T.H. (Territory of Hawaii), as Hawaii didn't achieve statehood until 1959. Roger was promoted to Private First Class in August; in letters to his family, he reports receiving a $16-a-month raise, now earning $46 a month. Every month, he sent a portion of his pay to his parents. *The Transcript* noted that he phoned home on November 11, 1940, and "is settling in at his new base."

A little more than a year later, the Japanese Empire would attack Pearl Harbor, just three miles from Roger's base. In a recollection of the attack, he wrote, "On December 6, 1941, a friend of mine, S. Sgt. C.L. Davis, a drill instructor at Bellows Field, invited me to stay over at his field, telling me that they had fried eggs for breakfast; something I hadn't had for breakfast in a year or so [versus the 'lousy' dehydrated rations offered at base]. I accepted his invitation after spending some time in Honolulu—lunch and a few beers—[and] we went to Bellows Field. In the morning, instead of having breakfast, we were rudely awakened by a strafing attack on our tent. From then on, it was strictly war—handing out guns with a quick lesson on how to load the rifle and setting up a machine gun on the airstrip, waiting for ammo while being strafed by Zeros, and later removing a body from a crashed B-17 and spending the night in the rain with a lot of small arms fire going on. The next day, we captured a Japanese Naval Officer from a beached one-person submarine. Later in the day, I returned to Hickam Field."

When the attack occurred, Roger's tent was shredded with bullets. Most of the soldiers around him were recruits, and no one had a weapon since guns were all locked up in the base armory. With no key available, they broke open the armory, grabbed some machine guns and Enfield rifles, and Roger gave a quick course on how to use the weapons while yelling for ammunition for the machine gun he had set up. No machine gun ammunition was available, so on the following Japanese sortie, he fired at the Zeros with his bolt-action Enfield rifle. Realizing his single shots were unequal to the Zeros' machine guns, who had spotted and were targeting the useless machine gun, he hit the ground.

Before returning to Hickam, while patrolling the airfield, he and his squad captured a naked and disoriented Japanese submarine officer. Roger persuaded his angry group of recruits, who wanted to kill the man immediately, that he might be valuable to Army Intelligence, so the sailor was tied up and turned over to the authorities.

Later information revealed that the captive's name was Ensign Sakamaki, and he was part of a "midget submarine" attack group. His submarine, designated HA.19, was a two-man, 78-foot-long, five-foot-wide sub, one of five midget subs ordered to sink US warships in the harbor. It would have been launched from a much larger vessel, ten miles offshore and intended to deploy its two torpedoes before sinking itself with explosives. This HA.19 was discovered and shelled by US naval vessels, grounded on offshore reefs, and washed ashore.

The shell-shocked and exhausted Ensign Sakamaki evacuated his sub and crawled to shore. The other crew member drowned, and his body washed up days later. All five submarines were sunk, and Ensign Sakamaki, captured by Roger and his squad, became the very first Japanese prisoner of war in WWII.

Investigators closely examined the grounded sub, finding aboard detailed maps of the locations of all the US ships, heightening security concerns.

As a curious aside, the tiny sub was taken to the US mainland and trotted about on War Bond drives. In 1991, it was moved to the National Museum of the Pacific War in Texas. Sakamaki, who in later years became an executive at the Toyota Motor Corporation, visited his sub in Texas.

On December 8, Roger returned to Hickam and discovered that the top floor of the barracks, his bunk, and the guardhouse where he worked had all been destroyed by bombing. He never forgot how blood ran down the stairwell of the barracks, describing the difficult job of carrying out the dead and collecting body parts.

Much later in life, Roger would reflect on how his desire for Sunday morning fried eggs saved his life.

On December 8, Roger sent a telegram to his parents saying, "I hope you received my Radio Gram and that you didn't worry about me too much. I am all in one piece," letting them know he survived the bombing. *The Transcript* noted on December 8 that "Pvt. Roger Dennett, stationed at Hickam Field, Honolulu, reported a scene of heavy casualties...."

Roger received a commendation letter for his actions from the Air Corps Commander, part of which stated, "Your actions at that time (December 7, 1941) and all times since has been highly commendable. You fought valiantly against a foe who had superiority in everything but courage...."

Roger resumed his duties at Hickam Field and was promoted to Corporal. He then was accepted into the Army's pre-flight training program. Cadet Dennett left Hawaii in early 1943 to begin attending the Army's nine-week pilot program at Santa Ana, California. Upon completion, Roger received his first set of wings. He and a buddy had a chance to visit Los Angeles and walk the streets of Hollywood, marveling at the fifty-foot iconic sign HOLLYWOODLAND on the mountainside. (In 1949, when rebuilt, LAND was removed from the sign. *Hollywood Land* was initially promoted as a housing development.)

In May, Roger was in line waiting to board a plane to attend flight school in Fresno, California. As the first aircraft became filled, Roger was assigned to the next one. While Roger's plane sat in the queue for take-off, the first plane took off and rose to several hundred feet before falling out of the sky, crashing, and killing all aboard. Roger later acknowledged that he always "seemed to be one step ahead of the Grim Reaper."

Disappointedly, after several weeks, he was diverted from flight school to the Buckley Field Armament School in Colorado. Roger spent the next few months at Buckley and Lowry Airfields. In August 1943, now-Sergeant Dennett completed the Aircraft Armorers (bombardment) school.

Roger was transferred to a six-week gunnery course at Tyndall Field in Panama City, Florida. He spent countless hours disassembling and shooting .30- and .50-caliber machine guns as well as learning how to identify aircraft. The students were repeatedly drilled on aircraft identification to help them rapidly recognize friendly versus enemy; models of enemy planes hung in their classrooms, mess halls, and in Roger's barracks. He passed his final test with true flying colors: firing a machine gun from the air at a cloth target being towed by another plane.

With his successful completion of gunnery school, Roger earned a second set of wings. Among the thousands of students trained at Tyndall Field, one of its most famous was actor Clark Gable.

For the remainder of 1943, Roger flew to and from different US bases, accumulating flying time and gaining familiarity with his gunner/armorer role.

In early 1944, Roger wrote home, letting his parents know he had been promoted to Staff Sergeant, which came with a further $16-a-month pay raise, and he would increase his allotment to them. He also told them he would be leaving for England the following month.

After a two-week boat ride, Roger reached England on March 7, 1944, assigned to the 642nd Bombardment Squadron within the 409th Bombardment Group (light), all part of the 9th Air Force. The group and several other groups that included fighters and bombers were based at the Royal Air Force Airfield Little Walden. Opened in 1944, it was located about 40 miles north of London.

The 409th Bombardment Group included Roger's squadron (the 642nd) and the 640th, 641st, and 643rd. The group was activated in 1943 at Will Rogers Field in Oklahoma. Each of the squadrons had twelve aircraft and would fly out of Little Walden for the next six months, attacking occupied airfields, coastal defenses, V-2 missile sites, and railroad yards in France as preparation for the upcoming D-Day. Roger's 642nd boasted D6 markings on its fuselage and a yellow stripe on its rudder to distinguish itself. The D6 marking, used in radio conversations, identified the squadron.

Roger began almost daily missions as a gunner on an A-20 Havoc, a medium bomber. The 48-foot-long bomber, nicknamed "Boston" by the British, was manned by three crew members (pilot, bombardier, and gunner) and excelled in low-level bombing and strafing. With four forward-facing .30-caliber machine guns and three others placed about the plane, it was devastating to small surface ships, supply dumps, and enemy troops in the open. Pilots liked the plane's maneuverability and handling. It felt like flying a fighter aircraft. With its 1600-horsepower engines, it was capable of speeds over 300 miles per hour and a range of 1100 miles, carrying a bomb load of 1800 pounds.

Missions were busy times for Roger, manning and maintaining seven machine guns. Always under withering anti-aircraft fire (he recalled to his daughter), as they approached their targets on one mission, his two-engine bomber was hit hard with shrapnel, and the pilot told the crew to prepare to bail out. Roger discovered his parachute had been shredded by fire and was useless. He responded to the pilot, saying, "If you are going to jump, I won't be joining you," and holding up his mangled parachute. That made the pilot decide to try to land the plane and at the last minute, it gained power and leveled off from its nosedive. The crew, inspired, coaxed it back for an emergency landing at the airfield. No one would be swimming in the ocean that day.

Once, when the crew received several days of liberty, Roger and his buddies headed to London to see the sights. One of their first stops was at Madame Tussaud's Wax Museum, which has operated since the 1830s. It featured life-like wax statues of well-known celebrities, and the group was amazed by likenesses of Napoleon, Jesse Owens, Vincent van Gogh, and Charles Dickens.

Likely, they also visited Big Ben and the Tower of London, ogled the many pretty English girls, and stopped at several pubs before returning to base.

Roger in his dress uniform, possibly on liberty. (Courtesy of Dennett family)

Quickly back in action, Roger's squadron supported the D-Day invasion, carrying out massive bombings as part of Operation Overland, the invasion of France. The unit hit bridges, communication centers, enemy troops, flak gun sites, and ammo/supply dumps.

On August 7, 1944, *The Transcript* noted, "Sgt. Dennett Awarded Air Medal - Veteran of Pearl Harbor Bombing - Now Fights as Gunner on Medium Bombers in England."

Several months after the successful invasion, Roger's group moved closer to the action, departing England for the Brétigny-sur-Orge Air Base in France. The French airbase was captured in 1940 and used by the German Luftwaffe until it was liberated in August 1944 and quickly converted to a US airfield supporting the 3rd Army. It was at this time that each crew member was issued a silk map in a waterproof pouch, in the event they were shot down. Roger's daughter still has his map.

That autumn, the A-20 Havocs were replaced by the Douglas A-26 Invader, a devastating light bomber and ground attack aircraft. Powered by twin 2000-horsepower engines, yet still manned by a crew of three, it had considerably more weaponry than the A-20. With eight .50-caliber nose guns and six more .50-caliber machine guns under its wings (3 on each side), all 14 guns were forward-facing, with two additional dorsal and two ventral guns. An additional upgrade: the A-20 had only .30-caliber machine guns, while the A-26's were all .50-caliber.

The fully functioning array of machine guns allowed them to conduct devastating, sustained, hot-lead strafing runs on groups of enemy troops. When all forward guns were in action, the cockpit was filled with smoke and the smell of cordite. Maintaining twenty machine guns was a daunting task for Roger; changing worn-out barrels and replacing broken parts took many hours.

Roger once pensively told his daughter how, on one mission, his plane came upon a battalion of German infantry and their vehicles in a field. He and his crew destroyed their trucks and killed almost every one of the hundreds of infantrymen. Even though the Germans were on their way to repel Allied forces, he later understood the extraordinary loss of life of young men just like himself, all of whom were serving their country.

In December 1944, Roger's squadron supported the Battle of the Bulge, bombing tanks, troops, and supply lines, and played a critical role in defeating German forces.

Roger left Europe in mid-January 1945 and arrived home eight days later. After a furlough, he was initially assigned to Tyndall Airfield, then moved to Kingman Airfield in Arizona, where his accumulated points qualified him for discharge. Roger returned to Fort Devens, Massachusetts, and was honorably discharged on June 8, 1945, arriving home to Williamstown two days later. His two-year enlistment in 1940 had stretched to five.

In World War II, a point system was devised to equitably release service men and women from active duty. Points were given for months of service, months overseas, campaigns served, actions of valor, and the number of dependent children. Roger's time in service and overseas, plus 60 missions, qualified him for release. His military awards included the Good Conduct Medal, an Air Medal with twelve clusters, the American Defense Medal, the Victory Medal, a European–African–Middle Eastern Medal, the Asiatic–Pacific Campaign Medal (with 1 star), and two Aviation Wings.

After five years of service, Roger was anxious to get on with his life and learn a trade. Using the GI Bill, he enrolled at McCann Technical School in North Adams, completing courses on pipefitting. Over the years, he would become a licensed journeyman pipe fitter, gas fitter, and refrigeration technician.

In addition to his education, Roger continued forth with his social life as well. He soon met Phoebe Carson, who worked at McCann. They began dating, got engaged, and then married on July 12, 1947. He and Phoebe had two children, Susan and Michael.

During and after school, Roger worked at different jobs to support himself. For a while, he worked in construction, then at one point with his uncle at a jewelry and picture-framing shop. He bought Phoebe's engagement ring at that jewelry shop. In later years, he would use the knowledge he gained at the shop to make frames and mat pictures for the family.

HAND SAWS FILE ONLY	.75
HAND SAWS SET ONLY	.50
HANDSAWS FILE & SET	1.00
HANDSAWS RETOOTH FILE SET	1.50
MITRE-BOX SAWS FILE SET	1.35
MITRE-BOX SAWS FILE; SET AND RETOOTH	1.85
BACK SAWS FILE & SET	.75
BACKSAWS FILE SET RETOOTH	1.25
RETOOTH ONLY HAND SAWS.	1.00

TACONIC SAW WORKS
10 ARNOLD ST.
WILLIAMSTOWN, MASS
ROGER DENNETT

Roger's handwritten price sheet. (Courtesy of Dennett family)

From 1950 to 1956, he served in the 9243 Volunteer Air Reserve Training Squadron. During this time, he also opened a home business called the Taconic Saw Works, where he earned extra money sharpening lawnmowers and saw blades. One of his price sheets still in existence shows he charged $1.35 to sharpen mitre box saws and $1.00 to set and file hand saws. If a customer seemed needy, he wouldn't ask for any payment.

In the 1950s, Roger began a thirty-two-year career as a serviceman with the Berkshire Gas Company. Often called out at night in cold weather, he would spend many hours at people's homes fixing gas connections to their stoves or furnaces. Dedicated to his job and focused on people's needs, he would remain at someone's house and make sure they were helped. Sadly, later in life, he would struggle considerably with asbestosis, a disease likely contracted from his work with old furnaces.

Early in their marriage, Roger and Phoebe purchased a 100-year-old farmhouse that needed considerable repair. Roger drew up blueprints for the rehab and bought the lumber, and he and Phoebe worked side-by-side for long hours and many years updating the house. While he was building the fireplace using stones found on the property, for example, Phoebe was mixing and carrying mortar to him. Roger also installed the furnace and water heater. Their $7,000 purchase became a cozy home for the family.

Roger was good with his hands, and his inquisitive nature never wanted to throw something out that he could fix. He enjoyed working with wood and, when his grandchildren were born, made cradles for them, followed by beautiful toy boxes, bookcases, and shelves. His bird-watching led to his crafting wooden birdfeeders.

Often described as naturally warm and humorous, his tastes were simple. Regarding cars, he drove four-door sedans, usually Plymouths or Dodges. At one point, he bought a Volkswagen Beetle to commute to Pittsfield when the gas company's headquarters moved there.

The family made several trips to Québec and spent a week on Cape Cod once a year. Otherwise, vacations were spent at local swimming holes or occasionally a short trip to Frontier Town or the Catskill Game Farm in nearby New York.

From his time in the military, he was an avid reader. He enjoyed reading various genres, from WWII history and forensic mysteries to books on nature, explorers, and ships, and distant countries. He enjoyed teaching Susan, his daughter, about the stars.

Roger, proud of his military service, belonged to the local American Legion Honor Guard, and newspaper photos show him serving at the funerals of local veterans. In December 2001, as a member of the Pearl Harbor Survivors Association, Roger was honored by the Legion with a remarkable gift: to return to Hawaii, with Phoebe alongside him, and attend the 60th anniversary commemoration of the Japanese attack on Pearl Harbor.

By this time, Roger was the only Berkshire-area Legion member still alive who had been at Pearl Harbor on the fateful day in December 1941. It was Roger and Phoebe's first true vacation as a couple, and they had the opportunity to visit the USS *Arizona* memorial and hear that President George W. Bush declared December 7 as the National Pearl Harbor Remembrance Day.

Roger adored his two grandchildren, Trista and Amanda, crafting toys with them and telling them stories. He would often be the topic of their school projects, as they were proud to tell everyone of their grandfather's military service.

As Roger's health declined, he and Phoebe moved to Westfield to be with their daughter. His friends in the Williamstown American Legion continued to visit him. Mike Kennedy, the former veterans agent and a close friend, described the diminutive Roger as the "biggest little guy I ever met...."

This Pearl Harbor survivor and airman with sixty combat missions who always seemed to be "one step ahead of the Grim Reaper" passed away in 2010, followed by Phoebe eight years later. After sixty-three years of marriage, the war hero was buried with military honors in Williamstown's Eastlawn Cemetery. A caring, kind man with a natural sense of humor and a knack for telling jokes, Roger Dennett enlivened the lives of all those he met.

Frank F. Falbo
Radio Operator
168th Engineer Combat Battalion

In December 1944, artillery and tank fire poured down upon American forces during a surprise attack by massed German forces. Days of fearsome hand-to-hand combat ensued during the bloodiest confrontation of World War II, the Battle of the Bulge. During some of the coldest days of the war, men fought, froze, and died in the onslaught. At one critical intersection in a small eastern Belgium city called St. Vith, tens of thousands would be wounded. Frank Falbo was in the center of this maelstrom.

FRANK FRANCIS FALBO WAS born in Jamaica, New York, on October 16, 1913, to two young parents, recently emigrated from Italy. His dad, Dominic Falbo, and mother, Luigia (Ricada) Falbo, had met and married in Catanzaro, Italy, a city in southern Italy, part of the Calabria region located near the tip of the Italian peninsula, often called the "City of the Two Seas," with the Ionian Sea on one side and the Tyrrhenian on the other. Luigia, a devout Catholic, had given Frank his middle name after Saint Francis of Assisi.

Immigrating together through Ellis Island, Dominic and Luigia settled briefly in Jamaica, New York, in the borough of Queens. After some years there, they became concerned that some of their four children were coming under the influence of the local gangs and suspected one of their younger sons was already doing favors for the local group. Deciding to move, they were attracted to northwestern Massachusetts, near some of Dominic's relatives living in the Springfield area. After stopping there briefly, they heard about work opportunities in North Adams and moved there permanently in the early 1920s.

Dominic quickly found work as a fireman at Sprague Electric Company before working until retirement in the Windsor Mill boiler room. Although he once owned an older black sedan, Dominic enjoyed walking to work from Nelson Street, where the family resided.

His greatest passion was making wine and grappa in the basement of his home. Although often chided by Luigia for spending hours on end in the basement with his concoctions and cigars, for Dominic, it was his retreat. He also enjoyed growing tomatoes, and a news article from the local paper notes, "Three tomatoes were exhibited at the *Transcript* office this morning by Dominic Falbo…weighing five ¾ pounds...these are the biggest he has ever seen…their weights are two, two and a half, and one and a quarter pounds" (9-18-43).

The diminutive Luigia, shorter than five feet tall, was a busy homemaker and became an avid crocheter, making numerous lacy countertop doilies and, occasionally, a beautiful bedspread, all without patterns. Every Sunday, she made sure the family was dressed smartly in their best clothes when they walked to church for Mass. Luigia often led the way in a black dress coat and feather-trimmed hat, toting her Italian prayer book and rosary beads.

Frank, who had begun elementary school in Jamaica, Queens, completed his primary education at Johnson School in North Adams. He enjoyed roaming the neighborhood with his bike and new friends. At one point, he became a member of its newly formed Boy Scout Troop #1, then a member of the Eagle Patrol; he quickly memorized the Scout Pledge and loved the drill of learning to tie knots. The troop met every Wednesday night at the school, a gathering he looked forward to.

After graduating from Johnson School, he briefly attended Drury High School before leaving to work in the mills, wanting to help support his family and learn a trade. He quickly found employment at Arnold Print Works, tending a singeing machine that processed raw cloth. Frank would ensure that the fabric was processed smoothly without burning. He spray-painted the factory walls one time, always looking for overtime opportunities.

In the late 1930s, Frank was introduced to Evelyn Mae Berard by his brother Pasquale (known as Patsy to everyone), who was dating Evelyn's sister. Eventually, the brothers married the sisters, with Frank and Evelyn walking down the aisle at St. Patrick's Church in Williamstown on July 8, 1939. The couple honeymooned with a trip to the 1939 World's Fair held in Flushing Meadows, New York, just a few miles from his birthplace. At the World's Fair they witnessed R.C.A.'s introduction of a new phenomenon, the black-and-white television.

In late 1941, with war being declared with Japan and, shortly afterward, Germany, the need for servicemen and women became acute. In June 1943, a large group that included recent Drury High School graduates and married men was part of that month's quota. Frank volunteered, and alongside the group, had the customary physical exam in Springfield, Massachusetts, then two weeks of furlough before entering the Army on June 30, 1943. Evelyn lived with her parents when Frank left, then later she found an apartment in the Dowlin block of downtown North Adams.)

Frank underwent basic training at Camp Edwards in Massachusetts, earning the Army's Marksmanship Badge, then was transferred to Camp Carson in Colorado, assigned to Company C of the 168th Engineer Combat Battalion, where he began his radio technician training. Subsequently, in the fall of 1943, Frank was selected to attend an advanced 16-week course in communications at Fort Monmouth, New Jersey.

Fort Monmouth and The Signal Corps School

FORT MONMOUTH, ESTABLISHED IN 1917, was designated the site for the Signal Corps School and its vastly important Signal Corps Laboratories. During WWI, the Corps successfully

Pvt. Frank Falbo, in his dress uniform with unit patch. (Courtesy of Falbo family)

recruited operators from the Bell Telephone Company to train as Army communications specialists. Interestingly, some of the land used for the Fort was originally owned by the Marconi Wireless Telegraph Company, an American subsidiary of a British-owned company, the first to successfully transmit signals across the Atlantic Ocean, in 1901.

Frank would attend the Replacement Training Center for Radio Operators, which opened in 1941. The one-year course was initially designed to train 5,000 soldiers, but the pressures of the war changed its annual quota to 7,000 men and reduced the training time from one year to sixteen weeks.

The center was a small city with over sixty barracks, officers' quarters, infirmaries, a base theater, a chapel, eight mess halls, and twenty classrooms for training officers and enlisted men. Pictures from the era show men in rows at desks on teletype machines, learning Morse code and improving their typing speeds. They also learned to climb poles, string wires, repair radios, and train carrier pigeons.

Few knew that the Fort housed the Pigeon Breeding and Training Center, which trained pigeons to carry messages and to fly and return in darkness. It was used throughout WWI, WWII, and the Korean War. During WWII, pigeon hobbyists supplied over 50,000 birds to the Signal Corps. In several cases, the pigeons saved hundreds of lives with their messages. Eventually, with the advent of more sophisticated ways to communicate, the last 5000 birds were sold for five dollars per pair.

Much of the radio equipment used during WWII was developed at Fort Monmouth, including field radio equipment, such as the SCR-510 (the first F.M. backpack radio), radio relay sets, walkie-talkies, and RADAR (Radio Detection and Ranging). RADAR and radio relays were considered weapons systems that greatly affected the outcome of WWII.

After training, Frank rejoined the 168th in Colorado; the unit had just returned from maneuvers in Tennessee. In the early months of 1944, the men of the 168th were involved in long forced marches and tactical training, including crossing rivers, patrolling, rifle qualifications, and bivouacking outside.

In May 1944, the combat engineers boarded US Army Transport *Henry Gibbons* in New York and departed for overseas. Later that same month, they landed in England and were billeted at Wrexham, where their training would continue until boarding the SS *Robert L. Vann* in mid-July and landing on Utah Beach. It was July 24, 1944, more than a month after D-Day.

The 168th Engineer Combat Battalion was a unique group within the Army. Often noted as an orphan group and not assigned to a particular division, usually led by a Major, it would receive the more difficult assignments that no one else wanted. Over the next many months, the 168th would serve in four different armies: the 1st, 2nd, 3rd, and 9th; and three Corps: the 8th, 11th, and 16th. Most of Frank's time in the unit was with the 8th Corps.

Frank, assigned as the radio operator for Company C, was surprised by the amount of destruction he saw as his battalion worked its way to the front lines. Even a month after the D-Day invasion, there were still rotting animal bodies in the fields; occasionally, they passed a German soldier long dead, and many of the houses and barns that served as German barracks or gathering points had been leveled.

During the summer months, the battalion moved and battled through St. Malo, Brest, and other small French towns; at one point, they provided security for the recently captured Morlaix Airport. They were often under attack from German artillery or strafing and bombing runs by enemy planes. Although Frank was designated the company radio operator, he was also a rifle marksman, often used in combat roles during some of the company's advances.

Frank worked closely with Company C's commander, communicating daily via radio with the battalion, providing situation reports and requesting supplies and replacements. The 168th worked continuously under the most challenging conditions, building POW stockades, repairing roads, removing anti-tank obstacles, blowing up roadblocks, and clearing fields of box mines. Enemy mortar and machine gun fire often accompanied their efforts. In August, several soldiers had their feet blown off while trying to clear a German S-Mine. S-Mines, also known by American troops as "Bouncing Bettys," were deadly steel cylinders loaded with TNT and shrapnel. The Germans buried the mine in the ground with a protruding sensor, designed to launch under 15 pounds of pressure. They would explode in four seconds at about three feet above the ground, spraying shrapnel in all directions. Tens of thousands of mines were buried by German forces to slow the Allied advance into France and Germany.

The combat engineers' dangerous job was to clear the mines using metal detectors or probing with bayonets, then disarm them. When available, the 168th would use German POWs to clear mines.

In September 1944, after the surrender of Brest, Company C was charged with securing and maintaining the town's power plant. Later in September, the 168th left France, first passing through Versailles and Paris, and arriving at Houffalize, Belgium, near the German border, on October 1, 1944.

Company C's platoons worked in gravel pits extracting rocks and fill, and others at sawmills cutting and hauling logs to help with construction work. The platoons worked under the most stressful conditions of artillery shelling, strafing from enemy planes, heavy rains, and muddy, partially destroyed roads.

In November 1944, the battalion built tent floors for the 23rd Infantry Division, a road for the 15th Field Artillery, and Company C in particular worked on a 2nd Division Rest area at Norn, Belgium.

Frank, left, with his friend Dutchie, dressed for liberty. (Courtesy of Falbo family)

Road building continued into December 1944 in support of 8th Corps operations.

Frank, now working as a radioman for the company commander, Major Nungesser, began accompanying him in a command car during his duties. The command car was a four-wheel-drive, ¾-ton Dodge WC (Weapons Carrier) equipped with a radio and used as a communication center. The Signal Corps radio set was in the rear seat, and a whip antenna was mounted on the left side. The convertible and its 76 horsepower, 6-cylinder motor had a maximum speed of 54 miles per hour and a range of 240 miles.

In late December, the unit moved near St. Vith, a city in eastern Belgium. No one immediately realized the unit had been dropped in the middle of a critical intersection, one that the Germans would soon target in one of World War II's largest battles.

Battle of the Bulge

ON DECEMBER 16, DURING dense fog and snow, more than seventeen divisions totaling 200,000 German troops and up to a thousand Panzer tanks attacked Allied lines, hoping to stop the Allied advance and drive to the English Channel, splitting the Allied armies. Striking a quiet sector along a 75-mile front, the Germans broke through American lines, wreaking havoc, death, and destruction. Combating both Germans and blizzards, many GIs froze to death and thousands more suffered frostbite from freezing rain. If they could be held, two of the most vital areas that could disrupt and delay the German juggernaut were Bastogne, a small Belgian town, and St. Vith, where Frank was located.

The German plan called for St. Vith to be captured on the first day of attack: December 16, 1944. It was the center point for five main highways and three rail lines, all crucial to the enemy's armor, infantry, and supply lines.

Quickly realizing St. Vith's importance to the enemy, General Jones of the 106th Infantry Division, to which the 168th Engineer Combat Battalion was then attached, directed a colonel to defend the town with two engineer battalions, the 168th and 81st, and a headquarters staff. These non-infantrymen would be the only troops in the path of overwhelming odds. They were sent forward on December 17 with instructions to proceed until they encountered Germans, then dig in and hold.

Beginning on December 19, Panzer Divisions supported by infantry began striking the area with great force. After repeated and intense infantry, tank, and artillery attacks, including hand-to-hand combat, the 168th was able to deny the Germans access to St. Vith's highway and railroad center for the next six days. It was enough to disrupt the German schedule and, before withdrawing, the 168th would inflict significant losses on the besiegers…but not without heavy casualties.

By December 20 and 21, holding St. Vith was no longer possible; under relentless pressure from the Germans (artillery, infantry reinforcements, and tank attacks), a strategic retreat began. The 106th Infantry begrudgingly retreated, still fiercely battling tanks with hand grenades and bazookas.

In an oral history recording by Frank, he noted that his unit was attacked in the Ardennes Forest and taken "completely by surprise: We were in bunkers dug in for the winter with bunks." (Though the conditions were miserable, they'd built primitive beds, expecting to be there for a while.) When describing the attack, he thought of the line from "The Star-Spangled Banner" about "bombs bursting in air."

Earlier on December 21, the 168th had lost communications with headquarters, so Frank and several from his squad took a command car, found a break in the electrical line, and repaired it. The small group returned to the bunker area, and his squad was sent somewhere else while Frank was left to operate the radio. Shortly after that, a colonel ordered Frank to take the command car and lead a caravan of vehicles in retreat.

Initially objecting, wanting to wait for his company commander, Frank said he needed to stay near the radio, but the colonel gave him a direct order. With Frank in the lead, the caravan of vehicles quickly crossed open fields, ran through fences, and, as dark approached, pulled into a small town.

The caravan's leader noticed a light on in town and told Frank to run over and shut it off before the group was targeted by artillery. As he approached the house, Frank noticed a woman on the second floor holding a lamp, a terrible mistake. When she saw Frank, she quickly doused it…but it was too late. Attracted by the light, enemy artillery started shelling his group, and Frank was hit almost immediately. In his oral history, he said, "The first shell got me, and then I told a friend *I'm hit, go get help*."

Frank had been struck by a 150mm shell fragment which penetrated both legs, shattering his femurs and bursting his eardrums. The German 150mm heavy howitzer was a standard artillery piece for the German Army. Its crew of twelve could fire four high-explosive rounds per minute. Each giant round weighed 96 pounds, could travel over eight miles, and was devastating to vehicles as well as soldiers in the open.

The large piece of shrapnel that wounded Frank so badly, here displayed next to his dog tag. (Courtesy of Falbo family)

A Jeep bearing a stretcher arrived, and so began Frank's long road home. Records show that he was evacuated and evaluated at the Battalion Aid Station in Neuberg, Belgium, where his admission document titled *Chief Complaint—Condition on Admission—Previous Personal History* reads: "W.I.A. - 21 Dec, 1944 - 1900hrs - Neuberg Belgium - was struck by 150mm shell fragment sustaining perforating wound of right leg & F.C.C. of femur - upper 1/3 & penetrating wound on left thigh. He is in a body cast." (F.C.C. is the acronym for Fractured Compound Comminuted, meaning the bone is broken in at least three places, the skin over the wound is not intact, and usually, the bone is exposed.)

Amazingly, the family still has the heavy, jagged piece of howitzer shell taken from Frank's legs and an original drawing of his body that outlines his injuries and shows where bone/skin grafts were taken from hips and legs.

After Frank was stabilized, he moved to the 56th General Hospital in Liege, Belgium, for eight days, then on to a hospital in Paris, eventually arriving at the 109 General Hospital in Chester, England, in January 1945, where he underwent additional surgeries. He left England on May 25 aboard the hospital ship *Acadia* and was sent to Stark General Hospital in Charleston, South Carolina, as noted in a *Transcript* article dated May 5, 1945: "Pvt. Frank F. Falbo is at Stark Hospital—Dowlin Block Boy Wounded in Belgium December 21."

The USAHS (United States Army Hospital Ship) *Acadia* was built in 1932 and converted from a passenger ship in 1943 to the US Army's first WWII hospital ship. The interior was reconfigured to accommodate over seven hundred wounded and a 150-person medical staff.

In addition to Frank, the 168th casualties would include 23 killed in action, 130 wounded in action, and 199 missing in action. Many of the missing turned up months later as captured soldiers. Frank's engineer battalion strength of 600 would drop to 356 after the Battle of the Bulge; it was replenished in the following weeks.

Overall, in the Battle of the Bulge, the Americans would suffer

Form 55 B
Medical Department, U. S. Army
(Revised May 21, 1929)

CHIEF COMPLAINT—CONDITION ON ADMISSION—PREVIOUS PERSONAL HISTORY

Name Falbo Frank F. Grade Pfc Ward 24

Chief complaint: W.I.A - 21 Dec 1944 - 1900 hrs - Heubeerg, Belgium - was struck by 150 mm shell fragment sustaining a perforating wound of rt leg c F.C.C. of femur - upper 1/3 & penetrating wound of left thigh

General appearance and condition on admission: adult male - white - age 31 yrs - right leg covered by double spica body cast - apparently comfortable and in good general condition

Occupation: Civilian - spray painter & radio repair man
Army - engineers

Tropical service:
France, Belgium, Luxembourg & Germany - 1 year

Habits (alcohol, tobacco, drugs):
Moderate use of beer & whiskey. Smokes about 15 cigarettes daily - no drugs

Family history:
Mother & Father - L & W. 2 brothers & one sister - L & W
Sister is suffering from Diabetes Mellitus
No history of T.B. Ca. Asthma or Insanity

Previous personal history:
childhood - Measles, Mumps
No serious adult diseases
Operations - none
Has had trouble c discharge from both ears since induction into the Army.
Soldier is married 6 yrs. - no children

Injuries:
None

Venereal diseases

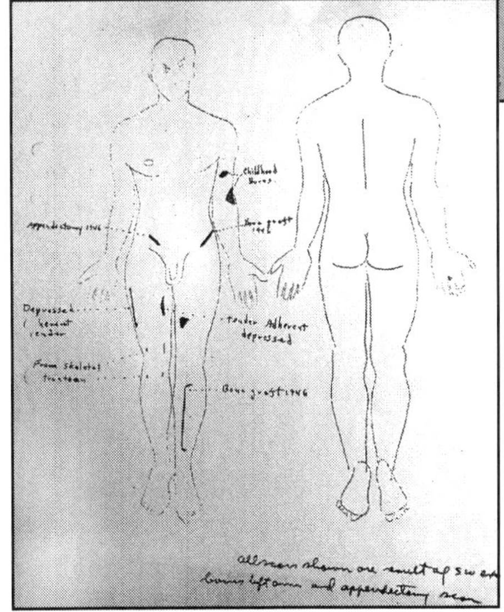

The original documents from Falbo's injury. (Courtesy of Falbo family)

19,000 killed, 47,000 wounded, and 23,000 captured or missing in action. On January 23, 1945, a month after the 168th retreated, the 7th Armored Division attacked and retook St. Vith.

After the war's end, in November 1945, the 168th Engineer Combat Battalion returned to New York and was inactivated, with its remaining personnel reporting to separation centers.

Frank had been assigned to the Tilton General Hospital at Fort Dix, New Jersey. He continued to undergo surgeries, removing more shrapnel and undergoing more bone grafts, trying to repair his severely damaged legs. The hospital staff were not encouraging and said he would probably never walk unaided again. It was predicted he would need to wear braces and use crutches or a cane.

Frank was placed on terminal leave from May 23, 1947, until honorably and medically discharged on July 21, 1947, at Tilton General Hospital, Fort Dix, New Jersey.

His decorations include the Purple Heart, the Good Conduct Medal, the American Theater Medal with four bronze stars and an arrowhead, the World War II Victory Medal, the European–African–Middle Eastern Campaign Medal, and the Belgian Croix de Guerre. Frank wouldn't know it then, but his unit would be awarded the Presidential Unit Citation for the defense of St. Vith.

His discharge papers noted that Corporal Falbo served in the European Theater of Operations and participated in the Battles of Normandy, Northern France, The Ardennes, and The Rhineland. His forty-eight months in the army would include four months in the infantry, fifteen months as a radio operator, and twenty-eight months as a patient.

Not long after his discharge, Frank's dad, Dominic, died. Luigia, his mom, who spoke little English and did not drive, moved in with Frank and Evelyn. During this time, Frank and Evelyn decided to start a family, and were blessed with a daughter. Frank's daughter has fond memories of helping her Italian grandmother make spaghetti and meatballs, stuffed peppers, and lasagna. She enjoyed the contrast with her mom's meat and potato meals.

Once released, Frank quickly found work as a salesman for Fowler Real Estate of Manchester, New Hampshire. In addition to selling property, he painted and wall-papered homes on the side. Then, he found a better-paying job as a laborer for Hanson Construction and worked in that capacity until he was involved in a severe accident on the way to work. The truck he and twenty laborers were driving in crashed through a guard rail and rolled over several times, spilling the men out all over a hillside, killing one. Frank, fortunately, escaped with minor injuries. A *Transcript* article dated 6-6-1950 reported, "Mr. Falbo, who had spent months in hospitals after being wounded badly in Belgium on December 21, 1944, during the Army's bitterest fighting in Western Europe, telephoned his wife immediately after being released from the hospital. He assured her he was unhurt but considered himself extremely lucky."

For years since his release from the army, Frank wore a metal brace on his right leg. It attached above his ankle and went over his knee, often creating sores and infections that required treatment at the VA hospital in Albany, New York. His family remembers him often rubbing his leg near the area where metal pins had been inserted. His wound was apparent whenever he wore shorts; there was a big hole in one leg and a dent in the other. The family also recalls that despite his nagging injuries and ongoing pain, Frank never complained.

After years of wearing leg braces and receiving treatment for the effects, one day Frank decided he'd had enough, took them off, and never wore them again, to be left with a slightly bowed gait. His visits to the VA would continue most of his life, usually to remove bits of shrapnel that continued to surface or to battle infections. When at the VA, he would also visit an audiologist since his eardrums had burst when the artillery shell hit him. Even today, long after his passing, the braces and crutches remain hanging on his garage wall, a memorial to his service.

Shortly after the construction accident, Frank accepted a new position at the North Adams Cascade Company, an office and school supplies wholesaler. He became a production supervisor on the second floor at the main plant on Brown Street. The building formerly housed the Gale Shoe Company.

Frank oversaw the crew that processed huge rolls of paper into lined pads and formed reams of paper for schools. He would arrive at work around 4 a.m. to turn on the machinery and ensure the ink was warm when employees came to work. When needed, he was always ready to help maintain the machines. Frank retired from Cascade after working there for thirty-three years.

Frank enjoyed bowling with ten pins at the Valley Park Lanes. He was in an independent church league as a member of the St. Anthony team. Local news articles note that he made the Team Honor Roll for bowling a Triple (score) of 332. He was the team's representative, and his daughter remembers him bringing home scoresheets and tallying his team's scores.

The family often picnicked at nearby Cheshire Lake, at the old Boy Scout Camp. They vacationed at Iron Gate Lodge in Bristol, New Hampshire, every summer, enjoying New Found Lake and its twenty-two-mile shoreline. After making new friends, the families began coordinating their summer schedules and would book a cottage for the same week of vacation. The week of adventure included using row boats for fishing, sunbathing, dance parties, and eating all three meals in the main lodge.

Later in life, Frank and Evelyn were smitten with the game of golf and became longtime members of Mount Anthony's Country Club in Bennington, Vermont. After Frank's retirement, two of their golfing friends invited them to spend a week in Florida at a golf resort. Thus began Frank and Evelyn's annual trip South, usually from January to Easter, when they would vacation at different locations, all featuring golf.

Frank belonged to the VFW and served as an American Legion Vice Commander. He stayed in touch with war buddies, and some visited occasionally; one became his daughter's godfather. He always participated in or attended local parades. He also loved to sing at home and in church and proudly taught his daughter the Pledge of Allegiance.

Frank and Evelyn were social and often played canasta or pitch with friends (when not golfing). Their daughter remembers New Year's Eve was always a special event, an evening out dressed in their best clothes, cocktails, dinner, and dancing. In 1989, the couple would celebrate their 50th wedding anniversary with family and friends.

After sixty-four years of marriage, in 2003 Frank passed away. He was buried in Eastlawn Cemetery in Williamstown with full military honors, a tribute from a firing squad, and a flag presentation to Evelyn. The love of his life would join him there in 2018 when she passed away at 100 years old.

The boy from Jamaica, Queens, who had been brought to North Adams by his parents to avoid street gangs, embraced the Berkshires as his home in more ways than one. He will always be remembered by his family as a kind, loving patriot, gravely wounded in the defense of his country and its European allies, a man who suffered much but never complained.

Charles B. Haley & George H. Haley
Gunner's Mate, USS *Henrico*
Rifleman, *38th Infantry Division*

Growing up as farm boys, two brothers entered the service a few months apart and found themselves fighting for their lives in the Pacific. While one was operating a 5-inch anti-aircraft gun on an assault ship and fighting off a flurry of kamikaze *attacks, the other brother was seven hundred miles away, charging enemy machine guns and trying to save his decimated squad caught in a deadly ambush.*

BOTH GEORGE HAYDOCK HALEY and Charles Benson Haley were born at home to George W. and Mary (Haydock) Haley in Williamstown, Massachusetts. George, the oldest child, was born on June 5, 1918, and his brother Charlie almost four years later, on May 24, 1922.

Their father, George W., had also been born in Williamstown in 1896, attended local schools, and was a hardscrabble dairy farmer and carpenter. Later in life, after his son George H. returned from World War II, they bought the Williamstown Ice Company, which included the pond and icehouse on Cold Spring Road, as well as trucks and equipment (*Transcript*, 12-9-47).

To make ends meet, George W. had a trash-collecting business that serviced Williams College, and one day during his rounds, he met Mary Haydock, who cooked and cleaned for a college professor. Mary hailed from Dungannon, in County Tyrone, Ireland, where she'd been born in 1896, attended Irish schools, and immigrated to the United States in 1914 at the age of eighteen.

They married not long after meeting, and over the next decade and a half, from 1918 to 1932, they had seven children, five sons and two daughters. Initially, Mary kept her cleaning job and was able to bring home leftover food to feed their children. The family subsisted on a seven-acre farm, selling milk from their two cows, raising pigs and chickens, and growing and canning vegetables from their large garden.

The Haleys lived in a worn, brown-shingled, 1200-square-foot farmhouse built by George W. himself, and, as the family grew, Mary transitioned to working solely as a homemaker. Growing up, all the children worked. The girls helped their mom in the house and with canning, and the boys helped their dad with tending livestock and cutting hay. The latter was a chore they heartily disliked: tiring, sweaty work using scythes to cut hay, gathering up loose straw, always on the watch for snakes, and throwing it on a wagon drawn by an equally tired horse. There was no automatic baling for them.

All the children attended Mitchell Elementary School and Williamstown High School. Charlie also had a paper route, and both he and George worked as apprentice carpenters before entering the military.

George completed high school, and Charlie attended for one year. Charlie had a brief run-in with the law when he and three other juveniles were convicted of stealing some belongings out of cars parked near a fraternity house during the 145th Williams College commencement weekend. Because of his age, Charlie was given a suspended sentence and one year of probation (*Transcript*, 6-27-39).

Charlie was the first to enter the military, enlisting in the US Navy on April 10, 1942, just before his twentieth birthday. He tried talking George into joining alongside him, but George wanted to continue working on the farm and doing carpentry work. That didn't last for long, and not surprisingly, George was drafted into the Army four months later, on August 18, 1942.

Two of the family's three other boys were too young to be drafted, and the third was classified II-B for having flat feet. He would tease George and Charlie jokingly, saying *I'll "B" here when you leave and "B" here when you get back.*

Charlie "…has been sent to Springfield, then to Great Lakes Training Center," noted *The Transcript* on April 17, 1942. After his recruit training at the Naval Training Station at Great Lakes, Illinois, he was selected to serve in the prestigious President's Honor Guard in Washington, DC.

Before he sees a real ship, Charlie poses before a mural of one. (Courtesy of Haley family)

The Ceremonial Honor Guard, established in 1931, was comprised of 200 sailors who would represent the United States at White House functions, visits by Heads of State, inaugural parades, wreath-laying ceremonies, and burials of fallen sailors. The sailors served as casket bearers, color guards, and firing parties.

The Navy's selection requirements for the Ceremonial Guard were rigorous. Seamen needed to be six feet tall, carry themselves well, and be of a sober nature. If selected, training was arduous. Those on the Guard were trained to stand motionless for extended periods for long ceremonies and continuously practiced the manual of arms (how to execute rifle drills), precise marching, and instructed how to maintain spotless uniforms.

Charlie would wear his white and blue dress uniforms (white for winter, blue for summer), complemented with white cartridge belts and a silver-plated bayonet, leggings, and depending upon the occasion, he might carry a 1903 bolt-action Springfield rifle.

"We used to go up to the White House. We attended all the parades and funerals at the Unknown Soldier's Tomb.... When the Secretary of Navy died, we marched six to eight miles from Union Station to Arlington Cemetery" (*Transcript*, 8-18-95).

One of his responsibilities was to act as a "chaser," picking up sailors who had deserted or were absent without leave (AWOL) and return them handcuffed back to the naval brig. He was armed and cautious around the prisoners. True or not, as he understood them, the rules would require him to serve the man's sentence if he let him escape.

While in Washington, since his classification was 3rd class gunners' mate, he was forced to make a choice. Change to a lower rating to stay, or be shipped out (*Transcript*, 8-18-95). Not wanting a reduction in pay from the $21 per month, he successfully tested for a gunner's position and returned to the fleet.

George Haley was drafted officially into the Army in September 1942. His four months of basic training in South Carolina were hot and miserable; more than once, he wished he had followed Charlie's advice and joined the Navy. George wrote his mom to see if she could get legal help so he could be discharged and return home to work on the farm. It was not to be, and his mom was probably content to have one less mouth to feed.

For his four months of basic, he would train at Camp Croft Infantry Replacement Center as a member of Company C, 31st Infantry Training Battalion. The Camp trained 60,000 recruits a year and served as a prisoner of war (POW) camp. George's 13-week basic training cycle included discipline, customs, and weapons training, focusing on the M1 rifle, Browning Automatic Rifle, anti-tank rockets (bazookas), and infantry mortars. He would run obstacle courses, learn hand-to-hand combat techniques, process through the Army's gas chambers, and practice amphibious landings.

In December 1942, Pvt. George Haley was transferred to the Army's replacement training center at Fort Meade, Maryland, where

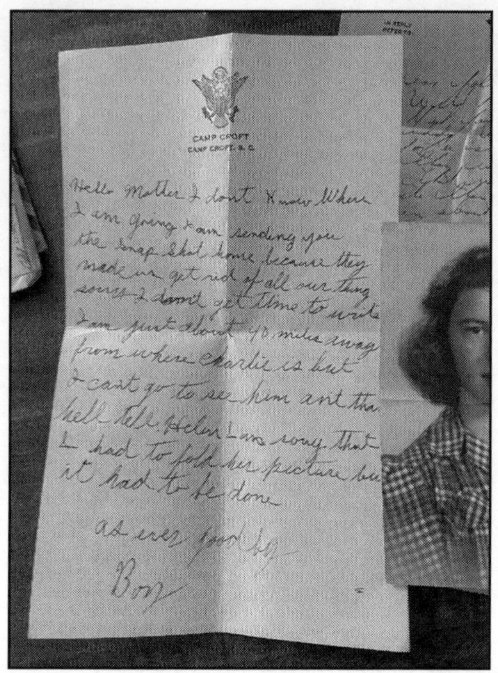

CAMP CROFT
CAMP CROFT, S. C.

Hello Mother I dont Know Where
I am going I am sending you
the snap shot home because they
made us get rid of all our thing
sorry I dont get time to write
I am just about 40 miles away
from where Charlie is but
I cant go to see him aint that
hell tell Helen I am sorry that
I had to fold her picture but
it had to be done

as ever your boy

Boy

George sends home a photograph "because they made us get rid of all our thing*[s]*," and he's only forty miles away from Charlie "but I can't go to see him ain't that hell." (Documents courtesy of Haley family, photo by the author)

he was assigned to the 38th Division. The 38th Division was nicknamed "Cyclone" during the early 1940s when a tornado damaged its Camp Shelby, Mississippi, training camp. Formerly part of the Indiana National Guard, the 38th was founded in 1917, and its soldiers served as replacements for units decimated in France. It was a particularly dangerous assignment.

George received further assignment as an infantryman to Company E, 2nd Battalion, 151st Infantry Regiment of the 38th Infantry Division.

While George was preparing to go overseas with his division, Charlie had been assigned to USS *Henrico*, an attack transport ship or APA (Amphibious Personnel Attack). The transports could carry about 2,000 servicemen (soldiers, Marines, and the 500 sailors who crewed the ship). The *Henrico* sailed to Scotland, where the crew began training for the invasion of Normandy. Now a 2nd Class gunner's mate, Charlie was assigned to the 5-inch gun.

This powerful anti-aircraft gun could fire 42-pound shells and required between 15 and 20 men to operate and feed the gun. There were two 5-inch, single-barrel, pedestal-mounted deck guns on the *Henrico*, one forward and one aft. Charlie was assigned to the aft gun. The 5-inch guns were mainly used as an anti-aircraft gun (but also anti-ship). Historians consider it one of World War II's best dual-purpose naval guns, especially when attached to a fire control system.

USS *Henrico* Patch. (Courtesy of the author)

The gunners would put up a barrage curtain, creating a "wall" of shrapnel to down enemy planes with shell fragments. Even at its best, it took, on average, 1,000 rounds per aircraft kill.

A well-trained crew of up to twenty sailors could fire up to 22 rounds a minute, hand-loading the heavy projectiles and gun powder bags into the gun's 2,000-pound barrel. The gun's horizontal range was over ten miles, and it could shoot vertically at aircraft as high as 37,000 feet.

Charlie, because of his rank, likely served as a gun captain. He would be responsible for ensuring the gun was in a constant state of readiness, checking/lubricating bearings, maintaining fluid levels, cleaning the gun sights, and cycling the equipment to ensure the firing systems were in the best condition. Once firing began, he would oversee the actions of the powder and projectile men and rammer while they loaded the gun, and since he knew everyone's job, Charlie could step in to help when someone was killed or wounded.

Accommodations were tight on the USS *Henrico*. It was a 700-foot long, seventy-foot-wide ship. Sleeping accommodations resembled a can of sardines. In a small room, about 20 feet by 15 feet, 75 men would be packed in bunks stacked high.

In a 1995 interview with *The Transcript*, Charlie offered a vivid description.

"There was barely enough room between bunks. It was impossible to sleep on your side," Haley recalled, shaking his head at the recollection. "Forget it; if you had a heavy guy lying above you a big bulge would hang down on top of you." He added, "Don't forget. A ship rocks. So, you'd learn to make a little roll with your clothes underneath the thin mattress on either side, to create a gully to keep you from falling out" (8-18-95).

Charlie's original 1944 hammock. (Courtesy of Haley family)

To avoid the crush, some sailors slept in hammocks, which Charlie describes as "three pieces of string with netting: The hammock would flip you out until you learned to balance. All someone had to do was touch it, and over you'd go." Charlie's family still has his hammock. Conditions were so tight that the sailors stored personal items in the smallest lockers during the day.

While Charlie was settling in on the USS *Henrico*, George had been training with his unit for months at Camp Livingston in Louisiana. Finally, the 38th Division shipped out in early January 1944, landed in Hawaii for more training, and served as defense for Oahu.

In late January 1944, the 38th deployed to New Guinea and spent months killing or capturing by-passed Japanese troops: "Private

First-Class George Haley is serving with the US army infantry struggling in hand-to-hand combat with the Japanese in New Guinea," read *The Transcript*. In December 1944, the division moved to Leyte, Philippines, again mopping up and supporting security operations.

In the meantime, Charlie had taken part in the famous D-Day landing. Through heavy seas and under enemy fire, *Henrico* landed the 16th Regiment of the 1st Infantry Division on the Easy Red sector of Omaha Beach. The ship also picked up wounded troops and returned them to Portland, England.

There was to be no idle time for the ship. It continued rehearsals for amphibious landings and, in July 1944, landed troops in southern France, then departed for Oran, Algeria. For the next two months, it continued shuttling more troops to France.

In a letter home, Charlie wrote:

> *.... we have made two invasions so far, Normandy and one in southern France.... We took the first assault troops to the beach in each one. There were a few planes after us, which was pretty exciting. Otherwise, everything went along fine. Lost a lot of sleep. I had to man the guns all the time. (*Transcript, *8-31-44).*

The local paper also noted that he was the only local man to have participated in both invasions.

In late January 1945, George's regiment made a combat landing on the Island of Luzon and then secured the Bataan Peninsula, including Corregidor and Manila Bay.

By February, George's 2nd Battalion was charged with clearing out the remaining Japanese defenders on Corregidor. Once Corregidor was secured, his battalion was quickly sent to assault and capture Caballo Island in March.

On March 27, 1945, Company E made an amphibious landing on the small island of Caballo, Manila Bay, Philippines. George's company secured the beachhead under heavy fire from machine guns, mortars, and 20mm cannons. Pushing inland, Company E used scaling ropes to climb a 200-foot hillside under fire, digging in atop the hill. Resupply and evacuation of the wounded were possible only with ropes. The climb alone cost George's company the loss of 42 men from falls and sliding boulders.

The next day, Company E pushed on to the next mountain. Now exhausted, short of rations and water, it continued to move forward and, after hand-to-hand fighting, gained the apex, suffering heavy casualties. *The Transcript*'s 1995 retrospective piece described it in great detail:

> *Staff Sergeant (then PFC) G.H. Haley Awarded Bronze Star…. during an advance across an open draw between Hill One and Two on Caballo Island, the squad of which Sgt. Haley was a member, and a small group of engineers were cut off from the rest of the platoon by heavy enemy machine gun fire which held up the advance temporarily. The resulting fire killed two members of the squad and two engineers and seriously wounded several others.*
>
> *Although in an open area and constantly subject to enemy fire, Sgt. Haley maneuvered himself into a position to bring bazooka fire to bear on machine gun positions situated in a small tunnel. With utter disregard for personal safety and although drawing heavy fire upon himself, he single-handedly loaded and fired 37 consecutive rounds of rocket fire into the tunnel, which had an opening of about three feet by four feet, scoring 35 hits at a range of about 75 yards destroying three machine guns and their crews. His continuous fire allowed the squad to rejoin the platoon without further casualties and accomplish its assignment.*

What is notable about George's heroics is that he fired

thirty-seven high explosive rounds from a bazooka without a loader while exposed to enemy fire, a significant accomplishment.

George, right, one of a number of heroic soldiers receiving the Bronze Star from a commanding officer. (Courtesy of Haley family)

The bazooka, nicknamed "stovepipe," was a five-foot, 13-pound aluminum tube. It was cumbersome to carry, although its shape charge was deadly within several hundred yards of the target. The finned, nine-pound rocket with two pounds of TNT was designed to be used against tanks but was most effective against enemy fortifications and machine gun nests. The rockets were loaded from the rear by an assistant who was aware of the weapon's dangerous backblast. Somehow George performed both jobs by himself.

A *Transcript* article dated May 7, 1945, "George Haley Promoted to Sergeancy on Luzon" provides further detail:

> *...promoted from private first class to sergeant following his recent performance on the recent Caballo Island operation.*

> *Sgt. Haley, a veteran of the liberation of Bataan, now becomes an assistant rifle squad leader in his company of the 151st Infantry Regiment.*

His battles continued, and as *The Transcript* noted,

> *Sgt. Haley's unit kills 19 on Luzon—Trudging through 12 miles of dense jungle and bamboo thickets a rifle company of the 38th Division including Sergeant George H. Haley, recently bagged 19 Japanese and captured many enemy weapons...the patrol made its kill when it surprised the Japanese cultivating a rice field. They grabbed their guns as the company approached but to no avail.*

Amid the continuous combat, the USS *Henrico* docked in the Philippines, and Charlie noticed a soldier with the 38th Infantry Cyclone patch. He told the soldier that his brother was in that same unit, with the Company E 151st Regiment. The soldier knew where the unit was. He went and found George, and there was a shipboard family reunion. The ship's mess fed George the best meal he had eaten in days, and a few hours later, he returned to the battle.

George's 38th Infantry Cyclone patch. (Courtesy of the author)

In June 1945, fighting continued. Wrote *The Transcript*, "Sgt. Haley Fights Way Out of Ambush—Successfully smashing out of an ambush.... with his squad...kills ten Japanese, and destroys stores of ammunition and supplies in the mountains east of Manila.... Patrolling in the front-line area, the squad was halted by two snipers who were quickly eliminated. Moving farther up the trail, the patrol was ambushed, and in the ensuing fight, eight more Japanese were wiped out. The 151st patrol returned to their lines with no casualties" (6-25-45).

Then, the division shifted back to Manila, fighting and finally ending all opposition. They received the nickname "Avengers of the Philippines" for their efforts in clearing the Philippine islands. During the battle for the Philippines, 12,000 Americans were killed in action, often fighting side-by-side with Filipino Army regulars, of whom 20,000 died. Civilian fatalities were in the hundreds of thousands; some estimates indicate 5% of the country's total population was killed.

The 38th was in combat until the war's end on August 14, 1945, ending 198 consecutive days of combat. The division continued to mop up diehard Japanese soldiers and capture prisoners through September 1945. The division faced 80,000 enemy soldiers throughout their combat, killing many and capturing almost 40,000. George's regiment would earn three battle streamers for New Guinea, Leyte, and Luzon.

While George was in almost constant combat, Charlie on the USS *Henrico* had been participating in numerous amphibious exercises, preparing for the invasion of Okinawa. The ship landed troops there in late March 1945, under continuous Japanese air attack.

Charlie is quoted in the same 1995 *Transcript* newspaper interview that during the Battle of Okinawa, "Japanese planes would taunt the sailors by flying within 15 miles of the 20-mile radar range which protected the ship, then flying back out" causing the gunners to be on constant alert at their battle stations, often sleeping on or near their guns: "When they figured they had you all tired out, they'd attack you."

On April 2, 1945, the ship's luck ran out, and it was hit by a *kamikaze*, a Yoksuka P1Y "Frances" attack bomber. The suicide bomber crashed into the ship's bridge, and three bombs exploded below deck.

Charlie recounted, "When we got hit in Okinawa, we'd been on standby in a cove we'd found, but there was only one narrow channel to get in or out, and the ships had to move in a single file. So, there was no protection for each ship at this point." Then, in their haven, a Japanese plane spotted them. "He dropped three bombs. One hit the bridge. I was going on watch at 7:30. I was on the bow, and that's where the plane was coming in. I could see the plane go by. There was a big explosion, and it killed all the power on the ship. The guns use hydraulics because they are so big, so they didn't work. Three planes came back and strafed us. We loaded the 5" guns by hand, but it moved too slowly to do any good."

He had just come off the bridge and said, "If I'd had been on the bridge, I'd have been killed."

Several of his close friends were killed, even though he marveled at the ship's luck. "We were filled with gasoline and ammunition (and it never ignited)…and had just offloaded 500 soldiers. If they had been on the ship, we would have lost a lot of lives."

The sailors hit on the bridge were incinerated or burned to death and initially sealed in by the tremendous heat. Charlie recounted in the *Transcript* article, "There were 8 to 10 guys right by the door all burnt. There were pieces of people all around. You couldn't identify them. There was the torso of one guy, who was stuck in a door…and the smell of burnt bodies…it was horrible."

Forty-nine sailors were killed, including the ship's captain, and many wounded.

When the disabled *Henrico* was towed to San Francisco in May for repairs, Charlie was transferred to the USS *Goodhue*, which would then transport occupation forces to Japan and be the first US ship to enter Tokyo Bay in late August 1945. (The USS *Goodhue* was part of the same Okinawan amphibious force as the USS *Henrico*. It was hit on the same day by a *kamikaze* during the Battle for Okinawa, and bombs killed 27 crew members.)

The USS *Goodhue* would be charged with transporting 1,000 American, British, Dutch, and Norwegian rescued prisoners-of-war to Manila on their first step home.

Charlie noted, "We weren't allowed to bring them home immediately. We took them to different ports because they were so skinny.

We kept them out to sea to fatten them up so people in the States wouldn't see how bad they looked."

Later, the USS *Goodhue* would make several round trips from Manila, ferrying returning war veterans home. After the war, it was decommissioned in 1946 and used for commercial purposes until scrapped in 1981.

The USS *Henrico* would continue to serve, participating in the atomic tests at Bikini, transporting troops in the Korean War, standing by to be part of a naval blockade of Cuba during the early sixties, and then it would serve in the 7th Fleet supporting amphibious landings throughout Vietnam. The twenty-five-year-old USS *Henrico* was decommissioned in February 1968 and scrapped in 1979.

At war's end, George was discharged in November 1945, and Charlie just one month later. George was awarded the Bronze Star Medal, Combat Infantryman's Badge, WWII Victory Medal, Asiatic–Pacific Ribbon, and the Philippine Liberation Ribbon.

Charlie's service awards included the Philippine Liberation Ribbon, the Asiatic–Pacific Ribbon, the Philippine Presidential Unit Citation, and the European–African–Middle Eastern Campaign Medal, and he also earned the WWII Victory Medal and Good Conduct Medal.

After the war, Charlie became a union carpenter, storing his tools in the trunk of his sedan as he traveled to different work sites. He built houses for the Haley Development and worked on the Mount Greylock High School and the Shaker House. Charlie married Edith Babcock shortly after the war, though disappointedly, they did not have any children. Edith passed away in 1988 after almost forty years of marriage.

Over the years, Charlie's reputation as a craftsman grew, as he designed and built beautiful kitchen cabinets for his customers.

Charlie would continue to relive in his dreams the attack on the *Henrico*. He vividly remembered the Japanese *kamikaze* flying over his head and seeing the "red meatball" on the underside of its wing before it crashed into the bridge of his ship. Even up until his death, he told a nephew that his dead shipmates kept coming to see him. After the war, the almost six-foot-tall rail-thin veteran took to drinking, eventually stopping but never ending the memories that haunted him. Charlie died in December 2010 at eighty-eight years of age.

George, who had contracted malaria in the tropics, would suffer from the effects of the disease for a short time after returning home. His brothers remember George sitting outside in hot weather covered with a blanket, freezing. The largest of five sons at 6'6" tall, he was 260 pounds when he went off to war. When he returned from the Pacific, he weighed 160 pounds.

After the war, George worked as a mason tender for a company involved with the Sterling & Francine Clark Art Institute and as a heavy equipment operator and truck driver. He married Grace Dickinson, who tragically died in 1972, suffering a heart attack while mowing the lawn. They had a daughter and two sons.

George liked to tinker with his red and white two-door Scout and, for relaxation, always had a large garden and enjoyed cooking. He is described as happy-go-lucky, always laughing, and a nice guy. At times, though, he was a worrier who could anger quickly and yell at people. His family surmised that he suffered from the aftereffects of his months in battle and the numerous close-up fights with an unrelenting enemy. George died after a short illness in December 1980 at age 62.

These two brothers, George, the oldest, and Charles, the Haley family's third child, served heroically during World War II's most difficult years. Leaving home as young men, they each personally saw the horrors of war…and forever carried memories that would haunt them for the rest of their lives.

Both men shared their military experiences with their families, for which we are grateful today. Though harrowing and haunting, the stories are valuable in their telling. In the words of one nephew who fondly remembered Uncle George and Charlie, "their stories took me there."

Richard T. McKnight
Navigator
554th Army Air Force

Richard McKnight was an experienced navigator who had flown hundreds of missions across the globe, but nothing like this new assignment. He was now ferrying planes, parts, people, ammunition, supplies—and most dangerously, aviation fuel—to secret, special operations airfields from India to remote areas of China. The dangerous part was flying over the Himalayas, known to aircrews as the "Hump" or the "Aluminum Trail" because of the hundreds of aluminum cargo aircraft, just like his, that had been forever lost, disappearing in its deep canyons or dense forests.

Flying a non-insulated, thin aluminum, converted passenger aircraft, usually overloaded, at altitudes of 20,000 feet through a maze of mountains from India to China and back was a daunting challenge for aircrews. With oxygen masks on, the men wore heavy coats and gloves, forgoing the plane's open-flame propane heater because often the crafts also carried 55-gallon gasoline drums.

The weather and cold presented the biggest risks; at the heights flown, ice forming on the wings could bring down a plane. Darkness, high winds, and frosted windshields often necessitated instrument flying—essentially flying blind.

This was the situation that greeted Richard as World War II was coming to a close. Would he and his crew be one of the final sacrifices to the Aluminum Trail? He found himself day after day in deadly combat, battling not just the enemy but also the unforgiving elements and terrain.

WILLIAM T. McKNIGHT, RICHARD'S father, born in the late 1800s, began the family military tradition with his service in the US Army during World War I, spending almost a year in France and Germany with the 9th Army Engineering Corps. The Corps was deactivated in May 1919, and William headed home to Mishawaka, Indiana, one month later. William's World War I helmet is still on proud display to this day at the family home.

Not long after returning stateside, William met Mildred B. White; they soon married and moved to Akron, Ohio, attracted to the area by employment opportunities in the lucrative tire and rubber industries.

It was in Akron that Richard Thornton McKnight was born on April 13, 1921. His parents chose his middle name in hopeful tribute to a generous wealthy relative. Richard Thornton was quickly nicknamed Dickie. As an only child, he was beloved by his parents.

Tragedy struck the family in 1929 when Dickie's father, William, died at the age of thirty-three. At seven, Dickie remained fatherless until his mom remarried and the new family moved to Cleveland. As a youth, Dickie would spend his summers with his maternal grandparents in Indiana. He attended local grammar schools and, in 1939, now going by Dick, he graduated from John Marshall High School in Cleveland, Ohio. Afterward, he worked as an inspector at a machine shop that made fuel pumps while attending Fenn College, the predecessor of Cleveland State University.

Dick, always fascinated by flying, decided to join the Army Air Corps and become a pilot. It was amid World War II, and the demand for aircrews was high. At Dick's induction physical, he weighed 120 pounds and was rejected as too thin. The five-foot-ten-inch candidate was determined to join, however; Dick stopped smoking, focused on a diet of cheeseburgers, reached 129 pounds, and was accepted into the Air Corps. He later told his children that after being inducted, he returned to smoking, and his weight dropped back to 120 pounds, for a time.

After additional testing, Dick was disappointed once again. His scores were not a match for a pilot designation but perfect for training as a navigator. So began his military service. From July 1942 until July 1943, he was an enlisted soldier in the Cadet National Guard, attending and graduating from Preflight/Bombardier/Navigator School at the Selman Airfield outside Monroe, Louisiana.

Selman Army Airfield was constructed at the beginning of World War II and, by war's end, would train 15,000 navigators. The eighteen-week Preflight and Advanced training course would have three enlistees and an instructor flying on Beechcraft AT-7s to learn their trade. Their credo was simple: "Get them there and get them back." The navigators spent considerable time learning to navigate by four methods: landmarks, dead reckoning, radio beacon, and celestial bodies.

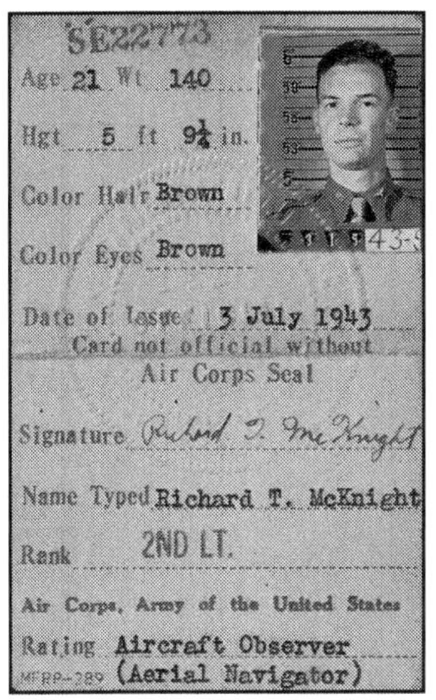
SE22773
Age 21 Wt 140
Hgt 5 ft 9¼ in.
Color Hair Brown
Color Eyes Brown
Date of Issue 3 July 1943
Card not official without
Air Corps Seal
Signature Richard T. McKnight
Name Typed Richard T. McKnight
Rank 2ND LT.
Air Corps, Army of the United States
Rating Aircraft Observer
(Aerial Navigator)

The newly commissioned navigator. (Courtesy of McKnight family)

Upon graduation in July 1943, Dick was commissioned a 2nd lieutenant and received the designation of Navigator-Operations Officer. His commissioning letter stated that his officer appointment is effective "for the time being and for the duration of the war and six months after."

Several months after graduation, Dick was assigned to the 4th Ferry Group, part of the Air Transport Command (ATC). He left for England in November 1943, arriving there three weeks later on December 18, 1943.

Air Transport Command (ATC)

THE ATC WAS CREATED in July 1942 when the United States realized it needed an international transportation system to support its troops overseas and its allies. The ATC network stretched worldwide and was involved in ferrying everything from newly manufactured planes to their units to supplies of ammunition, fuel, and equipment. It also delivered service members where the need was greatest. In support of these efforts, it built airports around the world. By war's end, the Air Command had grown to hundreds of thousands of airmen and civilians, with over 3500 planes serving Allied forces across the globe.

There was a heavy reliance on C-47 and C-46 cargo planes to support the North African and Middle Eastern Campaign. The route originated in Florida, flying south to Brazil, and then across the Atlantic to Africa and the Middle East.

As part of Dick's first ATC assignment, he would operate out of the Nashville, Tennessee, Airport with the 4th Ferry Command transporting new aircraft to embarkation points or directly overseas. In addition to new aircraft, the crew would also fly needed supplies to their destinations.

Still stateside, Dick does a bit of shopping. (Courtesy of McKnight family)

Depending on his route, Dick often stopped at airfields on Ascension Island in the South Atlantic, or later in the Azores, to refuel and break up thousands of miles of continuous open-water flying. He navigated aircraft to dozens of countries throughout almost every continent, frequently operating in the Caribbean, Central America, South America, Africa, Canada, Europe, Asia, and the Pacific Theater. He once told his daughter he had been in every country in the world but two.

On one of his missions, his crew and the plane needed to stop to refuel on Ascension Island. The plane had just enough fuel to get

Formal service photo of Lt. McKnight in dress uniform. (Courtesy of McKnight family)

there. Dick was trying to navigate by the stars on a cloudy night; as the time approached when they should have reached the island, nothing loomed on the horizon. Instructing the pilot to climb above the clouds, Dick used a sextant to determine their location, returned below the clouds, and led the formation of five C-26 aircraft to the island.

He later related to his daughter that the crew asked if he was certain about the navigation, and her dad replied that he was, but they should have reached Ascension by now. He said, "A heaviness came upon them all, as I'm sure they contemplated what this meant, running out of fuel, missing the island, and a watery death." As their concerns mounted, Ascension Island rose into view dead center in front of them, and everyone sighed in relief.

His logbook for 1943 shows him and the crew ferrying C-47 aircraft and supplies throughout the Caribbean, crossing the Atlantic Ocean to Brazil, and making long flights and numerous stops in Africa.

The men were never in one place long enough to establish a base camp. They often laid over in frontier-like towns, featuring dirt streets and shabby hostels with primitive plumbing. When not exhausted from hours of flying, they'd stop by local bars or dance halls. At the airfields, they lived three-to-a-tent with mosquito nets—or a step up, in "bashas," a structure with hard floors and a thatched roof. Their meals often consisted of the same three items: rice, powdered eggs, and a version of SPAM.

In the first part of 1944, Dick's logbook shows back-to-back trips to Brazil, Liberia, Senegal, Morocco, Egypt, Sudan, and the country next to Venezuela that was known then as British Guiana. After making his delivery and handing over his plane, he'd return as a passenger to Florida to pick up another plane to deliver. In April, he was helping ferry new aircraft from Tennessee or Miami-based manufacturing plants to airfields in North Africa, Brazil, and Egypt. When on the ground, coolies (the term at the time for local laborers) unloaded their planes, at times with the assistance of elephants.

His first flight to India was in February 1944, and he hopped a ride on a C-54 to return to the United States. At the time, he did not know that India and China would play a significant role in the last months of his military service.

In June 1944, the 4th Ferrying Group was moved and assigned to the 554th Army Air Force Base Unit, and Dick was promoted to 1st Lieutenant the following month. He continued to serve as a navigator, traveling to Greenland, Labrador, England, Africa, and the Middle East.

Early in 1945, he made a number of trips to the Pacific, landing in the Solomon, Marshall, and Gilbert Islands (known today as Kiribati). That spring, his travels began focusing on Asia, flying from India into China, supporting Allied and Nationalist forces in their opposition to the Japanese.

China-Burma-India (CBI) Theater: "The Forgotten Theater of WWII"

IN 1942, LESS THAN a week after Pearl Harbor, the Japanese invaded Burma (now called Myanmar), quickly securing Rangoon as its capital and pushing out Allied forces, and in the process, created a blockade sealing the only land supply route from India to resupply Chinese troops fighting the Japanese.

In 1937, Japan had invaded China, and both Nationalist and Communist forces were trying to halt further incursions. The remarkable coalition of British, Communist, and Chinese Nationalists

Postcards collected during Dick's time in China, showing famous scenes in Shanghai. (Courtesy of McKnight family)

opposing the Japanese and Thai forces now required supplies to be flown from India to remote, primitive airfields in China. The coalition decided to open an air corridor that launched from thirteen airbases in northeastern India's Assam Valley to Kunming, the capital of Yunnan province in southeastern China, and other nearby secret airfields. Allied motives were not altogether altruistic. America wanted to keep the one million Japanese soldiers occupied and out of the Pacific Theater. Britain wanted to regain control over Burma, while the Chinese Nationalists, looking ahead, were hoping to defeat the growing Communist element within the country while fighting the Japanese.

In 1942, the Allies had established a supply route over a treacherous portion of the Himalayan Mountains that wove itself from India over the daunting peaks and through the maze of mountains, with crew members often looking up at the towering masses. The corridor would be 200 miles wide with a 25,000-foot ceiling.

In July 1944, Richard was appointed as a navigation, intelligence, and briefing officer in the Burma Theater, helping to fill the need for a desperate shortage of airmen, especially navigators. This would be his most challenging and dangerous assignment. He would fly on a C-47, C-46, or C-87 Liberator cargo plane, or their variants. He would repeatedly cross over what the flyers called the Hump, an air corridor initially 50 miles wide and over 500 miles long to bring supplies to desperate forces.

The Army Air Force would provide a critical role in resupply to both British and Chinese Nationalist forces and to a small group of American volunteers flying Curtiss Wright P-40B fighter planes, a group that became known as the Flying Tigers. The Tigers boasted a notoriously famous shark's mouth insignia and would be credited with destroying over 600 enemy planes.

Before Dick's arrival, a number of C-46s from the organization had been shot down by Japanese fighters based in Burma. The fighters were less of a threat by 1944, after many of their airfields were destroyed by US bombing. Nevertheless, the danger still existed, and when a cargo plane faced an enemy fighter, there was usually only one result.

Dick's unit also supported many special operations groups that maneuvered behind enemy lines, including the Chindits, a group composed of British and Indian soldiers and named after the Burmese word for "lion," as well as the Mars Task Force, consisting of Chinese and American commandos.

It was during this time, in the summer of 1944, that the first recorded use of a helicopter in combat occurred. Four crewmen were rescued from behind enemy lines in Burma on a recently developed, frail-looking, single-rotor Sikorsky helicopter with a tiny tail rotor.

The Himalayan corridor was, without question, one of World War II's most dangerous air routes. The often fuel-laden, overloaded cargo planes needed to negotiate some of the world's highest mountains under unbelievable, everchanging weather conditions, including winds reaching 125 to 300 miles per hour. Over the course of the war, 600 planes and thousands of airmen would be lost, many never found. When the ATC started its India-to-Burma flights, aircraft mechanics and spare parts were in short supply. Maintenance was often deferred and then conducted outside in the weather. At times, crews went into the Himalayan foothills to scavenge parts off crash sites.

Later in life and more than once, Dick, a quiet man, acknowledged to his daughters that he was lucky to be alive and that trips over the Hump required great skill and constant vigilance. There was no rest during the arduous, nearly four-hour, 500-mile flight from India to China. After arriving in China, Richard and his crew would often be redirected to other remote airfields, sometimes making five or six landings daily, flying eight to twelve hours before returning home.

The hazardous weather was magnified by icy conditions, few navigational aids, rudimentary maps, and only local towers for traffic control. Reliance on homing beacons at every airfield was severely affected by the extreme changes in weather. Crews operated in almost year-round bad weather. From May to October, the monsoon season brought heavy clouds, fierce rains, and severe thunderstorms with turbulence. Late fall and winter meant freezing cold ground fogs. The crews quickly realized the importance of instrument navigation. It seemed like every flight was a final exam, resulting in life or death.

Dick's logbook, along with survival booklets and silk map carried by all air crews. (Courtesy of McKnight family)

The Planes

DICK SPENT HUNDREDS OF hours navigating on the military's C-47 cargo plane. Introduced in October 1941 by Douglas Aircraft, it was a camouflage version of the popular civilian DC-3. The twin-engine plane had a 95-foot wingspan and was 64 feet long.

It cruised at 155 miles per hour with a range of 1600 miles. The crew of three included a pilot, copilot, and navigator.

The plane was not armed, insulated, or pressurized, requiring the crew to wear oxygen above 10,000 feet. It could carry about 5,000 pounds of supplies, eighteen stretcher cases, or twenty-eight paratroopers. Everyone wore heavy jackets and gloves at higher elevations, breathing frosty air. The plane was considered easy to fly and maintain, especially at remote airfields, but was not suited to carry heavy loads at high altitudes. It's notable that the C-47 was later used in the 1948 Berlin Airlift, the Korean War, and Vietnam. In General Dwight D. Eisenhower's memoirs, he is said to have called the C-47 one of the top four pieces of equipment that helped the United States win World War II. The others were the rocket-propelled bazooka, the Jeep, and of course the atomic bomb.

Dick also navigated on a four-engine C-87 Liberator, which climbed poorly and was the subject of many takeoff crashes. In addition, its electrical and hydraulic systems could freeze in high altitudes, causing it to spin out of control. Its saving grace was an ability to reach a higher ceiling than the C-47, which helped the crew avoid weather fronts.

Then Dick navigated on the C-46 Commando, a twin-engine workhorse that began flying China missions in 1943. The pressurized 76-foot-long aircraft, with a crew of four, could easily fly at 22,000 feet and was significantly superior in the amount of cargo carried than the C-47 and C-87. It wasn't without its dangers; mechanical failures like the carburetor icing over and instances of unknown fire origins or explosions, and the plane earned its nickname "Flying Coffin." Each plane often carried twenty-eight 55-gallon drums of high-octane aviation fuel. The explosions were eventually determined to be gas leaks in the fuel system and modified after the loss of many planes and men.

Dick spent over half of his accumulated flight time, 674 hours, navigating the C-47, C-87 and the C-46.

Dick had the least navigation hours on the C-54 Skymaster,

introduced in 1944. The four-engine plane would eventually replace the other cargo planes. Its large cargo box carrying five times the load of a C-47 was helpful, but it lacked the high-altitude capability of a C-46. The 93-foot-long Skymaster was manned by a crew of four, had a range of 4,000 miles, and was considered safer than its predecessors. In 1945, the C-54s took daily flights from Calcutta and Kunming, bringing back the critically wounded for medical treatment.

During a stopover on one of Dick's CBI flights, his crew became friendly with a Canadian aircrew, sharing a few drinks in the off hours. The following day, in line to take off, the plane in front of Dick's banked sharply and plummeted to the runway, killing all aboard. It was a sobering moment he remembered for the rest of his life. When he asked who was on board, he was told it was the Canadian group they met the night before.

In fairness to all four aircraft on which Dick navigated, they faced probably the worst flying conditions of any theater in World War II, in a constant battle with terrain and weather. The Himalayas' critically dangerous winds featured updrafts or downdrafts that could move a plane thousands of feet in seconds. The six-month monsoon season also created quagmires of mud and heightened difficulties in transporting supplies to air bases and loading planes—never mind how the rains complicated efforts to fly and stay on course.

Aside from the peril of flying, on-the-ground conditions were often primitive. Tents or huts didn't fare well in the monsoon season, coupling hot temperatures with high humidity. Clothes and bedding remained mildewed, sanitation was problematic, and malaria and dysentery were prevalent. All of these remote bases had to purify the water, a time-consuming process, and C rations were often the day's fare.

In January 1945, Air Command had its worst day. With its twenty-four-hour, around-the-clock, all-weather aerial supply operation, they lost fifteen aircraft and their crews to severe weather. An announcement in March did not improve morale: ATC's commanding general changed the airmen's rotation policy, from 650 flight hours over the Hump to 750 hours and twelve months. Crews had been doubling and tripling their daily flight hours so they could leave as soon as four months. The twelve-month rule was harsh, but it increased safety; tired crews trying to achieve 650 hours had become accident-prone, resulting in dramatic and tragic losses.

After three and a half years of continuous operations, the Air Command's mandate to resupply and support military troop movements was discontinued in August 1945 with the surrender of Japan. Celebrations were raucous, with extra liquor rations, racing Jeeps, and shooting guns.

During the following months, bases were closed, and the ATC transported 48,000 US servicemen back over the Hump from China to Karachi to return home. The Air Transport Command had become the largest international airline in the world. By the end of the war, the United States had bought, used, and eventually sold thousands of aircraft to the civilian population and trained thousands of pilots who were recruited to create America's worldwide airline system.

The unit's multi-year operation and accomplishments were noteworthy. President Roosevelt awarded them the Distinguished Unit Citation. At the time, it was the largest and longest resupply mission in history, supplying 50,000 tons per month to Allied forces. The herculean efforts in delivering over 600,000 tons of cargo were not without a cost. ATC lost over 600 aircraft, 1500 crew members who died, and 300 more who were never found. The losses were higher than in any other non-combat aviation unit—and more than in many combat units. It was estimated that a third of the pilots (and crew) who flew the Hump were killed, badly injured, or permanently missing.

After the war, many of the planes were repurposed to provide continued support for Chiang Kai-shek's troops battling the communists in China; air-dropping supplies to soldiers in the Indochina, Korean, and Vietnam Wars; and even used in the Bay of Pigs invasion, 1961. Most cargo planes were inactivated in the late 1960s.

The crews who served in this dangerous, unsung theater returned home with little fanfare, and many would struggle to readapt to America's culture and from the effects of their harrowing experiences.

Dick left India on January 14, 1946, and arrived in Florida eight days later, traveling through Iran, Egypt, Morocco, Senegal, Ascension Island, Brazil, and British Guiana. He had survived and completed more than two years of overseas service.

He was promoted to captain just before his honorable discharge on March 10, 1946, and credited with completing the following campaigns: Air Offense Europe; China Defensive; China Offensive; India Burma. His 300 missions garnered him the following decorations: the European–African–Middle Eastern Medal with one battle star, the Asiatic–Pacific medal with 3 battle stars, a World War II Victory Medal, and an American Campaign Medal.

Dick McKnight was in fine company. Several other members of Hump aircrews became notable in their fields: Barry Goldwater was a pilot before becoming a United States Senator and presidential candidate. Robert McNamara was a statistician and analyst before serving as Secretary of Defense and a notorious architect of the Vietnam War strategy. Gene Autry was a pilot before achieving success as a film and television star.

After his discharge from the military, Dick found work with RCA as a radio/television technician and was subsequently promoted to the Missile Test Project, managing a tracking station in the Caribbean Sea. Dick would remain in the active Army Reserves until about the mid-1950s.

In 1957, with a strong desire to complete his college degree, Dick moved to Indiana, attending and graduating from Tri-State College in Angola, Indiana. His electrical engineering degree earned him a spot with the Sprague Electric Company in North Adams. While at Sprague, he joined its golf league and took up what would become a lifelong sport.

Back in North Adams, Dick, at this time a forty-four-year-old bachelor, met Elvy Johansson, the widow of one of his closest friends, at the local Friendly's restaurant. He sat with Elvy and her three children, chatted, and began a whirlwind romance, culminating with their marriage in 1966. Dick remembers picking up the check on the day they met.

The couple were married at the 1st Congregational Church and would soon have a daughter to add to their family. Elvy was fourteen years younger than Dick; she would graduate from North Adams State College in 1973 and become a local educator. She was also involved as a Girl Scout leader and taught Sunday school.

In the early 1970s, Dick accepted a position with Williamstown's Hoosac Water Quality District and would work there for the next twenty-nine years, beginning as a technician and eventually becoming the district's project manager and treasurer. He also served as a committeeman for St. Mark's Episcopal Church Boy Scout Troop 70, supporting the family's two boys.

Family life assumed a pattern: each day around 3:30, when Elvy and Dick returned from work, they would sit outside in lounge chairs, under the willow tree, and read the local news in *The Transcript*. Dick would have a Black Label beer, Elvy often wine or a cocktail. The couple would talk until 5:00 p.m. when she began supper. Dick, who had prepared his own meals much of his life, loved Elvy's cooking, especially her Swedish meatballs, Shepherd's pie, and homemade Sloppy Joes. Dinner conversations would certainly include discussions on the value of an education. Elvy and Dick were able to put all four children through college without burdening them with loans. After dinner, they would watch national news on one of the three available TV channels.

Dick, ever thrifty, preferred buying used Chevrolets or Fords several years old. He would not buy foreign-made cars, a legacy from his difficult war years. At one point, he had a yellow Pinto to commute the short distance to work, which Elvy made him sell when a warning was issued about its exploding gas tanks. Elvy was also a major influence in Dick quitting smoking; with the help of stick pretzels and Beeman's gum, he quit not long after they were married.

Family vacations were simple and local affairs, often involving extended family and friends. They did travel to Myrtle Beach and Niagara Falls and visit family in Michigan. Dick usually had a list of home projects, some deferred, but he would always paint one side of the family's two-story Cape every summer. Dick's favorite pastimes were golfing and music. Every Tuesday night, he and three lifelong buddies would swing their clubs at Waubeeka Golf Links in Williamstown. As a music lover and with his interest in electronics, Dick built the family's stereo system, later upgraded to a cassette deck that played his pre-recorded tapes. He and Elvy would spend hours listening to Glenn Miller, Frank Sinatra, and Herb Alpert. At the time, the family loved to watch the TV show "Name That Tune." His musical interests also included playing one of the various harmonicas he had collected.

Sadly, Elvy passed away in 1983 at the age of forty-eight. Dick's best friend was gone forever; he would never remarry. One of his daughters remembers that on her own 44th birthday, her dad sent her a card noting his life began at 44 (when he married Elvy).

Dick would continue to work until he was eighty years old. At one point, his children bought him a riding mower, but he continued to use his push mower for exercise, and said it was just simpler to maintain.

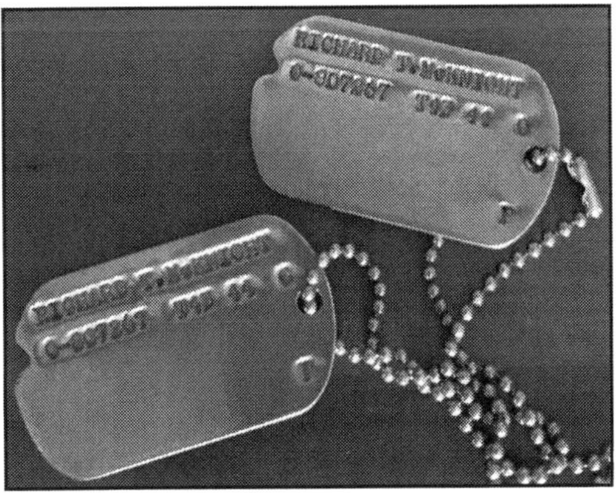

The McKnight family cherishes the memorabilia of his wartime years. (Courtesy of McKnight family, photo by the author)

Dick, described by his children as humble, kind, and a family-loving person, passed away in 2003 and was buried in Eastlawn Cemetery in Williamstown, Massachusetts, with full military honors. He did share some of his war experiences with his family, reminding them that "freedom was worth fighting for." However, he kept his military items, the detailed logbooks, silk crewmen escape maps, medals, and wings, along with his World War II coin collection, tucked away in the bottom drawer of a bookcase. In contrast, the wedding picture of him and Elvy was on display for all to see.

ELIZABETH J. MCNICOL
COMBAT NURSE
98TH GENERAL HOSPITAL

Assigned as a charge nurse managing other nurses and hundreds of wounded patients, Betsy cared for some of the more critically injured soldiers of World War II. She had extra training as a neurosurgical nurse, a specialty that was highly in demand. She followed Patton's 3rd Army from England through France and Germany, staying near the front in order to respond to catastrophically wounded battle casualties. At great risk to themselves, Betsy and her nightingales provided solace and critical care to tens of thousands of soldiers and POWs recovering from traumatic injuries.

ELIZABETH McNICOL WAS BORN to Elizabeth and Mathew Steveson "Steve" McNicol on September 25, 1921. One of three children, she would be called Betsy, named after her mom.

Mathew had been born in Providence, Rhode Island, then came to the Berkshires as a boy, moved to Williamstown, and married Elizabeth Welch at St. Patrick's Church in 1915. He would work at Williams College for more than forty years and, at one point, was the Assistant Director of what was then known as the Lawrence Museum of Art.

Elizabeth Allen Veronica Welch, Betsy's mother, had been born in Williamstown and, after attending local schools, also worked for many years at Williams College, at the former Psi Upsilon Fraternity. Elizabeth was a founding member of St. Patrick's Church Women's Guild.

Betsy's grandfather and Mathew's father, James McNicol

A pensive moment for Betsy in Williamstown. (Courtesy of McNicol family)

(originally spelled MacNicol), had been a coal miner from Scotland. He had married Thomasina Whyte and emigrated with her in 1892, eventually settling in Williamstown. In 1915, the couple was notified that one of their sons, Sergeant Alexander McNicol of the Gordon Highlanders, had been killed in action in France—one of the first from the Berkshires to die in World War I.

Betsy's maternal grandparents, Thomas and Katherine Welch, both born in Ireland, emigrated separately in the late 1800s. They met, married in 1890, settled in Williamstown, and had four children. Thomas was a gardener for sixty years, renowned for his roses. He also designed and built the family's home on North Street. Katherine, "Katie," was well known for her charitable acts to needy people.

Betsy and her family grew up in the house on North Street with her grandparents, amidst the smell of the abundant rose bushes her grandfather had cultivated on their vast lawn. As a little girl, she was always ready to help her grandfather plant and weed his sizeable vegetable and flower gardens. When she was very young, Betsy picked lupines and gladiolas from the big field across the street and would sell them to neighbors and friends.

Already something of a tomboy, she loved fishing with her grandfather for trout in the stream on the farm across the street, which was nicknamed "Doctor Brook." She and Grandpa caught their share of dinner meals, and Betsy was always hunting frogs to catch for her grandmother (Nana), known for cooking up tasty frog legs.

Betsy was always busy during her adolescent and high school years. In a pop concert sponsored by the Hi-Y Club, she performed an "aerobatic dance" and won prizes in local flower shows. She and her mom were also deeply engaged in Girl Scouts. Betsy, a member of Troop 3, acted in the play *Tenant*, attended Winter Reunions, and at one Girl Scout Rally, her troop was commended for destroying the largest number of tent caterpillar nests!

Proud of her Scottish heritage, Betsy learned to play the bagpipes at an early age. She and her cousins all dressed in tartan kilts, Glengarry bonnets, and scarves with badges affixed, and would play for their families.

At Williamstown High School, she was a cheerleader for the athletic program, at one point spraining her hand trying to do back flips during a basketball tournament. Not one to remain still for long, Betsy was a member of the Dramatic Club, the Glee Club, the Camera Club, and served as Class Historian and Librarian.

After graduating in 1939 from Williamstown High, she entered the Henry W. Bishop Memorial School of Nursing in Pittsfield, Massachusetts. After three years of study, practical application, and serving as the class Vice President, she graduated from Bishop on May 19, 1942, with a degree in nursing. Then Betsy began working at the nearby House of Mercy Hospital. During her training, a surprising accident occurred when a janitor using a buffer lost control, breaking Betsy's right ankle. She recovered quickly, although she would have multiple surgeries on it the rest of her life, and at one point, the ankle was fused, giving her a slight but detectable limp.

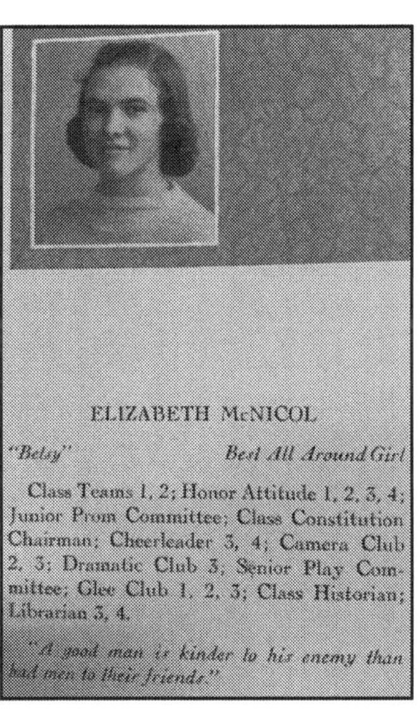

ELIZABETH McNICOL

"Betsy" *Best All Around Girl*

Class Teams 1, 2; Honor Attitude 1, 2, 3, 4; Junior Prom Committee; Class Constitution Chairman; Cheerleader 3, 4; Camera Club 2, 3; Dramatic Club 3, Senior Play Committee; Glee Club 1, 2, 3; Class Historian; Librarian 3, 4.

"A good man is kinder to his enemy than bad men to their friends."

Betsy's yearbook photo and accomplishments. (Courtesy of McNicol family)

While in school, she met a lieutenant by the name of John J. Kennedy, though no relation to the more famous family, and attended his graduation ceremony from flight school in New Mexico. The couple announced their engagement in March 1944. John earned his silver wings and was assigned to a bomber squadron as a navigator.

With John assigned overseas, Betsy applied for the Army Nurses Corps, was accepted, and entered the Army on July 5, 1944, headed to Fort Devens for basic training. Applicants for the Nurses Corps needed to be between 21 to 45 years of age, unmarried (although that requirement was changed in 1942, allowing married women to apply), a graduate of a three-year nursing program, a US citizen, between five and six feet tall, and possess both a certificate of health and letters stating their moral and professional excellence.

At Fort Devens, the first activity during her four-week orientation program was issuing uniforms and dog tags, and getting haircuts and inoculations. Classwork would go on to cover military customs and courtesies, administration, and ward nursing. In the outdoor training, she would be digging foxholes, purifying water, studying field sanitation, learning about airplane identification, and planning what to do during chemical or mechanized attacks. There would always be daily drills (marching) and long hikes with knapsacks, canteens, and gas masks. She loved keeping her mom updated on her new experiences.

US Army Nurse Corps

WHILE NURSES HAVE SERVED in some capacity since the Revolutionary War, tending soldiers under George Washington, they were volunteers and not considered part of the Army. In 1901, the United States established a permanent Army Nurse Corps, and during World War II, the corps grew from fewer than 1,000 nurses to over 55,000. The government quickly realized it would need a massive influx of nurses to staff the growing number of hospitals serving millions of new soldiers and sailors. Before war's end, there would be hundreds of general, station, evacuation, and field hospitals established all over the world treating US military personnel.

Given the Army's sudden need for nurses, it made efforts to decrease the number one reason for discharges: pregnancy. The units took great care planning where they located the nurses' barracks, discouraged drinking, and encouraged nurses to stay in groups. The nurses used the acronym PWOP (pregnancy without permission) to describe a fellow member being released from active duty. The second highest reason for discharges was fatigue: from long hours, extreme working conditions, and witnessing the number and gravity of the wounded they attended.

Interestingly, due to prevailing discrimination, only a limited number of black nurses anxious to serve were allowed to do so, totaling just five hundred by war's end. They were often restricted to working with black patients and POWs. Female physicians were also not admitted to the Army's Medical Corps. Male nurses were never accepted in the US Corps of Nurses. If a man had a nursing degree, he became a medic.

Not long after 2nd Lieutenant McNicol completed her basic training in November 1944, she departed for overseas headed for her first assignment at a general hospital in England. Tragically, shortly after her arrival, she would receive word that her fiancé, Lieutenant Kennedy, was missing in action over Hungary. While he was serving as a navigator on a bomber, his plane failed to return to base.

After months of anxiety, 2nd Lieutenant Kennedy's parents received a telegram notifying them that "Second Lieutenant John J. Kennedy, 24, previously listed missing in combat over Hungary November 20, has been reported killed the same day" (*Transcript*, 3-7-45). The confirmation of his death was disastrous news for Betsy. She had now officially lost her beloved fiancé, and she grieved for his parents with whom she had become close, referring to John's mom as Mother Kennedy. Betsy would visit them several times after the war.

Upon arrival in England (November 1944), Betsy was assigned

to the 3rd Army and would work at the 98th General Hospital near Newbury, serving there for the next seven months. The 3rd Army was led by the aggressive and successful General George S. Patton, Jr, known for his motto "When in doubt—attack." His division would roar across Europe in eight campaigns beginning after D-Day, taking them through France, Belgium, Luxembourg, Germany, and Czechoslovakia. While his battlefield successes were lauded, the 3rd Army would ultimately suffer 16,000 killed and over 100,000 wounded. Many of those were treated at Betsy's hospital.

Lt. McNicol arriving at barracks with her duffel bag. (Courtesy of McNicol family)

Betsy settled in at the large hospital, with its hundreds of beds, focusing on longer-term care and providing specialized treatment for brain, eye, chest, or psychiatric injuries. The patient wards were huge, and she witnessed the agony of row after row of soldiers. Betsy was there when the hospital received a large influx of patients after D-Day, many arriving by LSTs (Landing Ship, Tanks converted to transport wounded) from France. The soldiers were triaged on the dock after being unloaded and then treated at her hospital. Battle tags on their extremities gave her some indication of the type of wound and any treatment given in the field.

During her time in England, Betsy also helped care for many grievously wounded German POWs. She was assisted by male medics and female Red Cross nurses' aides; armed guards watched the Germans.

When not working long hours, she returned exhausted to a spartan barracks. With few amenities, it was cold in the winter—the coal stoves never seemed to provide enough heat—and blistering hot in the warmer months. The nurses washed and set out their clothes to dry, and it wasn't uncommon to see nylons hanging from the rafters. In the little time between work and rest, a few of her friends bought bicycles and explored the countryside.

CHAIN OF EVACUATION

BETSY WAS AT THE end of the Chain of Evacuation, which began when a wounded soldier was treated on the battlefield by a medic, brought to a casualty collection point, and initially triaged. Those beyond help were given morphine and made comfortable until they died. Potential survivors were moved to battalion aid stations, usually a mile from the front, and often given plasma, splints, additional dressings, and morphine before being moved to mobile field hospitals where emergency surgery would be performed in hopes of stabilizing the wounded soldier.

Then, the seriously wounded were sent to evacuation hospitals, possibly station hospitals, for further treatment. Finally, those needing more surgical intervention or long rehabilitation ended up at Betsy's general hospital, the last stop in the chain. With all the benefits of a well-established civilian hospital, like electricity and running water, they would receive the most comprehensive care. They eventually returned to duty via a replacement depot or were evacuated to the United States for additional care, recovery, or discharge.

Nurses were part of every link in the chain of evacuation in every area of war, both the Pacific and European Theaters. Their jobs were emotionally draining: working long shifts, caring for thousands of seriously wounded patients, often haunted by the patients they couldn't save. Helping with transfusions, calming or restraining delirious patients, and treating/debriding the many burn cases were just a few of their tasks.

Some innovations and practices reduced the types of morbidity seen during World War I. Antibiotics played a crucial role in reducing sepsis and gangrene. Sulphonamide (Sulfa) powder was dusted into wounds on the battlefield, slowing the infection rate, and penicillin was introduced to surgical units in 1943. Blood transfusions and debridement (removing dead tissue) lessened the danger of infection, resulting in fewer amputations; all helped reduce mortality rates and hasten recoveries.

Betsy's job wasn't without some lighthearted moments. One morning, after she and several other nurses were recovering from a long-overdue, late-night party, she began one of her morning chores of shaving wounded soldiers. At one point, a soldier told her she was using toothpaste instead of shaving cream! Without close inspection, it was a natural error; both were kept in similar tubes.

Sometime in the late summer or early fall of 1945, Betsy traveled across France and was finally stationed with the 98th General Hospital supporting the 3rd Army outside of Munich, Germany, probably in the town of Nuremberg (Nurnberg in German). She was to remain there for six months, treating the recovering wounded of the 3rd Army and numerous POWs.

On the back of this photo, Betsy wrote: *Newbury, England, June 1945. Still in pretty good condition - don't you think?* (Courtesy of McNicol family)

The Nuremberg Hospital was formerly a complex that included a German military hospital, barracks, and mess halls. It was dedicated by Adolph Hitler in the late 1930s. General Patton's 3rd Army captured the complex in April 1945, quickly repaired its war damage, and turned it into a US hospital. Not all the damage was visible: Strong rumors indicated that when the hospital had been under German control, Dachau concentration inmates were experimented upon with frightening procedures, including underwater immersion.

Betsy was now assigned as a charge nurse to a neurosurgery ward in the spinal cord injury (SCI) unit. After the high mortality rates in World War I, SCI was created to manage spinal cord and brain wounds. It was quickly determined that using antibiotics, early surgery, and especially debriding wounds of metal and bone fragments would yield much better outcomes.

As a charge nurse, she was responsible for other nurses, each of whom had ten to fifteen patients; she ensured the ward was heated and ventilated, that orderliness was maintained, and that linens were changed. Even as a charge nurse, she gave baths, shaved patients, brushed teeth, and handled bedpans. All of the nurses served meals and fed the more severely wounded patients. When necessary, they gave alcohol rubs to immobilized patients in order to avoid bed sores.

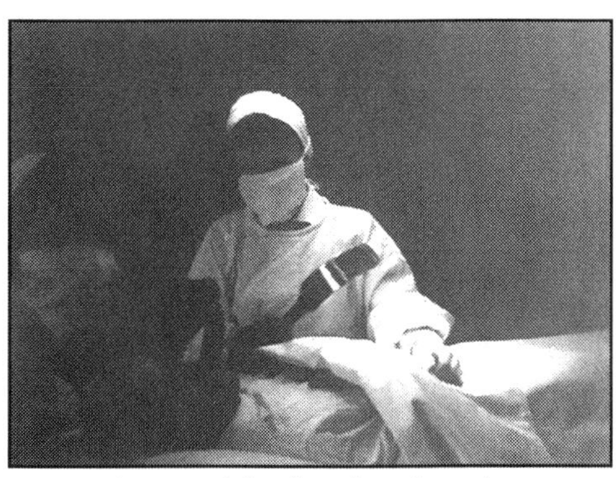

Betsy, at the patient's head, works with another nurse to save a soldier's life. (Courtesy of the McNicol family)

Nurses also gave intravenous medications and started fluids. This was at a point in time when syringes were sterilized and reused, and surgical gloves were often washed and used again, which created a great deal more labor.

The War in Europe ended in May 1945. Betsy continued to serve recovering soldiers and POWs. She was promoted to 1st Lieutenant in November. As her patients returned home, she had several chances to visit the nearby towns of Gamisch and Berchtesgaden, enjoying the natural wonders of beautiful lakes and mountains. She may have had a chance to see the recently captured "Eagles Nest," a redoubt of Hitler's in the mountains outside of Berchtesgaden.

Betsy returned to the United States by ship, nine months after the war had ended, in March 1946, and was honorably discharged at

Fort Dix, New Jersey, on April 24, 1946, having served overseas for sixteen months. Her decorations include the American Campaign Medal, European–African–Middle Eastern Campaign Medal, and World War II Victory Medal.

In the last two years of the war, European Theater hospitals cared for hundreds of thousands of wounded. Shells and bullets caused the most common injuries, but patients also suffered from second- and third-degree burns, broken bones, shrapnel wounds, brain and spinal cord injuries, nerve damage, paralysis, loss of sight, loss of hearing, loss of limbs, and combat fatigue.

Betsy seldom talked about her wartime experiences. She told her father, an Air Raid Warden during the war, "Daddy, you will never understand what I saw."

Later in life, she did share with her family that she and her fellow nurses treated thousands of soldiers, many with horrific wounds and countless of them requiring amputations.

She didn't take long to return to work at Putnam Memorial Hospital in Bennington, Vermont. The conversion to a civilian hospital experience from her wartime general hospital duties went smoothly, although she fondly remembered her independence in treating casualties.

At the hospital, she met her future husband, Joseph Fowler, who happened to be visiting his girlfriend. Inadvertently opening the wrong door, Joseph met and chatted with Betsy. Smitten with Betsy, he ended his former relationship and the two started dating. One of their early and sad connections was losing a loved one during the war. Betsy's former fiancé, John Kennedy, was shot down and killed over Hungary in 1944, and Joseph's older brother, Pfc. Harvey Fowler, a twenty-eight-year-old Marine, was killed in action by mortar fire on the Island of Guam in July 1944.

Joseph had returned from serving with the field artillery in the Asiatic–Pacific area. After his brother's death, he was transferred to Hawaii by War Department policy, as the family's only remaining son.

Months after their unintentional meeting, Betsy and Joseph were married on July 5, 1947, at St. Patrick's Church in Williamstown. They moved to Manchester, Vermont, where Joseph worked with his father and eventually took over the Fowler Insurance Agency, the oldest insurance business in Vermont and second oldest in New England, founded in 1858. Joseph himself would operate the business for almost forty years. It was eventually sold in the 1990s.

After moving to Manchester, Betsy and Joseph had two daughters, Shara-Lyn and Susan, and a son, Dana; Betsy became a homemaker and a much relied-upon community organizer with the organizational skills she'd acquired in the Nurse Corps.

The five-foot-four-inch-tall dynamo was the one people called on when they needed a chairperson for a community project. People would say, "Betsy will get it done."

Betsy was active with the 1st Congregational Church, leading fund drives and managing tag sales. For over fifty years, she served as a Girl Scout leader supporting, among many other things, their annual cookie drives.

She was also involved in local Red Cross blood donation drives and a great supporter of local carnivals. Her social involvement helped promote the Fowler good name, a great adjunct to the insurance agency. Joseph was involved with the Rotary Club, the Eagles Aerie of Manchester, and the International Quartet and was a lifetime member of the Veterans of Foreign Wars.

In the late 1950s, Betsy helped organize the Junior Instructional Ski Program (JISP) at Bromley Mountain Ski Resort. It provided an opportunity and equipment for elementary school children to learn how to ski. She would drive kids to the resort in her large Mercury station wagon. Betsy could no longer ski because of her ankle injury, but she enjoyed seeing her young charges learn the sport.

She continued her involvement in civic affairs as president and then a member of the Parent Teacher Association, as well as the local Planning and Zoning Board. She served for years on the Board of Directors for the now-defunct Ethan Allen College.

Betsy and her family lived in a two-story white house with black shutters and a sizable deck. The home was set on a large lot where she had a flower garden, as one "never afraid to get her hands dirty." She loved animals, and the family had a favored collie named Yankee. At one point, the kids even cared for a donkey.

Everyone would agree that Betsy was fun-loving, organized, sincere, and enjoyed entertaining at their home. She enjoyed baking pies and cakes around the holidays. She was also the family's take-charge person and expected the children's help.

Betsy did allow the children to wear her service uniform at Halloween for trick-or-treating. The little ones wearing her olive drab jacket skirt with its nurse's cap would bring a smile to her face and rekindle the better wartime memories.

Traveling in their station wagon, the family vacationed in Philadelphia and Washington, DC, visiting the nation's favorite monuments, and other times, they traveled to Maine, staying with friends and enjoying the beach.

Their most exciting trip was traveling to New York City in a sleeper car. They were going to be on the famous *Today* show invited by their personal friend, the show's news editor Frank Blair. Betsy and Joseph chatted with Dave Garroway, the first host of *Today*, about Manchester's Winter Carnival. The kids were excited and waved to everyone they met.

Later in life, Betsy found time for golf and became quite skilled. Spring and summer often revolved around her membership in the Ekwanok club and its tournaments.

At times, for a veteran of war, tragedy never seems too far away. Once, when her children were swimming at a local lake, Betsy, always alert, noticed her daughter, Lyn, had slipped out of sight. Quickly reacting, they brought the girl to shore; Betsy, seeing she was not breathing, performed CPR and saved her daughter's life.

Not long afterward in the early 1980s, unexpectedly and tragically, her thirty-three-year-old son Dana, a Vietnam veteran who served in the submarine service, died of an aneurysm.

Shockingly, Betsy too succumbed to an aneurysm a few years later, passing away at age sixty-six. She, Joseph, and Dana are today buried near each other in the Dellwood Cemetery in Manchester, Vermont.

The United States Red Cross recruited thousands of nurses during World War II; most nurses often wore their symbolic pins with pride. The pin was not allowed to be worn with civilian clothes, only while in uniform. This young girl from Williamstown, Massachusetts, who treated countless wounded during World War II, who returned, married, had a family, and fairly well organized her entire town, always reminded her family to return her Red Cross pin as she was instructed so many years ago. Today, Betsy's picture hangs in the gathering room at the Williamstown American Legion Post 152, forever etched in time as "Lt. Betsy McNicol WWII US Army Nurse—WHS Grad."

Lawrence B. Urbano
Fighter Pilot
VF-3 Fighter Squadron

He was in trouble; the Grumman Hellcat shuddered during his last strafing run, and now the controls would not respond. With great effort, Larry turned toward the last-known location of his carrier. With no radio contact, and separated from his sortie, he was in a desperate position.

Staring at the 2,000,000-square mile expanse of the Philippine Sea, the thought of locating the USS Yorktown *and its 870-foot landing deck seemed hopeless. It was nowhere in sight, and he could hear his engine struggling to keep him aloft.*

LAWRENCE BLANQUART URBANO'S AVIATION story begins much earlier, in Williamstown, Massachusetts, where he was born on May 8, 1923, to a World War I Aviator veteran, Raphael Urbano, and his wife Flora.

Raphael had served 18 months in France in the Air Corps. He was a Flight Sergeant with the 248th Aerial Bombardment, known as the "Crazy Black Cat" Squadron. Almost thirty years later, his son Lawrence would fight under the same insignia.

Lawrence's mother was Flora C. (Blanquart) Urbano. Flora was from North Adams, and Raphael, a native of Italy, had immigrated to the area at five years of age in the early 1900s. They had married in 1921 at Notre Dame Church in North Adams and moved to Williamstown shortly afterward. The couple had three children, two boys and a girl.

After World War I, Raphael was the service manager at Thomas

McMahon & Son Chevrolet for fifty years. In the 1920s until the mid-1950s, the dealership was located on Spring Street, and Raphael and a partner owned and managed the repair shop in the rear of the location. Raphael became very engaged in World War II initiatives, leading war bond campaigns and teaching auto mechanic courses to women, which would qualify them for the Motor Corps. At one point, he also served as the commander of Williamstown's American Legion Post.

Flora came from a large family of seven children, five boys and two girls. Flora's father and mother had each been widowed in their previous marriages. First, they adopted an infant boy, and then went on to have six more children together. In 1958, Flora's mother, Jeanne Blanquart, was voted "Mother of the Year" at age eighty years old, an honor bestowed by the Aeries of the North Adams Fraternal Order of Eagles.

Their son Lawrence attended Mitchell School and was very active in its pageants and plays. As a sixth grader, he had a central role in the school's Thanksgiving Program, "Simple Simon," a pantomime. He was also chosen to be a lieutenant on the school's student patrol, which guarded street corners and crosswalks, helping the younger children get to school safely.

Lawrence, by now called Larry, was also a member of Boy Scout Troop 65, receiving his First Class Award and merit badges for public health, scholarship, and swimming. Always on the go, he made the local paper when he broke his left arm roller skating near the Williams College campus.

While attending Williamstown High School, he joined the Stony Ledge Ski Club, was elected to its board of directors, was also a member of the National Ski Patrol, and helped plan the club's ski trips. During his high school years, he served as president of his class and the Pro-Merito Society, was on the Debate Club, and lettered in baseball and football, despite his diminutive size; at five feet six inches tall, he was quarterbacking over some towering competition. As the perennial underdog, the team only scored two touchdowns in the 1940 season.

He always found time to participate in school plays, and in his senior year, Larry had a leading role in "Once There Was a Princess." His senior yearbook describes him as a "genial wit with perpetual drive," the class's best dancer, a writer for the *Spirit* newsletter. It was reported that his best "Worldly Possession" was the "gift of gab."

Larry entered Williams College in 1941 with the class of 1945. In 1942, with World War II raging, he took the enlistment oath at the Selection Board in Boston to become a naval cadet. As a sophomore, he was allowed to complete the college year, ending in February 1943, though his official enlistment date was December 1942.

In March 1943, Naval Aviation Cadet Urbano entered flight school in Sheffield, Massachusetts, and upon successful completion, headed to the Navy's eleven-week pre-flight training in Chapel Hill, North Carolina. His training included naval history and essentials, military drill, and physical fitness.

Then, he went on to three months of primary flight training at the Naval Air Station in Olathe, Kansas, followed by more months of advanced flight training. Larry finally entered the last stage of his fighter pilot training at Pensacola, Florida, where he successfully graduated, was commissioned an ensign in the Navy, and received his gold wings in May 1944.

He spent several weeks home on leave before heading to San Diego in September 1944 to sail on a carrier. He was assigned as a Hellcat pilot. In October, ready to ship out, he sent his personal effects home, certifying the parcel contained "no live ammunition, hand grenades, explosives any kind or any other articles dangerous to life."

Initially, he was attached to the VF-100 squadron (VF denoting a fighter squadron), ferrying replacement aircraft, including the Corsair fighter, to different carriers and moving others to shore. The US Navy was replacing its Vought F4U Corsair fighter with the Grumman F6F-Hellcat, which had better handling and visibility for carrier work. The Corsairs would be reserved for land-based operations.

In November 1944, Larry was assigned to the aircraft carrier USS *Yorktown* (CV-10), known as the "Fighting Lady," named after the previous USS *Yorktown* (CV-5) that was sunk at the pivotal Battle of Midway in June 1942.

The newest *Yorktown*, commissioned in April 1943, carried a crew of over 3,000 sailors and aviators and 90 planes, a mixture of fighters and bombers. Her storied history and future would include some of the major battles of World War II, earning The Lady twelve battle stars and a Presidential Unit Citation.

She would later participate in the Korean and Vietnam wars and was also used as an *Apollo 8* recovery ship. The ship itself starred in the 1970 movie *Tora, Tora, Tora,* featuring the infamous attack on Pearl Harbor. The *Yorktown* was decommissioned in 1970, donated to Charleston, South Carolina, and officially became a museum on October 13, 1975, on the 200th anniversary of the United States Navy.

Larry was glad to be aboard and delighted to fly the Grumman F6F-Hellcat, now attached to VF-3, known as the Felix the Cat squadron, or the Crazy Cats. He found the Hellcat rugged, reliable, and easy to handle, although slower than the Corsair; the Navy thought its capabilities would be an answer to the speedy Japanese Zero.

Larry thrilled to be at the controls of his Hellcat. (Courtesy of Urbano family)

An earlier member of VF-3, Edward "Butch" O'Hare, flying under the "Felix the Cat" insignia, earned the Medal of Honor for placing himself between nine oncoming enemy bombers and his ship. In the ensuing fight, he shot down five bombers and disabled a sixth. O'Hare International Airport in Chicago is named after him. Butch was later killed in action when his Hellcat was shot down in a subsequent mission.

An 18-cylinder, 2000-horsepower engine powered Larry's Hellcat, which possessed six .50-caliber Browning machine guns and six aircraft rockets, three located under each wing. Among the plane's most significant fighting advantages were a bullet-resistant windshield, an armored cockpit, and self-sealing fuel tanks, something the Japanese Zero did not possess. Postwar memoirs by Japanese pilots noted that the Hellcats withstood numerous machine gun hits without falling out of the sky. Conversely, unarmored Zeros often exploded after a burst of machine gun hits.

Throughout the war, the United States built over 12,000 Hellcats, which destroyed more enemy fighters than any other aircraft. It was credited with 75% of kills in the Pacific Theater, representing over 5,000 downed enemy aircraft.

Once *Yorktown* arrived in the Pacific, sorties began immediately. In November and December 1944, Larry's squadron, VF-3, raided airfields in the Marianas, New Guinea, and on Saipan. December found the Hellcats strafing targets on Formosa, Canton, and Indochina and conducting raids on Japan's outer defenses.

On one of the mid-December raids in 1944, flying in and out of heavy clouds that obscured the target, then finally flying low enough to see his target, Larry's aircraft was hit by antiaircraft fire during a strafing run on an enemy airfield. He knew his smoking, single-engine plane was mortally wounded and immediately turned around in the general direction of the *Yorktown.*

From 10,000 feet, he could see the vast, blue expanse of the Philippine Sea and realized he could not make it back to the carrier. He would have to ditch his plane, and he quickly debated whether to parachute or land the plane in the water. The water looked calm. With only seconds to decide, he lowered his flaps, made sure his wheels were retracted, tightened his safety harness, and landed tail-down in the water. Quickly retracting the canopy, he had just moments to clamber out and inflate his "Mae West" life preserver and raft.

Fortunately, his solo expedition was short-lived. He was, against all odds, rescued by an escort destroyer whose fire control officer was a graduate of Williams College. Larry recalled at the time saying to himself, "What's a little 'ole boy from Williamstown doing in the South China Sea?"

After being given some dry clothes and a day of rest, Larry was transferred to a tanker and headed back to the *Yorktown*. But his water odyssey was not quite over; as the tanker proceeded, it was caught in Typhoon Cobra, a devastating cyclone that would seriously damage the Pacific fleet known as Task Force-38. Before Larry could return to *Yorktown*, the storm would sink three destroyers, kill hundreds of sailors, and create raging fires that destroyed or damaged dozens of aircraft. The *Yorktown* itself was kept busy participating in rescue operations.

In late December, the tanker was able to return Larry to the naval base at Ulithi, where the *Yorktown* was refueling and resupplying. At the time, Ulithi, an atoll, was the largest naval base in the world, with berths for hundreds of ships supporting the war efforts in the Pacific Ocean. Seabees had built docking piers, camps, airfields, mess halls, and hospitals to support the 9,000 men stationed there and the many sailors visiting. The Navy also kept replacement carrier aircraft for those destroyed in battle. The *Yorktown* was berthed with five other carriers in a section nicknamed "Murderers Row." (At the time, Murderers Row was the nickname given to the New York Yankees' powerful first six batters and a serious part of 1940s American culture.)

In January 1945, the *Yorktown*, with Larry aboard, left Ulithi and resumed raids on Japanese airfields, knocking out parked planes and installations, low-level attacks subjected to withering antiaircraft fire. The air group supported bombers that would intercept convoys attempting to resupply Japanese ground forces; American bombers sunk six destroyers and four transports. While supporting the bombers, VF-3 downed thirteen enemy planes.

The action hardly ceased, and few days were spent off duty. On February 16, 1945, Larry's squadron was providing air cover for bombers hitting an aircraft engine plant only sixteen miles from the Japanese emperor's palace; they demolished it. During the sortie, Larry got into a dogfight with a Japanese Zero (nicknamed *Zekes* by the aviators). The enemy plane approached Larry head-on, giving him little time to think; Larry responded with his .50-caliber machine guns, shredding the cockpit. The Zero plummeted, smoking and unmanned, to the ocean.

He quickly swung around onto the tail of another enemy fighter interceptor and applied a barrage of machine gun fire that penetrated the plane's fuselage; the plane seemed to falter, then fell to the left in what became a death spiral. It, too, plummeted into the sea. Within a matter of minutes, Larry had downed two enemy aircraft, one Zeke, one Tojo. His pilot's log notes both kills.

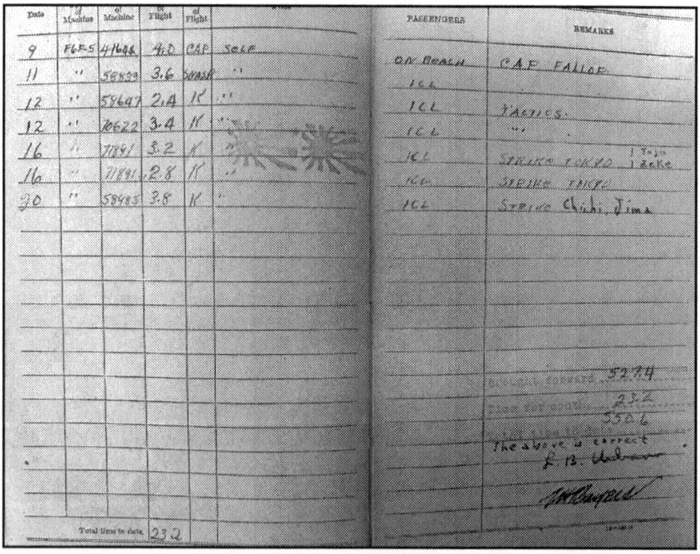

Larry's actual logbook showing flag symbols representing the two downed Japanese planes. (Courtesy of Urbano family)

The Japanese Mitsubishi A6M Zero had excellent maneuverability and long range, making it one of Japan's most vaunted aircraft, capable of being used on land or from a carrier. Early in the war, the plane had been one of the best fighter aircraft. By the time Larry arrived on the *Yorktown*, the Grumman Hellcat was more than a match for the nimble Zero, exceeding its firepower, armor, and speed. The Zeke had two 20mm cannons and two 7.7mm machine guns.

The Allies also encountered the Nakajima Ki-44 *Tojo*. A fighter-interceptor plane with excellent speed and rate of climb, it was a solid adversary to the Grumman Hellcat. Also equipped with four 12.7mm machine guns, it was used in air defense against incoming B-29 bombers as the Allies closed in on the Japanese homeland.

The May 1, 1945, *Transcript* cited early reports of Larry's heroic actions. The article's headline read, "Ensign Urbano Flew from the 'Fighting Lady'—Spring Street Boy Downed Two Jap Fighters." The article went on to report that "Ninety-one airplanes were shot down [by the Crazy Cats, part of Air Group III], with an additional 181 destroyed on the ground….Jap shipping suffered also….Planes from the 'Fighting Lady' sank 28 vessels, including a light cruiser and destroyer."

In a *Transcript* article dated September 21, 1945, it was reported that Larry received the Distinguished Flying Cross for his heroics, with headlines reading "Credited with Five Planes, Jap Lugger: Ensign Lawrence B. Urbano, USNR, of Spring Street presented the DFC and Gold Star in lieu of a Second Air Medal." (A *lugger* is a midsized fishing boat, often with two masts.) The article introduces him as "a 22-year-old, a former student at Williams College, where he had a varsity spot on the wrestling team."

The medals were presented to Larry in Norfolk, Virginia. The citation read as follows: "Capitalizing on excellent tactics and air discipline displayed by the entire division, which accounted for the destruction of five airborne planes, he shot down one enemy fighter from a head-on approach and then swung on the tail of a second plane and destroyed it." The article also mentions separate actions: "he is credited with destroying three planes on the ground and sinking a Japanese lugger by rocket attack off Formosa."

The ensuing months were marked by more raids on Japan and providing support for both the Iwo Jima and Okinawa invasions in

Larry's medals are on display today at the Williamstown Historical Museum, of importance from left to right, with Distinguished Flying Cross and Air Medal far left. (Courtesy of Urbano family)

order to degrade enemy air support, communications, and shipping. The enemy was not idle; in March, three dive-bombers tried to penetrate the *Yorktown*'s antiaircraft curtain of fire, and one succeeded in dropping a bomb that broke through the first deck and exploded near the hull, killing and wounding over thirty sailors. Larry was friends with many of the injured sailors, some of whom serviced his plane.

In April 1945, Larry's squadron continued to support the ground troops on Okinawa and, at one point, was diverted to attack an incoming Japanese task force. While providing coverage, the *Yorktown* bombers destroyed the battleship *Yamato* and a light cruiser. Larry and the Hellcats distracted, strafed, and set some of the escorting destroyers afire.

In May and June 1945, *Yorktown* and the Crazy Cats continued to support the Okinawa landing and resumed strikes on the Japanese homeland.

In July 1945, Lawrence returned home from overseas to undergo further training. He decided to return to college and remained in the Naval Reserves. After nearly four years in naval aviation, Larry's decorations included a Distinguished Flying Cross, two Air Medals, two Presidential Unit Citations, the Asiatic–Pacific Medal with three stars, and an American Campaign Medal.

Larry returned to Williams College, graduating Cum Laude in 1947, with a degree in literature. He and other returning veterans were allowed to remain members of the class of 1945.

He decided to pursue a law career and applied to Harvard Law School; in 1950, he graduated and passed the bar exam. Larry then worked as a law clerk to the Supreme Judicial Court, the State's highest court, for one year before becoming a research associate at Harvard studying the Massachusetts court system.

In the early 1950s, he met and married a well-educated medical secretary, Norma Ruth Ecklund. The young couple resided in Boston while Larry served three years as an Assistant US Attorney and then worked for a private law firm. Remaining in the Naval Reserves, Larry continued to fly on weekend drills and during a two-week summer training.

Though successful in Boston, Larry missed his hometown. He soon established a partnership with the Williamstown law firm owned by O. Dixon Marshall in the late 1950s, and he and Norma relocated to Williamstown in 1960. The law office was on the 2nd floor over the McMahon dealership on Spring Street, where his dad had worked for so many years.

Larry, second from left, checks with his pilots before a flight at Weymouth. (Courtesy of Urbano family)

In August 1961, Larry's squadron was unexpectedly called to active duty in response to the Berlin crisis. The VS915 squadron flew twin-engine sonar-radar equipped Grumman S2F Trackers and conducted anti-submarine patrols off the Atlantic coast from Maine to Cuba.

Based at the Weymouth Naval Air Station, Larry served nine months as the squadron commander and in this role was recognized by the Naval Reserve Association for his unit's outstanding performance. When he returned to his office in Williamstown, the unit was deactivated.

While he was serving in Weymouth, his law partner's health had declined, requiring Larry to return home on weekends to maintain client contacts and process legal paperwork. His partner died in 1962, and Larry assumed the business.

Actively involved in the Town's affairs, he assisted in seeking candidates for an open selectman position. With no one volunteering, Larry signed up a few moments before the deadline and served six years and three years as the group's chairperson. He also served as Williamstown's town counsel for many years.

Surprisingly and sadly, Norma, suffering from a long illness died unexpectedly on December 3, 1971, at the age of 44.

Larry immersed himself in his work, assisted by Ellen Eaton, who had worked for the firm for many years. Larry had known Ellen in high school, and she had been the mainstay behind the firm during O. Dixon Marshall's long illness and Larry's call to active duty. After working together for so long, Larry and Ellen developed a fondness for each other and were married on May 20, 1972. After their marriage, they continued to work together in the law office for years.

Williamstown honored Larry with its 1974 Hayden Memorial Award for his accomplishments as a soldier, lawyer, and citizen. Over the years, he served on many special committees and task forces for the local community as well as the state. Larry was on the Board of Directors for the Williamstown Theater and Buxton School and was a trustee at the former Williamstown National Bank and North Adams Hospital, in addition to the numerous charities he supported with his time and money. He loved his community and provided free financial counseling seminars for the elderly. Once, he dressed up as Ephraim Williams, the Town's founder, to march in Williamstown's bicentennial parade.

In 1980, recognizing his judicial excellence, the state appointed him Associate Justice of Massachusetts Superior Court, and he and

Ellen moved to Worthington, Massachusetts, to shorten his rotating judicial commutes. For the next ten years, he would act as magistrate over a plethora of issues ranging from drug trafficking and armed robbery to homicides.

An anecdote that few know is when celebrating his judgeship appointment at a friend's house, Larry choked on a piece of steak. His host saved the day by successfully applying the Heimlich method, in the process breaking three of Larry's ribs. Once recovered, Larry jokingly asked his friend to go a little easier the next time and maybe a bit higher on his torso.

In 1983, Larry retired as a Lieutenant Commander from the US Naval Reserve. All in all, he served in the Navy for over forty years, thirty in the active reserves and ten years inactive. He earned the Naval Reserve Medal.

Now living full-time in Worthington, the couple enjoyed two pastimes together: golfing at the 10-hole Worthington Golf Club and visiting their summer home in Brewster, Massachusetts, near Cape Cod. On occasion, at the Worthington Golf Club, they would see one of its more famous members who lived nearby, George Shultz, former Secretary of State for Ronald Reagan.

Larry served ten years as a judge before contracting Parkinson's disease and passing away in 2001. His beloved wife, Ellen, lived another twenty years. Both are buried together in Williamstown's Eastlawn Cemetery.

Today, he is still remembered by the citizens of Williamstown for his remarkable ability, excellent legal mind, willingness to serve, and engaging personality. As one friend said, Larry was "the ultimate citizen; he served the nation and his community without question."

Joseph J. Zasloff
Radio Operator
26th "Yankee" Infantry Division

The Nazis had been waiting for them. As Joe's small squad forged ahead to the outskirts of town, they paused, hearing loud clanging noises. The noise seemed to be on all sides. Realizing Tiger tanks were coming for them, they frantically retreated to the center of the village, looking for shelter. Scrambling into the cellar of a nearby house, they had only moments before a tank swung its cannon in their direction.

JOSEPH JERMIAH ZASLOFF CAME into the world in Pittsburgh, Pennsylvania, on February 24, 1925, and left it nearly nine decades later, in his home-by-choice of Williamstown, Massachusetts.

His parents were Harry T. and Anna (Shuset) Zasloff, both Jewish immigrants. Harry, one of thirteen children, was born near Zaslav, Ukraine, the same native village as the parents of renowned actor Leonard Nimoy. Anna was from the historic region of Bessarabia, now part of present-day Moldova, near the border with Ukraine. They had emigrated separately in the early 1900s. Anna, ten years old, came with her mom. Both were looking for a better life and to avoid early European pogroms against Jews.

Harry's first wife had passed away. Some years after coming to America, he met and married Anna. From this first marriage, he had a daughter named Rose, and the couple would go on to have two children of their own, William and Joseph. Joseph was the youngest child. His middle name was misspelled at birth when the clerk omitted an *e*, leaving it *Jermiah* in perpetuity.

Harry was always busy. His entrepreneurial drive had him creating numerous businesses. First, he started a fish market, then shoe and jukebox businesses. He was especially interested in world events and often spent his free time hanging out with buddies, speaking Yiddish, and reading Yiddish newspapers. Anna was a great supporter of his endeavors and a busy homemaker.

Joseph, called Joe, resided with his family in a middle-class Pittsburgh neighborhood called Squirrel Hill, within a large Jewish community. He attended a public elementary school and the rigorous Allderdice High School. Always a popular student, Joe was elected class president in his senior year. His winsome ways did not translate to serious studies; however, he would admit later in life he wished he had studied harder.

Outside of school, Joe was busy. He worked for his dad in the shoe business and would make his way throughout Pittsburgh, changing records in jukeboxes. He also managed a paper route for extra money.

Joe's high school graduation came in the middle of World War II. He attended college classes briefly and then, at eighteen, found himself part of the April 1943 Army draft quota (*Pittsburgh Post-Gazette* 4-17-43). In May, at eighteen years old, he boarded a train to Fort Bragg (now Fort Liberty), North Carolina, for basic training.

Records show he was assigned to Battery B, 1st Training Regiment-Field Artillery Replacement Center (F.A.R.C.). Joe would comment later in life of the battery commander, Captain Rankin, "A fairer, squarer officer was never made. He is highly respected by the men."

Even so, the training was difficult for the recruits. They underwent long days of learning military regulations, close order drills, calisthenics, weapons, and bayonet training. They had few minutes to themselves when not in the classroom, drilling outside, or running obstacle courses.

Any free time was dedicated to washing their clothes, cleaning equipment, and writing letters home. Several men in his unit were

A happy soldier, having completed basic training. (Courtesy of Zasloff family)

hospitalized with acute diarrhea when, somehow, they got soap in their mess kits. Apparently, the soap was a strong laxative.

After weeks of training, graduation would involve a series of competitions, including drills and exercises, to determine the best battalion. It's unknown how Joe's unit fared.

While in basic training, Joe scored high on the Army's General Classification test and was placed in the Army's Specialized Training Program (ASTP) and sent to the University of Maine at Orono. ASTP was designed to train junior officers and soldiers in specialized skills. Joe would study radar, engineering, communications, and other technical disciplines.

Aside from the classroom, training was demanding. While attending university courses, ASTP soldiers maintained strict military discipline, including early morning reveille, calisthenics, eating at mess halls, and marching to class. All proudly wore the ASTP patch emblazoned with the "Sword of Valor and Lamp of Knowledge." Joe enjoyed his time there, mixing with other highly intelligent soldiers from across the country, and barracked at the Sigma Chi House.

Joe, on left, with friend Morty Haas attending ASTP training in Maine. (Courtesy of Zasloff family)

In the spring of 1944, not long after his arrival, the Army

decided it needed infantry replacements for casualties in Europe more than it needed technical specialties. Joe and most of his cohort were transferred to the 104th Infantry Regiment of the 26th Yankee Division. The group joined their new unit in Tennessee for spring maneuvers, and once the Division was up to strength, it headed to Europe.

Records indicate that around 500 men attended ASTP in Maine. Most were assigned to an infantry regiment where fighting and surviving was a daily effort. Education was of little value. Between 1944 and 1945, over 10% of the cohort was killed in action, and as many as 75% were wounded as their units fought through northern France and Germany. The ASTP program closed at the end of the war.

Note: Some of ASTP's notable alums, in addition to Joe Zasloff, include his friend Victor Lundy, a future architect; Bob Dole, a future US Senator; Henry Kissinger, future Secretary of State; and future authors Gore Vidal and Kurt Vonnegut.

Due to the Army's pressing needs, Joe's division was shipped directly from the United States to France in August 1944. Records indicate it was the largest convoy to sail from America to Europe, with over 100 ships. Over 9,000 troops were squeezed onto the converted passenger liner SS *Argentina*. It was a noxious experience, with miserable bathrooms and showers, long chow lines, and men sleeping in tight bunks stacked five high. Everyone tried to spend as much time on deck as possible to enjoy the fresh air.

The 26th Infantry Division, known as the Yankee Division, was formed in 1917 and consisted of units mainly from New England. The division had fought several renowned WWI battles, including Château-Thierry and Saint-Mihiel. Reconstituted in World War II, it comprised three infantry regiments: 101st, 104th, and 328th.

Joe was assigned to Company K, 3rd Battalion of the 104th Infantry Regiment. His unit landed on Utah Beach on September 7, 1944, and then was assigned to General Patton's US Third Army.

Each battalion contained three rifle companies and one heavy weapons company. Companies A, B, C, and D comprised the 1st Battalion; E, F, G, H, 2nd Battalion; I, K, L and M, 3rd Battalion. D, H, and M were the heavy weapons companies.

Joe was the company's radio operator and reported to a communications sergeant who worked for the company's executive officer. The communications group often worked from the company command post, liaising with battalion headquarters.

The radio Joe likely used was an SCR-300, often called a "walkie-talkie." Developed by Motorola, it is known for its ruggedness in cold or hot weather and wet conditions. The FM radio was used heavily on D-Day and throughout the European theater. It was the radio used by most infantry units.

Joe, on right, in a command vehicle with what appears to be his radio. (Courtesy of Zasloff family)

With his ability to grasp information quickly, Joe learned to tune, transmit, and receive. In addition to communicating with the battalion, the radios were often taken on advance patrols and used to keep in touch with the company commander. Companies usually had extra SCR-300s to communicate with individual patrols or to strip for immediate replacement parts.

The SCR-300 was carried on a soldier's back and had a line connecting it to a phone. It also sported a short or long whip antenna, with a range of three miles. The radio weighed 38 pounds with its large battery pack. Two soldiers often worked together, one carrying the radio and another using the phone to call in artillery strikes or report back from a reconnaissance patrol.

It would be in October 1944 that Joe and his unit were moved to the front lines. Sitting in a foxhole by himself, directly facing German positions, he was frequently under artillery fire. The unit's advance was stalled for several days, which gave Joe much time to think about his luck so far. Even in those early days in defensive positions, Company K lost people to mortar, artillery, and gunfire.

In late October 1944, the company's first large battle occurred at Moncourt Woods, a small forest the Germans used as an observation post to rain artillery down on the division. The regiment suffered many casualties when tree-top bursts of artillery fire sent shrapnel and large wood slivers downward on Joe's company, although Joe escaped injury. On the lighter side, several soldiers in the platoon witnessed a giant wild boar with threatening tusks bound through their line. They tried to shoot it, but all missed.

The unit then fought at Bezange-la-Petite, a series of five hills with good fields of fire that needed to be taken from the Germans. The regiment again incurred many casualties and was forwarded replacements after the hills were taken. The regiment and Joe's company then skirmished and fought through small northeastern French towns and villages with names like Hampont, Dédeling, Château-Voué, and Pisdorf.

Joe's 3rd Battalion often operated separately and parallel with the other battalions and continued to advance. In mid-November, the battalion fought a vicious eight-day battle in Rodalbe, France. Angling west, Joe's 3rd Battalion approached the town, not realizing the Germans had gotten there first. Company K was sent on ahead, and Joe, with his communication squad, was dispatched to the outskirts of town to report back on enemy activity.

Joe in one of the quaint small French villages, 1944. (Courtesy of Zasloff family)

Almost immediately, the squad

heard the loud clanging noises of enemy tank treads and realized they were facing ten to twelve tanks from the 11th Panzer Division. The tanks had the town center in its sights and were supported by two Grenadier Divisions.

The American battalion commander had sent a platoon from Company G to tell Joe's unit to withdraw, but it was too late. The trap had been set; Joe's unit could not be reached, and the rescuing platoon had to retreat.

Outmaneuvered, outnumbered, and dramatically outgunned, the soldiers sought protection in nearby houses. There was some hope that American tanks could reach them in time, but no one realized that the American Sherman tanks, with their narrow tracks, were mired in the mud and could not reach Rodalbe in time. Over the next few hours, many in Joe's company would be shot or taken prisoner. Joe himself was wounded on November 13, 1944.

In a 2012 email written to several of his former students, Joe describes his harrowing experience at Rodalbe. It reads as follows:

> *Our unit was engaged in a massive new offensive against powerful German resistance, which included artillery and at least a dozen Tiger tanks. Our Battalion of foot soldiers reached the point of attack well beyond the protection of our Sherman tanks. The Germans counterattacked, heavily shelling our freshly dug line of foxholes in the fields encircling Rodalbe. We were cut off from rear echelon support.*
>
> *Vic (a friend and future artist/architect) was in the company command post at the edge of the village. I was intermittently reporting on our situation by radio to the battalion commander and, on behalf of our company commander, asking for assistance, especially for evacuation of our growing number of wounded. By late afternoon, the German forces overwhelmed our dug-in comrades and ultimately took them as prisoners.*

When tanks roared toward our command post, those of us inside, including Vic and me, ran toward the interior of the village and found refuge in a cellar under a farmhouse. A tank followed us and fired into the cellar. Vic was badly wounded in the left arm. He made his exit from the cellar, with the help of one of our buddies, through an inside door and succeeded in struggling his way back to our lines. He was later sent to Walter Reed Hospital in the U.S.

I sustained a minor injury on my right foot and escaped through the outside door we had entered. I made my way to a nearby barn and hid part-time in the hay for three days as the Germans consolidated control over the village and its environs. On the third night, following a shelling of the German position by our artillery, creating noise useful for my escape, I slithered past a parked tank and hobbled several miles to reach our rear echelon. I was later sent to a military convalescent hospital where I spent a month and was then assigned back to my unit.

After fleeing the wine cellar, some of his comrades ran upstairs and were captured. Joe kept the radio on his back as he ran back out the cellar door, into the barn and lay in a horse's stall. With his feet propped against the door, he hid for three days and two nights, living on a can of K rations. He had already taken the precaution of throwing away his dog tags, which identified him as Jewish.

In the pitch black, he used a barn that was on fire as a directional device to get back to US lines. His perilous journey was not over yet; at one point he was challenged in German to halt. Joe froze and put his hands up until he realized it was a German American soldier who spoke in his native tongue.

When Joe crept back to his unit, even though wounded, he managed to bring back the radio. Ultimately, he was awarded the Bronze Star for "remaining at his communications post at Rodalbe,

France, and calling for help despite the fact the town was overrun by enemy tanks" (*Pittsburgh Sun-Telegraph* 2-8-45). He also earned the Purple Heart for his wound.

Another news article from Pittsburgh on February 8 mentioned "Pvt Zasloff…hiding in a barn barricaded the door so the enemy would think it had been jammed by shell fire and lived on K rations while he listened to the Germans outside." The Germans were so close, he heard a Nazi trooper being bawled out for reporting late for guard duty.

The Tiger I Tank used at Rodalbe had an 88mm main cannon that fired a high velocity HE (heavy explosive) round. It was amazing that Joe, Vic, and others escaped with relatively minor wounds. Victor Lundy, the architecture student, had been transferred into Joe's unit, and they became close friends. An accomplished artist, Victor sketched people, places, and scenes during his time with the unit (May to November 1944). His sketches survived the war, were donated to the Library of Congress, and are available online. Several

Lundy's sketches of Joe. (Courtesy of Zasloff family)

sketches of Joe reside in the collection. After the war, Victor had a distinguished career as an architect. He and Joe reconnected by phone later in life and shared what they had been doing since they last saw each other in the village of Rodalbe, cut off from their regiment by German tanks.

Shortly after his escape, Joe was again called into action while he was recovering from his ordeal and being treated in a field hospital for his wound. A disoriented GI threw a can of kerosene into an open fire, and the tent caught fire, endangering all the patients. With quick action, Joe put out the fire with several blankets. It is believed Joe received his second Bronze Star for his quick thinking in extinguishing the fire and saving the other patients.

During the winter months, Joe developed trench foot and would have poor circulation in his feet for the rest of his life. During this cold period of November and December, many troops were dealing with trench foot due to poor-quality boots that lacked waterproofing. Prolonged exposure to low temperatures and wetness caused thousands of casualties in the division.

After Joe's narrow escape, the battalion continued to move through France, crossing the Saar River, often fighting house-to-house in small towns. Then, they captured the Saar Union in early December and reached the Maginot line on December 5, 1944. Company K had the dangerous job of working with engineering units to destroy massive pillboxes that populated the line.

During a rest period, the battalion was called to the Ardennes, moving north through Luxembourg, to help stop the German counteroffensive, later named the Battle of the Bulge. Fierce fighting ensued, the men retreating and counterattacking until eventually pushing the Germans back.

In January 1945, they liberated the town of Grummelscheid in Luxembourg and then assumed defensive positions through March 1945. The unit crossed the Rhine on March 13, 1945, and house-to-house fighting continued at Hanau, Fulda, and Meiningen and moved southeast into Austria, capturing Linz in early May. The division was moving into Czechoslovakia when a cease-fire was announced.

One day later, Joe's division, accompanied by an armor unit, liberated the Gusen concentration camp in Austria, discovering an elaborate tunnel system created for aircraft production and intended during the German retreat to be demolished with the prisoners inside. The fast action by the 26th prevented the slaughter of the forced laborers. Today, the United States Holocaust Museum in Washington, DC, flies the division's colors at its entrance.

With hostilities over, the US Army repurposed several hotels and casinos to create an overseas university for GIs to attend while waiting to return home. In France, Joe attended one of the eight-week Biarritz American University courses. The school offered a variety of college subjects, plus sponsored an orchestra, a theater, a newsletter, and several sports teams. From August 1945 to March 1946, it helped many of the soldiers ease their transition to civilian life.

Just before returning home, Company K learned their Commanding General, George Patton, had died from a car accident when his driver hit an army truck. Patton, the only one injured, was paralyzed and lingered in the hospital for twelve days before dying and being interred at an American cemetery in Luxembourg.

During 200 days of fighting, the Yankee division lost 1800 soldiers killed in action, had over 7000 wounded, and 800 soldiers became prisoners of war; a number of these were captured at Rodalbe. The division would earn a Distinguished Unit Citation for its valiant efforts and had two soldiers awarded the Medal of Honor.

Joe, in addition to two Bronze Stars and a Purple Heart, would earn the Combat Infantryman's Badge, the Good Conduct Medal, a Meritorious Unit Award, the European–African–Middle Eastern Campaign Medal with four stars, an American Campaign Medal, and a World War II Victory Medal. He participated in four campaigns: Northern France, Rhineland, Ardennes, and Central Europe.

When a soldier returned from overseas, his departure was based on a point system, and with Joe's two Bronze Stars and Purple Heart plus almost 200 days of combat duty, he was spared reassignment to the Pacific and instead directed to LeHavre, France, for the boat trip home. Arriving on the east coast in late January 1945, he was entrained to the separation center at Indiantown Gap, Pennsylvania, and honorably discharged on February 1, 1946, headed home to a warm welcome.

Joe resumed his studies at the University of Pittsburgh, where he had briefly matriculated before being drafted. Using the GI Bill, he earned a Bachelor of Arts in Political Science in 1947 and his Master of Letters in 1948. Joe then returned to Europe and, in 1952, received his PhD in International Relations from the University of Geneva, Switzerland. His thesis focused on British policy in Palestine. Joe would always attribute his interest in international affairs to his army service.

In 1952, Joe returned to the cellar in Rodalbe. (Courtesy of Zasloff family)

While in Europe in the 1950s, he returned to the village of Rodalbe and met the owner of the house and cellar where he had hidden. The pock-marked farmhouse and shrapnel-riddled entrance to the cellar stood as a vivid reminder of how lucky he was on that cold November day in 1944, barely escaping death and capture.

In 1954, Dr. Zasloff began a forty-nine-year teaching career with the University of Pittsburgh as a professor of Political Science, before retiring to their summertime vacation home of Williamstown, Mass. During those years, he would instruct, lecture, and assist at many other institutions and colleges. Joe was sponsored on many foreign teaching assignments, beginning with a Smith-Mundt lectureship at the University of Saigon from January 1959 to June 1960, and then as a Fulbright professor at the University of the Philippines. He became an accomplished linguist speaking French, Yiddish, German, and Russian, in addition to his English.

In 1964, at 39, Joe would have described himself as a lonely bachelor when he had the great fortune to meet Tela Cohn on a blind date suggested by a former girlfriend. Tela recalled that when she first saw Joe through the peephole of her door, she said to herself, simply, "I like him." Her heart told her he was the one. Their first date was at a Middle Eastern restaurant. After one week, Joe offhandedly proposed when he said he was headed back to Vietnam to conduct a study for the RAND Corporation, and would she like to come. Tela immediately said yes. They were married in May 1964 and left for Saigon the next month. Joe now had a wonderful partner with whom to share his life in this world.

During the 1960s and 1970s, Joe served on several commissions, made trips back to Indochina, and was a sought-after lecturer on Southeast Asian political problems. In teaching and research, he worked for the US State Department, Peace Corps, and Agency for International Development. He worked for RAND in the capital cities of Saigon and Vientiane, conducting a number of studies and writing about issues concerning the Vietnamese communists and Pathet Lao through interviews with prisoners and defectors, often communicating in French.

He and his research partners presented the results of an extensive study on the motivation and morale of communist soldiers to

General Westmoreland, the US Embassy in Saigon, and the US State Department. In the end, their salient points were that the Vietcong and North Vietnamese were resilient and determined, unlikely to be defeated, and underscored the importance of nationalism to the communist motivation.

His in-depth research efforts were described in a 2014 remembrance as "measured, analytical, a historical view of the origin and nature of conflict, maintaining the importance of nationalism in the communist's motivation to keep fighting." Zasloff always looked for the rationale, motivators, and "intentions of behavior, especially during times of war."

Later in life, he told his wife Tela that one of the first things his own father had asked him privately upon his return from the war was, "Joe, did you kill anybody?" and when Joe answered no, his dad replied, "Good."

Dr. Zasloff wrote nine books; in addition to one on Great Britain and Palestine, he authored eight on Indochina with a focus and assessment on the struggles, growth, and effects of communism in Vietnam, Laos, and Cambodia. His list of research studies and articles is extensive. Several of his later books were co-authored with his friend and colleague, MacAlister Brown, a political science professor at Williams College, who introduced Joe and Tela to Berkshire County.

Zasloff's on-the-ground research, experiences, and writing made him a subject expert on Indochina. He was predominantly centered on the US foreign policy toward Indochina and, during the tumultuous 1960s and 1970s, was a speaker in much demand. During the Vietnam War, he spoke at many different public forums and, in the mid-1960s, proposed a negotiated withdrawal of US troops, realizing the weak South Vietnamese government was unlikely to unite its citizens in a concerted effort to resist North Vietnam. His conclusions were presciently accurate based on exposure to the populace and extensive interviews. Many reached the same conclusion, years and many lives later.

While Joe was teaching and researching, Tela would go on to

earn her doctorate in rhetoric and write several books. One of them, *Saigon Dreaming: Recollections of Indochina Days*, shares their experiences as a newly married couple in Saigon and Laos. She also did freelance editing and lectured on literature and writing at Carnegie Mellon University.

With the University of Pittsburgh as their base, Joe, Tela, and their four daughters occupied a three-story, red-brick colonial home close to the university. Often, a live-in student would take the 3rd floor, trading rent payments for help around the house.

Weekends usually involved Joe and the girls food shopping on Saturdays, with stops at the Giant Eagle supermarket, a bakery, a bagel shop, and a health food store. All their efforts went toward supporting his weekend breakfast smorgasbords, a medley of cold cereals, grits, and assorted toppings.

During the school year, the girls would enjoy swim, dance, or piano lessons, and the family would go downhill skiing at Blue Knob mountain or, often, partake in a less expensive hobby: cross-country skiing. The girls also ice skated locally.

Joe and Tela were strong proponents of experiencing different cultures, and in this regard, Joe would accept temporary teaching appointments in many places. Early in their lives, the girls traveled with their dad and mom and attended school in Manila, Beirut, Kuala Lumpur, and Nice.

The family spent summer breaks each year in Williamstown, so that Joe could collaborate with his best friend and coauthor MacAlister Brown. Joe usually rode his bike to an office near Mac's, while his daughters would enjoy area day camps, local tennis courts, a library, and the pond at Margaret Lindley Park.

In the 1980s, the family participated in several trips in the "Semester at Sea" program, a university study-abroad series that sponsored hundreds of college students to travel around the world on ships with ten or eleven ports of call and related field trips. Professor Zasloff and other educators would serve as teachers and chaperones and be allowed to take their families with them. Joe would teach classes on board the ocean liner and lead field trips in various countries, while Tela would take the opportunity to homeschool the girls, while teaching composition onboard. The family loved experiencing different cultures and foods during their visits to Morocco, Spain, Greece, Turkey, Russia, Egypt, Israel, India, Thailand, Indonesia, Japan, Korea, Taiwan, and Hong Kong.

In 2002, their daughter Beth and her husband visited Rodalbe. They talked with the elderly owner of the now well-maintained, two-story, cream-colored farmhouse and visited its adjoining cellar. When walking down the narrow concrete stairway into the cellar, with its low overhead and fieldstone walls, they got a sense of the conditions her dad felt so many years previously.

The next year, when Joe retired from the University of Pittsburgh, he and Tela moved to Williamstown permanently. They enjoyed dinner conversations with a close group of friends and, at one point, expanded the house to accommodate their activities. Joe, always a natural athlete, remained active, skiing and playing tennis and squash.

Joe and Tela celebrated their fiftieth anniversary in the spring of 2014. Sadly, Joe passed away in December 2014.

World War II and Vietnam encompassed the notable career of Dr. Joseph Zasloff. In both, his efforts could be characterized as valiant. His courageous conduct in World War II earned him two Bronze Stars, and he then dedicated much of his life to understanding and lecturing on the nature and motivation of human behavior during times of war. His early writings and lectures on Indochina stood out as a prescient warning of involvement in the Vietnam War and the perils of US efforts.

After living through the Great Depression, a harrowing World War II experience, and traveling to war zones as a scholar, Joe remained optimistic and upbeat about the world, settling down finally in his beloved Berkshires and always choosing to see the best in everyone—a wonderful way to be remembered.

FURTHER READING

Abbott D. Abbott

From Texas to Rome: Fighting World War II and the Italian Campaign with the 36th Infantry Division by Fred L. Walker (1969, reissued 2021).

Return to Cassino: A Memoir of the Fight for Rome by Harold L. Bond (1964).

A River Swift and Deadly by Lee Carraway Smith (1989).

The Texas 36th Division: A History by Bruce L. Brager (2002).

Albert Bachand

Adventures of a US Navy Seabee, 1942-1945 by Frank Wademan Coughtry; Henry W. Rauch, editor (2016).

The Seabees Speak: Interviews with the Can Do *Veterans of World War II* by Sharon A. Tolisano (2007).

The Seabees of World War Two by Commander Edmund Castillo, USN (1963, reissued 2010).

William F. and Madeline E. Beattie

The Battle for Manila by Richard Connaughton, John Pimlott, Duncan Anderson (2002).

Battle of Manila: Nadir of Japanese Barbarism, 3 February-3 March 1945 by Miguel Miranda (2019).

The War in the Pacific: From Pearl Harbor to Tokyo Bay by Harry A. Gailey (1995).

World War II Photo Intelligence by Col. Roy M. Stanley II, USAF (1981).

Ferdinando J. Berti

PT 109: An American Epic of War, Survival, and the Destiny of John F. Kennedy by William Doyle (2015).

US Patrol Torpedo Boats: World War II by Gordon L. Rottman (2008).

Robert I. Brown

The Battle of Okinawa: The Blood and the Bomb by George Feifer (1992, reissued 2020).

Coral Comes High by George P. Hunt (1946, reissued 2019).

With the Old Breed: At Peleliu and Okinawa by E.B. Sledge (1981, reissued 2007).

Dixon H. Daniels

Bitter Peleliu: The Forgotten Struggle on the Pacific War's Worst Battlefield by Joseph Wheelan (2022).

Brotherhood of Heroes: The Marines at Peleliu, 1944—The Bloodiest Battle of the Pacific War by Bill Sloan (2005).

Operation Stalemate: 1944 Battle for Peleliu by Daniel Wrinn (2021).

Roger J. Dennett

It Only Takes One: Memoirs of a Tail Gunner by Larry Stevens (2013).

Masters of the Air: America's Bomber Boys Who Fought the Air War Against Nazi Germany by Donald L. Miller (2006).

Frank F. Falbo

Hinder Forward: The 168th Engineer Combat Battalion in ZI and ETO from May 1943 through November 1945 by Dean F. Jewett (2001).

James G. Garvie, Jr.

The Armored Fist: The 712th Tank Battalion in the Second World War by Aaron Elson (2013).

The Finger of Fate: A 712th Tank Battalion mini book by Steve Krysko (2014).

Tanks for the Memories: An Oral History of the 712th Tank Battalion from World War II as told to Aaron C. Elson (1994).

Charles B. & George H. Haley

Attack Transport: The Story of the USS Doyen by Lawrence A. Marsden (1946, reissued 2020).

War and Resistance in the Philippines, 1942-1945 by James Kelly Morningstar (2021).

Ernest A. Jaworski

Artillery Warfare 1939-1945 by Simon Forty and Jonathan Forty (2020).

US Field Artillery of World War II by Steven J. Zaloga (2007).

Raymond W. Kelly

Love Company: L Company, 399th Regiment, of the 100th Infantry Division during World War II and Beyond by John M. Khoury (2018).

Robert T. Leitch

3rd Air Division, 8th Air Force USAAF 1942-1945: Flying Fortress and Liberator Squadrons in Norfolk and Suffolk by Martin W. Bowman (2009).

B-17 Flying Fortress In Action by David Doyle (2010).

The Bomber Boys: Heroes Who Flew the B-17s in World War II by Travis L. Ayres (2005).

William S. Linscott

See Naples and Die: A World War II Memoir of a United States Army Ski Trooper in the Mountains of Italy by Robert B. Ellis (1996).

Soldiers on Skis: A Pictorial Memoir of the 10th Mountain Division by Flint Whitlock (1992).

The Boys of Winter: Life and Death in the US Ski Troops during the Second World War by Charles J. Sanders (2005).

Reno L. Maselli

Always Ready: The Story of the United States 147th Infantry Regiment by Tom McLeod (1996).

Narcheeso "Cheeso" Massaconi

Battle Wounds of Iwo Jima by Thomas M. Brown, M.D. (2002).

Iwo Jima: The Dramatic Account of the Epic Battle That Turned the Tide of World War II by Richard F. Newcomb (1965).

World War II: Battle of Iwo Jima, A History from Beginning to End by Hourly History (2020).

Richard T. McKnight

Aluminum Alley: The American Pilots Who Flew Over the Himalayas and Helped Win World War II by Rory Laverty (2023).

Flying the Hump to China—The Early Days: The Humble Beginning of the First Airlift by James Paul Segel (2017).

Flying the Hump: The War Diary of Peter H. Dominick edited by Alexander S. Dominick (2022).

Elizabeth J. McNicol

Bedpan Commando by June Wandrey (1989).

Combat Nurses in World War II by Wyatt Blassingame (1967).

GI Nightingales: The Army Nurse Corps in World War II by Barbara Brooks Tomblin (1996).

A Half Acre of Hell: A Combat Nurse in WWII by Avis D. Schorer (2014).

If I Perish: Frontline US Army Nurses in World War II by Evelyn M. Monahan and Rosemary Neidel-Greenlee (2003).

Alfred H. Neveu

The Cross of Lorraine: A Combat History of the 79th Infantry Division, June 1942 – December 1945 by University of Wisconsin (undated).

Robert B. Nichols

A Gunner on a Battleship in World War II by Frank "Frenchy" Letourneau (2011).

USS Missouri: *America's Last Battleship* by David Doyle (2018).

USS Missouri *at War* by Kit Bonner & Carolyn Bonner (2008).

Bernard J. St. John

Intrepid Aviators: The American Flyers Who Sank Japan's Greatest Battleship by Gregory Fletcher (2013).

Intrepid*: The Epic Story of America's Most Legendary Warship* by Bill White and Robert Gandt, Foreword by John McCain (2008).

TBF/TBM Avenger: Grumman's First Torpedo Bomber in World War II by David Doyle (2020).

Torpedo 8: The Story of Swede Larsen's Bomber Squadron by Ira Wolfert (1943, annotated edition 2019).

Henry St. Pierre

Fighting Fox Company: The Battling Flank of the Band of Brothers by Terry Poyser and Bill Brown (2013).

Operation Market-Garden 1944: The American Airborne Missions by Steven J. Zaloga (2014).

Operation Market Garden in 24,389 Words: The Concise History of the Biggest Gamble of World War Two by Tom Leferink (2019).

US World War II Parachute Infantry Units by Gordon L. Rottman (2014).

George P. Taylor

The Liberandos: A WWII History of the 376th Heavy Bombardment Group and its Founding Units by James W. Walker (1994).

Lawrence B. Urbano

That Gallant Ship: USS Yorktown *[CV-5]* by Robert Cressman (1985).

Frank J. Wotkowicz

12th & 15th Air Forces by Gérard Paloque (2012).

B-25 Mitchell, Vol. 2: The G through J, F-10, and PJB Models in World War II by William Wolf (2022).

Joseph J. Zasloff

Apprentice Revolutionaries: The Communist Movement in Laos, 1930-1985 by MacAlister Brown and Joseph J. Zasloff (1986).

North Vietnam and the Pathet Lao-Partners in the Struggle for Laos by Paul F. Langer and Joseph J. Zasloff (1970).

Postwar Indochina: Old Enemies and New Allies edited by Joseph J. Zasloff (1988).

A Rescuer's Story: Pastor Pierre-Charles Toureille in Vichy France by Tela Zasloff (2003).

Saigon Dreaming: Recollections of Indochina Days by Tela Zasloff (1989).

About the Author

© 2021 GreenFlash Pro Photography

DENNIS G. PREGENT IS the award-winning author of *The Boys of St. Joe's '65 in the Vietnam War*, *Born in the Berkshires*, and *Berkshire Patriots: Stories of Sacrifice.* Born in Pittsfield, Massachusetts, and raised in nearby North Adams and Adams, Pregent enlisted in the Marines in his senior year of high school, at age seventeen.

After serving almost seven years of active duty with two tours in Vietnam, he returned to the Berkshires, graduated from North Adams State College in 1975 (currently Massachusetts College of Liberal Arts) and went on to receive his MBA from the University of Massachusetts in 1977 before embarking on a lifelong career in Human Resources.

For over thirty-five years, until his retirement, Pregent served in HR as an international vice-president for Evenflo/Spalding and ConAgra Food. His responsibilities were far-ranging, from domestic and foreign labor relations to international executive staffing.

Several years after his retirement in 2012, Pregent began researching and writing books focused on the beautiful and history-rich region of the Berkshires. *Berkshire Heroes in WWII: With Courage and Honor* is his fourth book. His debut, *The Boys of St. Joe's '65 in the Vietnam War*, recently won the Bronze medal from the Military Writers Society of America.

He and his wife Carol have six children and fifteen grandchildren and reside in Garner, North Carolina.

For further information or to contact him, please visit ***dennispregent.com***.